D0083374

COLD WAR
AND
DÉTENTE

The American
Foreign Policy Process
Since 1945

Paul Y. Hammond
University of Pittsburgh

COLD WAR AND DÉTENTE

The American
Foreign Policy Process
Since 1945

Under the General Editorship of
John Morton Blum
Yale University

Harcourt Brace Jovanovich, Inc.
New York   Chicago   San Francisco   Atlanta

Maps:

Pages 355, 357, 358, 359 © 1973/1974 by The New York Times Company. Reprinted by permission.

Page 354 from *The National Experience*, 3rd edition, by Blum, *et al.*, © 1963, 1968, 1973 by Harcourt Brace Jovanovich, Inc., and reproduced with their permission.

Pages 350–51, 352–53, 356, 359 (index map) Harbrace

© 1969, 1975 by Harcourt Brace Jovanovich, Inc. *Cold War and Détente* is the second edition of *The Cold War Years: American Foreign Policy Since 1945.*

ISBN: 0-15-507881-X

Library of Congress Catalog Card Number: 75–6281

Printed in the United States of America

Preface

Cold War and Détente is the second edition of *The Cold War Years,* published in 1969. The change in title reflects some of the significant changes in world circumstances as well as shifts in interpretation and emphasis over the past six years. The term *détente* refers broadly to a level of accommodation between the United States and Communist nations, particularly Russia, that transcends the rigid Cold War atmosphere. In this edition, *détente* is used to refer to these more cooperative relations, with the understanding that the possibilities of continued competitive or even hostile relations are not excluded by this stage. The term *postwar era* refers to the entire period from 1945 to the present.

This edition gives greater attention to the theses of the revisionists in assessing American foreign policy, particularly in exploring whether the course of the Cold War might have been modified in the early postwar era and in examining certain public pressures toward global American intervention as part of our "national" interest." More attention is also given here to the Eisenhower Administration's handling of the Soviet Union as well as to Eisenhower's tendency toward selective and restrained intervention abroad. New interest in this subject has been generated by the Nixon Administration's establishment of détente with the Soviet Union and our diplomatic rapprochement with the People's Republic of China.

The last three chapters are new: Chapters 10 and 11 cover the Nixon Administration, with a brief discussion of the Ford Administration. Chapter 12 explores prospects for the future from the vantage point of the mid-1970s.

A basic assumption of *Cold War and Détente* is that domestic political conditions greatly influence the ways in which American officials perceive and deal with foreign affairs; in addition, the traditions and machinery of the American governmental process further govern the specific responses of officials in making foreign policy.

This book is organized according to presidential administrations because the Presidency is the most important determinant of foreign policy and is normally the strongest influence on public opinion about foreign affairs. The main issues of American foreign policy are examined within the context of each President's strategies and style of political leadership in conducting foreign affairs, in choosing his principal advisers, and in relating to Congress and public opinion.

The emphasis on presidential leadership in foreign policy allows for closer examination of the traditional issue raised by populists—namely, that greater public attention to foreign policy would improve its quality. The course of public opinion throughout the postwar era suggests that sometimes an active public can have an important constructive influence on policy making. But at other times a high level of public attention has led to short-sighted or rigid foreign policies, especially when officials have either overreacted to external crises or avoided innovations for fear of arousing hostile public responses.

In particular, some of the rigid policy stances adopted by American administrations during the Cold War period persisted largely because public attention was so aroused over the menace of Communism during the early postwar era that it later became difficult to seek more conciliatory relations with the Soviet Union and China. On the other hand, public opinion can sometimes encourage the government to reassess its policies or can even become a direct and overwhelming force for innovation in foreign relations. The course of the Vietnam war from the Eisenhower era through the Nixon era illustrates both the rigidities and the innovations that public opinion may generate in foreign policies.

On balance, a more interested public can be a distinct asset in international politics. The stability and effectiveness of a government in an international crisis, for example, may depend on the resolve and active support of a relatively informed public. Yet each postwar presidential administration has faced the pitfalls of either a too actively aroused public or a too deferential one. The President who tries to mobilize public support behind foreign policies by dramatizing specific issues may find his later options restricted by the public's simplified expectations and its high level of attention to future developments. By contrast, the President who encourages broader public deference to government officials and less public attention to foreign affairs gains more latitude in handling complex foreign policy issues. But such an administration is particularly vulnerable to attack by rival political factions or to unexpected external events that provide an impetus for public alarm.

The need for an active and more informed public became particularly important after World War II with America's new postwar alliances, our new foreign programs, and our increased military expenditures. Yet it may be unrealistic to expect the public to be truly "well informed" about foreign policy issues. These issues are complex and not easily solved even by government officials who devote full time to them; the public is likely to devote less attention to these issues and to have less information for resolving them. If so, we must seek a more feasible role for the public in helping to form foreign policy—some balance of skepticism and trust that reflects the actual level of public attentiveness and comprehension of the policy issues involved.

The book, with its faults, is mine. The views expressed in it are my own and are not necessarily shared by the Rand Corporation. For the book's merits I have depended upon many friends and colleagues. For the present revision I am particularly indebted to John Morton Blum, Yale University; John Lewis Gaddis, Ohio University; and James Foster, the Rand Corporation. Barbara Bengen edited both editions with skill and patience. My children and wife, Merylyn, felt the full weight of writing and revision done in addition to my regular research duties.

PAUL Y. HAMMOND

To Brett, Wendy, Robyn,
Spencer, and Clifford

Contents

chapter 1

The Domestic Base
of Foreign Policy:
An Introduction

INFLUENCES ON FOREIGN POLICY

In the United States the President normally dominates foreign relations. It is true that he has no monopoly in the formulation or conduct of foreign policy: Congress can legislate important changes in foreign relations, particularly through its control over federal expenditures. It often appropriates much less than the President requests for foreign economic assistance and has frequently added provisos to foreign aid and defense appropriations.

The President also lacks exclusive control over the linkages with the external world. He cannot keep track of all connections of the United States government with other governments. Often he takes for granted the diplomatic ties with other governments maintained by the State Department as well as the military and functional economic ties maintained by other cabinet departments. Only rarely are these ties used to undercut presidential policies. More often they limit his choices of policies and thus, in practice, encourage continuity in American foreign relations.

As for other links with the external world, some—such as business and private communications—cannot be controlled by the President. Most other links, such as the mass media—newspapers, radio, and television—can be manipulated only for a high political price, for the press corps that interprets the news output of the government is diverse and suspicious. Yet no one but the President normally controls the major external linkages for *any* price.

In foreign affairs, more than in any other area, the President can avoid or appear to rise above party politics and divisive partisanship. This is not a statement about his virtues. Generally it is to his advantage to appear to stand above partisanship when he can, for that posture adds to his congressional and public support. Neither is it a comment on the virtues of presidential power in American politics. Presidential power and partisanship both have come under criticism in recent years from the political left, as they were from the right at the beginning of the postwar era, and indeed into the mid-fifties. The domestic constraints on his conduct of foreign relations are normally expressed in criticism and opposition, but not always along party lines.

This remark does not set foreign affairs apart from other kinds of political issues in the United States. With domestic as well as foreign policy issues, political leaders persistently compete for support across party lines. The lines of party identity are fluid, and political interest groups overlap. A textile worker, for example, may favor trade protection against Japanese and other imports, but he may want Japanese electronic and optical products to be fully competitive in the American market. He may be Polish or Hungarian and cling to the hope of a rollback of Communist power in Eastern Europe, while having preferred a diplomatic settlement in Vietnam because he has sons who were of military age during the period of direct military involvement in the Vietnam war. He will then be a protectionist and a free trader, a "hawk" and a "dove," all at once.

Many factors enter into the determination of a nation's foreign policy behavior. An in-depth study of a foreign affairs episode should cover such factors in great detail. However, the scope of the present work is too large to permit detailed treatment of all foreign policy "inputs." Accordingly, we will deal mainly with two: the Presidency and public opinion as it constrains that office. Opinion surveys and voting analyses indicate that the American voting public can be divided into several strata according to how much interest the voters normally have in foreign affairs, how well informed they are about foreign affairs, and how likely their voting behavior is to be influenced by foreign policy issues. Normally, foreign affairs have distinctly lower saliency for the voter than do most domestic issues. Usually, the constituency interested in foreign affairs and knowledgeable about it is very small; therefore, politicians correctly assume that domestic issues play a more important role in determining voting behavior and other political acts.

However, foreign issues cannot always be ignored. They have played an important role in certain critical elections. In the 1916 presidential campaign the supporters of Woodrow Wilson played successfully to the growing public perception of a potential external threat by adopting the slogan "He kept us out of war!" Franklin D. Roosevelt made a similarly successful appeal to the electorate in 1940. The wars that followed these election campaigns, it is clear, cut deeply into the public consciousness, though they ultimately had dissimilar effects on the political positions of the incumbent Presidents. Relating the issues raised by these wars to voting behavior is not easy with the available survey data. But we have rich and reliable data indicating that the Korean war, for example, was a salient political issue for millions of American voters in the 1952 presidential election. The messages in the mass media have a special impact when a personal followup occurs, such as the military draft. The economic recovery of Europe in the late forties meant little to millions of American voters. But the war in Korea was directly relevant because millions of voters or their kinfolk fought in it or expected to fight. It is also fairly clear that the more public attention Korea drew, the more impatient the public became. Protracted involvement was not popular, and many felt that we ought to end the war as soon as possible.

Similarly, the issue of Vietnam heavily colored the elections of 1968 and 1972. It induced President Johnson not to run in 1968, despite his landslide electoral victory four years earlier. It may well have affected the outcome of the election later that year in the swing of votes away from the Democratic candidate to a slender majority for Richard Nixon. But the positions of the two principal candidates on Vietnam were not clear during the election campaign in 1968, and the outcome was therefore ambiguous in terms of public sentiment on the war issue. Four years later the ambiguity of the outcome was even stronger. The Democratic and Republican candidates took strongly divergent positions on Vietnam, yet the incumbent, President Nixon, was reelected by an enormous electoral landslide. Vietnam had profoundly disillusioning and divisive effects on public moods and opinions, and since it did, it would have been reasonable to predict electoral defeat or setback for the incumbent. Quite the contrary occurred. In 1972 President Nixon managed to make his identification with the war into a political asset by convincing the public that peace was at hand on American terms, thus avoiding the appearance of being an appeaser.

World War II, by contrast, generated a high degree of public unity in this country—mainly because once involved in that war, the United States devoted all its energies (or seemed to) to ending it as quickly as possible. The public remained united by the objective of early military victory. Whatever its motivations or goals, the Roosevelt Administration succeeded in maintaining this wide public consensus when it chose to exclude as wartime issues the nature of the postwar political settlement and of the American postwar involvement in international affairs.

How much Roosevelt himself understood these postwar considerations is not our concern here, though the main lines of his wartime policy suggest that he did grasp them. Wartime planning in Washington, for example, was based on the accurate expectation that once the war was over, American public interest in foreign involvement—and support for it—would quickly subside.

An early wartime strategy was to create a network of treaties and other legal commitments associated with what became the United Nations that would institutionalize and routinize the international role of the United States. These commitments in effect legitimized our role abroad by requiring widespread public participation and endorsement so as to rise above postwar partisan controversy. At the same time these multilateral arrangements would assure that international demands could be kept minimal. It was a common American belief that the United Nations, not the United States, would keep the peace and protect the security of its members.

These were the circumstances facing the new Truman Administration in April 1945. When Truman left the White House nearly eight years later the United States had become broadly engaged in the military containment of the Soviet Union and had established military bases and allies throughout the world. A commitment for the maintenance of American troops in Europe had been made for the indefinite future; military alliances had been arranged from Norway to Turkey, and they would soon be extended from Pakistan through Indochina to Korea. American nuclear strategic power had also grown significantly in that period.

Some critics have argued that the Truman Administration responded too slowly to Soviet threats during 1945 and 1946; others have charged the contrary—that America's hostility to the Soviet Union, or more broadly, the propensity to expand American hegemony worldwide, caused the Cold War. All these views had been aired by 1950.

REVISIONISM AND AMERICAN FOREIGN POLICY

In the mid-sixties, during the malaise over Vietnam, a revisionist school of postwar American history revived the latter claims to argue that the Cold War was a product of certain long-standing characteristics of American foreign policy.

The revisionists encompass a variety of viewpoints, with emphasis on two major themes: (1) that the United States has been persistently and unjustifiably expansionist in its foreign policies, and (2) that its expansionism has been the special outgrowth of the capitalist economic structure—that is, that the American government has been dominated by private economic interests and its foreign policies have been directed toward achieving their aims.

Governments put the best face they can on their expedient behavior, and publics are inclined to adopt a convenient view of morality in foreign relations. The revisionists have made important contributions to the popular interpretation of American history by calling attention to the resulting cant and sham. They have also helped to *remind us of the strong pressures on any nation to become imperialistic when it has the power to do so,* as the United States had in particular after World War II. On the other hand, historical evidence suggests that American expansionism, to the extent that it has occurred, is not unique: most nations have tended to expand their perceptions and definitions of "national interests"—and of what is a salient threat to these interests—to match the reach of their international power. The United States has not been conspicuously better or worse than other states in its expanding vision of its vital national interests.

Revisionist theories have also tended to assume that the American government is composed of officials thoroughly in agreement with one another and focusing on the achievement of a consistent set of foreign policy objectives directly reflecting American economic interests. As the following chapters will indicate in more detail, the postwar period in particular was plagued by disagreements and open factionalism among American leaders in both the executive branch and Congress. In fact, one might argue that a major problem in the postwar period was that of too little consistency and forethought rather than too much.

As for the influence of business interests on foreign policy, the revisionists may have been correct in some specific instances. But their general assumptions have been questionable. They have assumed that American business enterprises have converging interests on most major foreign policy issues, and also that they perceive clearly where their interests lie. These assumptions appear to be somewhat oversimplified. For example, a major scholarly work has shown that even a single complex corporation can have interests *both* in maintaining and in reducing foreign trade barriers. Moreover, firms are often uncertain about what kinds of government intervention would help them when they balance their foreign interests against their domestic interests or when they consider the drawbacks as well as the benefits of government help with foreign markets and resources.[1]

This diversity of economic interests is multiplied significantly when many business corporations are involved in foreign policy legislation. Even more important, historical evidence suggests that the American political system is composed of sufficiently different political and economic interest groups so that their divergent demands ordinarily enable the government to avoid becoming the exclusive servant of any one set of interests. The independence of government from any one special interest group does not necessarily

---

[1] R. A. Bauer, I. deS. Pool, and L. A. Dexter, *American Business and Public Policy* (New York: Atherton Press, 1963), pp. 127–53, 230–42, 350–57, 396–99.

rest on government's virtues but on competition among interest claimants that the government can neither ignore nor fully satisfy.

It is also notable that as expansionist as the United States has been in its employment of power, it might have been even more so. It might have used its nuclear monopoly more than it has done to threaten and dominate, and it might have used its preeminent world trade position much more to prevent the recovery and growth of economic rivals. One need not ignore the criticisms of the revisionists in order to credit American foreign policy in the first postwar decade as reflecting a remarkably broad vision of self-interest and common interests with its allies. (As the last chapter will discuss, the decade ahead may fall far short of the latter standard.)

Nonetheless, the revisionists have enlivened historical interpretation by dramatizing the public values at stake in the complex relationships between internal political and economic factors and the nation's foreign policies. Examining these relationships will be a major task of this book. One of the risks of looking inside a country for explanations about foreign policy is that the effort encourages deterministic outcomes. With this warning in mind, however, a major task of this book will be to examine the domestic basis for American foreign relations, since the two arenas appear to be closely meshed in the postwar period.

In order to focus on the American political processes and behavior and their relationship to American foreign policies, this book will treat domestic Soviet developments only minimally. That is, the chapters that follow deal mainly with American *perceptions* of Soviet behavior rather than attempting to analyze or characterize Soviet conduct from other points of reference.

This book's thesis is that the course of the Cold War was broadly determined by strong political forces in both countries that directed each superpower into conflict with the other. In the postwar era the two rivals faced one another without intervening nations to maintain the equilibrium of the international power system or to reduce the potential threat that each superpower appeared to pose to the other. In fact, the disparity between each principal rival and its allies and clients was great enough to induce some of the latter to "fish in the troubled waters" of bipolar conflict, sustaining and exacerbating the rivalry rather than balancing and stabilizing it, as discussed later.

THE BEGINNINGS OF THE COLD WAR

In the World War II coalition against Germany, Italy, and Japan, the United States had been linked with the Soviet Union as well as with Great Britain, the British Commonwealth, the exile governments of the defeated European states, and China. As the war drew to a close, Soviet-American relations began to deteriorate. Wartime cooperation had not been close, and the war did not lead to integrated multilateral operations with the Russians or other channels for mutual give-and-take that might have reduced the stresses of ending the war and postwar adjustment.

Soviet-American wartime collaboration had consisted almost solely of an expedient alignment against a common enemy. With the defeat of Germany, opposing perspectives and interests generated first discreet and then open diplomatic conflict. Russia expected the defeat of Germany to bring security to her western frontiers through the establishment of friendly regimes in Eastern Europe. At the very least Moscow wanted Eastern Europe within her acknowledged sphere of influence. The British supported spheres of influence as one basis for postwar settlement. However, since Britain had gone to war to save Poland from Germany, she could hardly abandon the Poles to Russian control now. But Churchill and Stalin did agree to a line of division between a British sphere in the Eastern Mediterranean and a Soviet sphere in Eastern Europe, and Roosevelt went along with them, over State Department objections.

The war with Germany had established an American interest in European security that was not confined to the Western portion. This security could be ensured by a balance of power in Europe in which no single state dominated the continent—a Europe composed of stable, strong, independent states. In addition, American officials disagreed with the British and Soviet view that the acknowledgment of spheres of influence by the major powers could provide a stable postwar settlement. The State Department persistently advocated an ambitious new international system—what was to become the

United Nations—rather than regional spheres. (Amerian officials took for granted that Latin America was a regional American sphere.) The American interest in Eastern Europe had domestic political origins as well: Roosevelt evidently thought that if he lost Eastern Europe to the Soviets he would alienate the Poles and other ethnic groups among the American voters.

The American perception of Soviet power at the end of World War II focused mainly on the potential threat of Soviet armed force coupled with internal subversion in countries along the Soviet borderlands and in Western Europe where American and continental balance-of-power interests were involved. American interests were reinforced by the propensity in Washington to harken back to Woodrow Wilson and talk about a universalist postwar settlement—one that rested on universally accepted standards of justice. Russian regionalism and American interest in the balance of power in Europe thus collided head on. This conflict was aggravated by the universalist rhetoric of Communist dogma versus American democratic universalism and free trade capitalist ideology. Political commentator and journalist Walter Lippmann termed what followed the "Cold War"—a far-reaching hostility between the two superpowers.

Gabriel Kolko and Gar Alperovitz, two leading revisionist historians, both attribute to the American government a high degree of purposefulness, astuteness, and unity on the postwar international scene. Kolko depicts the United States as persistently seeking to restore the prewar powers, including Germany, Italy, and Japan, as bulwarks against Bolshevism. Alperovitz argues that at the end of World War II the United States used first economic weapons and then "atomic diplomacy"—that is, atomic blackmail—to construct an American-dominated world order that extended to Eastern Europe and the Far East.[2]

It does not appear, however, that Roosevelt's war aims or those of the United States government collectively were that focused. Roosevelt worked out mainly short-term accommodations with the British and Russians in wartime conferences at Teheran in 1943 and Yalta in early 1945 in order to avoid disputes among the converging

---

[2] Gabriel Kolko, *The Politics of War* (New York: Random House, 1969); and Gar Alperovitz, *Atomic Diplomacy* (New York: Simon and Schuster, 1965).

armies of conquest and occupation. The longer-term arrangements, notably the Soviet agreement to support new democratic governments in Eastern Europe and the special status of the Big Four in the forthcoming United Nations charter, had less immediate import, so they could readily be reopened for negotiation or ignored.

The attention devoted at Yalta to planning the United Nations could be interpreted along with the statements of American officials at the end of the conference to indicate that they hoped for a revolutionary change in the nature of foreign relations. Roosevelt's closest adviser, Harry Hopkins, said: "We really believed in our hearts that this was the dawn of the new day we had all been praying for and talking about for so many years. We were absolutely certain that we had won the first great victory of the peace."[3]

Roosevelt may have been less optimistic than Hopkins, but he did share Woodrow Wilson's vision of a new international order in its purest form. Yet at the same time, Roosevelt pursued quite traditional power political objectives as well. His arrangements for the United Nations allowed for a continued dominant role for the major international powers—defined as the United States, the Soviet Union, Great Britain, France, and China (although China's power and independence were not taken very seriously). He had also readily approved of Stalin's and Churchill's agreement that recognized a British Eastern Mediterranean sphere and a Soviet Eastern European sphere that overlapped slightly in the Balkans. Possibly Roosevelt had a consistent viewpoint about the postwar world that reconciled the Wilsonian rejection of spheres of influence with this actual acceptance of spheres. More likely he was applying to international affairs the eclectic style of policy development that characterized his leadership in domestic affairs—using the United Nations and Wilsonian rhetoric to sanctify a postwar international system dominated by the great powers.

Isolationism was a label used to characterize American foreign policy from the rejection of the League of Nations in 1920 until Pearl Harbor in 1941—or at least until Lend Lease in 1940. Viewed as a folly by political leaders of the forties, isolationism had achieved the status of a popular myth. However, neither Roosevelt

---

[3] Robert E. Sherwood, *Roosevelt and Hopkins* (New York: Harper & Row, 1948), p. 870.

nor the eighty-nine Senators who voted to ratify the U.N. Charter in 1945 gave specific meaning to what a postwar foreign policy that repudiated isolationism would be like. Wendell Willkie, the Republican presidential candidate whom Roosevelt had defeated in 1940, had argued for broad and active postwar international involvement by the United States. Within the Democratic party, the Vice President Henry Wallace had a similar viewpoint. Roosevelt discarded Wallace for Truman in 1944, however, and Wallace was only on the fringe of foreign policy making thereafter. Republican and Democratic leaders of weaker internationalist persuasion viewed the United Nations as a way to help limit the international role of the United States and thus reconcile "internationalism" with the domestic political constraints on America's external role. This apparent solution to how the United States could play an acceptable role as a world power was reinforced by another popular internationalist myth: had the United States maintained its support of the League of Nations after World War I, it held, World War II would not have occurred. By linking the outlook about America's world role at the end of World War II to participation in the United Nations, hard questions about American commitments and choices were avoided for the time being. Revisionist historians have quoted wartime and postwar American officials to indicate that the United States worked to counter Soviet power, talked of using American nuclear weapons as bargaining chips, and worried about the postwar economic position of the United States. On balance, however, the evidence appears to show an absence of common accord about postwar objectives among the most influential American officials at the end of the war.[4] The attention given by our officials to planning and arranging for the United Nations—an inordinate amount considering its limited potential as a tool of Amerian national interests—is one example of the American search for "easy answers" to hard questions about our postwar policies.

Historian John Blum has noted "an ominous blandness, a soft consensus rather than a hard commitment" in the United States

---

[4] The problems caused by selective evidence in the works of several revisionist historians—William Appleman Williams, D. F. Fleming, Gar Alperovitz, David Horowitz, Gabriel Kolko, Diane Shaver Clemens, and Lloyd C. Gardner—are highlighted in Robert James Maddox, *The New Left and the Origins of the Cold War* (Princeton: Princeton University Press, 1973).

Senate's nearly unanimous vote to ratify the United Nations charter. The ranking Republican foreign policy spokesman in the Senate, Arthur Vandenberg of Michigan, a former isolationist, spoke of the United Nations as a "mechanism for constant and friendly consultations" and denied that it encroached on American sovereignty or that United Nations operations would entail the use of force. Blum has recalled that Senator J. William Fulbright of Arkansas noted at the time the peculiar "docility" with which the Senate considered and approved the United Nations Charter. If American leaders believed the Wilsonian rhetoric about fundamentally changing the nature of foreign relations, Fulbright wondered at the absence of serious discussion of that change.[5]

Membership in the United Nations also had domestic political attractions: it would reduce the political risks and increase bipartisan support for the foreign policies of government by either party. By associating specific foreign policies with the United Nations, both Democrats and Republicans could more easily justify such policies as part of a broad consensus about peacekeeping under international law. When Roosevelt spoke at Yalta about the "end of the system of unilateral actions," he was appealing to his bipartisan consensus in favor of international legal and collective security institutions that would not only sanctify but also limit American involvement in international affairs.

Political scientist Hans J. Morgenthau has noted that if the United States had pursued its anti-Soviet objectives during World War II with the "single-minded political purpose which Professor Kolko attributes to it," the American armies would not have been stopped at the gates of Berlin or withdrawn to what are now the borders of West Germany. Washington "would have pursued a military strategy which could easily have kept Czechoslovakia out of the Soviet orbit and prevented Berlin from becoming an enclave in Soviet-controlled territory."[6] Similarly, had Roosevelt been forging an anti-Soviet diplomatic arsenal with calculated foresight, he would

---

[5] As quoted in John Morton Blum, "Limits of American Internationalism: 1941–45," in Leonard Krieger and Fritz Stern, eds., *The Responsibility of Power* (Garden City, N.Y., Doubleday, 1967), pp. 391f.

[6] Hans J. Morgenthau, "Historical Justice and the Cold War," *New York Review of Books* XIII (July 10, 1969), p. 12.

scarcely have placed such a high priority on the United Nations, as in the bargaining at Yalta, since effective United Nation action would require Soviet-American cooperation.

For many of its American supporters, the United Nations had offered the hope—or illusion—of minimizing political controversy over foreign policy and limiting the demands placed on the United States by foreign affairs. Given this assumption, it was but a short step from the United Nations to the North Atlantic Treaty Organization (NATO).

From the outset, NATO too had an appealing burden-sharing feature to it. The cooperative aspect of the NATO alliance and of the European recovery program also helped to legitimize foreign policy undertakings for the American public and encouraged the executive branch and Congress to support NATO by ratifying treaties, authorizing legislation, and appropriating funds.

The new institutions of postwar foreign policy—principally the machinery of foreign economic and military aid and national security planning—became part of the national foreign policy-making process of the United States government. During the late forties this machinery was strongly predisposed (as has usually been the case with any such group) to reduce the uncertainties of its tasks—in this case foreign affairs—by visualizing its responsibilities as mainly meeting the threats of a conspicuous and malevolent military rival and by demanding the resources to provide for superior military forces. It simplified matters for American government officials to interpret ambiguous evidence as a clearcut military threat by the Soviet Union. The political dynamics of the Communist nations were glossed over through the conception that the United States faced a monolithic, Soviet-controlled Communist bloc.

DOMESTIC CONSTRAINTS ON POLICY STANCES

The developments of the late forties exemplify a recurring pattern in American foreign relations. The construction of the American Cold War alliance system was largely the result of an effort to establish within the United States government a stable basis for the postwar international role that most opinion leaders in the United

States considered necessary for it to play. The governmental structure and processes of foreign policy making have often had to reconcile domestic political constraints with the perceived requirements of foreign relations, while sometimes producing less desirable consequences. The governmental processes themselves, then, are an important factor in explaining foreign relations.

The chapters that follow describe a growing American antagonism toward the Soviet Union in terms of the pressures of American politics, the constraints of the American governmental process, and the momentum of American foreign operations and programs. These pressures and constraints were applied largely by a coalition of Democrats and Republicans intent upon maintaining a major international role for the United States. Yet this coalition lacked detailed agreement about what that role should be and was worried about the political costs they would have to pay for maintaining it. From the outset, foreign policy leaders looked for ways to galvanize public support for external commitments, ways to reduce and limit commitments, and ways to routinize and institutionalize the commitments that were made.

The next two chapters deal with the deepening of the Cold War. As we shall see, until late 1950, the Truman Administration was not willing to make the full commitment of military resources necessary to turn the political containment of the Soviet bloc into military containment. The resource and political demands generated by the Korean war completed the Cold War polarization process that had begun in the last months of World War II. As historian John Gaddis has done, this book dates the completion of the polarization process as late as 1950–51.[7]

Both the Soviet Union and the United States were predisposed by internal forces to be antagonistic toward one another at the end of World War II. Russia was a modern dictatorship, ruled until 1953 by Joseph Stalin, a moody and paranoid dictator with extraordinary political power. Soviet foreign relations were plagued with suspicion and preoccupied with extending Russia's hegemony along her western borders. It is unlikely that Stalin and the Soviet gov-

[7] John Lewis Gaddis, "Was the Truman Doctrine a Real Turning Point?" *Foreign Affairs* Vol. 52 (January 1974), pp. 386–402.

ernment would have responded more positively had American policy been less defensive. Indeed, the American concessions that were made seem to have increased Soviet expectations of additional concessions. This response further exaggerated the American viewpoint that "appeasing" aggressors only increased their appetites. "Few things in history," the Soviet bloc historian Adam Ulam has concluded

> appear as inevitable as that there should have been tension and competition between the US and USSR following the conclusion of the war. The nature of both systems made it inevitable. How could Stalin's suspicion have been allayed even by a vast American loan and dispatch of sample atomic bombs? Here was a man who imprisoned hundreds of thousands of his countrymen merely for having been prisoners of war, who had executed his closest collaborators, exiled the families of those who continued being his faithful servants, like Molotov and Mikoyan, and was to turn against the leaders of Yugoslavia, until 1948 his most fanatical followers.[8]

On balance, the evidence indicates that the Cold War was the product of suspicions and actions on both sides. The Soviet Union and the United States after World War II were so predominant in their respective positions relative to the power of their own allies that, together, the two provided the main structure of international order—a bipolar power system that predisposed each to be suspicious of the other.

As a leading power realist, Hans Morgenthau holds that states ought to pursue their national interests, and if they do so rationally and consistently, the most preferred international order will result. Accordingly, Morgenthau agrees with Kolko that the Soviet Union merely pursued its own national interest after World War II while the United States in turn pursued counterrevolutionary ideological objectives reflecting its interests.

[8] Adam Ulam, "On Modern History—Re-reading the Cold War," *Interplay* (March 1969), as reprinted in U.S., Congress, House, Committee on Foreign Affairs, *The Cold War: Origins and Developments*, 92nd Cong., 1st sess., 1971, p. 25. "Could Stalin's fears have been appeased?" Ulam goes on to ask. He feels that, "if carefully qualified," the proper answer could be in the affirmative.

If one could know for certain what the "national interest" is at a given time, we could be more confident of the international outcome. Regrettably, all too often one is left to ask with the late political scientist Arnold Wolfers, "Which interest is the national [one]?"[9] As for Kolko, he does not, as Morgenthau notes, convince the reader of his argument that the United States should bear exclusive blame for starting the Cold War.[10]

The Cold War often appears to have been heavily "overdetermined"—that is, many explanations have been offered to explain why it *had* to occur. Yet not all aspects were inevitable. It need not have gone as far as it did or have been sustained for so long. It would not have taken a great deal to reduce marginally the antagonism between the two blocs, the risks run in their military competition, and their mutual hostility and suspicion. Such marginal reductions would have been valuable to both sides and might have become more significant in time. Doubtless on both sides suspicions and hostilities had grown reciprocally and therefore might have been abated by incremental steps. Negotiations and unilateral actions to ameliorate dangers and costly conditions were possible. Both sides could have pursued political solutions more persistently. Both could have moderated their hostility by changes in military and political positions within the bounds of their own domestic constraints.

On the other hand, it is important to consider that the Cold War could have been even worse than it was. The arms race could have been more competitive. Confrontation could have occurred more often and been more dangerous. Nuclear holocaust could have been more imminent. More actual warfare, disorder, and repression might have occurred. The Cold War may have been a mistake, but it was not exclusively or even primarily an American mistake. It was the result of shared errors and misperceptions by several nations, and it might have escalated further than it did.

This book devotes continuing attention to the internal processes and forces of American government and politics. The chapters that follow present a picture of American foreign policy making as

[9] Arnold Wolfers, "National Security as an Ambiguous Symbol," *Political Science Quarterly* XLVII (December 1952), pp. 481–502.

[10] Morgenthau, pp. 10f.

the product of conflicting forces and viewpoints within the government. These divergences in turn reflect nongovernmental interests that include public opinion, private economic interests, and other domestic forces. The government as national actor, while sensitive to outside pressures and interests, is usually able to hold the initiative in dealing with these varied interests. And the government pays special attention to these noneconomic interests that show up as votes in federal elections and are expressed as segments of public opinion.

chapter 2

Truman's First Term: The Beginning of the Cold War

At the onset of World War II President Roosevelt had taken care to bring Republicans into his Administration and establish an informal wartime coalition. When the war drew to a close, American executive branch officials—to say nothing of Congressmen and other public figures—differed widely in their political and ideological outlooks toward Russia. The tenuous coalition of viewpoints among American officials was held together primarily by the recognized need for cooperation with Russia. One faction, the power realists in the government, consisted mainly of the Joint Chiefs of Staff and the civilian lawyers and brokers on wartime service in the War Department, led by Henry L. Stimson and John J. McCloy. This faction considered cooperation with Russia a political necessity, and they were supported by liberal internationalists who considered it a moral imperative and leftists who sympathized with the Soviet regime. For example, when Henry Morgenthau, Jr., the liberal financier who was Secretary of the Treasury, protested in writing to Roosevelt in January 1945 over the concern of the War Department about Soviet power in Europe, his aim was to mobilize support for his plan to destroy the economic potential of Germany to wage war. He strengthened his case by charging that a soft peace for Germany was a policy advocated by those who would under-mine continued friendship with the Soviet Union. In this way, Morgenthau appealed to a wider constituency than if he had con-fined himself to his own well-known views about a punitive peace for Germany. While this document signals the postwar split over how the United States ought to deal with the Soviet Union, it is also evidence of a belief that friendship with Russia still commanded a wider consensus in Washington than did the issue of how severely to deal with Germany.

At the same time, other political factors were changing at a breathtaking rate. World War II had left Europe prostrate. In China the civil war between Chiang Kai-shek's Nationalists and the Communists resumed after being postponed for a decade by the Japanese threat. Elsewhere in Asia and in Africa, the war had set loose forces of national independence and political revolution by demonstrating that Europe's political dominance on both conti-nents could be challenged. The war launched an era of decoloniza-tion that saw Southeast Asia, the Indian subcontinent, and most of Africa divide into a variety of independent states.

This was the setting in which postwar American foreign policy developed. This international setting provided the stimuli to which American political leaders and public opinion responded. One can-not accurately interpret American postwar foreign policies without taking into account the perceptions of these external events held by the public and by political factions and leaders. Much of these leaders' efforts were directed at reconciling the foreign policy re-sponses they considered necessary with the restraints of public opin-ion and of factional conflict within the government.

SUCCESSOR TO "DR. WIN-THE-WAR"

Most major elements of the United States Cold War posture were developed during the Truman Administration (1945–52). Harry S. Truman was an experienced but colorless politician when he became President. His political career had begun in the medi-ocrity of the Pendergast machine in Jackson County, Missouri, where he was a county judge for ten years, and most of his Senate career had been undistinguished. Truman gained national prominence, however, from his chairmanship of a Senate investigating committee established in 1941 to deal with mismanagement in the defense effort. His handling of the committee hinted at a deep concern with the larger purposes of public life that became more apparent later, and he was largely successful in his efforts to avoid excessive congressional zeal in overseeing the war effort. Truman's nomination for the Vice Presidency on the Democratic ticket in 1944 left men of stronger views and bearing—among them James F. Byrnes, an able and ambitious South Carolinian, and Henry A. Wallace, the brilliant but erratic incumbent Vice President—standing in the wings.

TRUMAN'S FIRST CHALLENGES

Truman came to the Presidency without the broad experience in urban (and urbane) politics that Franklin Roosevelt had gained by 1933, without the solid international and national stature that Eisenhower had achieved by 1953, without the dazzling success of Kennedy in capturing control of the national Democratic party by 1960, and without the mastery of the Senate that Johnson had demonstrated. Truman was not a heroic figure. He could be wrong; he could be petty; and he could be highly partisan. In the largest issues of his Administration, however, he rose to the occasion, acting out his own schoolboy image of great Presidents. "History taught me. . . ," he wrote and said many times. Sophisticated historians could quibble about the validity of the lessons that Truman learned from history, but these lessons were an important part of his public philosophy. They helped to make him an overachiever in the Presidency.

Truman became President in April 1945, as the European phase of the war was drawing to a close. The Allied armies from the west, under the command of General Dwight D. Eisenhower, and the Soviet armies from the east had converged on Germany. Men and matériel were already being transferred to the Pacific theater to complete the defeat of Japan.

At first the war operations required little direction from the new President. An effort to structure the postwar international system with multilateral institutions was also in full swing. A more flexible international monetary system than had existed in the prewar era had been sketched out in international negotiations at Bretton Woods in 1944, and arrangements had already been made for establishing a formal United Nations organization. In his first press statement as President, Truman announced that the San Francisco Conference would meet as scheduled to write the United Nations Charter. The conference ended June 26, and the Senate ratified the Charter July 28. Meanwhile, Germany had surrendered on May 8, and Truman, arranging a meeting with Stalin and Churchill, had begun to address himself to the more pressing problems of the war's end.

The Big Three met in mid-July in Potsdam, the heart of defeated Germany, to settle the outstanding issues of their wartime alliance—primarily the future of Germany. Roosevelt's meeting with Churchill and Stalin at Yalta in the Crimea in February 1945 had produced some optimism in the American delegation about working with the Russians. The mood of the American delegation returning from the Potsdam Conference five months later, however, was much more grim. The diplomats had grappled with the issues growing out of the tightening grip of Soviet power in Eastern Europe—the question of what constituted "broadly representative" governments in Poland and the other new Soviet satellites, the exclusion of Western authorities from Eastern Germany, and the unwavering Soviet demand for large reparations from Germany. The American delegation had gone to Potsdam troubled by the developments in Eastern Europe but ill-prepared for the utter Soviet noncooperation that it encountered.[1]

As a diplomatic event, Potsdam proved to be a holding action for the Big Three. It settled nothing of consequence although it did forestall head-on clashes over rival interests in Europe when tragic outbreaks of violence between the two victorious sides were dangerously plausible. The heads of state dealt with most issues by referring them to a conference of foreign ministers or, as in the case of Poland, to future peace treaty negotiations (which meant, on the whole, an acknowledgment of the Soviet-dominated status quo).

[1] Paul Y. Hammond, "Directives for the Occupation of Germany: The Washington Story," in Harold Stein, ed., *American Civil-Military Decisions* (University, Ala.: Univ. of Alabama Press, 1962), pp. 434–35.

Soviet behavior sharpened Truman's antagonism. But it was easier to resolve to stop "coddling" Stalin than to discover and take the necessary steps to avoid coddling.

The Yalta agreements had already come under partisan attack with the charge that Roosevelt gave Eastern Europe to Russia. Potsdam came under similar fire. These charges about the wartime conferences opened a partisan breach in Washington. American negotiations with the Chinese Communists in 1946 to bring the Nationalists and Communists into a coalition government widened the partisan breach when they ended in failure and recriminations.

Unfortunately, though attacking the Roosevelt and Truman records in negotiating with the Russians was fair politics, this assault did not settle the central policy issue that was to confront this country over the next five years: what level and kinds of effort should the United States make to cope with what it perceived to be the Soviet threat? Equally important, though easier to lose sight of, was the question of how to minimize antagonism between the United States and the Soviet Union. A single answer came to be applied to both issues during 1946: the United States could get along best with the Soviet Union if it operated from a position of strength; the risk of Soviet hostility to American firmness would be more than offset by the stabilizing effect of American strength. Again, the analogy with the prewar appeasement of Hitler was often drawn in these early postwar years: giving in to aggressors only expanded their appetites.

The nation that Truman led as a new President in 1945 was one that was turning inward, tired of foreign burdens, yet aware of its central position as a world power. It became Truman's role to preside over the government in Washington while helping to recast public expectations substantially. And in 1945 he had few political assets beyond public sympathy to help in carrying out these tasks. A criticism leveled at Truman during his Administrations was that he set a low standard for future postwar Presidents. This criticism proved to be too optimistic a view of the future. No other postwar President—with the peculiar exception of Nixon—has surpassed the standard of achievement in foreign relations that Truman set.

When the Truman Administration began in 1945, Washington anticipated a much smaller effort in foreign relations than was actually made over the years that followed. Strong popular pressure to bring the troops home developed immediately after the Japanese surrender in August. As General Marshall, head of the United States Army and Air Force, explained to a joint session of Congress a month later, "The rate of demobilization has been determined by transportation facilities. . . . It has no relationship whatsoever to the size of the Army in the future."[2] Roosevelt's postwar plans had relied heavily enough on the United Nations to avoid hard questions about how to cope with major security issues. Truman at first accepted these plans as part of the presidential office thrust upon him. Even the deterioration of relations with the Soviet Union in no way affected the demobilization plans.

Churchill has written of the "deadly hiatus" between Roosevelt's fading strength and Truman's gradually tightening grip on world problems.

> In this melancholy void one President could not act and the other could not know. Neither the military chiefs nor the State Department received the guidance they required. The former confined themselves to their professional sphere; the latter did not comprehend the issues involved. The indispensable political direction was lacking at the moment when it was most needed. The United States stood on the scene of victory, master of world fortunes, but without a true and coherent design.[3]

GOVERNMENT POLICY FACTIONS

The reasons for what Churchill saw as a "melancholy void" went beyond Roosevelt's illness and Truman's inexperience. The war's ending exposed the new President to at least three distinct and unresolved lines of policy development. One was centered in the State Department, which by common consent would play the leading role in foreign policy in the postwar era. Throughout the war, the State Department had been reduced largely to handling the routine mechanics of diplomacy and writing papers about

[2] Quoted in U.S., Congress, House, *United States Defense Policies Since World War II*, H. Doc. 85:1, No. 100, p. 5.

[3] Winston S. Churchill, *Triumph and Tragedy* (Boston: Houghton Mifflin, 1953), p. 455.

postwar policy, while the important external actions of this country took place overwhelmingly in the military sphere. The State Department's main objectives were fairly conservative. Its plans for the United Nations favored the League of Nations model rather than a more forward approach. A position favoring a "peace of reconciliation" with Germany was directed toward reconstituting the structure of power in Europe and reviving the visions of independent democracies associated with the early twenties. Under Cordell Hull's leadership the State Department had also become a doctrinaire proponent of a liberal trade policy. Free trade had drawn its supporters in the thirties as a limited government solution to the Great Depression, an alternative or supplement to national economic planning. By 1945, however, free trade could have seemed plausible only to officials who were largely out of touch with the economic catastrophes and political upheaval brought by the war in Europe and Japan.

The major European protagonists, Germany and Britain, had forced their economies into massive war production (Britain sooner and further than Germany). At the war's end the British elected a Labour government intent upon economic planning and major social welfare programs, although the alternative Conservative party would also have carried out active government intervention in the economy and social welfare efforts. In practice, the liberal trade policies advocated by the State Department, with the active support of a Treasury Department faction, amounted to a hard line toward America's closest wartime allies, since liberal trading policies limit the extent to which national governments can implement national economic plans. The doctrinaire free trade policies promoted by the State-Treasury faction ran counter to the efforts of the British, French, and other Western European governments acting as managers of the economy and gatekeepers over imports and exports. Truman's abrupt cancellation of Lend Lease to Britain when the European phase of the war ended, accompanied by our new free trade policies, produced severe economic pressures on the British.

While the State Department's free trade policies represented a longstanding commitment to doctrine and a self-confidence about America's competitive trade position between World Wars I and II, war-induced economic changes had now made these policies a threat to America's allies. America's homeland, unlike that of all other major participants, had not been devastated by the war; and, unlike Great Britain, the United States had not liquidated the main assets of a vast empire to prosecute the war. From the position of commercial strength that the United States would enjoy after the war, the insistence of the State Department on doctrinaire liberal trade policies appeared threatening to British officials. When Churchill recognized the implications of American policies, he warned his Foreign Secretary: "We should certainly not be prepared ourselves to submit to an economic, financial, and monetary system laid down by, say, Russia, or the United States with her fagot-vote China."[4]

Meanwhile, a quite different policy line had been developing toward Germany, involving other factions within our government and originating from different premises. The American military, anticipating that they would at first be responsible for administering a defeated Germany, had been anxious to keep their sphere of action free of political constraints in order to concentrate on winning the war and avoid being associated with political objectives that might later prove unpopular. Roosevelt evidently had similar views. At any rate, he resisted pressures from several directions to commit himself to a definite policy about the postwar treatment of Germany. In the Treasury Department, however, a hard line had developed about the postwar treatment of Germany. The Morgenthau Plan proposed to dismantle Germany's industrial base in order to assure that Germany would never again be able to wage aggressive war. The "pastoralization" of Germany (in Churchill's phrase), if taken literally, would have forced the emigration of millions of Germans unable to make a living in a deindustrialized economy. War Department officials were determined that the American forces would not assume the burden of imposing such a revolutionary policy as civil affairs administrators in Germany. They had in fact become the leading advocates of economic pragmatism and were engaged in extensive relief activities in Germany when Truman became President. Thus in 1945 Truman took charge of a government divided by a State-Treasury faction that was hard line about America's wartime allies in the name of liberal trade, and a State-

4 Winston S. Churchill, *Closing the Ring* (Boston: Houghton Mifflin, 1951), p. 713.

War faction that was more flexible about the postwar treatment of our enemy Germany.

As Vice President, Truman himself had remained largely uninformed about these factional disputes and about the military and political issues of wartime negotiations because of Roosevelt's tendency to handle these matters personally. When Truman first became President, many government officials in the State Department, the Treasury, and the armed services were united in their view that it was essential to get along peacefully with the Soviet Union after the war. This belief was a carryover from a wartime judgment that after the war the Soviet Union would be the dominant power in continental Europe. Cooperation with the Russians was a matter of prudence, a major necessity. It depended not on trust but on the expectation that the United States could not or should not maintain enough power in Europe to permit us to follow any other policy. As Churchill suggests, therefore, the State and War Departments both obstructed an early shift to a more belligerent posture toward the Soviet Union in the spring and summer of 1945.

Churchill's warnings were undoubtedly heard in Washington, but they were discounted by some—particularly State Department officials—who viewed them as attempts to encourage a substantial American loan to the British, which they sorely needed. In addition, an articulate minority within our government took a harder line toward Russia. Averell Harriman, the American ambassador in Moscow, had been stating the case against the Russians, and Truman had unquestionably heard him. Harriman has recalled to historian Cabell Philips that he rushed back to Washington after Roosevelt's death to warn Truman about the Russians in order to stiffen our resolve to demand an independent government in Poland.

> I had talked with Mr. Truman for only a few minutes when I began to realize that the man had a real grasp of the situation. . . . He had read all the cables and reports that had passed between me and the State Department, going back for months. He knew the facts and the sequence of events, and he had a keen understanding of what they meant.[5]

[5] Cabell Philips, *The Truman Presidency: The History of a Triumphant Succession* (New York: Macmillan, 1966), p. 79.

THE SOVIET CHALLENGE

Harriman and Churchill were not the only voices in Washington warning of the Soviet challenge to Western interests. Stimson and McCloy in the War Department talked in terms of power and interests in Europe. They and the Wall Street lawyers they had recruited to man the civilian posts of the wartime military establishment hardly shared the hope about Russia prevalent in wartime Washington. Stimson and McCloy, fearing the creation of a power vacuum into which Russia could move, had opposed Secretary of the Treasury Morgenthau's proposal that the German economic apparatus be dismantled after the war. Still, they had backed General Marshall in his insistence that postwar politics not interfere with the efficient winning of the war.

In May, during the closing days of the war in Europe, Eisenhower proposed to withdraw the Allied armies under his command westward to the lines that would mark the occupation zones of Germany, established by agreement with the Russians eight months earlier. Eisenhower and the Joint Chiefs of Staff felt that United States compliance with the zone agreements would help ensure Soviet cooperation in setting up the joint machinery for the administration of occupied Germany. When Churchill protested, Truman, according to his later account, responded:

> We had no intention of extending ourselves beyond those zones. I took this position after consulting with our military chiefs. Russian tactics and aims were, of course, of much concern to us, and I agreed with Churchill on the seriousness of the situation. But I could not agree to going back on our commitments. Apart from that, there were powerful military considerations which we could not and should not disregard.[6]

With a seemingly awesome task ahead of them in Asia, the military chiefs wanted to concentrate on defeating Germany. They insisted that the Soviet Union be brought into the war in Asia to help, though Harriman wanted the Russians kept out. Truman's

[6] Harry S. Truman, *Memoirs*, Vol. 1: *Years of Decision* (Garden City, N.Y.: Doubleday, 1958), pp. 298–99.

decision in late July to drop atomic bombs on Hiroshima and Nagasaki reflected the same dominant concern with military objectives and military costs, particularly in terms of potential American casualties.

Roosevelt—"Dr. Win-the-War"—had shared these views, but he had never venerated military advisers as much as Truman did. *It was Truman's propensity to follow his military advisers, rather than his slowness in perceiving a Soviet menace to American interests in Europe, that contributed to the faltering political leadership that Churchill perceived when the military objectives of the war were attained in 1945.* Truman's support for the State Department's free trade goals accentuated the divergence between British and American views.

Furthermore, what Churchill perceived as a hiatus between Roosevelt and Truman was actually in part a gap between the Truman Administration's perception and its action. The Truman Administration's divergence from the wartime alliance with Russia began with growing complaints about Soviet conduct, such as Moscow's failure to comply with the Yalta agreements about the establishment of "broadly representative" governments in Eastern Europe. After the end of the war it became much more difficult to respond to the Soviet challenge to American interests in ways that met the diverse expectations in Washington about the postwar role of the United States in international affairs.

Despite the events of late 1945, the Administration could not abandon as easily as its critics the viewpoint that cooperation with the Russians was still a necessity. Truman could use tough language (or claimed to) in private, as he did with the Soviet Foreign Secretary, Molotov, in July 1945. Public utterances were more cautious, however. In June 1945 Truman responded to a reporter's question about the actions of the Russians in Eastern Europe by saying, "Be as patient with them as you possibly can," adding, "I don't blame them for wanting to have these states around them, just as we want Mexico and Canada to be friendly to us."[7]

The costs of losing all Russian cooperation were more immediate for officials who were responsible for administering occupa-

---

[7] Quoted in James David Barber, *The Presidential Character* (Englewood Cliffs, N.J.: Prentice-Hall, 1972), p. 270.

tion forces in Germany and Austria; who handled relief and rehabilitation problems in these countries, in Italy, and in the former enemy occupied states of Western Europe; or who worried about the vulnerability of Greece, Turkey, Iran, China, or Korea to Soviet military threats.

A glimpse of this problem can be seen in the diaries of Henry A. Wallace. In early August Wallace had recorded his view that President Truman, Secretary of State Byrnes, and the War and Navy Departments were not directed toward "strengthening our ties of friendship with Russia," and that "their attitude will make for a war eventually." Wallace would break with Truman over this issue, and it was to become a major aspect of Wallace's campaign for the Presidency in 1948 as a third party candidate.

Yet Wallace also recorded the vacillation of the Administration on the question of Russia. After the apparent hard line expressed against Russia in August, a September Cabinet meeting included a speech by Secretary of War Stimson defending the Soviet Union and stressing the hope of cooperation with them. Wallace recorded Stimson as saying that "throughout our history Russia had been our friend. . . . Our relationship with Russia during recent months had been improving. President Truman agreed to this. . . . The President then called on Dean Acheson, the Under-Secretary of the State, who indicated that he agreed with Secretary Stimson."[8]

The disparity Wallace noted in War Department behavior toward Russia—the hard line of August, the hopeful statement a few weeks later—reflected the uncomfortable position in which the War Department found itself after V-E Day: responsible for governing the American sector of occupied Germany and Austria and concerned about the safety and redeployment of American forces from the continent of Europe. Conscious of the problems that would be created for American forces in Europe if hostility with the Soviet Union grew, Stimson remained committed to a hopeful view about Russia as late as September 1945.

The problem was further complicated by disagreements between Secretary of War Stimson and Secretary of the Navy Forrestal. Forrestal, who had no responsibilities for civil affairs in Europe,

8 John Morton Blum, ed., *The Price of Vision: The Diary of Henry A. Wallace, 1942-1946* (Boston: Houghton Mifflin, 1973), pp. 475, 482.

listened to quite different advisers, and he moved rapidly into a position of more explicit hostility to the Russians.

Indeed, the postwar role of the United States, as visualized by the American public opinion elites, assumed not only that Russia would be cooperative but that the international system could be stabilized with a minimum of American involvement—such as through the United Nations. Our conflict with Russia over postwar objectives provided the impetus for adapting to a world that turned out to differ from the one we had anticipated in other respects besides the assumption of Soviet-American cooperation. American involvement abroad would have expanded during the postwar era even without the conflict with Russian interests. But it was easier to present government modifications of postwar policy as responses to Communist challenges than as adaptations to a variety of changing or new conditions.

As evidence of Soviet hostility mounted after Postsdam, the perception of the Soviet Union as our enemy became increasingly strong in Washington and among the American public. In 1946 Russia exerted military pressure in Iran and against Turkey to gain special privileges in the use of the Dardanelles. In response, Truman dispatched the Sixth Fleet into the Eastern Mediterranean on a diplomatic pretext. This was the first American military reaction to a Soviet military threat in the postwar era. It was limited to a redeployment of existing forces that cost practically nothing.

REACTING TO COLD WAR COSTS

The second phase in the Truman Administration's response to Soviet contentiousness was its effort to reduce the costs that Soviet noncooperation was adding to America's economic burdens in Europe. Since the war, the four occupying powers (the United States, the Soviet Union, Great Britain, and France) had each governed a separate zone in Germany. Mindful of the prospect that the four powers might not work together harmoniously, Byrnes had eliminated from the Potsdam protocol any grounds for direct Soviet collection of economic reparations in the Western zones. This of course did not eliminate the reparations themselves; it meant merely that they had to be delivered to the Russians by Western authorities. By the summer of 1945 it had become evident that the United States would have to prop up the economies of all three non-Soviet zones. Thus, much of the Western zones' share of the $10 billion in economic reparations that Russia was getting from Germany would, as Truman had bluntly told Stalin at Potsdam, be paid indirectly by the American taxpayer. Moreover, Soviet intransigence, combined with French determination to keep Germany divided, paralyzed the four-power occupation. Together these circumstances precipitated changes in American policy.

In May 1946 the United States zone commander General Lucius Clay suspended deliveries of economic reparations to the Soviet Union, thus ending Western cooperation with Soviet demands for reparations. In order to cope more effectively with the economic chaos of Germany, Byrnes offered to merge the American zone with the British and French and abandoned the agreed policy of holding German industrial production at 50 percent below the prewar level. At Stuttgart in September Byrnes gave a more positive tone to these steps: "Germany is a part of Europe and European recovery would be low indeed if Germany with her great resources . . . turned into a poorhouse."[9] Byrnes's speech supported long-held convictions in the State Department that mild peace terms with Germany were in the interest of the United States. In January 1947 the British (but not the French) agreed to the merger—the first step in the establishment of the Federal Republic of Germany (which eventually gained the necessary French cooperation).

Merging the American and British zones did not mean that we were abandoning all cooperation with the Soviet Union in Germany but rather that we were seeking new ways to cope with Germany's political and economic collapse. The merger was intended to make Germany not only self-sustaining but useful in the economic recovery of Western Europe as a whole. It was not a commitment by the United States to extend its power to Europe but rather a move that would enable us to reduce our forces there. The zonal merger pitted the American policy of reconstructing the German and other Western European economies against the Soviet appeal for German national unity. Such "unity" would have expedited the transfer of German plants, equipment, and current production

9 U.S., Congress, Senate, Foreign Relations Committee, *Documents on Germany, 1944–1959*, 86th Cong., 1st sess., 1959, Committee Print, pp. 35–42.

to Russia for reparations, effectively placing the German economy at the service of Russia. Implicit in the Russian plan was an acceptance of German and Western European economic chaos (and continued dependence on the U.S. Treasury) as compatible with Soviet interests.

Churchill, out of power, had already given classic expression to this phase in the break with Russia in a speech at Fulton, Missouri, in March 1946. He referred to the new Russian imperialism as an "Iron Curtain" that had descended across Europe, and he advocated a "fraternal association" of the United States and Great Britain, French reconciliation with Germany, and European political integration. The American press hailed the speech for its candor. Probably timed to win Congressional approval for a $3.5 billion loan to Britain, Churchill's speech invoked Soviet expansionism to solidify Anglo-American friendship. Truman, though having advance knowledge of the speech, later denied that he had known what Churchill would say; but many interpreted his presence on the platform as an endorsement of the Prime Minister's analysis.

Yet, it was one thing to sound the alarm and quite another to make effective responses. No one—certainly not Churchill, whose country was economically prostrate—had recommended the remobilization of national power in any form. Truman had followed an erratic course during 1945 and 1946—at one time firm and decisive, at another equivocal. He developed a firm and consistent position in dealing with the Russians only as the task of guiding government economic and military programs required him to do so.

MOBILIZING ACTION AND SUPPORT

Before the merger of the American and British zones of Germany could actually be accomplished in 1947, the Truman Administration had decided to increase its commitments in Europe. This action represented the third phase of its response to Russia. Now the Administration could exploit some of the advantages of the President's primary role in foreign affairs, but it also faced special problems in winning support from Congress and the public. In order to understand what those problems were we must examine the domestic side of the foreign policy debate that took place in 1945–46.

In September 1945, armed with a report from his war reconversion director that predicted "an immediate and large dislocation in our economy,"[10] Truman had called Congress into special session and presented it with a staggering program of domestic legislation. He asked for strong powers to cope with reconversion problems, a modest tax reduction, a large increase in congressional pay, and a full program of basic social welfare legislation and economic reforms. Included were several measures to deal with unemployment, stabilization of the peacetime economy, a huge housing program, and the expansion of programs for the development of our natural resources. Later, this program, somewhat restated, would be called the "Fair Deal." The breadth and magnitude of these proposals indicate the Administration's great concern about postwar domestic problems. (By contrast, when his Administration first came to grips with a peacetime military budget, Truman indicated that not more than a third of the federal budget was to be allocated for national defense.)

Republican leaders rightly considered Truman's legislative message the "kickoff" of the 1946 congressional campaign, for it was an aggressive partisan move by a President seeking a political base for his leadership. Truman's message also helped to alienate business leaders, who recognized it as an effort to perpetuate the significant powers that government had gained in wartime. Finally, it cast a partisan shadow across the Administration's efforts to cope with inflationary wage and price pressures over the next two years. By indicating that he intended to extend New Deal social and economic programs and, above all, to take the initiative in domestic politics, Truman had fired the opening shot of postwar partisanship in domestic affairs.

But he was not permitted to pick his own grounds for partisan battles. The Administration's posture toward the Soviet Union had become particularly vulnerable to partisan attack because the public perceived it as laggard in dealing with Russian challenges.

In time for the 1946 election, moreover, a venerable Republican leader who played a direct role in Truman's China policy dramatically broke with the Administration to supply its political rivals with a partisan issue. Patrick J. Hurley, a former Secretary of War, had been sent by President Roosevelt as ambassador to China

---

10 Quoted in Philips, p. 103.

in 1944 to help bring about some reconciliation between the Communist and Nationalist Chinese regimes. After a year in China, Hurley abandoned the effort, returned home, resigned as ambassador and charged (correctly) that State Department officials had been undermining his policies. His criticism was neither partisan nor ideological until he began to question the public loyalty of State Department officials, charging Communist sympathizing in the State Department. It was the beginning of a long and tragic vilification of the China specialists in the State Department in which distinguished and mediocre service alike were condemned.

Our China policy had been permitted to drift with Hurley's shift in attitude while serving there. To dispel the doubts raised by his disturbing and surprising resignation, the Administration reaffirmed its goal of a "strong, united, and democratic China" and dispatched General Marshall as ambassador to Chungking with instructions to broaden the base of Chiang's government by including representatives of other groups.

By March Marshall had negotiated a truce between Communists and Nationalists and returned to Washington for a visit. But the truce soon crumbled. By summer the Communist forces had gained substantial strength and confidence and paid little attention to the mediator from Washington. Thereafter, Marshall's role, like Hurley's, increasingly concentrated on the Nationalist government, persuading it to take conciliatory measures toward the Communists (which were ignored by Mao) and undertake internal reforms in the hope of winning wider mass support.

By November 1946, when the congressional elections occurred, the situation in China was still too confusing to serve as an effective partisan issue, but it did add to public anxieties about international affairs and provided Republican candidates with an occasion to state their suspicions about the State Department. Republicans leveled their main criticisms of the incumbent government at Roosevelt's handling of the Yalta Conference and at Truman's negotiations at Potsdam for making treaty concessions to the Russians—criticisms that implied that the Communist "menace" (as our conflicting postwar interests with Russia were increasingly labeled in public accounts) could be met without incurring costs to the United States. *It is quite clear that until after the 1946 elections both the Administration and its critics treated the objective of "get-*

ting tough" with the Russians as though it had little to do with the federal budget.

It should also be said that the Administration failed to back up its own increasingly tough statements about the Russians with tangible commitments: for example, the precipitate withdrawal of American armed forces from Europe proceeded unabated during the spring of 1946, at the very time that attitudes had hardened against the Russians. This inertia at first reflected genuine ambivalence about the Russian issue and then became intentional ambiguity as hope for Soviet cooperation faded. In fact, some degree of ambivalence would remain a characteristic of the Truman Administration until mid-1950, when the Korean war precipitated a consistent and explicit Cold War position in Washington.

The main source of ambiguity was doubt by the Administration that it could fully disclose its worries about dealing with the Soviet Union without incurring adverse political reactions. In September 1946, Clark Clifford completed a survey of opinions within the government concerning relations with Russia. The results indicated support for a global policy of containing Russia with all available means, including atomic and biological warfare if necessary. Congressional leaders were doubtless generally aware of these views. In all probability Republican campaign attacks on the Truman Administration that November were sharpened by this indication that the Administration considered itself cornered by the disparity between its assessment of American foreign policy responsibilities on the one hand, and its assessment about what the public would support on the other.

The 1946 congressional elections were a severe political setback for Truman. In response he replaced Secretary of State Byrnes with Marshall. Truman had high regard for Marshall, and it was a politically prudent move, with a Democratic Administration facing a Republican controlled Congress for the first time in sixteen years. Moreover, there had been vexing difficulties with Byrnes. They had climaxed after the Moscow Foreign Ministers' Conference in December 1945 when Byrnes attempted to arrange a radio address to the nation on the results of the conference without reporting first to Truman.

Two close observers of Byrnes's deteriorating relationship with Truman had been Dean Acheson, Under-Secretary of State, and

John Foster Dulles, a special Republican adviser to Brynes. Both men were to become Secretaries of State themselves, and both evidently learned from the firing of Byrnes that the Secretary of State is the President's man.

THE TRUMAN DOCTRINE: RESOURCES AND COMMITMENTS

With the convening of the 80th Congress in January 1947 under Republican leadership, it hardly seemed likely that the United States would make major new foreign commitments that would tax the federal treasury. House Speaker Joseph Martin promptly declared as a Republican goal a 20 percent cut in income taxes and commensurate spending reductions. The most reasonable prognosis was for two years of congressional dominance and financial retrenchment in Washington. Instead, what followed was a period of vigorous presidential competition with Congress in domestic affairs and strong and often challenged presidential leadership in foreign affairs that brought the United States major political and fiscal obligations abroad. Several circumstances produced this unexpected presidential success in foreign affairs: an economic crisis in Europe; the appointment of a new Secretary of State; and Truman's own leadership—often erratic, but tough in responding to the large issues of foreign policy and national security.

January 1947 brought a winter of record breaking severity to Western Europe. The Labour government in Great Britain, faced with economic difficulties long anticipated but little acknowledged, had calculated the nation's fuel needs only for a normal year. The result was a shortage that slowed down the economy, causing further economic difficulties. The winter revealed economic and political weakness on the continent too. "Last week," journalist Anne O'Hare McCormick wrote from Paris in the *New York Times* in mid-February

it was suddenly brought home to us that we are now in the front line. . . . The crisis in Britain and France pointed up a truth the United States knows but shrinks from facing. They are primarily economic crises, signs of the difficulty of treating postwar breakdown by democratic means. They reveal how battered and shaken are the old strongholds of democracy in Europe, and how few these strongholds are. Most of all they throw the ball to us, giving notice that if freedom as we understand it is to survive it's up to the United States to save it.[11]

In the same period, Marshall became Secretary of State and immediately began mobilizing the resources of the Department of ˙ate to meet the problems he saw. "Most of the other countries of world," he told a Princeton audience in an address on February 22

find themselves exhausted economically, financially, physically. If the world is to get on its feet, if the productive facilities of the world are to be restored, if democratic processes in many countries are to resume their functioning, a strong lead and definite assistance from the United States will be necessary.

This phase of American policy rested on the belief that Russia threatened vital American security interests, mainly in Europe, through a combination of political and military subversion, backed up by military blackmail, during conditions of economic prostration. This perception of a Soviet menace led Washington to shoulder definite though limited obligations and provide substantial resources to Europe while avoiding a direct confrontation with Russia.

Under Marshall's leadership, the State Department moved away from its preoccupation with free trade policy to work with reconstruction-oriented officials in the civil affairs organization set up in Europe after the war and now directed by the State Department. This new focus redirected State Department goals from the global objectives of liberal trade and multilateral peacekeeping to a regional emphasis on Europe's perceived human welfare and security needs.

During the first postwar year, Europe's national economies began to sag. In late 1946 the United States undertook quick action

11 Quoted in Joseph M. Jones, *The Fifteen Weeks* (New York: Viking, 1955), p. 84.

to prop them up and to encourage European economic development and integration. According to the State Department's key memorandum on the proposals that were developed, the threat to Western Europe was due largely to "the disruptive effect of the war" rather than to Communist activities. But, before these ideas had come into focus, the slumping economy of Western Europe had produced a power vacuum in the Eastern Mediterranean that required further American action.

In late February 1947 the British informed Washington that their economic hardships would force them to reduce their commitment to Greece and Turkey after March 31. In less than three weeks President Truman had recommended to Congress a $400 million military aid program for the two countries. Linked to it was the "Truman Doctrine," the tendentious and appealing idea that the United States must "support free peoples who are resisting attempted subjugation by armed minorities or by outside pressures," as President Truman put it in his nationwide radio address on March 12. "I believe," he continued, "that we must assist free peoples to work out their own destinies in their own way. I believe that our help should be primarily through economic and financial aid which is essential to economic stability and orderly political processes." The ideological cast of the Truman Doctrine was restrained, but unmistakable. The President ended by saying:

> The seeds of totalitarian regimes are nurtured by misery and want. They spread and grow in the evil soil of poverty and strife. They reach their full growth when the hope of a people for a better life has died.
>
> We must keep that hope alive.
>
> The free peoples of the world look to us for support in maintaining their freedoms.
>
> If we falter in our leadership, we may endanger the peace of the world—and we shall surely endanger the welfare of our own nation.

The Greek-Turkish aid program served a limited purpose: to help the Greek government against a Greek Communist guerrilla war supported by Albania, Yugoslavia, and Bulgaria, and to help the Turkish government withstand Soviet pressure for joint bases on the Dardanelles. It became a dramatic beginning of the Truman Administration's successful effort to assume the task that Marshall had referred to at Princeton in February. Because its purpose was to provide limited military aid to meet what seemed an urgent need, the Greek-Turkish aid program was a highly satisfactory rallying point for overriding the congressional mood of severe budget and tax cutting.

But the Administration was still careful to undertake prior consultation with congressional leaders. Having resolved to act, Truman had Marshall and Acheson help him explain the need for the Greek-Turkish aid program privately to congressional leaders. Republican Senator Vandenberg garnered further support from among his party colleagues.

At two White House meetings Vandenberg had indicated that the price for congressional cooperation would be a "full and frank statement" by the President. In effect, Vandenberg was asking for two things: that the President strongly commit himself publicly to the aid program and that the rationale for the program be described as an essential response to Soviet aggressive interests in the Eastern Mediterranean and beyond. Vandenberg also wanted Truman to point out the potential consequences for American security interests of not countering Communist threats. Vandenberg's first demand required only that the President play his presidential role, and Truman was happy to oblige. The second demand could have meant several things—a denunciation of historic Russian expansionism or of the world revolutionary aspirations of Communism; a description of the East-West struggle; an indication that the Greek-Turkish program was only the beginning of a larger and more costly effort; or reference at least to the trouble in Western Europe caused by economic chaos and domestic Communism. Vandenberg's essential concern, however, and that of congressional colleagues who supported him, was that American action be in pursuit of American interests, not humanitarian ideals, and that the easiest way to win political support for such action was to talk about the threat of Communism. "The problem of Greece," Vandenberg wrote a congressional colleague at the time, "cannot be isolated by itself. On the contrary, it is probably symbolic of the worldwide ideological clash between Eastern communism and Western democracy; and it may easily be the thing which requires us to make some very fateful and far-reaching decisions."[12]

In his public message, Truman did not describe Soviet expansion in the frank terms that he and Acheson had used privately with congressional leaders. Without being specific, he referred emphatically to the larger considerations that lay behind the Greek-Turkish program. The result, paradoxically, was a landmark Cold War statement about the ideological and political challenge of Communism and the American resolve to meet it. But the program itself in no sense typified this thinking in the American government in the spring of 1947. It was in fact a narrow and defensive program to improve the military power of two governments that were quite undemocratic by American standards. The purpose of the public message was not, as it appeared to be, to generalize from the Greek-Turkish situation to the military threat of Communism everywhere. On the contrary, the intent was to link the narrow response in Greece and Turkey with the political and economic problems of Western Europe that were receiving intensive attention at that very time. (Truman's rhetoric would nonetheless become a problem. Later it was cited as a precedent for universal intercession abroad.)

With Vandenberg's backing, the program gained wide bipartisan support both in and out of Congress. Vandenberg also promptly alleviated anxiety that the program would bypass the United Nations by amending the aid bill to provide for withdrawal of American aid if the United Nations were to take equivalent action. After giving it much attention, Congress passed the Greek-Turkish bill in mid-May under the impetus of the crisis in Greece and Turkey and the breakdown of the Big Four Foreign Ministers' Conference in Moscow in April 1947.

THE MARSHALL PLAN

Meanwhile, Marshall had returned from the Moscow negotiations convinced that the Soviet Union intended to aggravate the growing economic sickness of Western Europe and that the United

---

[12] Arthur H. Vandenberg, Jr., ed., *The Private Papers of Senator Vandenberg* (Boston: Houghton Mifflin, 1952), p. 340.

States had to act to bring about European recovery. He had found Acheson in agreement, convinced by the staff work begun in early March.

Their agreement was only one aspect of a remarkable convergence of informed opinion in Washington in the spring of 1947. Prominent Republicans had arrived at much the same conclusion at a more methodical pace. Within the wartime Roosevelt Administration in 1945 Stimson and McCloy had struck out against the Morgenthau Plan, arguing that German industry was too great an asset for postwar Europe to be thrown away. Byrnes had adopted their view in his Stuttgart speech. In January 1947 John Foster Dulles, the Republican State Department adviser, in an important speech cleared in advance by Vandenberg and by Thomas E. Dewey, leader of the Republican party, had advocated the integration of the industrial potential of Germany into Western Europe in such a way as to advance the economic unification of Western Europe. Dulles subsequently accompanied Marshall to Moscow as a special adviser. While they were there, former President Hoover released a report on economic conditions in occupied Germany and Austria that supported the Stimson-McCloy arguments, emphasizing the common problems of the European economy and the need for restoring productivity. (Concern over what the German occupation was costing the United States launched the Hoover study.) Leading journalists—Lippmann in particular as well as Reston, Childs, the Alsops, and the anonymous reporters of the weekly news magazines —wrote about European economic problems and the responsibility of the United States to act.

Acheson voiced the developing viewpoint of the State Department on May 8 at a meeting in Cleveland, Mississippi. But it was Marshall's speech at the Harvard Commencement on June 5 that launched the effort and gave it a name: the Marshall Plan.

Despite the name his proposal acquired, Marshall made clear that there was no plan:

This is the business of the Europeans. The initiative, I think, must come from Europe. The role of this country should consist of friendly aid in the drafting of a European program and of later support of such a program so far as it may be practical for us to do so. The program should be a joint one, agreed to by a number of, if not all, European nations.

On a calculated risk that paid off handsomely in muting left-wing opposition to the Marshall Plan in Western Europe, the Soviet Union had not been excluded from the invitation to participate in the program. Neither France nor Britain was eager to include Russia in the Marshall program. But the French government was hardly strong enough to face a showdown with the French Left if the Marshall Plan began to look like a Western coalition against the East, and similarly, the Labour government in Britain had no desire to divide Europe by making an issue of the Soviet Union's participation. For these reasons, Britain and France reluctantly invited the Soviet government to a tripartite meeting in Paris in late June 1947. It was a curious meeting. The Russian Foreign Minister, Molotov, brought eighty-nine technicians and clerks and a rigid position against a European program. Bidault of France and Bevin of England insisted upon a common European economic recovery plan, accepting European economic integration in principle. Molotov and his delegation, on a signal from Moscow, withdrew, taking with them any prospect for the Soviet satellites' participation in the Marshall Plan. Europe had been effectively partitioned—but without any onus on the British or French governments and very little on the United States. Sixteen nations now set quickly to work.

Meanwhile, in Washington several prestigious government committees helped the Administration demonstrate the need to aid Europe: a committee on natural resources; another to consider the impact of foreign aid on the domestic economy; a third, composed of distinguished private citizens and chaired by Harriman, now Secretary of Commerce, to advise on safe magnitudes of assistance. In the House of Representatives, a Select Committee on Foreign Aid, chaired by Massachusetts Congressman Christian Herter, undertook a series of reports about the prospective aid program. The select committee was a device for counterbalancing the more conservative Congressmen who held seniority and power in the standing committees. By December 19, 1947, when President Truman submitted draft legislation for the European Recovery Program to Congress, a remarkable array of political pressures could be brought to bear upon the legislative process.

The Marshall Plan thus brought together the War Department faction and the State Department, with its preference for a "peace of reconciliation," under the chief organizer of the war, Marshall. The State Department at last broke out of the fetters of its wartime quarantine to assume a policy leadership role, but it was ill-prepared to administer American reconstruction programs in Europe. The organization that administered the Marshall Plan, the Economic Cooperation Administration, was constructed outside the Department of State.

The policy isolation had ended for the State Department, but it would continue to have trouble maintaining a central role in foreign policy making because of its reluctance to administer the actual economic and military assistance programs that would be major instruments of American foreign policy for more than the next two decades.

The Russians had already helped by walking out of the Paris meetings; they were to help again. The Communist coup in Czechoslovakia in late February 1948 and the suspicious death of the Czech Nationalist leader Jan Masaryk in March dramatized the spread of Soviet power in Eastern Europe. Western anxieties over an impending Italian national election, in which the Italian Communist party stood a good chance of winning control of Parliament, and the growing tensions over the status of West Berlin also helped. (The Soviet blockade of West Berlin followed in June.) Congress approved the European Recovery Program at the end of March.

A persistent controversy about this early postwar period concerns the origins of this ominous Soviet behavior. Did it spring from Soviet expansionist objectives, or was it a response to what they perceived as threatening American actions in Europe?

The Soviet challenge was undoubtedly reactive in some degree to American and European behavior, as we in turn reacted to Soviet moves. The behavior of both the East and West was also greatly determined by domestic forces within each nation. In the United States, officials doubted the American public's willingness to support foreign policy actions in peacetime, public opinion was puzzled by the reports about tough negotiations with a wartime ally, and Europe was undergoing alarming political and economic collapse. On the Soviet side, where it was a widespread expectation that throughout Europe Communism would emerge as the dominant political force in the postwar era, the sustained American interest in Europe undoubtedly generated suspicion.

THE BIRTH OF THE WESTERN COALITION

Another phase of the developing American response to the Soviet challenge—military commitments to Western Europe—began at the end of 1947. As soon as Congress had authorized the Marshall Plan, the Administration began work with Republican leaders in the House and Senate foreign relations committees to lay the legislative groundwork for the North Atlantic Treaty. They emphasized bipartisan support, the goal of European unity, foreign self-reliance, and foreign initiative—factors that had made the Marshall Plan attractive in the United States. In June 1948 the Senate passed the Vandenberg Resolution by a vote of 64 to 4, expressing support from both Republicans and Democrats for the collective security measures taking shape in Western Europe. Ostensibly, the initiative for the North Atlantic Treaty came from the Republican side of the Senate; actually, the alliance had begun to take shape in response to signals from the Administration early in 1948 through discreet diplomatic channels. The British had initiated the fifty-year Brussels Defense Pact, which would become the nucleus of the North Atlantic Treaty.

By October 1948 the United States had reached tentative agreement with the Brussels Pact countries (Britain, France, Belgium, the Netherlands, and Luxembourg) and with Canada on collective defense arrangements. The seven countries decided to invite Norway, Denmark, Iceland, Italy, and Portugal to join them. The twelve signed the NATO pact in Washington in April; the Senate ratified the treaty in July, more than a year after the Vandenberg Resolution. The treaty received broad public and congressional support in this country—partly because the Truman Administration had carefully laid the groundwork for its acceptance, as it had done with the Marshall Plan.

When the North Atlantic Alliance first took shape in early

1948 few American officials expected the treaty to be followed by an American military assistance program to help the other members rearm. That summer, however, the Berlin blockade put immense pressure on the airlift capacity of the United States and focused attention on the conventional Soviet military threat. Originally, the alliance had been intended on both sides of the Atlantic as a way to counter Soviet military blackmail used to promote political instability in Western Europe. The Berlin crisis, however, quickly turned official thinking to narrower military problems. And American officials became concerned about Europe's military weakness and the limited American forces stationed in Europe. Broader political considerations had shifted to short-range military ones in response to a Cold War crisis—as would often happen in the future.

By the following spring, when the North Atlantic Treaty was signed, plans to proceed with a military assistance program were already well advanced. As soon as the Senate had ratified the treaty on July 21, President Truman requested $1.45 billion for military aid, most of it for the treaty countries. The Truman Administration was now prepared to arm its allies against what was widely perceived in Congress, the executive branch, and among private opinion elites to be the military menace of the Soviet Union.

THE CHANGE IN U.S. SECURITY POSTURE

From January 1947 to October 1949 the peacetime external posture of the United States changed dramatically. The Truman Administration had given up primary reliance on the United Nations for its security and had abandoned the expectation of cooperation with the Soviet Union to declare a general threat from Soviet power. The United States government had underwritten first the economic reconstruction and then the military security of Western Europe and had appropriated the first of the billions of dollars these tasks would require—all in spite of the congressional intent at the beginning of the period to cut the budget and taxes.

The vital votes on the Marshall Plan had occurred in 1948, when the prevailing view was that President Truman would not win reelection. These votes represented the high water mark of postwar bipartisanship, with careful joint preparations between the

Democratic Administration and the Republican leaders of Congress to win public support and legislative approval. The Administration could exploit the towering prestige of Senator Vandenberg on the Republican side and the high status that foreign affairs now enjoyed in both the Senate and the House. The behavior of the European states had made the political clearance problem in Washington easier. Their initiatives and visible interest in economic and military integration struck a responsive chord with American officials, who were inclined to see political and economic unification as the solution to Europe's weakness and chaos.

As the Administration moved into these massive commitments to Europe, it found the Republican leadership particularly cooperative. Senator Vandenberg and Thomas Dewey, leader of the eastern and metropolitan Republicans who represented the party's presidential constituency, were both attracted by the growing link with Europe. If anything, the eastern Republicans were ahead of the Administration in supporting the components of the European recovery and rearmament programs—the acceptance of Germany as an essential part of the European economy; reconstruction in order to end American material obligations; and European unification to achieve stability and prosperity.

Formally, the cooperation between the two parties rested on the commitment of both to bipartisanship. But bipartisanship depended upon much more than close White House–Congressional cooperation. Truman's economic and military foreign aid programs were ambitious enough to mute most claims that the Administration was neglecting the Communist threat abroad. They were also constructive enough to appeal to some public idealism or vanity and to avoid charges that the United States was unduly belligerent. They were broad enough to make it difficult for their opponents to invent appealing alternative policies. Above all, they gave the President the initiative. *In the postwar era nothing more quickly won the sympathy of the public than an Administration that seemed to be dealing vigorously with what the public perceived to be an external threat to this country's interests.*

This particularly salient political reality discouraged the Administration from examining more carefully alternatives to its expanding program for a Cold War alliance system. The alternative of greater patience and concessions to the Soviet Union, for which Henry Wallace came to be the leading spokesman, suffered from a special handicap. By 1947 Wallace had already been denied support from regular party leaders, so his only hope was to gain influence by winning public support for his policies. But the interest of a wider public in foreign affairs could more likely be aroused by a perception of external threats than by an appeal to patience.

Another choice—to aid Asia more and Europe less—was suppressed for the time being by the broad agreement in Washington that aiding Europe was urgent and primary.

A third choice, a more subtle and flexible one, was posed by an eloquent and prolific foreign service officer and Soviet specialist, George Kennan, in a widely read article published in July 1947 under the pseudonym "Mr. X." Kennan attributed Soviet conduct to historic Russian imperialism and to the ideology of Communism, both of which inclined the Soviet Union to be patient, flexible, and persistent in pursuing selected expansionist goals. As he later made plain privately within the government, Kennan wanted to stop short of military involvement with Western Europe and, at the same time, not substantially rearm the United States. His view was rooted in a grand and traditional conception of diplomacy: that American responses must be flexible. Only limited military force would be necessary. The political factionalism and nationalism within the Soviet bloc must be taken into account; the militants must be discouraged by the West, not strengthened by Western militancy. These views were pushed aside by an Administration intent on winning public support for building "situations of strength" from which to negotiate with the Soviet Union and puzzled by Kennan's seemingly mystical faith in diplomacy. Whatever the merits of Kennan's views, his policy suggestions were considered by the Truman Administration, but rejected. However, his published statement *was* read for more urgent lessons about Soviet aspirations.

CONCLUSION

During the three years from Potsdam to the Democratic convention of 1948 the Truman Administration had begun a profound change in the character and magnitude of the American involvement in world affairs. The war had seriously undermined the economies of the major powers of Europe, including the Soviet Union, while the American economy had expanded. By 1948 the fears of a postwar depression in the United States had subsided and America's economic preeminence had become unmistakable.

The change in our involvement abroad was more than a matter of recognizing that the United States had interests outside the Western Hemisphere that required us to play a major role in world affairs. Our role as a world power also changed. The instigator of the new role was Marshall, the professional soldier with the largest vision about the wartime effort. Characteristically, in 1947 he instructed the American officials assigned to develop a plan for Europe's economic recovery to "avoid trivia." By avoiding trivia Marshall had infused definite objectives into our enormous military effort during World War II, and in 1947, with commensurate vision, he set the guidelines for postwar American efforts to transform external conditions.

Traditionally (though with some important exceptions), American diplomacy, like British diplomacy, had been aloof and manipulative. Now, under Truman and Marshall, our diplomacy changed to bring American economic power directly to bear in Western Europe. The diplomat and his traditional function of maintaining contact with foreign governments were pushed aside by new American officials—young economists, lawyers, and business executives—who established direct working relationships for our government with the budget and treasury offices in European capitals. Traditional diplomatic methods and objectives also gave way to deadlines and targets, to programs and their management. These new organizational requirements produced new influences on foreign policies. They imposed a demand for clear and unequivocal doctrines to orient government programs and operations. In addition, the costs of these efforts and the American stake in their success made our foreign relations far more dependent upon domestic political consent, which became an important element in America's postwar experience as a world power.

When the United States became involved in the Korean war, these new forces predisposed the United States government to view the Communist bloc as a monolithic power structure with which one negotiated at his peril. The next chapter will trace the consolidation of this Cold War orientation from 1948 to 1952.

chapter 3

Truman's Second Term: Apex and Nadir

THE 1948 ELECTION

The Truman Administration's response to the Soviet challenge and to Europe's needs during 1947 and 1948 represented towering achievements for any administration, but domestic problems had brought Truman's popularity to a low ebb by the spring of 1948, as the presidential nominating conventions approached. He was able to thwart a Democratic "dump Truman" movement only because of his control over the party as President.

On the left, Truman had lost the support of many liberals in the party when he fired Henry Wallace as Secretary of Commerce (before the 1946 congressional elections) for public disagreement with the Administration on foreign policy issues. On the right, Truman lost the support of Southern Democrats by proposing a strong civil rights program in early 1948. Both these groups broke away from the Democratic party to run their own presidential candidates: Henry Wallace on the Progressive ticket and J. Strom Thurmond on the States' Rights ticket. Nonetheless, Truman was able to hold together some elements of the New Deal coalition through his civil rights commitment and his 1948 State of the Union message, which had included proposals for cutting taxes and for spending $10 billion on social legislation.

After his nomination, Truman called the Republican-controlled 80th Congress back into session and challenged it to enact the legislative program called for in the Republican campaign platform. The challenge was an unprecedented act of partisanship, admired for its audacity as much as it was resented. Congress failed to respond, and the "Do Nothing Congress," as Truman dubbed it, became a keynote of his campaign. On the positive side Truman further detailed his State of the Union proposals for extensive social and economic legislation—what was to become "the Fair Deal"—and staked his campaign strategy on intensive whistle-stop speech-making tours.

Foreign policy issues, ironically, had little impact on the conduct of the 1948 campaign or the electoral verdict. Bipartisanship prevented the President from capitalizing on foreign policy achievements, although their impression on public opinion had been weak anyway. The public perception of a Soviet menace, however, had been stronger and had served Republicans to advantage in the congressional elections of 1946. Because the President is in charge of the federal budget, he alone must make many difficult choices about the allocation of national resources. This constraint had kept the Truman Administration from responding to the Soviet challenge with definite programs to aid China and Europe as expeditiously as its critics had wished. But by the 1948 campaign Truman had made up for this deficiency, and the Republican presidential candidate, Thomas E. Dewey, did not find the President sufficiently vulnerable to make the "soft on Communism" charge a prominent part of his campaign attack on Truman. Dewey campaigned with the posture of the front-runner, using a strategy that was designed to appeal to Democrats and Independents while holding together the divergent elements of his own party. Attacking his opponent's record would only open schisms in what seemed to be a winning Republican coalition. Given these Republican inhibitions, the bipartisan and anti-Communist emphasis of the Truman Administration's foreign policy shielded it from becoming a major target of political attack.

Henry Wallace's campaign as the Progressive party candidate for President vainly attempted to raise the saliency of foreign policy issues for the 1948 electorate. Wallace had lost his place in the Cabinet over a speech in September 1946 in which he had attacked the nascent Western alliance and the prospects of postwar

American rearmament. Just about everything the Truman Administration had done in foreign relations since then except the Marshall Plan had run contrary to Wallace's position. Wallace did make foreign relations—particularly the growing antagonism with Russia—a campaign issue, but he intermingled it with an ill-defined program of radical domestic reform. Dewey, assuming a lofty bearing, made little effort to link Truman with Wallace and thus left Truman largely free to ignore Wallace. Truman made an exception in Los Angeles, where Wallace seemed to have made the greatest inroads into Democratic ranks, to lash at the Progressive party's Communist ties (though not at Wallace's own loyalty). Elsewhere, however, Wallace drew neither Truman nor Dewey into debate on foreign affairs.

In a surprising outcome, Truman won the election with a 2.2-million-vote plurality over Dewey, and the Democrats handily reversed the Republican majorities in the House and Senate. It seemed as though the Administration would now be able to institute the domestic welfare program Truman had proposed to hold the Roosevelt coalition together.

But appearances were misleading. In fact, the election outcome represented a personal victory for Truman as an underdog but only a tenuous public endorsement of his domestic programs. The election in no sense endorsed or repudiated Truman's foreign policy, since such issues had played little part in the campaign. Moreover, the low voter turnout—one of the smallest percentages of eligible voters since the Civil War—reflected the lack of public interest in electoral issues or political personalities.

Even more important, the Administration soon found that, to meet its own priorities, the federal budget had to accommodate prior foreign policy commitments before it could assume new domestic expenditures. The Marshall Plan and foreign military assistance cost $5 billion in a federal budget that totaled $39.5 billion for the fiscal year beginning in mid-1949 and included heavy fixed obligations. Such a large sum for external commitments undercut the prospects for the social welfare expenditures outlined in Truman's "Fair Deal" program. Throughout his second term the Administration's growing financial and political commitment to foreign problems would force the sacrifice of the Fair Deal. Truman's own priorities accounted for that sacrifice as much as external developments.

At the same time, the prospects for presidential success in foreign policy also diminished after the 1948 election. Bipartisanship is, among other things, an agreement among the leaders of the two major parties not to bother the public with disputes about policy. It not only induces public confidence but public inattention as well. Yet, in his effort to win the 1948 election Truman had aroused public attention with a slam-bang partisanship that strained the relations with Republican leaders upon which bipartisanship in foreign relations rested.

After 1948, both parties turned toward more partisan foreign policies. Dewey's defeat left the leadership of the Republican party in the hands of congressional leaders who were more partisan than he, for the Republican defeat also diminished the political value for the Republicans of bipartisan agreement on foreign affairs. Senator Vandenberg might have been able to prevent the trend toward partisanship in foreign policy, but his health began to fail. The strongly conservative Senator Taft of Ohio became "Mr. Republican" in foreign as well as domestic affairs, his partisanship enhanced by Dewey's defeat and by his own ten years as a leading member of the Senate opposition to Democratic administrations.

The Administration also assumed a more partisan stance in foreign affairs after the election. Acheson, a life-long Democrat with no popular national standing, replaced Marshall as Secretary of State. Louis Johnson, a politically ambitious right-wing Democrat, replaced Forrestal as Secretary of Defense. By 1950, when the Korean war shifted the principal immediate issues of foreign relations from Europe to Asia, the Administration found itself isolated not only from the Republican leadership in Congress but from important Democratic legislators as well. Despite these severe handicaps, however, the precedent of bipartisanship lingered on long enough to offer the Truman Administration some political support for his foreign policies from 1948 to 1952.

COMMUNISM AND CORRUPTION

The Republicans discovered that the lack of active public support for foreign policy programs gave them a chance to make partisan gains by raising issues that would undermine public confidence in the Truman Administration itself and thus—indirectly—

in the Administration's foreign policy record. It was this plummeting of public confidence in the Truman Administration (as contrasted with the high confidence in the Eisenhower Administration later on) that explains why, paradoxically, the Truman Administration was to become so vulnerable on foreign policy issues after it had in fact developed an impressive program of collective economic and military efforts abroad.

What factors contributed to the loss of public confidence in the Truman Administration? The Republicans were able to rally public support on two major issues after 1948: the "mess in Washington" and the fear of Communist subversion. The "mess" consisted of a series of disclosures, mainly through congressional investigations, of corruption and unethical behavior in the government by Truman's military aide, his appointments' secretary, and other members of the White House staff. "Influence peddling" to gain business loans from the government-owned Reconstruction Finance Corporation (RFC) and to "fix" tax investigations were the most invidious scandals. The Bureau of Internal Revenue, staffed by political patronage, was particularly susceptible to influence peddling. The opposition understandably exploited these scandals, and Truman remained pathetically loyal to his friends under attack. At the end of 1951, with evidence of the RFC and tax bureau scandals accumulating, he attempted to reorganize those agencies and to conduct a cleanup campaign within the government. His efforts—a comedy of errors—collapsed a few months later, just in time for corruption to figure prominently with Communism in the Republican campaign charges in the 1952 election.

The charge of being "soft on Communism" had been a political issue since the 1944 election, and it became increasingly effective when the wartime alliance with the Soviet Union visibly began to sour early in 1945. It had been used effectively in congressional campaigns as early as 1946. That year Richard Nixon, for example, defeated Democrat Jerry Voorhis. Nixon accused Voorhis of having Communist supporters, citing the latter's endorsement by the leftist Political Action Committee as proof. Nixon was to use this same technique in his successful bid for the Senate in 1950 against Congresswoman Helen Gahagan Douglas, publicizing charges that she had been a Communist dupe. Through the late forties, the subversion issue continued to develop.

President Truman established the Federal Employee Loyalty

Program in 1947. It showed his own concern about the internal security problem and forestalled the 8oth Congress from setting up more stringent surveillance over federal employees. Truman's program screened the vast majority of federal employees rather than concentrating on the small number of officials employed in jobs that directly affected national security or even on the somewhat larger number of government employees having access to classified documents. The mere existence of the loyalty program stigmatized the federal service and invited suspicion about government officials. But without the more sensational spy confessions and trials the loyalty program would have made little impression on public opinion.

Before 1948, two principal cases of possible espionage had come to light within the government. Both were initiated by FBI investigations; both remained inconclusive. One involved *Amerasia,* a scholarly journal that tended to favor the Chinese Communists. This case produced the arrest, but not the conviction, of a senior foreign service officer. The second case involved a government official named Harry Dexter White. He was Assistant Secretary of the Treasury in 1946 when the FBI presented their report about him to the President. With insufficient evidence for prosecution, Truman decided merely to keep him under special FBI surveillance. The next year White was called before the House Un-American Activities Committee, where he denied charges leveled at him, but he died suddenly before the investigation could go further.

It was a third case, however, that caused the government real trouble. Alger Hiss had left an impressive fourteen-year career in the State Department in 1947 to become the President of the Carnegie Endowment for International Peace. In mid-1948 the House Un-American Activities Committee learned of testimony then being given to a federal grand jury by two former Communists, Whittaker Chambers and Elizabeth Bentley. The committee called them as witnesses in public hearings, and Chambers named Alger Hiss as a Communist agent in his testimony. Hiss denied the charge under oath and challenged Chambers to repeat his charges where he was not immune from prosecution. Chambers did, and Hiss promptly sued for slander. Chambers in turn produced stolen government documents and microfilm copies of other documents that the Justice

Department then used to convict Hiss of perjury for denying under oath that he had passed State Department papers to Chambers. (Hiss was never prosecuted for espionage itself.) Hiss's conviction for perjury in January 1950 gave Republicans the evidence to charge that the Truman Administration was "soft on Communism."

By early 1950 the anti-Communist pot was boiling. The Senate Internal Security Subcommittee had reopened the *Amerasia* case. The Communist party had been convicted of criminal conspiracy. Judith Coplon had been proved a spy while employed in the Internal Security Division of the Justice Department. And Harry Gold and David Greenglass were under arrest, implicated with Klaus Fuchs, the confessed British nuclear scientist spy.

The junior Senator from Wisconsin, Joseph R. McCarthy, joining the ranks of the congressional Communist-hunters, added to the partisan clamor his special talents as a virtuoso demagogue. In his first speech on the subject in February 1950 McCarthy drove straight into the dark corners of public suspicion. "The reason why we find ourselves in a position of impotency" in the world, he told his listeners, is "because of the traitorous actions of those who have been treated so well by this nation." He singled out the State Department, where "the bright young men who were born with silver spoons in their mouths are the ones who have been most traitorous. . . ." Said McCarthy: "I have here in my hand a list of 205—a list of names that were made known to the Secretary of State as being members of the Communist party and who nevertheless are still working and shaping policy in the State Department."[1]

The technique of alleged evidence, wild charges, and "hit and run" tactics were formidable weapons in McCarthy's hands. He did not answer charges, he issued them. The Senate set up a distinguished subcommittee under Senator Millard Tydings, a respected conservative Democrat, to hear McCarthy's charges. McCarthy overwhelmingly won a publicity contest with this subcommittee, driving it to charge him with fraud. The Democratic-controlled Senate supported the charge against McCarthy on a strict party line vote. (On the other hand, even Senate Republicans who disagreed with McCarthy supported him out of party loyalty, which partly ex-

[1] Quoted in Eric F. Goldman, *The Crucial Decade* (New York: Vintage, 1960), p. 141.

plains his continued influence.) Finally, McCarthy was instrumental in the defeat of Senator Tydings in the Maryland elections that November, as well as the defeat of the Senate Majority Leader, Scott Lucas, in Illinois. With this demonstration of nerve and potency, McCarthy cowed his opposition. Throughout the remainder of the Truman Administration, McCarthy was the most militant opponent of Truman's foreign policy and a scourge on the State Department.

Like the corruption scandals, the danger of Communist subversion had some substance in fact. No doubt some American citizens recruited into Russian espionage rings have worked for the government. And probably government protections against Soviet espionage were improved because internal security became a partisan issue. Nevertheless, the controversy over the internal threat of Communism exaggerated it out of all proportion and led to costly and ineffective protective measures. No one was convicted of espionage or related crimes from evidence disclosed either by the elaborate Federal Employee Loyalty Program or from the congressional investigations of the late forties. Yet the effect of these investigations on the federal service—lowered morale, inhibited initiative, overly "safe" advice, and recruitment troubles—was overwhelmingly negative and long lasting.

THE LIMITS OF BIPARTISAN ENGAGEMENT

Truman's foreign policy became particularly vulnerable to partisan attack in this atmosphere of suspicion and low public confidence. The Republicans found that charges of corruption and subversion were more salient foreign policy issues to voters than the Atlantic alliance or economic assistance. For these charges linked the public's perceptions of external threats and difficulties with concepts with which they were more familiar—conditions at home and the loyalty and patriotism of Americans.

The Republicans were particularly successful in attacking the Administration's neglect of Asia, which they attributed to subversion in the government. In politics, the charge of subversion is a terrorist weapon because of its indiscriminate destructiveness. In leveling this charge against the government, congressional Republicans correctly predicted that their Democratic colleagues would stand by or even cooperate in the attack—particularly since the Administration had neglected to secure the endorsement of even congressional Democrats for its China policy.

The Truman Administration had decided in 1947 to give foreign policy priority to Europe over Asia. It had held to that choice with much the same steady purpose that had characterized the World War II strategy to defeat Germany and then deal with Japan. The decision favoring Europe reflected three assumptions: that Europe was more vital than Asia to American interests; that the money we could spend abroad was limited; and that the political effectiveness (and hence the future) of Chiang Kai-shek's regime in China was uncertain.

Truman's emphasis on Europe reflected a fundamental choice of long-range priorities and objectives—one of the few made by any Administration in the postwar era. Yet the Truman Administration suffered heavily for deciding not to pour more resources into China while it gained little politically for saving Europe. There are two explanations for this outcome. Quite understandably, bipartisanship in foreign policy spread credit for saving Europe among Republicans as well as Democrats, and Congress as well as the Executive.

On the other hand, the executive branch alone had to shoulder the blame for not saving China. The special role of the President in recommending the specific allocation of funds in helping to prepare the federal budget forced Truman to make visible policy choices. Congress, however, could to some extent avoid these visible priority decisions, because congressional action usually focused on the amounts and general patterns of allocations, rather than on a vote either for or against the funding of an area. Thus on the record, Congress had merely approved allocating our foreign aid to Europe; it had never formally voted *against* funding for China.

In addition, the Administration missed an important political opportunity to link Congress with its policies by failing to take advantage of the China Aid Act of 1948. This election year bill to provide additional arms to Chiang Kai-shek was passed by wide majorities of House and Senate Republicans and Democrats alike in an effort to clear themselves of responsibility for the declining fortunes of the Nationalist Chinese government. In fact, the additional aid it provided the Nationalist government could hardly have saved it from collapsing on the mainland in 1949. But through lax execution of even the statute's limited provisions, the Administration allowed both Republicans and Democrats in Congress to place the onus on the executive branch for not offering sufficient aid, thus disassociating themselves from the failures in China. The result was a cleavage between the executive branch and Congress. As the Communist forces in China took increasing control of the Chinese mainland in 1949 while the Nationalist regime moved to Taiwan, the Truman Administration came under heavy attack for abandoning Chiang Kai-shek. These attacks became a large political burden for the Administration and for the Democratic party.[2]

We have noted that specific foreign policy issues were not prominent among the salient issues of the 1948 election, and to a lesser extent the same thing could be said for the 1950 and 1952 elections. But the question of which party held the greater public trust and confidence in the general handling of foreign policy was a significant factor in both these elections. The public verdict favored the Republicans, and for several years the Republican party enjoyed a political advantage as the party the public considered better able to conduct foreign relations. This public assessment owed much to the Truman Administration's policies in the Far East, particularly the decision not to save Nationalist China in order to concentrate on saving Europe (despite our success in Europe). The high political cost incurred by declining to respond to a potential foreign threat made such decisions unpopular with future administrations. The fall of China would later have a bearing on American involvements in Korea and in Vietnam.

EUROPE FIRST AND DEFENSE CUTBACKS: THE AMBIVALENT STANCE

In the earliest postwar phase of the Soviet challenge, the Truman Administration had been at a disadvantage in meeting demands that it shift more quickly from alliance to opposition, for

---

[2] H. Bradford Westerfield, *Foreign Policy and Party Politics: Pearl Harbor to Korea* (New Haven: Yale University Press, 1955), pp. 266–68.

critics could advocate change without having to find the additional resources required to implement it.

Once the perception of a Soviet threat to postwar American interests in Europe had become widespread, however, the Administration would have found public support readily forthcoming had it chosen to allocate resources for direct American rearmament. But this was not the response the Administration decided upon. It concentrated instead on economic recovery and then minimum military rearmament of Western Europe. Only after the Korean war started did the Truman Administration throw itself into American rearmament, and when it did, as we shall see, public demands for ambitious military programs continued to outpace its effort. From 1947 until 1951 the Truman Administration was inhibited in seeking popular support for opposing the Soviets by the justifiable fear that the public response might get out of hand and force the Administration to rearm the United States at the expense of its support for European recovery and rearmament.

This was a ticklish situation. Once the Russians were widely viewed as a threat, rearming the United States would have been much more popular than rearming Western Europe. Instead the Administration appealed to the popularity of government economizing to hold back American rearmament while resting its case for building foreign defenses on the Soviet challenge as it was popularly perceived.

The early emphasis of the Truman Administration on economizing in the military establishment would make it highly vulnerable to partisan attack when it reversed that policy later. Two key appointments to the Truman Cabinet after the 1948 election accentuated the divergence of earlier and later views: new Secretary of Defense Louis Johnson flamboyantly exploited the political appeal of budget cutting the Defense Department from his appointment in early 1949 through April 1950. New as Secretary of State Dean Acheson, on the other hand, drew into focus a quite different line of thought within the executive branch, which began to take shape a year before the Korean war started. He emphasized a much expanded rearmament effort for the United States and its allies, although still favoring the rearming of Western Europe first because the main prize—and hence the main threat—was there.

Johnson had been instructed by the White House to hold the

defense budget to $12.5 billion, and he resolved to make the most of his mandate to economize. His severe budget cuts exacerbated service rivalries, which exploded into a public row between the Navy and the Air Force. Johnson defended his cuts, and the two armed services asserted their rival claims to funds and functions in congressional hearings a few weeks after the Soviet Union detonated its first atom bomb. The hearings demonstrated a preoccupation with large-scale nuclear war at the expense of less glamorous conventional warfare (such as would be conducted within a year in Korea). The claims of each of the three armed services were tuned to the predilections of its congressional and public audiences. The economizing pressures had forced them to concentrate on being able to perform the tasks that were easiest to justify and that least required the allocation of American resources to our allies. The result was an anachronism: we were increasing our reliance on a nuclear monopoly as an effective American deterrent force without taking account of the new Soviet nuclear forces. Congress remained preoccupied with interservice military rivalry, but the anachronism did not escape notice within the government.

The plight of the American military posture and Europe's military weakness had become apparent to the American officials planning the military assistance program for Western Europe in mid-1949. As a result, Acheson had assigned State Department planners to examine whether our economy could carry the burden of increased defense expenditures. The Soviet detonation gave urgency to the State Department's inquiries and touched off a bitter secret wrangle over whether to proceed with the crash development of a hydrogen bomb. The wrangle ended in January 1950 when Truman directed the scientists to proceed, but the fight left several high-ranking civilians in the government doubtful about military strategy and policy. Acheson had been an advocate of the bomb's development, and the heat of the dispute produced one of his strongest Cold War statements:

> The only way to deal with the Soviet Union, we have found from hard experience, is to create situations of strength. Wherever the Soviet detects weakness or disunity—and it is quick to detect them— it expoits them to the full. . . . When we have reached unity and determination on the part of the free nations—when we have eliminated all the areas of weakness that we can—we will be able to evolve working agreements with the Russians. . . . It is clear that the Rus-

sians do not want to settle those issues as long as they feel there is any possibility they can expoit them for their own objectives of world domination. It is only when they come to the conclusion that they cannot so exploit them that they will make agreements, and they will let it be known when they have reached that decision.[3]

The Truman Administration had difficulty presenting a united front in its response to the Soviet nuclear detonation. Democratic Senators Brien McMahon and Millard Tydings wanted to start ambitious summit negotiations with the Soviet Union, while Acheson belittled the value of any negotiations at that time. Louis Johnson had been carrying out the President's mandate to hold down defense expenditures only to find Acheson building a case for higher defense budgets.

Furthermore, Truman's decision to proceed with the H-bomb had given presidential support to Acheson's reassessment of military requirements, thereby widening the gap between the economizers and the mobilizers within the government. By April Truman had on his desk a report (called NSC-68) reflecting Acheson's view and urging a huge increase in military spending. It gave top priority to building up conventional forces in NATO and recommended that the United States assume the economic burden of doing so in order to ensure the prompt expansion of these forces. It asserted that the American economy could carry this much larger military burden. It predicted that the Soviet Union would have nuclear weapons deployed for fighting within an estimated two to four years. And by that time, the report argued, the United States would have to be able to fight small conventional wars.

This national security planning report was endorsed only tentatively by President Truman before the outbreak of the Korean war. It proposed a two- to four-fold expansion of American military expenditures with emphasis on conventional armed forces to meet anticipated new Communist-bloc military thrusts—"limited wars"— as the United States lost its nuclear monopoly.

Truman's decision to enter the Korean war turned the NSC-68 report into a program for rearmament, and its estimated costs and recommended allocations were translated into the congressional appropriations bills on which the Korean war rearmament was based.

[3] Department of State *Bulletin* 22 (March 20, 1950), pp. 427–29.

Acheson and his associates in the State Department recognized the political subtleties and diversity of the Communist movement, about which they had ready knowledge. At their elbows stood two highly competent Soviet political specialists, George Kennan and Charles Bohlen. But in order to gain public and congressional support for rearmament and for developing the H-bomb, Acheson concluded that the Communist threat needed to be presented in bold simple terms.

NSC-68 was not intended to be a public document. It surveyed the strategic position of the United States in relation to Russia's acquisition of nuclear weapons, which was proceeding much faster than had been anticipated in Washington. The NSC study was designed to foster a common outlook within the government and be a talking paper with congressional leaders. Accordingly, it did not set forth the divisions and issues of Communist-bloc politics or the several dimensions of Soviet motivations and objectives. Kennan and Bohlen objected to the paper as an unsuccessful effort to ignore and conceal the more sophisticated work accomplished by the Kremlinologists. Acheson, however, wanted clear and uncomplicated guidelines for concerted government action.

The simplification of the political dimensions of the Communist bloc can thus be attributed to the Truman Administration's efforts to popularize its rearmament plans and to unite foreign policy factions within the executive branch and Congress behind a common program.

The implementation of NSC-68 completed the American Cold War response: (1) the characterization of Russia and her allies as a monolithic bloc, and (2) the undertaking of a comprehensive military program to deal with the world expansionist threat attributed to the Communist bloc.

THE KOREAN WAR AND THE LOSS OF PUBLIC CONFIDENCE

From World War II the United States inherited the occupation of the southern half of Korea up to the 38th parallel, facing a Soviet-occupied North Korea. Unable to agree on the terms of unification, the two occupying powers established separate regimes.

The South Korean government more closely reflected historic Korean nationalism, but it was dependent upon American security guarantees against the North Korean government.

POSTWAR RELATIONS
WITH SOUTH KOREA

By 1948 Korea had become an embarrassment to the United States. With our limited military forces stretched thin around the world, the Joint Chiefs of Staff judged available American forces inadequate to defend Korea and recommended American withdrawal. They also proposed that the United States establish a "defensive perimeter" in the Pacific off the Asian mainland—that is, a line of strategic plans that would demarcate those countries in the Pacific the United States planned to defend in case they were attacked. Truman approved both recommendations.

Sixteen months later, with the American withdrawal from Korea completed, Truman and Acheson drew attention to the new defense perimeter's limits. In January 1950 the President indicated that the American defensive perimeter did not necessarily include Formosa. Acheson, speaking at a press-club luncheon, was more explicit: the line of American defense in the Pacific ran from the Aleutians through Japan and the Philippines, excluding Korea and the Asian mainland. Korea must depend for its defense, he indicated, upon the United Nations.

THE NORTH KOREAN INVASION

In June 1950 North Korea launched a well-prepared invasion of South Korea. Syngman Rhee's government in Seoul appealed to the United States and the United Nations for help. President Truman first offered military supplies and then committed American forces to the defense of South Korea in the belief that if we failed to respond to such obvious aggression we would encourage further Communist expansion in Asia and possible attacks in Europe. Almost simultaneously American diplomats had won ambiguous United Nations sanction for the American assistance: the Security Council had swiftly convened and called for the withdrawal of the

North Koreans to the 38th parallel. Two days later, after the American decision to intervene, the Council authorized U.N. members to aid South Korea. Russia failed to exercise her customary veto in the Security Council because she was boycotting the Council. By the time the Soviet delegate returned, the basis for the United Nations Command in Korea had been laid.

In his first acts to aid South Korea, Truman had ordered the Seventh Fleet to protect the island of Formosa, the new home of Nationalist China. The military justifications for protecting Formosa were not strong. More important was the political significance of the action, since it effectively committed the United States to the continued existence of Nationalist China. The move embarrassed United Nation member participants in the Korean war because it indicated to them that the United States was willing to act unilaterally to gain its objectives in the region. On the other hand, the action probably did soften the domestic recriminations over Truman's earlier treatment of the Nationalist Chinese government.

Truman's decision to defend South Korea and protect Formosa against invasion with American naval power raised the level of the American military commitment abroad to sums roughly equivalent to those contemplated in NSC-68. But the Administration again stopped short of a military escalation that could have won it more popular support and stilled some of its critics in the new circumstance of war. By September 1950—even before the Chinese intervention—the Administration was resisting those who were demanding full mobilization.

General Douglas MacArthur, commander of American forces in the Far East and proconsul of the United States occupation of Japan, directed the American forces in Korea and also became head of the U.N. Command, which consisted predominantly of American troops coupled with American-trained and supported South Korean combat forces. The Communist attack swept down the Korean peninsula. American forces were quickly deployed from Japan and later directly from the United States. Unable to stop the advancing enemy, MacArthur chose a strategic enclave defense on the East Coast at the bottom of the peninsula around Pusan. When he had received sufficient reinforcements, he struck back at the Communists, following up with a landing on the West Coast at Inchon that caught the North Koreans by surprise. His break-out from Inchon went sufficiently well to put the North Korean forces to flight. On October 1 South Korean troops crossed the 38th parallel. A week later, a United Nations resolution suggested by Washington instructed MacArthur to "take all appropriate steps . . . to ensure conditions of stability throughout Korea." This resolution appeared to give him the authority to unify the entire country by force of arms, and he proceeded to attempt this task.

The new drive was short-lived, however. Reinforcements of Red Chinese troops began to appear among the North Korean units in October, and in November a Chinese offensive struck the separated columns of MacArthur's advancing forces, sending them reeling. Once again troops from the North swept down the peninsula, though this time their advance was soon checked. The Chinese involvement forced both Washington and the U.N. General Assembly to fall back on the more modest objective of repelling the invasion of South Korea.

The Korean war inflamed partisan fires in Washington. Acheson's press-club speech the previous January was singled out as an American invitation to attack South Korea, and a leading Republican Senator charged, "The blood of our boys in Korea is on his shoulders and no one else." The Administration's abandonment of the Nationalist Chinese regime in the late forties came under new fire as contributing to the Korean war.

The criticism that the Administration had invited the attack by defining the American Pacific defense perimeter as excluding South Korea underlined a dilemma of the new full-blown Cold War posture: military clients of the United States evidently could not be left to their own resources without risking criticism of the Administration for "inviting" attack upon them.

This situation was of the Administration's own making. In popularizing national security issues the Administration had pictured much of the globe as a seamless web of security stakes. Any local war could be viewed as an expansive move by the Communist bloc. For the next two decades the term *limited war* came to refer to an episode in the worldwide Cold War struggle that was limited in its military scope but not its political implications. The prospect that such wars could be kept localized was utterly ignored in the Korean case. Contrary to a commonly applied metaphor, the North Korean attack was not like Nazi Germany's expansion into Czechoslovakia or Poland. The attack on South Korea was apparently undertaken through North Korean initiative and did not represent part of a broad plan for global conquest by Russia or China. Although Russia and China assisted North Korea, the interests of the three regimes in the war were scarcely identical.

North Korea had to bear the main burden of the war and her vital interests were more immediate than Russia's or China's. Furthermore, the failure of North Korea to achieve a quick military victory and the American intervention posed different issues for Moscow from those faced by Peking. Both governments had an interest (an emerging, though still latent, competitive interest) in supporting the ambitions of the North Korean regime to reunite Korea. Beyond that, their stakes explicitly diverged—largely because Chinese and not Soviet territory was threatened. The Chinese intervention, when it occurred, amplified the disparity in the interests of Peking and Moscow.

DOMESTIC UNPOPULARITY OF THE WAR

Truman's prompt decision to assist South Korea won him immediate public support, but the opinion surveys revealed that his popularity began to trail off in August 1950 as the limited scope of our rearmament became apparent.[4] In September Truman called General Marshall back into the government as Secretary of Defense to replace Johnson. After the Chinese intervention House and Senate Republicans also asked Truman to replace Acheson as Secretary of State because "he had lost the confidence of the country." The attacks on Acheson were to persist among national and even regional political figures.

The principal campaign issues of Republican candidates for the congressional elections of November 1950 were inflation, Communism, and corruption—all familiar domestic themes from 1946 and 1948—and, in addition, the Korean situation. Robert A. Taft,

[4] For statistics on answers to the question "Do you approve or disapprove of the way Truman is handling his job as President?" in polls conducted by the American Institute of Public Opinion (AIPO) from 1945 through 1952 see *Public Opinion Quarterly* 25 (Spring 1961), p. 135.

the leader of the Senate Republicans, blamed the Administration for high prices, high taxes, the loss of China to the Communists, and the Korean conflict itself. Former Minnesota Governor Harold Stassen and Senator McCarthy added to the campaign the charge of Communist subversion in Washington.

The 1950 elections can be considered only a moderate defeat for the Administration if we take into account the historical tendency in this country for the President's party to lose seats at the midterm elections. The Republicans gained only five seats in the Senate and twenty-eight in the House. But Truman's domestic programs lacked the support of conservative Southern Democrats, which meant that on these issues the Republicans enjoyed a 196–126 advantage (excluding Southern representatives) in the House. After 1950 Truman's social-economic legislative program lost all its momentum.

By early 1951 General MacArthur had stabilized the front just south of the 38th parallel. American casualties had reached 40,000. In the next six months, ending with a cease-fire agreement and the beginning of armistice negotiations, the struggle in the midsection of Korea cost the United States another 35,000 casualties and produced stronger demands in the United States for breaking the military stalemate by bombing bases in Manchuria and taking other military actions directed at Red China itself. The Administration, aware of the vulnerability of its supply lines and staging areas to air attack, was fearful of expanding the conflict. Further, Truman was sensitive to the views of our U.N. allies, who wanted to restrict the fighting as much as possible.

Administration critics found another rallying point in General Douglas MacArthur. Left in charge of the Japanese occupation after the war, MacArthur had maintained an extraordinary independence from the Administration. Truman was displeased with MacArthur's propensity to ignore directives from Washington, but not enough to remove him from command. Truman even shrank from a proposal to confine MacArthur to Japan and have the Joint Chiefs deal directly with the field commander, General Matthew B. Ridgeway.

However, on April 10, 1951, Truman finally did remove MacArthur, after House Minority Leader Joseph W. Martin, Jr., read a letter from MacArthur on the floor of the House that challenged the Administration's Korean policy on several points. For months

MacArthur's views had created lively partisan debate in Washington and embarrassment among our allies. In the Martin letter MacArthur failed to refer to the United Nations, speaking only of "Red China's entry into the war against us in Korea. . . ." Previous public statements from MacArthur referring to "abnormal military inhibitions" and other differences with the U.N. allies had, as Secretary Marshall later testified at the Senate hearings, "aroused their fears, their uncertainties, and made it all the more difficult for us to deal with them."[5]

The dismissal of MacArthur helped to overcome the crisis in our relations with our allies caused by the Martin letter. But, as Truman anticipated, his action set off a crisis in American domestic affairs instead. For General MacArthur returned to the United States for the first time in fourteen years to tour the major cities as a dissident national hero.

He addressed a joint session of Congress on April 19, displaying an oratorical skill fully equal to the dramatic occasion. In his speech, and later in his testimony before combined hearings of the Senate Armed Services and Foreign Relations Committees, he challenged the Administration's emphasis on Europe, its willingness to accommodate allies, its reluctance to widen the scope of the war, and its assessments of the costs of doing so. MacArthur wanted Nationalist forces to be used in Korea and to attack the mainland of China. He wanted to blockade the Chinese coast and use American air power on the Chinese interior. He estimated that the enactment of these measures would require no increase in American ground strength and only a small increase in our air and naval forces.

MacArthur's recommendations touched strong emotional chords in American public life, but in fact his proposals got nowhere. As there had been since the 1930s, there was a flurry of Republican interest in him as a presidential candidate in 1952, but nothing more developed. Moreover, although MacArthur supplied the Republicans with eloquent strategic rhetoric for the 1952 election

---

[5] U.S., Congress, Senate, the Armed Services and Foreign Relations Committees, Joint Hearings, *Military Situation in the Far East,* I, 82nd Cong., 1st Sess., 1951, p. 349.

campaigns, he was actually to influence defense policy under Eisenhower very little.

As for Truman, the most remarkable thing about his dismissal of MacArthur was how few direct consequences the action had. To his supporters, Truman came across well in defending his constitutional position as Commander in Chief of the American armed forces. Indirectly, however, the MacArthur incident may well have helped to weaken popular confidence in the Administration by calling attention to the erratic American foreign policy before and during the Korean war.

It seems likely that the Administration's periodic switching of signals contributed to the new low in public support for our conduct of the war during 1951. First the Administration had defined its Asian defense perimeter to exclude Korea; then it had reversed this decision when the North Koreans attacked and South Korea appealed to the United States for help. Once American forces and prestige were committed Washington's objectives soared in a few weeks from holding and defending South Korea to "liberating" North Korea; then our goals were sharply trimmed back to defending the South and settling for the *status quo ante*. The Administration raised public expectations only to dash them again. Other inhibitions were imposed by some of our U.N. allies, although press and broadcasting accounts showed the American public that the actual fighting was mainly a Korean-American affair. Finally, there was the calculated decision of the Administration to limit the war effort: to carry out only a limited mobilization and to fight a limited rather than a total war against South Korea's invaders.[6]

All these factors contributed to the unpopularity of the Korean war, and some of them could not even be openly debated with Administration critics. To defend its decision against extending the air war to North Korea and China, for example, the Truman Administration would have had to publicize American military vul-

---

[6] It should be noted that during the Korean war U.S. defense expenditures rose from $11.9 billion in 1950 to $37.2 billion in 1953. (Both figures are in 1950 dollars.) But the American economy expanded enough to absorb the increased military costs without a cutback in private consumption. During the Korean war the American public got both guns *and* butter. Public expenditures for domestic welfare, however, probably would have been greater without the war.

nerabilities, such as our extended supply lines from the United States through Japan.

Even the arguments that could be offered publicly by the Administration rested on disputable plans and contingencies that ranked Korea as a lesser part of a large strategic whole. A military engagement in Korea was regarded by the Chairman of the Joint Chiefs of Staff as "the wrong war, at the wrong place, at the wrong time, and with the wrong enemy."[7] This evaluation showed a commendable resolve not to overreact. But it was also disputable, for it rested on a comparison between a real military challenge in Asia and a potential one in Europe. No less an authority on Soviet behavior than George Kennan considered the potential military threat in Europe exaggerated. He argued that the Russians, believing that history and politics were on their side, could afford to be patient and that their record showed that in practice they were cautious in their pursuit of foreign objectives.

Had the Administration taken Kennan's view that the Soviet military threat to Europe was not dangerous, it would have been less reluctant to concentrate on a military enterprise in Asia. But Kennan also considered the Soviet threat to American interests in Asia doubtful and preferred to keep American forces mobile and small. American reactions to Korea showed that the Truman Administration was willing to answer a Communist military challenge outside Europe but was reluctant to become too deeply involved for fear of jeopardizing our European and other interests. Because the Truman Administration worried about the worldwide military threat of Soviet Communism, it was unable to respond decisively to a *particular* Communist military threat. Once again, as in the earliest postwar response to the perceived threat of Soviet Communism, the Truman Administration suffered the disadvantages not shared by its critics of having to set priorities in allocating limited military resources because it was in charge of foreign policy.

What had not been apparent in 1946, however, was the inflexibility associated with the broad involvement of the United States in world affairs by 1951. The United States had thrown itself into two world wars in the twentieth century untroubled by the prospect that it was neglecting other international commitments. Prior to

---

[7] *Military Situation in the Far East*, pp. 731–32.

World War I, our foreign commitments were negligible. Intervention in a given international situation, therefore, did not require jeopardizing other foreign commitments. The Korean war was different not only because it involved only limited American interests but also because the United States had established many other distinct interests. Washington's principal concern in Asia had not been Korea but Indochina. Early American reluctance to help the French recover their Asian colonial holdings there had given way to the indirect subsidy of French efforts because of mounting concern about Communist expansion in Europe and Asia. Acheson had decided in May 1950 to aid French forces in Indochina as a means of encouraging French support for NATO defense goals.

The fall of China had virtually eliminated sensible open discussion of the political facts of Asia as distinct from the ideological elements of Communist movements. Similarly, the need to unify government action had inhibited the laying out of all the complexities and diversity of the Communist challenge in NSC-68. The Pentagon Papers show that the Communist threat in Asia was depicted as monolithic as early as 1950 in Joint Chiefs of Staff papers.

This represented the conventional outlook within the government, and there were few incentives for dissent from it. The hunt for scapegoats within the government for the fall of China would continue into the mid-fifties. It was much safer to overestimate than appear to underestimate the Communist threat in Asia in view of the political usefulness of blaming the Truman Administration for China's fall. It was also imperative that military and economic planners within the government have clear guidance—a limitation that administrators like Acheson accepted with all its rigidities, oversimplifications, and artificialities. Communism, as a result, was treated as a single movement that defied the known rules of politics, of ethnic and geographic loyalties, of historically rooted nationalism, and of ideological diversity.

Communist cadres in Asia contributed to this misapprehension, as did their counterparts in Europe, with their propaganda, their ritual deference to Moscow and to Communist doctrine and rhetoric. In addition, there was the special status enjoyed by the Soviet regime as the leading Communist power. All these factors helped to nurture the common American view that Communism was a single force.

The Korean involvement itself made it more difficult to re-examine fundamental Cold War issues and American policy alternatives. The Truman Administration was inhibited by the pressing requirements of the war and by the heavy criticisms being leveled at it from openly exploring alternatives to its Korean war policies. Its critics, however, were not required to weigh all the consequences of the ventures that they in turn proposed.

Even allowing for the constraints that go with the authority and responsibility of incumbency, the Truman Administration deserved several additional criticisms. First, American policy in Asia could have been more consistent even without changing its European priorities. Second, the strategic military planning decisions of 1948 were not compatible with the political-military decisions of the President in 1950. Third, the escalation of war objectives during autumn 1950 and the complications they caused—the intervention of China and the discrediting of MacArthur's strategy by Truman— could not have been forecast, but the general dangers of a highly independent field commander could have been. These complications were the result of common but indefensible temporizing.

But the Truman Administration's shortcomings in handling the Korean war are overshadowed by the immense political disadvantages inherent in maintaining a balanced and restrained American fighting posture. Full American war mobilization probably would have popularized the war domestically if the mobilization had been accompanied by commensurate American militancy elsewhere in the world. If, for example, the Truman Administration hesitated to upset the worldwide balance by becoming highly militant in Asia, then it would have had to become more militant in Europe and endured all the complications *that* would have produced in our NATO alliance and the conflict with Moscow.

The militancy would have engaged the attention of increasing numbers of the American public faster than the Korean war actually did, probably accelerating the mood of the reaction that actually occurred—growing militancy and impatience to get it over with. The Truman Administration decided against this course of action, fully aware that it was denying itself a domestic political opportunity, though it was wrong in its belief that it could popularize its choice of limited war. The largest lesson of the Korean war—and indeed the legacy of Truman's Presidency—may well be that *American political leadership, out of courage or ignorance, is willing to manage wars as it thinks they should be managed, despite the domestic political forces that are set loose.* Another lesson of the Korean war is that *when war draws public attention, the public becomes impatient for results, and this impatience becomes a severe inducement for political leaders to escalate military efforts and "get it over with." Those lessons would later affect American conduct of the Vietnam war.*

NATO AFTER KOREA

The Korean war strained the Truman Administration's relations with Western Europe, but it also helped to translate the North Atlantic Alliance into an organized military effort. The North Atlantic Treaty Organization (NATO) and its principal area command, the Supreme Headquarters of the Allied Powers in Europe (SHAPE), under the Supreme Allied Commander for Europe (SACEUR), were supposed to provide for the military defense of Europe through supranational military planning and command. In practice, their main function became one of helping to win the support of domestic political audiences on both sides of the Atlantic by giving authoritative endorsements for national military rearmament programs.

SHAPE was the product of three converging forces: first, the growing anxiety about the inadequacy of Europe's defense capabilities; second, the growing concern about how to integrate West German troops into NATO so as to make German rearmament palatable to Bonn's European allies; and third, the eagerness of Europeans for visible, permanent commitments by the United States to the defense of Europe.

An integrated military force in Western Europe was discussed only in general terms before the beginning of the Korean war, but the subject was pursued in greater detail as European rearmament became more urgent in light of the war. At the NATO Council meeting in May 1950, the members unanimously approved the creation of a permanent executive committee. This committee, to be led by an American, was to coordinate the national economies of NATO members and plan for a balanced collective force that could be paid for without disrupting Europe's recovery. Two Americans with high prestige in Europe were mentioned for the post: Averell Harriman, head of the American foreign military and economic assistance programs abroad and a man with a towering bipartisan reputation in Congress, and General Eisenhower, hero of European liberation in World War II. At the time, the United States opposed the establishment of a supreme military command. The following December, however, the NATO Council worked out a supreme multinational command structure for Western European and American troops. German troops would be placed under this NATO command as part of the arrangement for German rearmament.

An integrated supreme command under an enormously popular international figure such as Eisenhower would offer several advantages on the domestic front for European governments: SHAPE would appeal to the centrist and right-wing political groups who were eager to rearm in the face of what they perceived to be a threat from the East. At the same time, national military expansion could now take the name of European integration through NATO, and governments could use the appeal of internationalism to counter opposition to rearmament from the leftist groups in their own countries. SHAPE also blunted the edge of left-wing criticism by demonstrating that the European governments were in fact gaining by their dealings with the United States—that they were not simply being "dragged too far behind the wheels of American diplomacy," as British Labour-party leader Aneurin Bevan had declared when he resigned from the government in April 1951.[8] And finally, SHAPE was established at a time when (despite the Korean war) American prestige from the accomplishments of the European recovery program could have an important impact on the military sphere.

In January 1951, immediately after his appointment as Supreme Commander, Eisenhower toured the capitals of the NATO countries. His triumphal return to Europe became a rallying point for NATO. The French government showed new confidence in dealing with its extreme left factions by blocking a Communist rally that threatened to interfere with the Eisenhower tour. Meanwhile,

---

[8] 487 House of Commons *Debates 38* (April 23, 1951), as quoted in Leon O. Epstein, *Britain—Uneasy Ally* (Chicago: Univ. of Chicago Press, 1954), p. 242.

the Labour government in London announced an ambitious plan to expand the British armed forces. In a burst of enthusiasm that was not fully sustained, the Netherlands (which had been criticized by the United States for its alleged low level of military effort) increased its defense budget. Back in Washington, Eisenhower assured Congress that Europe was determined to bear its share of the military burden of fighting Communism. Returning to Italy in April, Eisenhower spurred the Italian defense effort as well.

But European governments quickly discovered that their efforts to share the burden of rearmament had high political costs. In Britain, for example, the drain on the budget imposed by the Labour government's plan to expand the armed forces ultimately split the party and led to its electoral defeat in October 1951. Similarly, in May 1951, France's Defense Minister, Jules Moch, lost his seat on the Socialist party's national executive committee for supporting defense requirements at the expense of social welfare objectives.

Similar problems existed in other NATO capitals. Unavoidably, the political interests of the governments had become tied to the European recovery program. Officials feared that their own tenure in office and the future political stability of their countries were dependent upon the success of their national economic recovery. As Dirk U. Stikker, the Dutch Foreign Minister, posed the problem presented by precipitous rearmament in the NATO meeting in New York on September 18, 1950: "Any further lowering of the present living standard in Europe without the prospects of a rise in the near future will endanger the social peace on the home front which is so essential to our defense effort."[9]

Throughout 1950–51 communications among NATO members abounded with published threats and counterthreats. Typically, American spokesmen in Congress stipulated that the United States —specifically Congress—would not appropriate economic or military funds for NATO members if they did not meet some specified standard of performance. The European recipients of American aid, on the other hand, stipulated that they could not meet the standards of military support expected of them if additional economic support was not forthcoming from the United States.

All these demands could have been made privately, but stating them publicly demonstrated a government's determination not to

[9] *New York Times,* September 19, 1951, p. 6.

back down and thus strengthened its bargaining position. Moreover, this public dialogue was intended to show each government's domestic constituency the relationship between American assistance and their own efforts.

It was here that the Truman Administration performed competently the political function of winning consent and support for its foreign endeavors. What was said privately evidently kept the American public threats from carrying too strong a sting in European capitals. The need for the Administration to placate Congress was a fact of life the Europeans had to live with.

NATO, SHAPE, and SACEUR all served to ease the political burdens of Washington as well as those of Europe.

As Supreme Allied Commander of NATO, Eisenhower played a skillful role as international leader and broker, mediating between his European clients and the United States to encourage their support of a common undertaking. (This role was to end in May 1952, when Eisenhower resigned his NATO post to seek the Republican presidential nomination.)

Despite Eisenhower's efforts, however, by autumn of 1951 it had become necessary to seek a new device for dealing with the bickering among member nations over a fair division of military burdens. In October the NATO Temporary Council Committee, meeting in Paris for its first session, appointed a committee of three —"the three wise men"—representing the United States, Britain, and France, to work out an equitable distribution of burdens among the NATO allies.

A major milestone in the integration of NATO, the committee obtained in unprecedented detail political and economic data from the NATO member countries, laid down criteria for establishing the division of military burdens, and produced a report that applied these criteria quite concretely. But its most significant function was to ease the issue of burden sharing that had caused so much discord in NATO relations.

CONCLUSION

When Truman became President in 1945 neither the Soviet nor the Western bloc had taken definite shape. But Europe soon became divided between East and West, and parts of Asia looked either to Moscow or Washington.

The United States government had been the major force in developing the Western alliance against Communism. In part our efforts represented responses to hostile Soviet or Communist initiatives. But the converse was also true: the Communist coup in Czechoslovakia and the Berlin Blockade of 1948 were partly generated—possibly even directly triggered—by the Marshall Plan and the development of NATO. While the statement of the Warsaw Pact was only superficially a mirror image of NATO, the pact was unquestionably also a response to NATO. Finally, it is plain that after 1945 the growing American hostility toward the Soviet Union in turn helped harden the Soviet posture toward the United States. It would indeed be extraordinary if the Soviet-American rivalry did not have this reciprocal effect.

It is proper to question, as the revisionists have, whether a change in American behavior could have modified Soviet behavior. No doubt the United States could have done more to cultivate Soviet friendship—indeed the American leaders, in their concern with generating effective public support for foreign policy, generated a rigid public image of the Cold War. On the other side of the fence, however, the scene is even grimmer. First, there is no evidence that the Russians expected to reconcile their political or ideological interests after the war with those of the West or the United States. Second, given the German invasion of Russia in 1941, it is understandable that the Russians emerged with an enhanced determination to eliminate any European threat to their national security. Expectations of revolution in Western Europe reinforced this determination (as did the later hope that Russia could benefit from the chaos and aspirations of the underdeveloped world). Finally, the morbid suspicions of Soviet dictator Joseph Stalin assured that conciliatory gestures from the West would be largely discounted in Moscow.

But ideologies change and rulers pass away. The United States government needed to be clear about the fact that it was dealing with a dynamic political system that would not necessarily go on behaving the way its leaders said it would. The Truman Administration needed to (but rarely did) make its own predictions about Soviet behavior independently of Soviet claims.

The main obstacle to making such reassessments came from the domestic political environment. There was little risk that any American political figure would be criticized for being overly anti-

Communist, while it was difficult to make the point to a large and relatively inattentive public that, despite what the Russians charged about the capitalist West, they were likely to make certain accommodations to the United States as expediencies.

Both Harriman, the wartime ambassador in Moscow, and Kennan, who was also in Russia then, had warned Washington in 1945 about the difficulties of dealing with the Russians. If the United States was tough and firm, they argued, the Soviet Union would eventually see that it would have to accommodate the United States. In the end we would be able to settle the outstanding issues with Moscow.

Their advice was to be firm with the Russians—but to remain willing to negotiate. Above all, they said, Washington should not preclude negotiations, since, even if the Russians did not want a settlement, it was our task to put them in a political and strategic position in which they *would* want one.

Yet, by the end of 1951 the Truman Administration's efforts to mobilize the American and foreign publics against the Communist threat had in fact frozen American posture toward Russia into a rigid stance to counter aggressive Communism. To accomplish this goal the Administration worked to develop positions of strength from which to negotiate with Moscow without trying to specify for itself or for the public what the terms of a satisfactory negotiating position or settlement with the Russians would be.

4

Eisenhower:
Inertia or Restraint?

THE MANDATE OF THE 1952 ELECTION

"I shall go to Korea." Dwight D. Eisenhower's eleventh-hour campaign promise resonated with the American public's impatience over the stalemate in Korea and with its vast confidence in him. The 1952 election marked a change from limited to larger public deference toward government leadership; and the first five of the eight Eisenhower years that followed represented an era of "good feelings" about the President.

In 1952 both parties nominated candidates with potentially strong extrapartisan appeal. Eisenhower's career as an eminent military commander in World War II and as Supreme Commander of SHAPE had won him extraordinary public confidence. Republicans correctly saw in him a relative outsider to partisan politics who could win votes from Independents and Democrats, thus offsetting the numerical advantage of the Democrats as the majority party in this country since 1932. By nominating Eisenhower over Robert A. Taft, Senator from Ohio, the Republicans moved away from the conservative wing of the party and chose to play down the criticisms leveled by Republican Congressmen against Truman's foreign policies.

The Democrats too chose to minimize party alignment in this

election in order to reduce their identity with the Truman Administration. They selected the incumbent governor of Illinois, Adlai E. Stevenson. Like Woodrow Wilson, Stevenson had entered state politics on a reform ticket. Like Eisenhower, he was a fresh face in his party's leadership ranks. Stevenson had no connections with Truman before the campaign and labored to avoid them during it.

The voter turnout in 1952 (62.7 percent) was much greater than in 1948 (51.5 percent), attesting to the stronger appeal of both candidates as well as to the degree of political controversy surrounding Truman's second term. Eisenhower won 55 percent of the popular vote—a landslide not achieved since Roosevelt's victory in 1936. (Eisenhower was to surpass his own record in 1956.) The result attested to his unique popular appeal as a trustworthy and likable public figure.

Surprisingly, the low public confidence in the Truman Administration and the partisan attacks on its handling of Korea, China, and the internal Communist menace failed to dominate the Republican victory in 1952.[1] Foreign policy issues affected the outcome of the election indirectly, mainly by adding weight to the value of Eisenhower's presumed personal ability to resolve them effectively. It helped that he was a Republican, since voters almost universally attributed to the Republican party the superior ability to deal with international problems. Even so, the opposition's criticism of Truman's China policy had little direct impact on the voter in 1952, and even charges that we had Communists in the government made very little impression in comparison with the domestic issues of internal corruption and excess government spending.[2]

Why, then, such an interest in Eisenhower for his expected capacity to settle the Korean war? The issue of Korea was vastly

[1] A. Campbell, G. Gurin, and W. E. Miller, *The Voter Decides* (Evanston, Ill.: Row, Peterson, 1954), pp. 58–67.

[2] "The most interesting fact . . . is that only 3 percent of the population mentioned the argument that the Democratic administration had been 'soft on Communism' and was 'infiltrated with Communists,' in spite of the fact that this argument was very prominent among the campaign stimuli to which the voters were subjected." *Ibid.*, p. 52; for additional evidence see Samuel A. Stouffer, *Communism, Conformity, and Civil Liberties* (New York: Doubleday, 1955), pp. 86–88.

different from that of Communism or China because it was a war. For two years the general public had been exposed to grim evidence that the United States was fighting a war on the mainland of Asia with American troops while its public leaders disagreed about the war's purpose. Evidently Eisenhower appealed to the general voting public as a President to whom it could delegate with confidence the complex issues that perplexed and alarmed it. The partisan clamor had predisposed the voters to want solutions, particularly in Korea, but not to favor specific solutions. "A central aspect" of Eisenhower's appeal "was his presumed ability to do something personally about Korea."[3] It was not, as political scientist Kenneth Waltz has shown, an unreasonable assignment for the electorate to give its President.[4]

THE EARLY PROSPECTS FOR CHANGE

Normally, a new presidential administration brings an impetus to change public policy. New ideas have been generated in the campaign, and a new winning coalition has been forged. The electoral results are likely to reveal new popular constraints and mandates for the Congress and the President; and new faces appear in key positions of the executive branch. Eisenhower's accession to the Presidency was no exception. His was the first Republican administration in twenty years, and the campaign had provided even more than the normal opportunities for policy changes.

Eisenhower's landslide brought congressional cooperation within reach. To be sure, it gave the Republicans a majority of only one in the Senate and eight in the House—margins that scarcely assured him Republican control of the Congress. (Two years later the Democrats would regain control of both houses for the remainder of Eisenhower's Presidency.) Yet Eisenhower's popularity stretched well beyond party lines. Voting for the President's program could be attractive for many Democratic Congressmen, especially with respect to foreign relations. The bipartisan tradition

---

[3] Campbell, Gurin, and Miller, p. 67.

[4] In James N. Rosenau, ed., *Domestic Sources of Foreign Policy* (New York: Free Press, 1967), p. 282.

legitimized interparty cooperation over foreign policy, and Democrats were free to help Eisenhower reshape foreign policy without admitting error, since they had avoided taking much responsibility for the Truman Administration's policy. Finally, no President in the twentieth century has enjoyed greater public confidence—particularly in his ability to conduct foreign relations—than Eisenhower during his first five years.

Administration officials and congressional leaders alike were disposed to make changes or give the appearance of change. Some prominent Republican leaders wanted radical change—major cuts in the budget, major reductions in foreign commitments and operations, and major changes in foreign relations. Reflecting the general public's mood of frustration over the Korean war, Republican spokesmen wanted to achieve a great deal more in foreign relations for much less money and with fewer commitments than had the Truman Administration. Senator Taft, for example, the leading contender against Eisenhower in 1952 for the party nomination, expected major cutbacks in domestic programs. Senator William F. Knowland, who was to succeed Taft as the Floor Leader of Senate Republicans in 1953, wanted to promote a Chinese Nationalist invasion of Red China and expand the Korean war, while reducing the federal budget. John Foster Dulles, Eisenhower's first Secretary of State, had talked about taking the "psychological and political offensive" against the Communists and insisted that the United States openly declare its intention to liberate the captive peoples of Eastern Europe.

Given the impetus for change on both parties and the public confidence in Eisenhower, one of the most striking features of the Eisenhower Administration was how little America's foreign policy changed during it. The Korean war was settled, of course, and certain consequences followed that settlement. Yet, most goals Republicans voiced in 1952 had not been realized by 1960. Much had transpired, but little had changed. On balance, foreign commitments had not been cut back; if anything, they had been expanded. The defense budget had been reduced but was rising again. American naval forces still stood between the Chinese Nationalists on Taiwan (Formosa) and the Communists on mainland China in Peking. The captive peoples of Eastern Europe remained firmly within the Soviet bloc. If anyone had taken the "psychological offensive," it was not Washington, but Moscow—led by the exuberant Soviet Premier Khrushchev. In 1960 the American public was still worried enough about the Soviet military menace to induce both presidential candidates to advocate better military preparedness. Communist China remained isolated; working relationships with the Soviet Union remained unimproved; and NATO had not yet been assigned the military forces that member nations had agreed to provide nearly ten years earlier.

The lack of change in American foreign relations during the fifties can be accounted for in several ways. First, despite some claims and charges during the campaign in 1952, the Republicans had already opted against radical change when they nominated Eisenhower. He identified with the more progressive internationalist wing of the party and with three major tenets of Truman's foreign policy—the American commitment to Europe, the strategic primacy of Europe over Asia, and the reality and unity of the Communist menace. Eisenhower's nomination also assured that a general withdrawal of the United States from its extensive world commitments would not be given serious consideration.

Foreign policy changes, furthermore, would probably have required strong presidential leadership and additional government activity. Eisenhower had the political support for both but the inclination for neither. His belief in a more limited role for the President and for a government that had already overshadowed the private sector restrained him from asserting strong leadership in domestic and foreign affairs. Eisenhower accepted a conservative economic view that Truman had agreed to in principle. It held that the federal budget should be balanced and federal taxes cut. A balanced budget and reduced taxes were widely sought by businessmen. Businessmen favored ensuring economic stability through a "sound" dollar (that is, one that would remain constant in value) and claimed that economic growth would occur by encouraging business investments through tax cuts and the elimination of inflation. This theory was discarded by the early sixties in favor of one that emphasized the need for a positive role by the government in creating pressure for expansion in the economy.

These views reflected Eisenhower's conventional midwestern Republicanism. His belief in presidential self-restraint was perhaps reinforced by his experience as a military officer between the two world wars. To Eisenhower's critics he had little appreciation of the stresses and challenges of the mid-twentieth century. Yet there was clearly more to Eisenhower than this. One cannot explain his performance during World War II and in NATO or his recurrent interest in blunting the Cold War rivalry with Russia without crediting him with more political insight. No disclosures by Eisenhower's political intimates have revealed his inner workings as a political man. He was more than just another general at the head of a modern government; yet how much more remains unclear.

This is the puzzle about Eisenhower. He remained publicly above American partisan disputes throughout two terms in office that vacillated from deep anxiety about foreign affairs through deferential inattention to foreign and domestic problems back to a growing concern about both. His critics complained about his lack of vigorous leadership in foreign affairs; yet the standards of both Republican and Democratic criticism in the mid-fifties assumed the need for vigorous American leadership abroad—a view that Eisenhower did not wholly share. Not until the shattering experience of Vietnam did Eisenhower's kind of self-restraint in the Presidency gain much support among the attentive and articulate foreign policy publics. The puzzle of Eisenhower, then, is closely linked to the questions that have come to be asked more conspicuously *since* his Presidency: what restraints should the United States impose on its own exercise of power in the international system? How much did Eisenhower think in these terms?

EISENHOWER'S EARLY LEADERSHIP

The 1952 campaign had suggested two issues on which the Republicans could be expected to take decisive action if elected. The first was the settlement of the Korean war. Prior to Eisenhower's election, armistice negotiations with North Korea and the Chinese Communists had dragged on for more than a year before being suspended in October 1952 at Panmunjom. When Eisenhower took office he faced the major stumbling block to agreement: the question of whether the repatriation of war prisoners should be forcible or voluntary. The United States had insisted upon the right of prisoners *not* to return home if they did not wish to.

Negotiations resumed, and when they appeared to be breaking down, the Eisenhower Administration threatened to break them off and "carry on the war in new ways never yet tried in Korea." Dulles privately suggested to India's Premier Nehru, who was in contact with Peking, that we might use atom bombs. Within less than two weeks the Communists accepted the final proposals from Washington and signed an agreement on the repatriation issue. The armistice went into effect on July 27, 1953, and with the settlement of the Korean war the public agitation over foreign relations that had plagued the Truman Administration subsided.

The second issue, that of the "captive peoples" of Eastern Europe, had emerged from the Republican campaign rhetoric. The foreign policy plank of the Republican platform had promised to "repudiate all commitments contained in secret understandings such as those of Yalta which aid Communist enslavements." In the ensuing presidential campaign, to Eisenhower's dismay, Dulles talked of liberating the "captive" states of Eastern Europe.

The captive peoples issue seemed ideally suited for demonstrating the differences between a Republican and a Democratic administration, particularly since nothing more than verbal declarations were required to underscore this point. Yet in fact the issue proved embarrassing. After he took over the State Department Dulles learned that the Yalta and Potsdam protocols were useful not only to Russia but also to the West. While the Russians cited the Yalta agreement in support of Soviet satellite regimes in Eastern Europe, Yalta and Potsdam also underwrote the legal status of West Berlin and of West Germany. A congressional resolution, when finally drafted, merely proclaimed a "hope" that captive peoples would one day be free. With these mild phrases it languished and died.

These two early Republican initiatives led to reduced Administration efforts to base foreign policy on a broad and active public consensus. The Korean settlement eliminated the most visible foreign policy issue for the public, and the Administration would hardly call public attention to the fact that it had abandoned the popular idea of rolling back the Communist empire and liberating captive peoples. Public attention to foreign affairs declined through the mid-fifties. Even opinion leaders accepted without question the Administration's handling of foreign relations.

Eisenhower's political status and style, along with his personality and personal background, accentuated this trend. He had a confidence bred by success in politics, yet he preferred to take important matters out of politics. Whereas Truman had relished being the national leader arousing the public to support the government in time of crisis, Eisenhower wanted to stabilize the execution of foreign policy so that problems would not have to be treated as crises in order to win the political support needed to deal with them. The burdens of foreign affairs had to be limited to commitments that could be sustained in the long run, and their handling would have to be reorganized.

Eisenhower's formative experience for the Presidency had been his wartime command of the Allied Expeditionary Forces in Europe during World War II. As allied commander he had been able to rely on massive military resources to defeat Germany. As President he was assured of a high level of political support. In neither role was he in desperate straits, forced to improvise solutions or to exploit crises to gain needed resources. Eisenhower generally had at hand resources that Truman often lacked—from military weapons to public support. Truman and Eisenhower agreed in principle about most foreign policy issues, but circumstances cast them into quite different roles. The Truman Administration's officials were mobilizers of political support and improvisers of foreign policy initiatives (including long-term foreign policy undertakings). Eisenhower was a more effective vote gatherer, yet disinclined toward political mobilization and strongly inclined to limit commitments to available resources.

The application of Eisenhower's views, however, depended mainly on John Foster Dulles, Secretary of State from 1953 until 1959. Eisenhower held Dulles in high esteem and treated him as a government expert on foreign policy. Dulles, a highly successful New York corporation lawyer, had also long been recognized as the leading authority on foreign affairs by the Republican party.

On the other hand, Dulles had practically no experience in government administration and was less confident than Eisenhower about controlling the forces of public opinion. His own political experience was disappointing. He had served briefly as an appointed U.S. Senator in 1950 but had lost his seat when he stood for election as an incumbent. He also failed to establish the relationship with

Congress that he hoped for. When he became Secretary of State he resolved to get along with Congress better than had Dean Acheson. He yielded to congressional attacks on the State Department and aimed at holding the support of the powerful Senate Foreign Relations Committee. His relations with the committee began on a cordial note but by 1954 had become rough and contentious.

"PACTOMANIA"

As noted, Eisenhower held a deep conviction—perhaps traceable to his military background—that foreign relations should rest on a more stable base than crisis-induced public consent. Dulles shared this aim but made it virtually impossible to achieve by the way he conducted foreign policy.

Both his lack of experience and his temperament disinclined him to delegate responsibilities in carrying out foreign policy making. He insisted that all matters be cleared through him and he was inclined to manipulate and maneuver rather than confer with other officials. He also avoided advance consultations with influential Congressmen—an essential precondition of strong bipartisan support in Congress. Much to the consternation of State Department officials, Dulles conducted foreign policy mainly from his hat.

The new Administration, like Truman's after mid-1950, saw Communist China as the obedient agent of the Soviet Union. When this premise of Sino-Soviet unity was coupled with the Republican determination to do better in Asia, the objective became the "completion" of containment—that is, the building up of American defense capabilities from NATO's right flank in Greece and Turkey, through the Middle East, across South and Southeast Asia, and up through the Western Pacific offshore line to Korea.

Military and economic strategists within the government had begun to plan for the completion of containment even before Eisenhower was elected President. Their plans became the basis for additional military pacts. Without Marshall or Acheson to stress the primacy of Europe, containment spread. It became an indiscriminate search for potential American allies among states in the regions adjacent to Communist powers.

At the same time, the Republicans were determined to meet

the widely shared perception of a Communist menace with a lower cost in United States manpower and material resources than had the Truman Administration. (In effect, the Republicans were returning to a pre-1950 Democratic position.) The Truman Administration's policy of containment avoided the rhetoric of "rolling back" Communism from Eastern Europe and of military confrontation because it assumed that time would erode the cohesion and hostility of the Communist bloc. Yet the most eloquent expositor of this view, George Kennan, considered the Truman Administration's policies needlessly belligerent, while the more militant Acheson wanted the United States to create "situations of strength" in Europe and elsewhere in order to demonstrate to the Russians that they would have to come to terms with the West. Acheson had seen the threat in Asia declining as Sino-Soviet unity disintegrated. Most of Eisenhower's advisers on foreign affairs, however, rejected Kennan's view that the Soviet regime would change from within as well as Acheson's prediction of friction within the Soviet bloc. They considered Russia's control over the bloc too firm to permit its breakup.

American efforts to achieve flexibility in Asia after the Korea settlement emphasized the use of indigenous forces coupled with strategic reinforcement by regional allies rather than American forces. The Eisenhower Administration began to build up local military forces in Taiwan, the Philippines, Vietnam, Thailand, Pakistan, Iraq, and Iran, and to tie these states into regional alliances.

In September 1954 the United States signed the Manila Pact, a loosely knit collective security arrangement with Great Britain, France, New Zealand, Australia, the Philippines, Thailand, and Pakistan that came to be known as the Southeast Asia Treaty Organization (SEATO). This treaty covered aggression (privately, it was understood to be only Communist aggression) in a territory that also included non-SEATO members—Taiwan, Cambodia, Laos, and South Vietnam. Then, early in 1955, two Middle East states on the southern rim of the Soviet bloc, Turkey and Iraq, signed the Baghdad Pact. They were joined by Pakistan, Iran, and Great Britain in an alliance that became CENTO (Central Treaty Organization). Not anticipating that Great Britain would join, Dulles had promoted the pact in order to ensure a military alliance against the Soviet Union that would avoid American embroilment in Arab politics and be independent of the British. Critics dubbed his preoccupation with military alliances "pactomania."

SEATO and CENTO had little substance beyond the license that went with their membership to expect more military aid from the United States. Regional members found little basis for cooperation among themselves and came to regard their open alignment with the West (implicitly against the Communist bloc) as a service that entitled them to rewards. This view that SEATO and CENTO helped to complete containment for the West more than it helped individual regional members was not groundless. Members of the Baghdad Pact, for example, did become embroiled in Arab politics because Iraq was a member, and the Iraqi government itself in 1958 fell to a coup as a result of its alignment with the West.

In retrospect it appears that the military-economic aid programs and the multilateral treaty chain stretching from the Philippines through the Middle East and Europe and across the Atlantic to Canada encouraged a literal and rigid application of the policy of containment, with no alliance member inclined to question whether the level of American effort was too high or too low or whether American efforts should be oriented in another direction altogether. United States military and economic aid proved to be powerful incentives to go along with American policy.

Dulles' pacts were scarcely comparable to NATO, since they lacked a combined military command and staff organization. SEATO and CENTO provided a symbolic rationale for American audiences of bilateral military aid and "defense support" programs. They were intended to offer member nations confidence-building assurances of American support. But the SEATO and CENTO treaties were expanded and confused by a network of official and semiofficial statements, collective declarations interpreting their significance, and bilateral and unilateral American declarations and explanations.

Intended to add flexibility to the American policy, on balance, the effect of these pacts in Asia and the Middle East was the opposite. They imposed a "friend-or-foe" test on the developing states of these regions that was awkward and inappropriate. They also created more commitments than the United States could meet, which generated anxiety among our allies and uncertainty among our rivals.

Moreover, the American security treaty network was used by the powers it involved—allies, clients, rivals, and the United States—in ways that increased the rigidity of Cold War alignments and confrontations. For example, the treaty network made public and explicit to allies, clients, and adversaries obligations that Washington could not fail to honor without some cost to the credibility of our other commitments (a cost that Washington estimated as very high, in part because its clients often raised the issue of credibility). Furthermore, these declared obligations allowed both clients and rivals to take initiatives at Washington's expense. For revisionist client powers such as Pakistan, Taiwan, and South Korea (with aspirations to change the political status quo in Kashmir, mainland China, and North Korea, respectively) a formal treaty commitment was a limited license to entangle the United States in the pursuit of its revisionist objectives. For revisionist rival powers such as North Korea or North Vietnam, America's formal treaty commitments helped them to predict contingent American military action. Rivals could then ask, What circumstances can we choose that will minimize the likelihood of an American response or will assure that the circumstances in which a response occurs are unfavorable to the United States? The conspicuousness of American commitments had the effect of leaving the initiative to others.

DOMESTIC PROBLEMS OF THE
FIRST ADMINISTRATION

The Eisenhower Administration, viewing the Soviet-bloc challenge as a long-term one, favored the adoption of policies that Congress and the American public would support for an extended time. The problem of ensuring domestic support for the stand against international Communism was to be solved by cutting defense outlays and manpower (so that fewer sacrifices would be asked of the public) and by deferring to Congress in foreign policy—permitting it to play a more prominent role in governing than it had in recent years. Both economizing and presidential self-constraint were prominent (though hardly exclusive) Republican ideas.

EXECUTIVE DEFERENCE
TO CONGRESS

As the new Administration discovered, deferring to Congress was not necessarily a way to win friends there. Congressmen were not interested simply in getting their views adopted as foreign policy: they were interested more broadly in governing, and that included the delegation of authority and the fixing of responsibility. When the President leads, he assumes responsibility; when he defers to Congress, he may be seeking to share a responsibility that Congress does not want to accept. This congressional ambivalence helped Eisenhower and Dulles to ride out the onslaught that Senator John W. Bricker of Ohio led against presidential discretion in foreign relations during Eisenhower's first term.

In 1953, Senator Bricker introduced a proposed amendment to the Constitution in the Senate. His proposal, known as the Bricker Amendment, called for severe curtailment of executive agreements that did not require congressional approval. It also provided that treaty ratification require not only the approval of two-thirds of the Senate but authorizing legislation as well, which would require majority votes in both Houses of Congress.

The Bricker Amendment stemmed from a long history of isolationist efforts to place strict constitutional limits on presidential discretion in foreign relations. The proposal was supported by a variety of conservative Republican groups that had been increasingly concerned about the broad exercise of executive power first under President Roosevelt and then under President Truman. The amendement was designed to appeal to popular distrust of the expanding presidential power during these Democratic administrations. Its proponents hoped to avoid the recurrence of what they considered "disasters," such as the wartime conferences at Teheran, Yalta, and Potsdam.

Opponents of the Bricker Amendment saw it as a threat to effective executive initiative in foreign relations. In particular, they feared that the requirement for majority votes in both Houses, while not necessarily harder to achieve than the present ratification process, would encourage amendments to treaties that would undo the negotiated agreements represented.

The Bricker Amendment, supported by several influential Republicans, was only narrowly defeated in the Senate in 1954. Efforts to revive the proposal continued for the next several years, but with decreasing impetus. The presence of a trusted Republican in the White House—and the fact that Eisenhower himself refused to endorse the amendment—helped to defuse the issue by 1957.

Eisenhower also deferred to Congress by letting them take responsibility for dealing with Senator Joseph McCarthy, though with more unfortunate consequences. Eisenhower had avoided conflict with McCarthy during the presidential campaign of 1952, and he continued to do so in office. When the Republicans gained control of the Senate in 1952 McCarthy became head of an investigating subcommittee and continued to pursue his earlier charges that the State Department was riddled with Communists.

The efforts of Eisenhower and Dulles to avoid a confrontation with McCarthy left State Department officials vulnerable to his broad attacks, severely undermining the operations of the Department. Initiative, morale, and responsiveness in the State Department —already discouraged by Dulles' preference for handling matters himself—were even further reduced. Officials tried to protect themselves by avoiding policy decisions that might be investigated or misinterpreted by McCarthy's powerful subcommittee. Increasingly, foreign policy became a matter handled personally by Dulles at a level high enough so that for the time being it was least vulnerable to public or congressional scrutiny.

McCarthy was later to shift his investigation to the Army and ultimately to offend the Senate, bringing down a motion of censure against him in 1954 for his behavior toward his fellow Senators. His influence was negligible after his fall from grace in the Senate, and he died in 1957.

MILITARY STRATEGY AND DEFENSE ALLOCATIONS

The Eisenhower Administration's effort to recast American defense posture and military doctrines was a puzzling combination of moves and intentions. Before he became Secretary of State, Dulles had talked of taking the "psychological and political offensive" and he argued that the United States should use the threat of aerial atomic retaliation as a deterrent to Communist aggression or expansion. The air power reference opened old wounds for an Army man. Eisenhower insisted that Dulles' statement about atomic retaliation be deleted from the Republican platform and criticized in his campaign the advocacy of exclusive reliance on retaliatory air power.

At the same time, Eisenhower was skeptical of the claims made by the armed services about what forces and equipment they needed. (Since he had once been Army Chief of Staff, he could claim some basis for his skepticism.) He also wanted to economize in the government and cut taxes. He did not flinch when George Humphrey, his Secretary of the Treasury, advocated a one-third cut in the budget, "using a meat ax" where necessary, as he put it.[5]

Eisenhower understood that most of the cuts in the federal budget would have to be made in the area of defense. In the campaign he had talked of a defense posture that would "keep our boys at our side instead of on a foreign shore." This idea evidently meant that the United States should withdraw forces from overseas—primarily from Asia—and hold them in reserve. After the election he found that Admiral Arthur W. Radford, the Commander in Chief of the Pacific fleet, shared his resolve to effect major economies in the defense budget and to withdraw American ground forces from overseas. He called Radford back to Washington and named him Chairman of the Joint Chiefs of Staff.

For Radford, however, bringing the troops home and cutting the defense budget held a different meaning: a nearly exclusive reliance on strategic air power—the very thing that Eisenhower opposed. This emphasis would make it unnecessary to build up a central military reserve—the very thing Eisenhower favored. Yet, as a practical matter, Eisenhower did not disagree with Radford about budgets and manpower requirements because he doubted that the military's estimates of its requirements were sound. It was Radford's views about military strategy, rammed past the opposition of the armed services (particularly the Army), that became the "New Look."

Dulles was at first dubious about cutting defense spending by relying more on nuclear weapons. Before the year ended, however, he joined Eisenhower and Radford in emphasizing that the changes

[5] Emmett J. Hughes, *The Ordeal of Power* (New York: Atheneum, 1963), p. 72.

advocated in strategy meant direct savings in defense spending. Even while promoting SEATO and CENTO, Dulles wanted to free the United States from reliance on local forces. Reflecting a crucial decision by Eisenhower at the end of 1953 that permitted military contingency planners to count on using nuclear weapons, Dulles restated on January 12, 1954, his preference for strategic air power. He linked this strategy with economizing: "We need allies and collective security," he said in a speech in New York. "Our purpose is to make these relations more effective and less costly. This can be done by placing more reliance on deterrence power and less dependence on local defensive power."

Eisenhower, however, preferred to stress local defense forces, strengthened if necessary by American forces from the central military reserve. "Our first objectives," he indicated in a policy directive to the Defense Department at the beginning of 1955, "must be to maintain the capability to deter an enemy from without and to blunt [such an] attack if it comes. . . . to provide for meeting lesser hostile action—such as local aggression not broadened by the intervention of a major aggressor's forces—growing reliance can be placed upon the forces now being built and strengthened in many areas of the free world."[6] Eisenhower, then, did not agree with the emphasis placed on strategic air power by Dulles and Radford, but he did not repudiate them.

Radford was thus free to push the conventional force cutbacks through the military establishment with single-minded determination while promoting with equal vigor military assistance agreements to build up local forces in Asia. Dulles, in turn, was well aware that the New Look would encourage our NATO allies to weaken their conventional forces while our policy was to get them to strengthen these forces; yet he too supported the New Look. (Greater reliance on local defense forces would later become the theme of the "Nixon Doctrine" in 1969, in response to a similar mood of withdrawal after a perceived overcommitment in Asia.)

Eisenhower and Dulles never explained these disparities between their convictions and their policies. They both evidently accepted the New Look as the product of a realistic assessment about the resources available to buy military strength. Neither would have

[6] As quoted in *Army-Navy-Air Force Journal,* January 8, 1955.

gained much from exposing these disparities. Both would have had to acknowledge that economic and political constraints played an important role in the determination of defense policy. Had they done so, defense policy would have become a much more partisan issue. Both preferred instead to claim a more authoritative basis for the determination of military and foreign policy. Military budget levels and force levels were set to meet the "requirements" of national security. Similar considerations applied to foreign relations. In this way, Eisenhower and Dulles avoided arousing public anxieties and attracting public attention to national security policies.

Their style was consistent with one interpretation of Eisenhower's electoral popularity: the public wish to turn foreign relations over to a trustful figure so that public attention could turn elsewhere. It also reflected the inclination of an incumbent administration to minimize public involvement in foreign relations when it is not optimistic about its capacity to explain its policies.

COPING WITH FRIENDS AND ENEMIES

The New Look was the Eisenhower Administration's recasting of Truman's national security policy. The Truman Administration had resolved that America's capacity to shoulder the economic burdens of national security was much greater than supposed, though no actual measurement was attempted. It undertook not only to rearm the United States but to assume for the time being the economic burden of rearming America's allies. In the characteristic manner of the Truman Administration, urgency served to win support at home and abroad for the new undertaking. It also enabled Washington to avoid answering two questions: what the actual capacity was of the United States and its allies to carry the burden over the long term, and how that burden should be shared among our allies, and us.

The New Look and the new military pacts were distinctly American answers to these questions. Republican criticisms of Truman's rearmament effort had generated a strong impetus to develop an overall rationale for American foreign policy. But consistency was not to be the hallmark of the new American national security policies. Rather, the policies were responses to the demand for economizing in military programs, while our dependence on the estimated requirements for our military security remained unchanged. To economize, Washington chose a specialized role for the United States among her allies—to provide the nuclear umbrella while they would build up a local conventional force capability with American assistance.

It now became American policy, as stated by military planners and endorsed by the President after consultation with his National Security Council, that the armed forces of America's allies would supplement American military forces while we concentrated on high technology forces—mainly the nuclear strategic role. It is not unreasonable for friends to take into acount what each can do for the other—for a homeowner to anticipate borrowing his neighbor's garden hose if his house catches on fire—to use a famous example of Franklin D. Roosevelt. However, the disparity in power between the United States and its allies assured that the American view of interdependency would carry much further than that. American policy in the mid-fifties assumed that other states would accept the special tasks assigned them by American military planners according to doctrines formulated in Washington. The New Look was designed to reconcile America's distinct combination of economic, political, and military constraints and aspirations. But it was exported as a Western Cold War posture that American officials assumed had validity for her allies as well. By extending its application in this way, American planners denied to allied governments and statecraft their function of reconciling *their own* distinct political, military, and economic constraints and aspirations through their own national doctrines and force postures. Nowhere was this more evident than in Europe.

NATO, EDC, AND GERMAN REARMAMENT

The difficulties that beset NATO throughout the fifties had several origins. One was, as Dulles had anticipated, the New Look. It was the first of two major recastings of American policy that treated NATO as an appendage of American military policy. To sustain or improve NATO's effectiveness, its members needed to increase the size of their conventional military forces. But American reductions in military manpower and defense expenditures could only make it difficult for NATO allies to carry on their own armament efforts and more difficult for the United States to press them to do so.

Another difficulty was the disparity in economic and military power between the United States and other NATO members. Seemingly secure beside the towering United States, no other NATO member worried much about its own lack of military defenses. Furthermore, anxiety over the Soviet threat declined with the 1953 Korean armistice and with ensuing developments in the Soviet bloc.

When the Eisenhower Administration had come to power, the Soviet bloc was a tightly knit military and economic alliance (although Yugoslavia, expelled from the bloc in 1948, had firmly established by 1953 that it could survive as a Communist state outside Russia's aegis). Stalin's death in early 1953 led to a protracted succession crisis in Russia. After the first tensions of the crisis passed, Soviet foreign policy became more flexible and conciliatory as a program of "de-Stalinization" got under way. The Soviet Union displayed its new flexibility by increasing its support of nonbloc nationalist forces (at the expense of local Communist movements) and by undertaking new programs of foreign economic and military aid abroad. It softened its conditions for neutralizing Austria, enabling completion of a four-power agreement that ended the occupation of that country in 1955. It also offered substantial concessions at the Geneva disarmament negotiations in 1955—concessions that the American delegation was unprepared to respond to.

Moscow underscored its apparent shift from military to economic and diplomatic initiatives in May 1956 when it announced the reduction of Soviet armed forces from 4 million to 2.8 million men and depicted this as a major unilateral step toward disarmament. Western skeptics saw this act instead as a belated effort to effect economies in the Soviet military establishment, much like the New Look in Washington. (Doubtless it was.) Nonetheless, the Soviet thaw reinforced the sentiment of West European officials that the military need for NATO rearmament was less urgent than Washington claimed—a view that was probably also true.

Before taking office, Eisenhower and Dulles had resolved to

confront the issue of what form the German military contribution to NATO should take. A treaty establishing a European Defense Community (EDC) had been signed in 1952, but France and Italy had delayed their ratification of it. It provided for a unified defense force that would permit the rebuilding of a German army only as part of an integrated Western European force. As President-elect, Eisenhower used a public New Year's greeting to cite the unification of Western Europe as a major objective of American foreign policy. The message was clear enough in Western Europe. "Within my first few hours in office," Eisenhower later reported, "I had read messages from Bonn and Paris describing meetings between Chancellor Adenauer of Germany and Foreign Minister Georges Bidault of France in which assurances were given of the support of both their governments for the principle of the European Defense Community."[7] On his first foreign trip as Secretary of State, Dulles was dispatched to Europe at the end of January to press the case of the EDC, and he continued to promote its cause privately with European officials at every opportunity. Yet at year's end the EDC remained an unratified treaty. Dulles now threatened more pointedly: if the EDC were not ratified, the United States would have to undertake "an agonizing reappraisal" of its commitments to Europe.

The threat caused a flurry of anxiety abroad. Even statesmen in Paris and Rome who supported the EDC believed that American public threats could only make their work more difficult by inflaming nationalist feelings.

In April 1954 Eisenhower promised a long-term commitment of American ground forces in Europe, provided the EDC treaty was ratified. But neither sticks nor carrots were sufficient. On August 30 the French National Assembly rejected the EDC treaty, for practical purposes killing it.

Washington's bluff had been called. When the EDC failed, Dulles offered a long-term American troop commitment as inducement for an alternative arrangement to bring West Germany into NATO. The arrangement turned out to be a loose aggregation of military forces, incongruously called the Western European Union (WEU).

---

[7] Dwight D. Eisenhower, *The White House Years*, Vol. 2: *Waging Peace, 1956–1961* (Garden City, N.Y.: Doubleday, 1965), p. 140.

The Eisenhower Administration's threats over the EDC issue were ineffective in part because they were not believed: the United States wanted a strong NATO as much as anyone did, and that required American commitments to Europe. In fact, the "agonizing reappraisal" Europeans might well have worried about would be the one that would probably have occurred if the EDC *had* come into effect. For Washington supported political integration and EDC in order to reduce Western Europe's dependence on us, whereas an important attraction of NATO to most of its members was that it tied American military power to their defense. The EDC, by providing an effective conventional military force in central Europe, would have permitted the United States to concentrate even more on nuclear weapons at the sacrifice of conventional forces.

INDOCHINA AND THE DULLES PARADOX

Since World War II American economic and military aid to France had been designed to avoid our direct support of the French struggle to regain and keep control over Indochina after the Japanese surrender. Even before the outbreak of the Korean war, Washington was inclined to view Indochina as only one of many theaters in an overall conflict with Communism. By adopting an optimistic outlook about France's ability to hold Indochina in early 1950, the Truman Administration was able to avoid confronting the issue of whether we could allow Indochina to fall into Communist hands. But the situation had deteriorated badly by early 1954.

The Eisenhower Administration, after careful consideration of direct intervention, resolved to sponsor a mutual defense treaty directed against Communist aggression in Indochina and Thailand —what later became SEATO. Since the U.S. Army estimated that successful intervention in Indochina would require from seven to twelve American divisions, Eisenhower made American involvement contingent upon (1) the military participation of allies, (2) a declaration of French intent to speed the granting of full political independence to the three states of Indochina (Laos, Cambodia, and Vietnam), and (3) congressional approval, which was correctly thought to require allied commitments.

Before a collective defense pact could be put together, however, the French government declared that without help its military position in Indochina would collapse in ten days and called for immediate armed intervention by American aircraft carriers. Radford and Dulles supported the request, but congressional leaders warned that congressional support was contingent on lining up the support of foreign allies first. Eisenhower accepted this proviso and insisted on British support in particular as a prerequisite. But the British demurred.[8]

Radford's policy, which advocated an air power venture in Indochina as well as the build-up of local forces in Asia, had won only partial endorsement. He lost because congressional leaders refused to be stampeded into unilateral action and because Eisenhower remained skeptical about military involvement in continental Asia and insistent on congressional endorsement. Direct American intervention in Indochina accordingly did not materialize in the spring of 1954.

Despite the Administration's resolve to exploit American strategic superiority and military flexibility, it had in effect demonstrated that the United States was unable to deal even with what it perceived to be Communist initiatives along the containment perimeter. Before the French appeal for American air strikes, Dulles had stated that nuclear deterrence was not appropriate where there had been no open aggression. In this way he ruled out the applicability of "massive retaliation" in meeting the main challenge in Asia.

In May 1954 the French bastion at Dien Bien Phu fell to the Vietminh. The French government settled at Geneva with representatives of Ho Chi Minh for a North-South partitioning of Vietnam at the 17th parallel. (It should be noted that Ho Chi Minh was not only the leader of the Communist Vietminh but a man with widespread popularity throughout all Vietnam as an anti-colonialist, nationalist leader.) The French and the Vietminh also completed armistice arrangements for Cambodia and Laos—the other two states in French Indochina. Neither the United States nor

---

[8] *Senator Gravel Edition: The Pentagon Papers,* 4 vols. (Boston: Beacon Press, 1971), vol. 1, pp. 88–107, 434–503.

the South Vietnamese government signed the agreement on Vietnam.

The Geneva agreements provided for elections in South Vietnam within two years, an arrangement that many delegates at Geneva interpreted as a graceful way to let Ho win. Washington, however, quickly became determined to save the anti-Communist government in South Vietnam. Dulles also immediately pushed ahead with the plans for a Southeast Asia Treaty Organization.

THE SUEZ CRISIS

PRECRISIS DISCORD

The Suez war brought the Anglo-American relationship to its postwar nadir and fueled French resentment over Britain's special relationship with the United States. For both Britain and France the Suez incident was an act of defiance against the United States. For France it was a desperate venture that reflected the stress of domestic political instability and the strain of a contracting empire. For Britain, which was more stable domestically and more reconciled to her shrinking world status, Suez revealed deteriorating relations with the United States and the personal alienation between Dulles and British Prime Minister Sir Anthony Eden.

The French were also antagonistic toward Dulles. They resented the pressure he had exerted on France to ratify the EDC Treaty, and they remembered his role in their withdrawal from Vietnam. Dulles had in fact intentionally remained aloof from the Geneva partition of Vietnam in 1954, but the French viewed him as presiding over the dissolution of their Asian empire by withholding American support.

Gamal Abdel Nasser, ruler of Egypt since 1954, had set out to make Egypt the dominant unifying force in the Middle East, exploiting popular resentment over Israel's statehood and British control over the Suez Canal and the Sudan. To pursue development and reformation he adopted a "positive neutralism," seeking help from both the Communist and Western power blocs.

The aspirations of Egypt's new regime divided Washington

from Paris and London. While at first the United States tried to ingratiate itself with Nasser, partly in order to meet the Soviet competition for his allegiance, Britain and France regarded Nasser as an adversary. Britain had commercial and strategic interests in the Suez Canal—but perhaps even higher stakes in its own national prestige. French commercial interests were also heavy, and France's position in Lebanon and Israel was threatened by Nasser's ambitions. Moreover, Egypt had become an important source of arms for Algeria in its fight against France.

In July, 1956, after the announcement of an Egyptian arms agreement with the Soviet Union, Washington (followed by London) backed away from a major commitment to help Egypt build the Aswan Dam. Nasser responded promptly by nationalizing the British controlled and partially French owned Suez Canal. Britain and France demanded in turn that the Canal be put under an international authority. Dulles played a major role in devising schemes for international control, but in an effort to win Egypt's compliance he undermined the impact of threats from London and Paris issued to Nasser. Eden saw Nasser as another Hitler. Impatient with the delays introduced by the United States, he resolved to act.

THE SUEZ ATTACK

On October 29 Israeli forces swept across Egypt's Sinai Peninsula toward Suez. Britain and France quickly joined in thinly veiled collusion with Israel on the pretext of protecting the Canal. Their objective was to seize the Canal and shatter the Nasser regime. The British attack, however, suffered major failures in execution. Its invasion force took a week longer to mount its attack than Prime Minister Eden had been led to believe. The delay was critical, for it permitted Washington to bring pressure to bear in stopping the attack.

President Eisenhower immediately condemned the tripartite action, took the matter to the United Nations General Assembly, and applied monetary and military pressures. With American support, the General Assembly approved a resolution calling for a cease-fire, while American naval and air forces in the Mediterranean harassed the British invasion forces.

Britain was also particularly vulnerable to monetary pressures because the pound sterling was one of the world's reserve currencies. Only the International Monetary Fund could save the pound, but the United States withheld the Fund's help. When Moscow threatened a nuclear strike against France and Britain, Washington responded ambiguously and then cut off further communication with British officials.

Under these combined economic and military pressures, Eden caved in. The French Premier, Pineau, followed suit. The war ended within eight days of the initial attack and hardly more than hours after the actual engagement of British and French landing forces.

IMPLICATIONS OF THE SUEZ WAR

The British and French had expected that the United States would not block the Anglo-French effort—a colossal misunderstanding of American intentions. London attributed the "misunderstanding" to Washington's deliberate deception, while Washington attributed it to puzzling stupidity on the part of Britain and France.

London and Paris evidently missed a major point about American behavior throughout the crisis. By attacking Egypt without United States approval, Britain and France were challenging American leadership in the Atlantic alliance and the American role in the Middle East. Washington reacted with genuine indignation. In a national television address, Eisenhower appealed to the rule of law in the world community, condemning aggression "no matter who the attackers, no matter who the victim."

Blame for the failure of both London and Paris to understand the American viewpoint lay with both sides. Dulles must have been insensitive to the personal stresses under which Eden and Pineau labored. And they, in their hostility toward Dulles, may well have underestimated his grasp of the American interests at stake in the planned venture and his determination to pursue these interests.

Above all, Britain and France failed to recognize that the United States faced special constraints as leader of the Western alliance: for if the United States could be dragged into foreign ventures by second-level members of its alliances, then it was in a vulnerable position as a world power. Thus Washington had to disassociate itself from the venture. French and British officials were inclined to explain away the American opposition as part of the problem of dealing with Dulles, or more broadly, as the result of the American prejudice against French and British colonial interests. Dulles was aware, however, that while the United States could take no action or responsibility for the venture, the Franco-British invasion would have served certain genuine American interests, provided our allies were willing to undertake and complete the task entirely on their own. At least it appears that Dulles had seen the possibility, for it has been reported that when Selwyn Lloyd, the British Foreign Minister, went to see Dulles after it was all over, the first question Dulles asked him was, "Why did you stop?"[9]

The Suez war made the Baghdad Pact a source of embarrassment to the United States, left NATO in disarray, and antagonized many neutral states. The caving in of Britain and France displayed the weaknesses of these states, diminishing the prestige of the NATO powers and of the United States, which suffered indirectly through its traditional association with the French and British. Conversely, Nasser's standing in the Middle East skyrocketed, and the Soviet position in the region improved, partly because Britain and France had agreed to a U.N. cease-fire order the day after the Soviet nuclear threat. The apparent knuckling under of Britain and France to Soviet nuclear power in turn diminished the confidence of Europeans in the American strategic umbrella.

The failure of the Suez venture brought down Prime Minister Eden in Britain, though not the Conservative government. The French government, already annoyed by Britain's special ties with Washington, resented Britain's submission and Washington's aid to the British afterward. These events added to the fiercely nationalistic, anti-American, and anti-British attitudes upon which De Gaulle would soon draw.

The effects of the Suez crisis on European cohesion, however, cannot be entirely isolated from the events occurring in the Soviet Union and Eastern Europe at that time.

[9] Richard Gould-Adams, *The Time of Power: A Reappraisal of John Foster Dulles* (London: Weidenfelt & Nicolson, 1962), p. 222.

THE HUNGARIAN REVOLUTION

In the struggle for succession after Stalin's death in 1953, the new ruling group in Moscow had helped to stabilize its collective leadership by denigrating the myth of Stalin's greatness. Premier Khrushchev accelerated this effort early in 1956 at the Twentieth Party Congress with a remarkable secret speech telling of Stalin's malevolence and abuse of power during his reign. The contents of this speech not only became known throughout the West but sent tremors reverberating throughout the regimes of Eastern Europe. All the East European Communist leaders had depended heavily on Moscow during the Stalin era. All had relied on the Soviet government as a model to legitimize their own authoritarian rule. To discredit Stalin was to discredit those Communist officials in the satellite regimes who were most closely associated with Stalin and his narrow autocratic model. In solving the succession problem within the Soviet Union, the Russian leaders were creating other problems for their satellites.

In June 1956 workers in Poznań, Poland, struck against a regime that had only recently been "democratized," setting off a national upsurge that installed a new regime and withstood Russian threats of intervention in October.

While the Soviet leaders were still dealing with the challenge to their authority in Warsaw, Hungarian students touched off a revolt in Budapest. Soviet troops intervened but were quickly forced to withdraw. As they left Hungary, Imre Nagy, the new premier, pledged free elections and an end to the one-party system. However he also added a potentially explosive declaration of Hungarian autonomy in promising "no interference in our internal affairs"— in effect a repudiation of Soviet hegemony that went well beyond the Polish stand. Four days later massively reinforced Soviet forces returned, quickly installed a new regime, and began a ruthless purge that Nagy, among others, did not survive. If the concessions to Polish nationalism marked the potential liberalization, the brutal repression of Hungary marked its limits.

Dulles correctly concluded that American pressure would only have hurt the Polish cause by provoking the Russians into retracting the concessions they had already made. Given the Russian brutality in Hungary, on the other hand, it would seem that little more could have been lost through American pressure on Moscow to moderate its actions there. In fact, the United States did inadvertently become involved in the Hungarian Revolution. Radio Free Europe, a CIA-supported private propaganda organization, proved unresponsive to the hands-off policy adopted in Washington with tragic results. It encouraged Hungarians to expect American intervention, provoking them to take futile risks while Washington could in no way lend support to the courageous Hungarian stand.

The Suez crisis upset the Atlantic bloc; the Hungarian crisis, the Soviet bloc. Both crises resulted in the bloc leaders temporarily asserting their dominance.

The repression of Hungary in 1956 delayed and limited the prospects for a liberalized Soviet bloc but did not destroy future possibilities. Moscow could not tolerate the challenge to its dominance of the bloc, but neither was it pleased with the inept and costly satellite regimes run by little autocrats (such as Ulbricht in East Germany) that the Stalinist era had produced. Once the repression of Hungary had marked the limits of permissible de-Stalinization among the European satellites, Moscow could then permit political liberalization with increased assurance that changes would not threaten Russian hegemony.

CONCLUSION

Eisenhower is remembered largely for his self-restraint in foreign policy: the Korean war, reducing United States defense expenditures and modifying our military posture, refusing to save the French military position in Indochina, and avoiding involvement in the Middle East over the Suez crisis.

Yet acts of self-limitation were only part of the Eisenhower record. His Administration had permitted clandestine CIA intervention in Guatemala to prevent a left-wing takeover that was abetted from abroad. Furthermore, Dulles had considerably expanded American economic and military obligations along the borders of China and Russia through the creation of SEATO and the offer of American military assistance to members of SEATO and the Baghdad Pact. The reasons for these actions were articulated in alliances, treaties, executive agreements, and the Cold War rhetoric of American foreign policy. The reasons for nonintervention, on the other hand, remained largely unarticulated throughout the Eisenhower Administration. Nonintervention (such as in the 1956 Hungarian Revolution) was at best explained as unfeasible.

This bias in favor of developing doctrines that justify action while not explaining inaction can be attributed to political conditions. Opinion leaders have found it convenient to sustain the popular myth of an omnipresent Soviet menace. To do so, they have found it necessary to concentrate in public statements on explaining foreign policy actions, while avoiding drawing public attention to decisions against taking action. As noted earlier, the Truman Administration's problems in trying to justify its inaction in China and its refusal to press for victory in Korea served as a lesson to American officials: visibility when choosing not to act in threatening situations is severely hazardous politically. As results of this asymmetry in incentives to explain and to act, the criteria for selective intervention have remained an unexplored subject in American foreign policy, and the United States appears to have expanded its perception of its interests to coincide with the reach of its power.

chapter 5

Eisenhower: The Inertia of the Second Term

INTRODUCTION

Three events—the Suez war, the Hungarian Revolution, and a year later the launching of the first satellite, Russia's "Sputnik"—marked a change in the Eisenhower Administration's posture in foreign affairs and in turn affected its domestic status. Eisenhower was to write to a friend in November 1957:

> Since July 25th of 1956, when Nasser announced the nationalization of the Suez, I cannot remember a day that has not brought its major or minor crisis.[1]

This comment effectively distinguishes the second phase of Eisenhower's foreign policy from the first. In the first phase, the United States worked actively to impose its policies on foreign affairs; in the second period, our policy making seemed to consist mainly of responses to events.

The 1956 elections might have been a time to move into a new

---

[1] Dwight D. Eisenhower, *The White House Years*, Vol. 2: *Waging Peace, 1956–1961* (Garden City, N.Y.: Doubleday, 1965), p. 226.

orientation toward international affairs. The Korean war had long since been settled. The public anxieties over it had abated. McCarthyism had subsided. Broad public confidence in government had grown. The shibboleths of Republican opposition had been put aside. Eisenhower's self-restraint in partisanship and his style of governing had created an era of good feeling that the election of 1956 only confirmed.

The election itself scarcely assured innovation in foreign relations. The Administration played upon established popular themes rather than using the campaign to imbue the public with a new understanding of foreign affairs. Eisenhower may have been confident of his capacity to win elections, but he did not display high confidence in his capacity to persuade the public that he was right. He took public opinion in foreign relations mostly as he found it— deferential to the Administration's handling of foreign relations.

The 1956 presidential campaign reflected this quiescence in public debate. The Democrats again nominated Stevenson. In order to win he needed to arouse the public—even to alarm it—over Eisenhower's conduct of public affairs. Even before the Suez war began he accused the incumbent of "irresponsibility and deception" in foreign affairs and of stating only half the facts on questions of war and peace. In late October, barely two weeks before the election, the American news media headlined the outbreak of war in the Middle East and uprisings in Poland and Hungary. Stevenson pressed his attack, charging the Administration with "mistake after mistake." By the eve of the election Washington had frustrated the Anglo-French (though not the Israeli) attack against Egypt and had stood motionless while the Soviet Union crushed the Hungarian revolt. These events might have caused a wavering of confidence in Eisenhower for not better controlling international conditions or for not responding with greater energy to perceived threatening situations. But for the time being, the public reaction appeared to be quite the opposite. The electoral results, which gave Eisenhower an even larger majority than in 1952, showed that Stevenson had not shaken public confidence in the President. In fact, Suez and Hungary actually contributed some votes to the Eisenhower landslide, confirming the electoral value of Eisenhower's strategy of restrained leadership in foreign relations and reflecting the reduction in public attention to foreign affairs. Eisenhower started his second term with 79 percent of the public approving his handling of the Presidency, according to a January 1957 Gallup poll.

SPUTNIK AND THE DECLINE OF AMERICAN CONFIDENCE

In the mid-fifties Moscow and Washington each made secret decisions about the pace at which it would develop two successive new generations of weapons: liquid-fueled and solid-fueled nuclear rockets of intercontinental range. In 1957 it became clear in Washington that Moscow had developed powerful and relatively accurate liquid-fueled rockets and that the Soviet Union had the technical and economic capability to produce enough nuclear-tipped missiles to destroy or seriously weaken the capacity of the United States to retaliate. If the Russians concentrated on developing their capabilities further, they might well be able to neutralize an American second-strike nuclear deterrent, thus allowing a safe Russian nuclear strike at the United States. Or Russia might be able to deter a nuclear attack *from* the United States so effectively as to free *conventional* Russian arms to undertake aggression.

By 1957 the Eisenhower Administration had committed itself to a limited deployment of liquid-fueled intercontinental ballistic missiles (the Atlas and Titan) in order to press on with the development and deployment of the solid-fueled missiles (the Minuteman and Polaris) with their promise of greater economy and better performance. The earliest Administration decisions in favor of the solid-fueled missiles evidently reflected an estimate that the Russians were far behind the United States in strategic nuclear strength. However, surprising advances in Soviet missile technology raised the alarming prospect in 1957 that the Russians might build a missile force that could deliver several times more explosive power than the American force could.

Two groups faced this issue in 1957. The Gaither Committee was a study group of prestigious businessmen and scientists organized by the White House, with access to many government secrets. It concluded that the growing Soviet strategic nuclear capability raised the requirements for American armed might. The other group was privately sponsored by the Rockefeller Brothers Fund under the direction of a young Harvard professor, Henry Kissinger. It came to similar conclusions and advocated several annual $3-billion increases in the defense budget.

Sputnik I, the world's first artificial earth satellite, was launched by the Soviet Union on October 4, 1957. Six weeks earlier Moscow had announced the successful test of an intercontinental ballistic missile (ICBM). American reports on the missile test indicated impressive accuracy. Two days after lofting Sputnik I, the Russians tested " a mighty hydrogen warhead of a new design," as they put it. A month later Sputnik II, weighing 1300 pounds, carried a dog into orbit and safely back, and, in doing so, demonstrated a very large payload capacity for Soviet rockets.

The impact of the Soviet space feats on public opinion throughout the world was immense. Among the publics in every country for which survey data are available, Soviet scientific and technological prestige soared dramatically—at the expense of the United States. The impact caught both Washington and Moscow by surprise. The Soviet Union exploited its space achievements for maximum propaganda impact and launched a diplomatic offensive by threatening the Western status in Berlin once again. Premier Khrushchev indicated that Russia might negotiate a separate peace settlement with East Germany and called for a summit meeting.

Even in the United States, opinions shifted significantly. Sputnik brought a new awareness—and new illusions—of Soviet scientific prowess. It also destroyed some old illusions about America's technological superiority upon which confidence about military security had depended. Furthermore, by raising the public perception of threat from abroad, Sputnik diminished public confidence in the Eisenhower Administration.

A survey in Washington and Chicago a few weeks after Sputnik reported that 43 percent of the sample agreed that the Russian satellite was a "serious blow to U.S. prestige."[2] This percentage appears to be an indication of significant disturbance in public attitudes. A more satisfactory indicator would be a survey run repeatedly over time to trace secular changes. One poll taken several times a year measures public perceptions of how well the President is doing his

[2] American Institute of Public Opinion (Gallup poll), October 27, 1957.

job. The percentage of the national sample who approved of Eisenhower's "handling of his job as President" had been sliding in 1957, but it dipped to 57 percent in the first poll after Sputnik.[3]

At the same time, in November 1957, 53 percent of a national public sample wanted to "take a new look at our defense policies," and only 26 percent were satisfied with them.[4]

A national survey shortly afterward in January 1958 on whether the Russians could wipe out most American cities with their new rockets showed a high 51 percent agreeing, 35 percent disagreeing, and 14 percent with no opinion.[5] Public confidence appears to have been considerably shaken by Sputnik.

The Eisenhower Administration further disconcerted the public by emphasizing that, regardless of Sputnik, it would continue to hold down government expenditures as before and limit its use of presidential leadership. Privately, Eisenhower talked of the public reaction to Sputnik as revealing the "psychological vulnerability of our people" and producing "a measure of self-doubt." He hoped that this stimulus would reduce congressional "balkiness" in supporting his legislative programs. Dulles too found a bright side to Sputnik. In an address he made on January 16, 1958, he referred to the public reaction to Sputnik as a mood that was producing "a more serious appraisal of the struggle in which we are engaged and an increasing willingness to make the kind of efforts and sacrifices needed to win that struggle."

The orbiting of Sputnik had in fact caught the Administration in the middle of an effort to reduce its defense programs. The economy effort was not abandoned, but the Administration did undertake a series of limited responses to Sputnik. It reorganized the Defense Department and established a special agency to manage nonmilitary research in outer space. These steps did not shift any government priorities, but they were intended to demonstrate the Administration's concern over Sputnik and to mollify its critics. The Administration also attempted to shore up NATO's military defenses against the newly revealed Soviet missile capability and

[3] American Institute of Public Opinion, as compiled in *Public Opinion Quarterly,* Spring 1961, Princeton, N.J., p. 136.

[4] American Institute of Public Opinion, November 24, 1957.

[5] *Ibid.,* January 29, 1958.

NATO's diplomatic solidarity against a new Berlin crisis. To strengthen NATO's nuclear might it sought to place Thor and Jupiter intermediate-range ballistic missiles (IRBMs) on the territory of NATO allies. Only Britain, Italy, and Turkey ever accepted any. It pressed NATO diplomatic initiatives by directing attention to the semiannual NATO ministerial meeting in early December 1957. Eisenhower attended, despite a stroke barely three weeks earlier (his third illness in twenty-six months). The meeting was dramatic but unsubstantial. These steps did not convey a picture of government concern grave enough to offset the public anxieties raised by Sputnik. On the contrary, they transformed this public anxiety into prolonged malaise that was reinforced by Soviet diplomacy.

In exploiting the worldwide reaction to Sputnik, Soviet leaders claimed to have rapidly growing missile strength based on Soviet nuclear prowess and the awkward but powerful rockets that had launched the orbital satellites. Khrushchev gave the erroneous impression that Russia had undertaken a crash program to build and deploy these first-generation ICBMs.[6]

Before Sputnik—in fact, before the Democratic presidential nominating convention of 1956—Senator Stuart Symington had publicized the fears of Air Force generals that Russian air power would overtake and surpass United States air power. But the generals failed to spread alarm or to help Symington win the Democratic nomination. After Sputnik, air power enthusiasts returned to this issue. They were joined by Eastern internationalist Republicans and prominent Democrats, particularly Senators. The Republican criticism was fortuitously coherent. The Gaither Committee had submitted its secret conclusions to the White House before Sputnik. When Eisenhower failed to publish them or to act, some members of the committee leaked their findings to the press, which reported them widely. The Rockefeller report was not published until January 1958, after Sputnik. These two documents were unquestionably authoritative statements, as far as informed public opinion groups could determine. The information reported about them contrib-

6 Allen Dulles, *The Craft of Intelligence* (New York: Harper & Row, 1963), p. 163.

uted to a restlessness among active and authoritative public opinion elites.

In the Senate, the Armed Services Preparedness Subcommittee conducted a wide-ranging and heavily publicized investigation of military preparedness issues under the leadership of Senator Lyndon B. Johnson. Symington, persisting with his charges that American air power had been neglected, was joined by Senator Henry M. Jackson in the claim that the Soviet Union had achieved superiority in the long-range missile field. (Both Senators had major aerospace firms among their constituents.) Senator Hubert Humphrey sought escape from interest group politics by advocating a pooling of Western Alliance scientific know-how and by successfully promoting the establishment of an arms control agency. John F. Kennedy, the youthful Senator from Massachusetts, reflected interest group pressures in opposing budget cuts but at the same time tried to escape their constraints by linking preparedness questions to broader issues.

The congressional attack on Eisenhower's defense policies indicated that Congressional leaders had been emboldened by Sputnik to challenge Eisenhower's authority in military matters. They began by attacking the Administration's defense program, then moved on to challenge its conduct of foreign relations, and, finally, to charge Eisenhower and Dulles themselves with inflexibility and complacency.

As congressional demands for substantially increased defense expenditures developed in both Republican and Democratic ranks, Eisenhower still argued that there could be no "security" without "solvency." In fiscal years 1958 and 1959 Eisenhower rode out congressional pressures for major defense increases, but the severe congressional scrutiny and certain alterations in defense programs by Congress left a residue of public anxiety. These successive years of apparent underresponse to perceived external threats eroded the confidence of Congress and of other public opinion leaders in Eisenhower's external policies.

The moods of broad public opinion fluctuated noticeably after Sputnik. After its first impact, attention and anxiety declined through the spring of 1958, to be aroused again in December by Khrushchev's announcement that he would sign a peace treaty with East Germany to turn over control of the Western access routes to Berlin to the East German regime. Nonetheless, the Administration's critics had lodged, at least with a small attentive public, the suspicion that arbitrary budget ceilings prevented the government from considering foreign and defense policies on their own merits.

Eisenhower could deny—as he did in a television address in March 1959—that he was subordinating defense to budgetary considerations and that defense was based on the "best composite judgment available." But public statements by military spokesmen and published information about the Gaither and Rockefeller reports had already provided contrary evidence. No composite military judgment considered the American defense posture adequate. Furthermore, no less an authority than Army Chief of Staff Maxwell D. Taylor had testified that the Administration permitted military experts to judge defense issues only within the confines of rigid budget ceilings imposed in advance.[7]

Taylor's criticisms, together with the Gaither Committee report and testimony before Johnson's Senate Preparedness Subcommittee, had publicized differences within the Administration itself over defense preparedness. Eisenhower was unable to present a united Administration front in the face of post-Sputnik criticisms.

Eisenhower himself had encouraged internal opposition to his views by appointment of the Gaither Committee members, who were preponderantly establishment "hawks." Their findings were predictable: faced with the same evidence that the military planners were, they drew the same conclusions. Yet Eisenhower himself had adopted a more favorable assessment that reflected his skepticism about military estimates of the strategic balance. The Gaither episode represents a real puzzle: why did Eisenhower not appoint a committee that would be more sympathetic to his own viewpoints? Like Truman after the Czech coup in 1948, Eisenhower after Sputnik had to cope with mounting pressures from a hawkish faction within the government promoting expansive defense postures that he was unwilling to agree with or repudiate. Evidently he could find no outsiders prestigious enough to be taken seriously who were committed to his own viewpoint.

By 1959, however, the public apparently regained some of its confidence in American military strength and appeared to reflect

[7] U.S., Congress, Senate, Committee on Government Operations, *Organizing for National Security*, Hearings, Part V, 86th Cong., 2nd sess., 1960, p. 769.

more of Eisenhower's optimistic view. A poll taken in March 1959 showed that 49 percent of a national sample agreed that the United States was either keeping ahead of the Soviet Union in military power or staying even, while 34 percent said the United States was dropping behind.[8]

THE MISSILE GAP

Spokesmen for the Army, Navy, and Air Force complained that the limited capabilities they had been permitted to acquire would not enable them to perform the combat tasks assigned to them. Such complaints are endemic to military establishments, as Eisenhower doubtless knew. Another complaint was new, however, and ominous: in the future, the Soviet Union would be far ahead of the United States in deployed strategic nuclear missiles.

The "missile gap" had been an ailment associated with the Sputnik malaise. It became a public issue in its own right when on January 12, 1959, an article in the *New York Times,* purportedly based on interviews with numerous authorities on the defense effort, forecast that by 1960 Moscow would have three ICBMs for every American one. It further claimed that this ratio would increase to fifteen to one in 1964 before the Polaris and Minuteman missiles would enter the American force in sizable numbers.

The Secretary of Defense, Neil McElroy, confirmed the Administration's projection of a missile gap two weeks later when he stated that the United States did not intend to match the Soviet Union "missile for missile." His statement, coming the day after Premier Khrushchev had indicated that Soviet missiles were in assembly line production, caused severe reactions. One widely read authority on military affairs termed it a "disastrous announcement that the United States has withdrawn from the missile race."[9]

The missile gap added to the anxieties that had been nurtured over the two preceding years, preparing the way to make national security policy an issue in the 1960 election. Eisenhower had been

[8] American Institute of Public Opinion, March 6, 1959.

[9] Hanson Baldwin in the *New York Times,* reprinted in the *Congressional Record* (February 5, 1959).

challenged in the area in which his judgment was the most authoritative. And in fact when the Kennedy Administration later repudiated the "missile gap" as groundless, it appeared that Eisenhower's refusal to become alarmed about the apparent Soviet threat during 1958–59 did have some basis in facts. Nonetheless, this was an area in which challenges of the government's conduct of external relations could be the most rewarding politically. To pose the question of the adequacy of American defense, particularly after the spectacular demonstration of Soviet technical prowess, was to address the element of foreign relations most salient to broad public opinion.

NATO AFTER SPUTNIK

Western Europe had followed its own impetus toward integration by setting up a common market in coal and steel in 1954 (the European Coal and Steel Community), and a common nuclear power research and development effort (the European Atomic Energy Commission—EURATOM) in 1957. The more ambitious idea of a customs union, or a general Common Market, highlighted the split in Europe that the Coal and Steel Community and EURATOM had foreshadowed. The "inner six"—West Germany, France, Italy, Belgium, Holland, and Luxembourg—proceeded with the market. Great Britain, having refused to join, organized an "outer seven" in a feeble effort to offset the disadvantages of her self-exclusion.

The first tariff reductions among the inner six were scheduled for January 1, 1959. But in anticipation of these tariff reductions, economic activity expanded among these countries. With the Japanese economy also expanding rapidly, American exports shrank, producing an international payments deficit for the United States of more than $3 billion in 1958—the first substantial deficit in the postwar era. The imbalance was to persist through the sixties and into the seventies, despite the efforts of four administrations to cope with it.

These events form the background for the remarkable development of French national assertiveness in the late fifties and its impact on NATO. Before General Charles de Gaulle took power in

1958, France interposed no special obstacles to the achievement of American objectives in NATO. Like other members of the alliance, she had certain national interests that conflicted with the needs of NATO, and she had fallen short in military contributions. Under De Gaulle, however, France became a formidable obstruction to United States policies in NATO.

The French National Assembly turned to De Gaulle in 1958 in a desperate effort to meet extreme political pressures from the French Army, which had ominously independent goals. De Gaulle extricated France from Algeria, suppressed the unruly army, established his dominant position in French politics, expanded the nuclear weapons program of the preceding Fourth Republic, and recast France's diplomatic posture to raise the country's international prestige. The stability of the French political system now ceased to be a major problem.

After 1958, in foreign relations De Gaulle was France. No ruler of a Western power since World War II dominated the external relations of his country as much as De Gaulle did. He used his power to pursue two closely related objectives: to stabilize France internally and to acquire major world power status for France. The close personal identity of De Gaulle with these objectives was misleading, for it led his critics to underestimate his behavior as personal pique and idiosyncrasy. In fact, his behavior amounted to far more than that. He adopted an aggressive diplomatic posture that improved France's international standing, helped consolidate his position as ruler of the French Fifth Republic, and stabilized the new French regime. At the same time, he used his extraordinary domestic position to pursue external objectives. He could stare down Bonn or freeze out London through his use of the veto and the boycott. Until 1968 his government was relatively secure at home and he was constitutionally able to act arbitrarily whereas the British, German, and other Western governments were not. Above all, he was willing to run the risks entailed in his methods, such as jeopardizing European integration. European integration served other European political leaders by reconciling the demands of domestic politics with the requirements of foreign relations. But De Gaulle was not dependent on political integration for his purpose, and he demonstrated that integration was vulnerable to the veto of any political leader able to do without it.

As part of its NATO policy throughout the fifties, the United States sought to discourage the acquisition of nuclear weapons by other members of the alliance. The British, who had already detonated their first nuclear device in 1952, were an exception.

After the Suez fiasco, Harold Macmillan, the new British Prime Minister and a wartime friend of Eisenhower, had set about restoring relations with Washington and reestablishing Britain's lost military prestige by substantially revamping her military posture along the lines of the American New Look. Since the British government was in severe financial difficulty after Suez, Macmillan economized by sharply reducing British military manpower and increasing British reliance on nuclear weapons.

To help, the United States immediately sold Britain sixty intercontinental ballistics missiles. We also agreed to cooperate with a British program for developing a missile that could carry nuclear warheads from Britain to Russia (and thus give credence to Britain's claim that it was a major nuclear power). Officials in Washington were discomforted by the extent to which the British government was capitalizing politically on what were limited American commitments for help with the new missiles. Nonetheless, Washington went along with the Macmillan government's efforts to score quick points in its domestic political struggles.

When De Gaulle came to power, the British were on their way to achieving a second generation strategic nuclear weapon system. But rising costs forced the cancellation of this effort, and Britain then arranged to purchase the Skybolt, a new American missile still in early stages of development. American technical aid was expanded further through amendments in the United States Atomic Energy Act in 1958, which increased the President's discretion in handling nuclear technology secrets.

But American cooperation with the British did not alter the two dominant tenets of American nuclear policy: (1) the United States would not give up custody of its weapons or permit others to decide when to fire them—in practice, the United States would maintain a veto over those of its weapons assigned to allied forces, and (2) the United States would not give aid in nuclear technology to a "non-nuclear" power.

The second tenet had originally been based on the view that producing nuclear bombs or warheads per se made one a full member of the nuclear club. According to this interpretation, only Britain qualified for aid at the time. By the time France sought entrance to the nuclear club, however, Washington had adopted more stringent requirements for offering technical aid.

Barely five weeks after taking office, De Gaulle told Dulles of his determination to develop nuclear weapons, with or without the assistance of the United States.[10] He also quickly made clear his desire to modify NATO substantially by establishing a tripartite directorate—France, Great Britain, and the United States—to replace what he called the Anglo-American directorate. He refused to allow American missiles not directly under his control to be stationed on French soil. Six months later, in June 1959, he forced the removal of more than 200 NATO fighter bombers from French bases because they carried nuclear weapons the French did not control. The French Foreign Office made clear that these acts were related to the failure of Britain and the United States to treat France as their equal in NATO and that it resented in particular the American failure to assist France's nuclear weapons program.[11]

De Gaulle's was a voice for national independence in a Western Europe that had diminished confidence in the United States nuclear umbrella after Sputnik. Western European skepticism about American nuclear power was an odd combination of nationalism and pacifism, born of the growing prosperity and the terrible prospects of nuclear war in Europe. On one hand, European critics of the United States feared that it would start a nuclear war needlessly, but on the other hand, they wanted to rely on the American nuclear deterrent capability rather than raise the level of their own defense efforts. But even before De Gaulle, France began to raise a new question: would the United States *fail* to strike even if Europe were threatened?

In 1958 NATO adopted plans to use tactical nuclear weapons supplied by the United States as ground force equipment. This deployment of nuclear weapons to NATO members would include West Germany, which alarmed the many Europeans who were already worried about German rearmament. Yet the persistent failure

[10] *New York Times,* July 6, 1958.

[11] *Ibid.,* June 14, 1959; *Manchester Guardian,* June 9, 1959.

of members to meet NATO's force requirements made it necessary to rely on German divisions along NATO's crucial central front.

France evidently faced unanimous opposition within NATO to its refusal to integrate air defense forces. In early 1960 it yielded on this point, an indication that it was not oblivious to the rationale of military analysis or to international political realities. The United States, in turn, began to show signs of modifying its nuclear sharing policies.

The first signs of change in Washington were reports that the powerful Congressional Joint Committee on Atomic Energy was conducting secret hearings on a plan to supply some allies with nuclear weapons. Asked about it, Eisenhower endorsed the idea.

Ten days later, in mid-February, the French exploded a plutonium bomb—their first nuclear detonation. Changing the statutory limitations on nuclear sharing now became urgent if the United States hoped to head off De Gaulle's establishing an independent French nuclear force.

From the outset, the White House agreed with Congress that the United States should keep its veto. The main change in sharing, then, would be to give our allies a veto too. Proposals to share control of some nuclear weapons would assure Europeans that their governments could prevent the use of the nuclear weapons assigned to the shared forces.

But they still could not prevent the United States from the veto-free use of its own nuclear forces, which were considerably larger, and the United States would continue to exercise a veto over the use of the shared nuclear weapons. In preliminary soundings, De Gaulle flatly rejected the proposal for a shared force.[12]

The proposal to share strategic nuclear forces exacerbated fears about giving German troops more nuclear weapons (particularly among the left wing of the British Labour party). The Germans, along with the other NATO forces, had already acquired tactical nuclear weapons through bilateral arrangements with the United States.

French forces were being withdrawn from NATO control, and British troop strength in NATO was being trimmed, while the

[12] See for example Joseph Alsop, *New York Herald Tribune,* May 27, 1960.

German divisions were being almost doubled. Anti-German reactions were a serious problem. One way to moderate these reactions was to emphasize the multilateral character of a shared strategic nuclear force as proposed by General Lauris Norstad. At the NATO Council meeting in December 1960, Secretary of State Christian Herter, now representing a lame-duck administration, proposed the establishment of a multilateral but fully integrated nuclear force under NATO command. His action assured that the subject would be carried to the agenda of the Kennedy Administration.

By the time Eisenhower left office, the import of Gaullist France's foreign policy for NATO had become quite clear. France's determination to become a nuclear power and De Gaulle's insistence that France have equal standing with Britain and the United States in NATO affairs had already proved disruptive. For the time being, De Gaulle tacitly accepted the integration of French forces in a mobile nuclear task force, but French opposition to integrated forces delayed for a year the establishment of an integrated air defense system for Europe.

As the predominant French leader through the sixties, De Gaulle would continue to challenge the American vision of one supranational Western European state: his goal was a Europe of strong national states no longer divided between East and West. American policy since 1947 had strongly favored the political and economic integration of Western Europe. But the proposal for an integrated NATO nuclear force, which had acquired the official mantles of both Washington and SHAPE headquarters by the end of 1960, would be laid aside quietly five years later, partly because of De Gaulle's opposition. In addition, the impact of the French government's stand against integration was greatly increased by the inconsistencies of the American policy in NATO and the weak expediencies upon which many of NATO's most impressive achievements had been built.

De Gaulle's challenge, in short, exposed other basic weaknesses in the movement for European integration. First, De Gaulle was correct in perceiving that American leadership in NATO tended to favor Great Britain, the NATO member that had traditionally been least amenable to European integration. Furthermore, though the United States talked of integration within NATO, we were actually moving toward greater independence from the Alliance by promoting a division of labor between us and the rest of NATO. And, most fundamentally, De Gaulle challenged European political integration because it would encourage national political leaders of democratic states to avoid dealing with troublesome national issues they must otherwise face by turning these issues over to military and economic technocrats in supranational agencies.

De Gaulle's challenge of Western policy, like the man himself, was of classic dimensions. His own vision of a Europe of nation states may have been tattered; but he demonstrated that the vision of an integrated Europe was no more heroic, for it was based largely on hopes of escaping from, rather than solving, the problems that inevitably arise within *democratic* national politics.

THE POLITICAL COMPLICATIONS OF
SAYING "NO"

The question of geographic priorities in American foreign policy persisted for Eisenhower throughout his eight years, but they were particularly troublesome with respect to two areas: the Middle East after the Suez crisis and the Formosa Straits. By contrast, the best examples of the Eisenhower Administration's selectivity and self-restraint were the decisions against American involvement in Africa and Latin America. This section will examine the Eisenhower Administration's policies in these four major areas.

For the Eisenhower Administration, the Anglo-French attack on Egypt posed a direct challenge to American leadership of the Atlantic alliance. Eisenhower's refusal to go along with London and Paris was in effect designed to enforce discipline within the Western alliance structure and reassert American dominance over it.

The disparity in power between the United States and its allies produced problems of discipline and dominance that were comparable in certain respects to those in the Soviet bloc. In their power aspirations, Moscow and Washington were not easily distinguishable. Washington, however, accepted more pluralism internally and externally, reflecting the more competitive political systems of the United States and its principal allies in Western Europe. In general, the United States dealt with its allies and clients in a distinctly less authoritarian manner than did Moscow.

The British and French had acted on their own in attacking Egypt because they had concluded that they could not otherwise get the United States to be sufficiently helpful to them. The Eisenhower Administration, beginning before Egypt's seizure of the Canal, had attempted to minimize American involvement in the Middle East, and it avoided committing resources or accepting obligations in this area. Yet we continued to be carried along by the rhetoric of active anti-Communism as we attempted to pick up the pieces of our own policy in the Middle East. Thus the Eisenhower Administration encouraged a situation much like one it had inherited in Asia from Truman's Presidency: a predisposition to become heavily involved in a distant local situation in the name of anti-Communism. The Lebanon and Formosa Straits crises both demonstrated the potential of our small client states to draw the United States into solving *their* problems *their* way—regardless of American interests—and in doing so, to tie down United States forces and risk committing the United States still further. Both situations involved American interests only indirectly; yet in both, the United States acted in haste and to its eventual embarrassment.

THE EISENHOWER DOCTRINE

American intervention to halt the British-French-Israeli invasion of Egypt in the fall of 1956 had severely burdened American diplomacy in Europe and the Middle East, as discussed earlier in this chapter. In an effort to recoup, Eisenhower asked Congress in January 1957 for a joint resolution that would "authorize" the President to use American armed forces "as he deems necessary" to defend the Middle East nations "requesting such aid against overt armed aggression from any nation controlled by international Communism." This resolution was to become known as the Eisenhower Doctrine.

The President's request was a way to share political responsibility with a reluctant Congress. Critics charged that Congress was being asked to sign a "blank check" that would authorize unspecified future actions. Besides, they argued, the Eisenhower Doctrine had missed the point of the Suez crisis—that the pressing threats to

American interests in the Middle East were not those of overt Communist military conquest but of expanding political influence. After much delay and some revision, Congress passed the resolution.

The method of securing approval for it partially frustrated its purposes. With so much controversy surrounding its passage, the resolution hardly demonstrated the solid backing in Washington that the White House had sought. Eisenhower's appeal for advance congressional support, furthermore, was not much appreciated by either Democratic or Republican legislators, who were unwilling to take responsibility for Eisenhower's foreign policy.

However, the Eisenhower Doctrine served a more immediate purpose: it helped Washington abandon Nasser and construct a pro-American, anti-Communist, anti-Nasser bloc—forcing the states in the Middle East to choose between Cairo and Moscow on one hand, and Washington on the other. The members of the Baghdad Pact—Turkey, Iran, Iraq, and Pakistan—expressed early support for the Eisenhower Doctrine. Lebanon, Jordan, Saudi Arabia, and Libya also supported it. Egypt and Syria drew closer together as a somewhat isolated leftist-nationalist faction, forming the United Arab Republic (U.A.R.) federation in 1958.

This division between "pro-American" and "pro-Soviet" states had certain drawbacks for American diplomacy, as illustrated by the Lebanon crisis. Rioting broke out in Lebanon in May 1958. The Lebanese government accused the new United Arab Republic of causing the conflict. Iraq, facing similar difficulties, also blamed the U.A.R. In July a bloody army coup in Iraq liquidated the royal house and the government before the U.S. Sixth Fleet could act, throwing the neighboring governments of Lebanon and Jordan into panic. A day after the Iraqi coup, U.S. Marines were dispatched to Lebanon and British troops were sent to King Hussein in Jordan to forestall further trouble.

But when the Iraqi troubles did not spread, Washington and London soon found themselves under attack from domestic critics who charged that military intervention was unnecessary. Soviet and pro-Nasser propaganda made the most of Western discomfort, and Moscow called for a summit conference. United Nations spokesmen wanted to get the troops out. India, the leading neutralist, protested the military intrusions. By August, when the United Nations

General Assembly met, the danger of violence had abated, and Washington faced the real prospect of a United Nations censure. The General Assembly, however, neither censured nor supported the Anglo-American action.

Once in Lebanon, the United States found itself caught between a sagging government and its leftist opponents who, though aided by Syria, were an integral part of national Lebanese politics. Before the United States could withdraw, it had to unite the two factions behind a candidate of national conciliation for the impending election.

The disadvantages of Washington's predilection to view complex international issues as a simple struggle between freedom and Communism were never more evident than in this Middle East crisis of 1958. Leftist Arab nationalists found themselves courted by Moscow and pushed toward the Soviet Union by the polarity underlying the Eisenhower Doctrine. The polarized political climate in the Middle East in 1958, for example, cooled the relations of Iraq, Saudi Arabia, and Lebanon with the United States. Yet these countries had by no means ignored the domestic threat of Communism. In addition, according to a well-informed judgment, even Syria had joined with Egypt in order to counter the growing influence of the Communist party in Syria.[13] Similarly, Nasser, though willing to exploit the link between Communism and Arab nationalism in other states, suppressed Communist activity in Egypt.

Initially, the Eisenhower Doctrine, coupled with American military and economic assistance, had produced an impressive lineup of Middle East states allied with the United States. Yet within a year leftist Arab nationalists had isolated Jordan, overthrown Iraq, and virtually destroyed the utility of Lebanon and Saudi Arabia as American allies.

THE INTERVENTION IN QUEMOY

The Eisenhower Doctrine had translated American goals in the Middle East into oversimplified opposition to Soviet Communism at a time when Arab nationalism was mixing with left-wing radicalism to produce a rich spectrum of political ideology and faction-

[13] Philip E. Mosely, *The Kremlin and World Politics* (New York: Vintage, 1960), p. 554.

alism. By contrast, on the island of Taiwan, the seat of government for Nationalist China since the Communist conquest of the Chinese mainland in the late forties, the Communist/anti-Communist line had been clearly drawn for American policy well before Eisenhower's inauguration.

As an early gesture of change in our Asian policy, Eisenhower had "unleashed" the Nationalist Chinese armed forces by withdrawing the U.S. Seventh Fleet from acting as a "shield against the mainland." The Nationalist regime could scarcely hope to invade the mainland successfully; but its forces were capable of harassing the mainland, which it did. As a result, the tiny island groups of Quemoy and Matsu, offshore from the Chinese mainland in the Formosa Straits and under Nationalist control, came under persistent Communist attack in late 1954. At Eisenhower's insistence, Congress authorized the President to "employ" the armed forces "as he deems necessary" to protect "Formosa [Taiwan] and the Pescadores against armed attack." The crisis abated by April 1955, though it remained unresolved.

In August 1958 the mainland batteries opened fire again. Dulles and Eisenhower quickly made two points in response: (1) there would be no retreat from American commitments to Taiwan in the face of Communist aggression and (2) the shelling was "an ambitious plan of armed conquest," as Eisenhower charged in a national television address, that "would liquidate all of the free-world positions in the Western Pacific area and bring them under captive governments."

The initial American position was tough and rigid. But within the month much happened to encourage a more flexible position. Public reactions to the tough line laid out by Dulles and Eisenhower in the midst of the congressional campaign were important. The Administration expected some partisan criticism and got it. But the public itself showed wide opposition to a showdown over the Formosa Straits. The State Department added to the Administration's embarrassment by announcing that 80 percent of the letters received were critical or fearful about the Administration's stand.

On the diplomatic level, the Administration got little support for its original stand. Events in Asia also encouraged its reconsideration. The shelling from the mainland was so intense as to prevent resupplying the islands without full-scale United States military support. Yet Washington had decided that the Navy would escort island-bound Nationalist ships no closer than the three-mile limit. The prospect that ammunition would soon be exhausted brought Dulles under heavy pressure from Taiwan to go further. The aging Chiang Kai-shek had every reason to involve the United States in an invasion of mainland China. His regime lived for the day it would return to the mainland and defeat the Communist government there.

At a news conference on November 30, Dulles denied any American obligation to defend the offshore islands or to help Chiang return to the mainland. A week later, under Soviet pressure, Peking announced a temporary cease-fire, which it later extended. In effect, Peking acknowledged its inability to take the islands by force at that time. Dulles' statement meant that the United States would not support the Nationalist government if it maintained a military buildup on the offshore islands to prepare for an invasion of the mainland. Peking in turn gave up preparations to take the islands by force. In a joint communiqué from Taiwan in late October, Dulles and Chiang renounced the use of force to recover the mainland. Through this act, Dulles had once again "leashed" Chiang Kai-shek.

The Eisenhower Administration's policy toward Nationalist China had now come full circle. Even more significant was the fact that Peking and Washington had achieved a point of agreement about the status of Taiwan.

THE ELECTIONS OF 1958

The 1958 congressional elections showed that the Administration's vulnerabilities in responding to crises at home and abroad could be exploited for partisan purposes. Domestic issues doubtless contributed much more than foreign affairs to the election results: the economy was just recovering from a recession, and a scandal had forced Eisenhower's key assistant, Sherman Adams, to resign. But foreign crises did have some impact on the election: the external threats implicit in Sputnik; the Formosa Straits crisis, which contributed to the militancy of the campaigns; the intervention in Lebanon; and the hostile reception given to Vice President Nixon in Venezuela affected the public and were reflected in the criticisms of opinion leaders in Washington.

While Eisenhower played a partisan role in the campaign, repeatedly charging Democratic irresponsibility in spending, the leading spokesman for the Administration was Vice President Nixon. Eisenhower's role in foreign policy and partisan affairs had failed to give the public the impression of an active and concerned President supported by national public opinion leaders.

As a result, the Democrats returned the heaviest majority to Congress since 1936: 282 to 153 in the House and 62 to 34 in the Senate. Most important in explaining these results was the fact that Eisenhower himself was not a candidate. The 1958 election confirmed what had become apparent in 1956—that Eisenhower's great personal popularity did not help Republican congressional candidates very much. The lesson for Democratic and Republican Congressmen alike was that grappling with the President in the next two years would not be as important as grappling with the other party in Congress. These factors moderated the partisan divisions between the President and Congress from 1959 through 1960, but they did not prevent an increase in partisanship on Capitol Hill.

LATIN AMERICA AND AFRICA: THE EFFECTS OF SELF-RESTRAINT

As we have noted, a primary concern of the Eisenhower Administration was the question of how best to allocate limited financial, military, and economic resources in order to further American foreign policies without overextending ourselves in the long run. The Administration's basic answer was to concentrate its resources and attention on the geographic areas in which confrontation with Soviet expansion seemed the most urgent. This decision led to our hands-off policy in both Latin America and Africa. This policy was reflected in the disproportionately small outlays we made to Latin America and Africa in government economic and military assistance. During the first five years of the Eisenhower Administration we spent $12.6 billion on military and economic assistance to Asia and the Middle East, while we spent only $1.9 billion in Latin America and only $350 million in Africa.

The Administration's determination to minimize its involvement in Latin America throughout the fifties was expressed in its major premise that, more than anything else, Latin America needed investment capital and that sufficient capital could be provided only by private American and other investors. This argument represented a justification for (1) not attempting to encourage political, social, and economic changes in Latin America and (2) not making heavy commitments for economic assistance to these countries.

In 1953 Eisenhower sent his brother, a well-known college president, on a tour of Latin America. Milton Eisenhower reported that these countries needed more stable economic conditions and more capital. He recommended substantial increases in United States government grants and loans but emphasized that primary reliance must be on private investment.

The Administration delayed its response to the report because it did not want to divert attention from the pressing issue of Communist turmoil in Guatemala. (Squabbling within our government over how to administer loans for Latin American economic development also contributed to the delay.) In 1954 the United States intervened covertly to stop a Communist supported takeover in Guatemala. At the Tenth Inter-American Conference that year the United States had won some support for its preparations to deal with the developing problem in Guatemala, but it had failed to establish a clear policy for economic and military assistance. By then, however, the budget ceilings for external affairs were weighing heavily on the State and Defense Departments. The Administration decided to rely primarily on private trade rather than on economic and military assistance. It encouraged American private investments in Latin America through guarantees and other incentives and by encouraging Latin American governments to change legislation that discouraged other foreign investments.

Latin American governments wanted more United States government loans and United States subsidies to stabilize their export market prices. Because each nation's economy depended heavily on the export of a few primary products, such as coffee or tin, it was highly vulnerable to price fluctuations. In 1957, at the Inter-American Economic Conference in Buenos Aires, the United States delegation encountered strong pressure for an additional commitment of resources. The Secretary of the Treasury, Robert B. Anderson, countered with the argument that foreign capital would be insufficient and that the Latin American governments would have to finance much of their economic development from domestic sources.

Unfortunately, grantors and recipients of economic assistance have no commonly accepted standards about sharing the burdens of economic development. Anderson's statement raised a serious point about the financing of economic development. Typically, capitalists in underdeveloped states invest their accumulated wealth abroad. When their governments seek development assistance from the United States, therefore, they are asking the United States to invest where their own investors will not. This phenomenon suggests that economies needing development usually have some features that make them unattractive to foreign investors, public and private, as well as to their own investors. Washington found ample reasons not to commit much public capital to Latin American development throughout the mid-fifties.

After Sputnik, however, United States policy in Latin America attempted to redress the neglect of previous years. But to the extent that our change in posture was noticed at home or abroad, it reinforced the public impression that our foreign policy was reactive rather than innovative.

In 1958 Vice President Nixon toured Latin America on a goodwill mission, but hostile crowds in Caracas, Venezuela, and Lima, Peru, threatened him with physical harm. Officials in Washington knew about the volatile protest movements in Latin America, and the Vice President had been briefed to deal with student demonstrations, but not with violence. The Nixon riots shocked Washington into action by suggesting strongly that the low priorities we had accorded to Latin America during the fifties could be truly dangerous to American interests.

The hostilities in Caracas may well have resulted from American identification with the dictatorial Jimenez regime, deposed in early 1958. United States policy now shifted to avoid identification with dictatorial regimes, to the benefit of a young left-wing political entrepreneur in Cuba, Fidel Castro. His revolutionary group would overthrow the harsh authoritarian regime of Fulgencio Batista in January 1959 (discussed in Chapter 7). Our foreign policy also shifted to permit the establishment of an Inter-American Development Bank, a proposal that Washington had long resisted because of the Bank's expected call upon the United States Treasury for operating capital. As the sense of urgency about Latin America grew during the late 1950s, major political changes of a quite different character were occurring in Africa. At the beginning of the decade European colonial powers still governed south of the Sahara. Through the mid- and late fifties the African nations rapidly became decolonized. Britain and France were less reluctant to let go of their African colonial interests than their Middle East interests (except for the British white-settler states, the Rhodesias and Kenya), and no pan-African movement united against the colonial powers. Consequently, these powers remained influential in the area and on fairly good terms with their former colonies. Soviet and American influence in the region remained minimal.

One exception to these circumstances occurred: in 1960 the Belgian government abandoned the Belgian Congo to independence, and chaos and violence soon broke out. The Soviet Union promptly intervened to support local leftist challengers of central authority and the United Nations took up peacekeeping operations supported by the United States. Except for this case, however, Soviet influence in Africa did not pose threats to which Washington had to respond, and we were happy to leave the continent mainly to others.

SUMMITRY AND DISARMAMENT

To attempt fundamental changes in international conditions, the Eisenhower Administration had three choices. First, it could intervene directly in regions and countries to effect changes. But the Administration was inhibited from broad activism by budgetary constraints and by doubts about its ability to change social and political conditions abroad (as well as at home).

Second, the Administration could assume a more aggressive military and psychological or political posture. But this choice was foreclosed when the rhetoric of "rolling back the captive nations" was surrendered during the early months of Eisenhower's tenure.

Third, the Administration could try to change its relationship with the Soviet Union—a choice to which Adlai Stevenson devoted much attention in his 1956 campaign. It is plain from the way

Eisenhower nurtured disarmament proposals in the White House that this option had a special place in his thinking as well. However, Eisenhower's experiences with disarmament negotiations represent an appalling record of government unresponsiveness to his guidance. This lack of response was due partly to bureaucratic problems but largely to the fact that Dulles was much less interested than Eisenhower in the prospects for negotiations with the Russians. In fact, the disarmament issue illustrates well the Eisenhower Administration's difficulties in dealing with the Soviet Union when Dulles and Eisenhower had different viewpoints.

In its early disarmament negotiations with the Soviet Union, the Truman Administration had at first taken the position outlined in the Baruch Plan in 1946: that the United States would not give up its nuclear weapons monopoly unless it could have absolute assurance against nuclear proliferation in return. The effect, of course, would be to keep Russia from getting nuclear weapons. Faced with this plan at the negotiating table, the Soviet Union needed only to delay agreement until it could get better terms as a recognized nuclear power. Disarmament negotiations had degenerated in the face of this deadlock into a propaganda battle, soiling the record for both sides.

The United Nations established a Disarmament Commission in January 1952, and the Western powers began developing a new disarmament program. But the American position remained unchanged on the vital issue of nuclear control: an acceptable agreement would have to provide a reliable method of accounting for all nuclear fuel production and all nuclear weapons.

Once hopes for improved relations with the Soviet Union began to rise in 1953, prospective summit meetings became politically important. In France, and particularly in Britain, a summit meeting promised enhanced status for the heads of state who attended.

As we have noted, Eisenhower put a far higher priority than Dulles did on disarmament negotiations and summit conferences. This difference of views led Eisenhower to establish a separate avenue for initiating proposals in these areas—the one exception to his almost complete reliance on Dulles' handling of foreign and military matters.

Throughout most of Dulles' tenure, Eisenhower assigned a presidential aide to work on proposals that might change the

United States relationship with the Soviet Union—in particular, proposals for disarmament and summitry. The first man to play that role was C. D. Jackson, who took Eisenhower's own idea for the "peaceful atom" and developed it into a set of proposals that Eisenhower presented to the United Nations General Assembly in December 1953. These proposals are of particular interest because they recognized that it was no longer possible to account for all nuclear fissile material, a position that had been the bedrock of American nuclear control policy since 1946. Eisenhower's new scheme simply provided that the nuclear powers would contribute to a United Nations pool of nuclear fuel. The new plan attempted to focus on the quantities that would be disclosed and put under international control, rather than on the impossible task of accounting for all fuel possessed by the nuclear powers.

Eisenhower's 1953 speech before the General Assembly marked the abandonment of the long-held American demand for comprehensive disarmament in favor of partial but immediately realizable measures that would be confidence-building. Yet Eisenhower's proposal was not followed up by the development of a unified negotiating position among the Western powers, nor was it even reflected in the positions taken by our own negotiators for more than a year at the disarmament conferences. At United Nations Disarmament Commission meetings, both the East and West experienced considerable difficulty in addressing the same issues at the same time, partly because disarmament remained a secondary objective to both. During 1954 and early 1955 it looked as though a summit meeting would be necessary if disarmament negotiations were to be fruitful.

The United Nations disarmament conference of May 1955, however, provided one breakthrough: the Soviet delegation finally moved away from the long-standing Soviet position that nuclear weapons must be eliminated as the first step in any disarmament plan, and the Russians invited the West to discuss partial measures of disarmament that might reduce tensions and lead to more complete agreements. The British, French, and American delegations all recognized the importance of the new Soviet proposals. A leading international authority on disarmament termed this "the moment of hope."[14]

[14] Philip Noel-Baker, *The Arms Race; A Programme for World Disarmament* (London: Atlantic Book Publishing Co., Ltd., 1958), chapter 2.

Unfortunately, despite their optimism over this new possibility, the Western delegations were unprepared to deal substantively with the Soviet proposals. The Western powers were unable to act because they had not yet evolved a unified negotiating position on disarmament issues. Eisenhower, despite his proposal of December 1953, was unwilling to move ahead without the specific agreement of our allies on an official negotiating stance. And in fact even the United States State Department and our own negotiators failed to follow up Eisenhower's initiatives.

The Soviets thus met with confusion and disunity among the Western delegations in response to their May 1955 proposals. This disarray offered the Russians tempting propaganda opportunities that they were to exploit during the next year.

In July 1955, two months after the eventful disarmament meeting, a summit meeting among the major powers was held in Geneva. The Geneva summit had been scheduled before the disarmament conference, partly because British enthusiasm for Geneva had overcome Dulles' resistance to summitry in this case. After the disarmament conference, the Soviet proposal became a major agenda item for the Geneva meeting.

In an effort to meet the Soviet initiative of May, Eisenhower made a dramatic proposal at the July summit meeting: that the United States and Russia exchange complete blueprints of their military establishments and permit one another to make aerial photo reconnaissance flights over the other country in order to reduce the prospect of surprise attack. Both powers were thus moving away from traditional positions on disarmament, although not toward actual agreement. Eisenhower's "open skies" proposal had real substance and was also an appealing counterproposal designed to match the earlier Soviet propaganda gains.

Eisenhower, however, was still constrained by the problems he had met earlier, after his December 1953 proposal. The other Western powers were unable to agree on Eisenhower's proposal, as they had been on the Soviet proposals. The Geneva summit was thus unable to surmount the disunity among the Western delegations over a disarmament negotiating position.

At a more general level, the Geneva summit conference undermined the military spirit of NATO by making the threat from Russia seem more remote. The negotiations had also raised expectations in West Germany for possible reunification with East Germany, since Russia had agreed to an Austrian State Treaty in April 1955. These hopes were dashed by the outcome of the Geneva negotiations, causing partisan political troubles for the aged German Premier Konrad Adenauer. In fact, the summit had complicated the politics of NATO, much as Dulles had feared.

Eisenhower nonetheless continued an independent office for the development of new disarmament ideas in the White House. Nelson Rockefeller had succeeded Jackson as head of the office, and it was the Rockefeller staff that had prepared Eisenhower's "open skies" proposal with virtually no clearance from the State Department. The fact was reflected in the problems Eisenhower had in achieving compliance with his policies to the point of active implementation by the State Department and by disarmament conference negotiators (perhaps partly because of Dulles' difficulties in administering the department). The dual problem of disagreements among American officials as well as among the Western delegations meant that not until mid-1956 was the West able to put forth an official negotiating position on disarmament issues. During 1955–56 the Soviets took advantage of this lag to propose a wide variety of first steps and partial measures that strained and divided the Western delegations still further.

After 1955, American negotiations were simply suspended, and it was not until Eisenhower's second Administration that the United States disarmament delegation was prepared to reenter serious negotiations.[15]

By spring of 1957 it became apparent that the Russians had again been reappraising their disarmament policy and seemed amenable to fruitful negotiations. Pressing for the agreement that now seemed possible, the President's special assistant for disarmament (now Harold Stassen) undertook to negotiate privately with the Russians in London. But in doing so he overstepped his mandate and caused consternation among Western European governments, particularly West Germany. The Adenauer government was in the midst of an election campaign in which the opposition party,

---

[15] Bernhard G. Bechhoefer, *Postwar Negotiations for Arms Control* (Washington, D.C.: Brookings Institution, 1961), pp. 398–429.

the Social Democrats, had been advocating direct negotiations with the Soviet Union on German reunification. Stassen's direct negotiations embarrassed Adenauer, and fissures appeared in the NATO alliance. Dulles seized on the complaint from Bonn to thrust Stassen aside and take over negotiations himself. He hammered out a comprehensive disarmament plan that won the agreement of all NATO allies and healed the breach caused by Stassen. But the package, composed mainly of proposals already rejected by the Russians, effectively ended negotiations with Moscow.

Dulles now appealed to the General Assembly in an effort to score against the Russians with a resounding vote there. The appeal had a negative effect for experienced negotiators on both sides, for they had learned to assess the seriousness of the other side's proposals by its self-restraint in using the proposals for propaganda appeals. In no negotiation had propaganda been absent on either side. Yet never before had a delegation appealed from the negotiating table to the General Assembly. The result "was virtually to destroy years of painstaking efforts within the United Nations."[16]

Sputniks I and II orbited while the General Assembly was in session. Their worldwide impact enhanced Soviet truculence over Dulles' appeal to the General Assembly. Khrushchev, after the space triumphs of late 1957, called for a summit meeting. It was a recognized way of putting Washington on the defensive.

A year later, Khrushchev increased the pressures on Washington. The West now placed a high estimate on Soviet strategic capabilities; the 1958 American congressional elections were over, and the Formosa Straits crisis had cooled off. Khrushchev took the opportunity to reopen the old issue of Berlin by placing a six-month deadline on starting negotiations over its status. He was prodding Eisenhower toward the summit. As the Berlin deadline approached, however, Khrushchev postponed the time limit, thus turning Berlin into a rolling crisis.

The atmosphere in Washington was flaccid. Eisenhower's public statements about nuclear war gave the impression that American military policy was adrift. On March 11, 1959 he stated publicly that there could be no "ground war" in Europe, and that

16 *Ibid.*, pp. 432–35.

nuclear war was "self-defeating." "What good would it do," he said, "to send a few more thousands or even a few divisions of troops to Europe?"

Eisenhower hardly needed to be told about NATO's political as well as military significance. His reactions to the Berlin crisis, however, suggest an overconcentration on the military purposes of NATO—to the detriment of the American political negotiations with Russia.

In 1958 the three nuclear powers stopped testing unilaterally. At the conclusion of a series of Soviet nuclear tests in the spring of 1958, Khrushchev declared that Russia would stop testing nuclear weapons in the atmosphere, provided the West followed suit. It was a brilliant gesture, partly because it caught Britain and America out of phase—both countries were planning tests later in the year. They demurred, tested again in August, and announced their own voluntary suspension for one year, effective November 1. The Soviet Union resumed tests again in October, but quit on November 3, and the test ban went into effect. A year later Eisenhower announced that he would not renew the ban, but he did not authorize new testing. The reciprocal test suspension remained intact until after Kennedy became President.

The Soviet announcement of a test suspension in 1958 marked a change in Soviet diplomacy. Khrushchev now dropped his demands for a summit meeting (although, at the end of the year, he issued a six-month ultimatum for a summit meeting on Berlin). The prospect of a Soviet-American summit affected Western states' interests differently. British participation at the "high table" has been an attractive prospect to every British government since Churchill first proposed a heads-of-state meeting in 1951. In the early fifties, the summit offered West Germany the brief hope of unification, but beginning in 1955 the prospect of Soviet-American agreement appeared threatening to Bonn because it might entail abandonment of German unification as a goal. For Khrushchev, a successful summit conference could help with hard-line cold warriors in his own government. But since Soviet bloc expectations could never be wholly realized by a Soviet-American settlement, the prospect of summitry also posed risks for Russia. Similarly, the United States government could lose a great deal both as a bloc leader and as a partisan administration at home if the summit negotiations dashed expectations.

Dulles' attitude toward negotiating with the Russians changed to reflect the new mood of sobriety in Washington about Soviet power, induced by Sputnik and Khrushchev's venturesome diplomacy. In January 1959 he suggested that a settlement of European problems with Moscow that placed Russia at a political or military disadvantage was not realistic and that the Soviet Union would have to be treated with greater consideration than it had been before.[17] Had Dulles lived, this late softening of his own attitudes about a general settlement with Moscow might have been clarified.

By the end of 1958 Dulles was seriously ill with cancer. With a national election pending in Great Britain, Prime Minister Macmillan took the initiative for a summit meeting. He visited Moscow in February 1959. Eisenhower moved slowly: he resented the pressure from London. Only after Macmillan's electoral victory in October did he agree to a meeting, and then conditionally. He insisted that thorough groundwork first be laid by preliminary negotiations at the working level and that no negotiating could occur under a Russian threat over Berlin. De Gaulle was in even less hurry. Before going to the summit he wanted to visit Moscow, and he wanted France to win nuclear status through detonation of her first bomb.

In the meantime Khrushchev, on Eisenhower's invitation, visited the United States for twelve days in September 1959. He addressed the United Nations General Assembly, toured the country, and conferred privately with Eisenhower at Camp David, the presidential retreat. Camp David hardly met Eisenhower's prerequisites for the summit meeting, but it eliminated his chief objection to the conference, for Khrushchev now dropped a fixed deadline for negotiations on Berlin. But the main achievement at Camp David was symbolic—a demonstration that the two heads of state could talk in confidence. The "spirit of Camp David" became a reference point in Soviet negotiations. It had no specific content but connoted better things to come. It also encouraged Eisenhower's pref-

---

[17] Department of State *Bulletin* (February 2, 1959), pp. 157–59.

erence for personal diplomacy—to undertake state visits aimed at modifying broad public attitudes in other countries in favor of the United States.

After Camp David, a summit meeting was scheduled for mid-May 1960. On May 1, a Soviet rocket brought down a secret, high-flying American photo-reconnaisance aircraft, a U-2—complete with uninjured pilot—on a planned intrusion into Soviet air space from Pakistan. Khrushchev chose to publicize the incident dramatically four days after it occurred. Washington had already issued the pre-arranged official lie to cover the operation—a lost aircraft on a weather observation flight. But the details released by Moscow quickly discredited the lie, aggravating Washington's embarrassment. Eisenhower now decided on a policy of full disclosure and stated that he took personal responsibility for the flight.

Barely a week later, the summit conference aborted at the opening session in Paris. Khrushchev demanded that Eisenhower apologize for the U-2 flights and punish the wrongdoers responsible for them. But since Eisenhower had accepted personal responsibility for the flights, he could "punish" only himself On the other hand, Eisenhower's failure to maintain the official lie may have put Khrushchev in a difficult position with the more militant factions within his own government that did not want him negotiating with Eisenhower. Critics considered Eisenhower's acceptance of personal responsibility unnecessary, the result of inappropriate personal compunctions. He has stated more expedient reasons: how could he negotiate effectively in Paris if he would not take responsibility for activities that were the subject of negotiation?[18]

According to one interpretation, Khrushchev seized on the U-2 incident to cancel the conference, having learned from information obtained from the spy plane that the United States would have been able to collect sufficient intelligence data during such missions to know that the Russians did not have the ICBMs they claimed to have.[19] While that would be an overriding cause for calling off the meetings, both sides had taken deliberate actions that had boxed the other side in, making the meeting impossible.

[18] Eisenhower, *The White House Years*, Vol. 2, pp. 550–53.

[19] Arnold L. Horelick and Myron Rush, *Strategic Power and Soviet Foreign Policy* (Chicago: University of Chicago Press, 1966), pp. 122–23.

Moscow exploited the U-2 incident, stridently condemning American duplicity and imputing that Washington did not want a summit meeting. For the American public, approaching the summer presidential nominating conventions, the Eisenhower Administration appeared again on the defensive, responding to the initiatives of Soviet diplomacy and fumbling.

The desire for major changes in international affairs—such as disarmament or some other step to moderate the Cold War—had produced few results by the last year of the Eisenhower Administration, despite Eisenhower's personal interest. Indeed, his own concern with moderating the Cold War—his willingness to meet with Khrushchev and his moderation in pursuing the arms race—only contributed to the impression that his Administration was on the defensive.

In fact the Eisenhower Administration was on the defensive, particularly with respect to the Cold War. Eisenhower never explained what the political basis of an accommodation with the Soviet Union might be. He failed to put aside the rigid ideological interpretation of the Cold War that he had inherited with the Republican nomination for the Presidency. His interest in accommodations with the Russians attests to the fact that his own thinking was not blocked by rigid ideology, but his policies never escaped its constraints. To accommodate Moscow was to go on the defensive in American domestic politics, since the public perception of a significant Russian menace in the fifties made it far easier to take a hard line with Russia than to attempt conciliation. (Khrushchev seems to have had similar difficulties in the Soviet political system.)

CONCLUSION

It is difficult to judge the Eisenhower Administration's handling of foreign policy because of the disparity between its pronouncements and its actions. This disparity permeated all Eisenhower's foreign policies. The rhetoric of policy was active, even aggressive; but the actual policy was usually restrained. Confronted with the Administration's rhetoric, one has difficulty evaluating how selective and how wise—how discriminating—Eisenhower was in choosing when and where to act.

The expansion of military alliances throughout the Middle East and Asia was hardly discriminating. Yet, after the formalities were over, as the Administration began to face the annual costs of military and economic aid to the Baghdad Pact and SEATO members in 1955 and 1956, it quietly cut back its support. In the course of building the military alliance network, the Administration had embroiled itself in several intractable regional conflicts—between Pakistan and India in Asia and among the Arab nationalists (complicated by the Arab-Israeli conflict) in the Middle East. Yet it had exercised some restraint even at the height of its entanglement.

In Western Europe, seeking a more effective military capability for NATO and a more flexible position for the United States, the Administration had become more closely identified with West Germany—to the discomfort of its other allies. It had also provoked a strong parochial nationalism in France by its favors to London and its preference for Bonn. In all these cases it had pursued a more flexible position only to become more entangled. The effort to extricate usually produced further constraints on future actions.

The Administration's Cold War rhetoric helped draw it into rigid support for loudly anti-Communist regimes while initially neglecting important non-Communist states such as India. The rhetoric of activism, similarly, was too general to commit the Eisenhower Administration in any one situation, but it sometimes predisposed the government to act in haste, as in Guatemala, Lebanon, and the Formosa Straits.

The New Look began as a serious effort to take advantage of technological developments in order to make the best use of limited military resources. But this strategy went astray in two respects: in the inadequate American defense budgeting and planning and in the facile and imprecise spinning out of strategic concepts.

The largest disappointment in the Eisenhower Administration's foreign relations record is its performance in handling the domestic political elements that influence foreign policy. Despite all the assets his Administration held at the beginning for reconciling public opinion to foreign relations, and despite all its efforts to do so, Eisenhower, like his predecessor, came to suffer a loss of public confidence in foreign policy.

It is true of course that the Eisenhower Administration suffered much less from popular alienation than did the Truman Administration. The impact of the perceived threats that it had to meet in external affairs were hardly comparable to the impact of the Korean war on American public opinion. Eisenhower started from a stronger political base than did Truman, and his popularity never drifted as low. Yet, the remaining similarities between the Administrations are still striking. In the end the Eisenhower Administration suffered from a growing chorus of criticisms from the interested and active public, and from unarticulated anxiety among the less attentive public. Both Truman's and Eisenhower's difficulties marked a significant gap between the governed and their governors—though the gap had been much wider in 1952 than it was in 1960.

In Eisenhower's second term, moreover, he failed to adapt his leadership to accommodate the heavy Democratic majorities in Congress and became increasingly partisan, evidently reflecting the alienation of the men around him from the Democratic congressional leadership. As for the broad public, their anxiety had been triggered by Sputnik and nurtured by critics of the Administration who were themselves responding to less widely known events—the mishaps in American alliance policies associated with the Suez crisis, the unrest in Latin America and Japan, and the Lebanon and Formosa crises. The public at large was not willing to grapple with these details, but it did assess the general posture of the government according to its own perceptions of external conditions. The Administration's critics were able to reduce confidence in the Eisenhower Administration because its posture seemed unduly complacent even to a largely inattentive public.

The appearance of complacency—some of which was real—derived principally from two sources. One was Eisenhower's self-imposed inhibitions in governing—his restrained executive leadership and deference to Congress and his belief in limiting the level and scope of government action. The other was his attitude toward competition with the Soviet Union. Eisenhower never fully articulated this attitude, although it was plain enough in his persistent commitment to disarmament and summitry, his reluctance to push the arms race ahead full tilt, his skepticism about a potential missile gap. These policy positions cannot be laid simply to his fascination with budget balancing. He played a cool game with the Russians—cooler than he could even make explicit. In the end, this game contributed to the growing uneasiness in broad public opinion over Eisenhower's handling of external affairs.

We will never know how much Eisenhower would have eased the way for his successors in their dealings with the Chinese and Russians had he made plainer a willingness to consider détente seriously. We do know that the years of good feeling he provided, though they soured somewhat at the end, built a mood of trust in public life that was to be drawn upon in the late sixties. Had he articulated and publicized his inclination to moderate the arms race and be conciliatory to the Russians—a generally unpopular view in the fifties—he might have paid an even higher political price than he did in domestic effectiveness and public trust.

On the other hand, had Eisenhower been willing to take on the role of foreign policy innovator he might have been able to break out of the constraints of domestic politics and significantly modify the Soviet-American (or even the Sino-American) relationship—as Nixon was able to do in the early seventies on the basis of considerably less public trust.

Eisenhower's Presidency remains puzzling because Eisenhower as a political leader is puzzling. The main questions concern his political acuity and his exercise of power. How politically motivated was he as President? How conscious was he of the issues of political power with which the Presidency was unavoidably embroiled?

Few men rise to the American Presidency as experienced as Eisenhower in large-scale organizations. As commander of the Western Allied military effort in World War II, then Army Chief of Staff, and later as the Supreme Commander of the Central NATO Headquarters, Eisenhower had extraordinary experience running military affairs in a complicated international and political environment and at the top of the American armed forces. In these roles he dealt with sensitive political issues—for example, how much to accommodate British interests in the way he directed the war against Germany, or how much to play the partisan Army spokesman against Navy competitors in the American interservice rivalries of the late forties. We do not know, however, how much he appreciated the political dimensions of the issues he handled, for he often made it look easy, and in military affairs the sensitive political issues were best grappled with discreetly. He remained disinclined to discuss the political dimensions of public issues when he come to deal with them as President.

Another puzzle of the Eisenhower Presidency arises from his handling of the larger questions about America's world role. In Eisenhower's view, foreign policy should avoid crises where possible, and his Administration attempted to do so in several ways. It paid increased attention to the policy formulation and planning conducted in the government's National Security Council. It also broadened the network of defense treaties and treaty organizations around the rimland of the Communist bloc in the Middle East, South Asia, and Southeast and East Asia. It pursued major economies in American military expenditures by using technology to reduce foreign policy efforts to a level that could be supported without crises.

These efforts all fit conventional Cold War strategies and the characteristic Republican concern about not overburdening the national economy with public expenditures. Eisenhower also attempted to reduce arms racing. Dulles effectively hobbled these disarmament efforts, but Eisenhower's concern about reducing tension with Russia suggests that some of his other policy stances might have been designed to moderate Soviet-American rivalry in more oblique ways. If so, the New Look may be a prime example: Eisenhower may have viewed the reductions in American armed services as another way to reduce the pressures for competitive escalation.

The main puzzle of the Eisenhower Presidency, then, is what his intentions were about making foreign and national security policy more flexible, more stable, and more acceptable over the long term. We can supply a partial answer to this question.

Eisenhower decided against a major undertaking to explain to the American public that the United States was engaged in serious long-term arms competition with the Soviet Union and the Communist bloc (the contemporary view of the "military threat") because it would alarm the public without offering it a clear solution. He did not challenge the objective of the proposed "Operation Candor," although he evidently worried about controlling an alarmed public opinion—a problem that in fact developed for him by late 1957.

Eisenhower was quite ruthless with his former military associates in making them work within tightly constrained budget ceilings. His reluctance about "Operation Candor" appears to have reflected a comparable skepticism about military analysis and planning. Eisenhower appears to have been reluctant to depend either on an aroused public opinion that could be exploited for other purposes (as it was by Senator Joseph McCarthy) or on the claims of Defense Department planners that our military effort was insufficient to meet the Soviet military threat.

Eisenhower's reluctance to take decisive action also fit in with other views he held, mainly his belief in the restrained exercise of presidential power on the grounds of constitutional principle and his preference for a foreign policy that would serve for the "long pull," as he termed it. Evidently he viewed vigorous assertion of presidential power as a temporary expedient but not a reliable governing mechanism in the long run.

chapter 6

The New Frontier:
Innovation and Crisis

THE 1960 PRESIDENTIAL CAMPAIGN

John F. Kennedy was a bold political entrepreneur who gained his political seasoning during the Eisenhower Administration. He was thirty-three and a first-term Congressman when Eisenhower was inaugurated President. In his political career he had never settled down to maintain a safe majority in a local or statewide constituency, and in 1956, as the junior United States Senator from Massachusetts, he set about becoming President before many people thought he was ready. To do so, he turned his attention from the Senate to the task of building a national constituency, and in 1960 he went to the Democratic nominating convention with an impressive record in the state presidential primaries, winning the presidential nomination on the first ballot.

Running against Richard Nixon, the incumbent Vice President, Kennedy won the 1960 election by a tiny plurality—less than .2 percent. But his electoral victory left him with some political assets for conducting foreign policy. The campaign had fostered a mood of expected change without producing sharp partisan issues in foreign relations. Both candidates had confined themselves to general talk about the need for new initiatives. For Nixon this approach represented a way to dodge criticisms of the Eisenhower

Administration without repudiating it. For Kennedy, the promise of general action represented the kind of campaign commitment that was unlikely to prove embarrassing later and thus would keep his future options open if he gained office.

In keeping with this approach, Kennedy was more of a hardliner on foreign policy than Stevenson had been in his 1952 and 1956 campaigns. Kennedy did not, for example, attack Eisenhower's failure to negotiate with the Russians. Instead, he exploited the stagnation of the post-Sputnik doldrums—the "missile gap," the slow-down in the economy, the evident drop in American prestige abroad, and the Eisenhower Administration's seeming reluctance to act. During his campaign, Kennedy gradually settled on a simple message of arousal and optimism: to get the country moving again. "I have premised my campaign," he said

> on the single assumption that the American people are uneasy at the present drift in our national course, that they are disturbed by the relative decline in our vitality and prestige, and that they have the will and the strength to start the United States moving again.

Getting things moving again was a young man's appeal—the young candidate telling a young electorate and a new, prosperous and optimistic middle class that controversial issues could be resolved and problems mastered. This theme would soon be adopted by other candidates in state and local campaigns and even in other countries—a tribute to Kennedy as a politician. Kennedy used his theme to link foreign and domestic affairs: Wilson, Roosevelt, and Truman, he said, were "successful around the world because they were successful here, because they moved this country ahead, because only in this way could America show a watching world."

KENNEDY'S PRESIDENTIAL STYLE

"The Chief Executive," Kennedy told the National Press Club after his election, "must be the vital center of action in our whole scheme of government."[1] Probably no one has entered the White

---

[1] Arthur M. Schlesinger, Jr., *A Thousand Days* (Boston: Houghton Mifflin, 1965), p. 120.

House more self-conscious about his role of leadership than Kennedy. Roosevelt's chaotic administrative methods had been given new respectability by two studies of his leadership.[2] Thus Kennedy came to office with new respect for what had been too quickly dismissed as Roosevelt's "administrative chaos" and for the need to avoid being cut off from independent sources of information. "I can't afford to confine myself to one set of advisers," he told historian Richard Neustadt during the campaign. "If I did that, I would be on their lead strings."[3] Reacting against the methods of the Eisenhower Administration, Kennedy promptly dismantled much of the White House staff organization, although he later rebuilt part of it as needed for orderly procedures.

Kennedy's preferences for keeping his policy options open, maintaining diverse channels of communication, and developing maximum flexibility in policy making were elements of his presidential style, and they directly affected his conduct of foreign policy. Whereas Dulles had come to depend increasingly on his capacity to manipulate other governments in order to maintain flexibility in foreign relations, Kennedy's flexibility and initiative abroad began with his manipulation of men, ideas, and resources at home.

Advised that Eisenhower had lost the political initiative in 1953 because of the difficulties of taking over the government, Kennedy got a running start on the Presidency after the election, quickly making key appointments, searching for additional talent to fill the appointive posts of the executive branch, and preparing for legislative proposals (and aiding the talent search) by establishing a series of task forces to report to him on major areas of public policy.

Kennedy, like Eisenhower, took over from a predecessor whose foreign policy had lost momentum, and like Dulles (for Eisenhower), Kennedy came to power determined to take the initiative. Truman's foreign policy had become fixed by the military objectives of the Cold War and paralyzed by the loss of domestic political support and the demoralization associated with the Korean war.

---

[2] Richard E. Neustadt, *Presidential Power: The Politics of Leadership* (New York: Wiley, 1960); Arthur M. Schlesinger, Jr., *The Age of Roosevelt,* Vol. 2: *The Coming of the New Deal* (Boston: Houghton Mifflin, 1959), Chaps. 32–34.

[3] Schlesinger, *A Thousand Days,* p. 123.

Eisenhower's foreign policy had become static under Dulles' autocratic hand; when Dulles died, it remained quiescent in the post-Sputnik malaise.

Kennedy sought departures in foreign policy by taking a broader view of the presidential role than Eisenhower had done. Eisenhower's foreign policy can be explained largely in terms of his own outlook and his relationship to Dulles. But Dean Rusk, Kennedy's Secretary of State, did not play a comparable role, and if we were to explain Kennedy's foreign policy in terms of the men around him and their influence, our list would be long. It would be drawn from Democrats in exile and in office who were associated with the National Advisory Committee of the Democratic party, divided into Truman and Stevenson factions. It would include the development economists, principally from Harvard and MIT, and others from Harvard, principally McGeorge Bundy, Arthur Schlesinger, Jr., and John Kenneth Galbraith. Kennedy had stayed aloof from the factional fights within the National Advisory Committee between the hard-liners (headed by Acheson), who wanted to reemphasize Europe, rebuild the NATO alliance, and reestablish American superiority in nuclear strategic power, and the Stevensonians, who wanted to emphasize economic and political development in the underdeveloped areas and take steps to reach a détente with the Soviet Union.[4]

Kennedy drew these men into association with his Administration, neutralizing and restructuring these two factions by adding other people as well. Rusk was the president of the Rockefeller Foundation, and although he had been an Assistant Secretary of State under Truman, he too had remained aloof from the Democrats in exile. Kennedy made Chester Bowles Undersecretary of State and appointed Acheson as a special adviser. To Adlai Stevenson, whose correspondence discloses a long record of dissent from the hawkish priorities that prevailed, he gave the prestigious ambassadorship to the United Nations. At the head of his White House staff for foreign affairs he placed McGeorge Bundy, a Republican who had written foreign policy speeches for Dewey in 1948. Walt W. Rostow, an MIT economist and a hard-liner on foreign policy,

[4] *Ibid.,* p. 200.

joined Bundy's staff and later went to the State Department to head its policy planners.

Eisenhower had been a nonpartisan leader with a partisan Cabinet. Kennedy was a vigorous partisan leader who, like Roosevelt, sought Republicans for his Cabinet. He appointed as his Secretary of the Treasury a former sub-Cabinet officer under Eisenhower, Douglas Dillon, a New York investment broker. Kennedy also tried to bring two prominent Republican Wall Streeters into his Administration, but when he failed, he appointed Robert S. McNamara, the new president of the Ford Motor Company, as Secretary of Defense.

KENNEDY'S OPTIMISTIC ECONOMIC PROGRAM

Kennedy's inaugural address on January 20, 1961, was a sermon on public duty and national peril. Ten days later he began to unfold his program. Not since Truman's legislative message after V-J Day had a President with such enthusiasm for public action laid before Congress the outlines of a general effort.

"The present state of our economy is disturbing," Kennedy said. "We take office in the wake of 7 months of recession, 3½ years of slack, 7 years of diminished economic growth, and 9 years of falling farm income." He concluded, "In short, the American economy is in trouble. The most resourceful industrialized country on earth ranks among the last in the rate of economic growth." He prescribed an expansionist economic policy: "We must show the world what a free economy can do—to reduce unemployment, to put unused capacity to work, to spur new productivity, and to foster higher economic growth within a range of sound fiscal policies and relative price stability."

"Efficient expansion at home" was to be the linchpin of domestic and foreign programs alike. More than anything, moving ahead that first year meant getting the economy going. Kennedy's legislative program included some social welfare spending proposals. But its core was a strategy of induced economic expansion. In the next four years federal spending increased by $20 billion, taxes were cut about $20 billion, and the supply of money and credit increased more than 10 percent per year. Kennedy's objective —to manage the economy for maximum utilization and growth— reflected a profound shift of attitudes about economic policy.

Nowhere did Kennedy's strategy of induced expansion mark a sharper contrast with the fiscal and economic policy of the Eisenhower Administration than in dealing with the balance of payments problem that had plagued this country since 1958. For ten years after World War II the world demand for American products had greatly exceeded the domestic demand for foreign products, providing a comfortable margin between American dollars earned abroad and dollars spent. The Marshall Plan, the military and economic assistance programs of the fifties, the Korean war, and the costs of stationing American forces abroad all helped to deplete our dollar credits. But the persistently favorable balance of payments firmly established the dollar as the preeminent reserve currency. Dollar creditors throughout the world remained confident that the dollar was the currency least likely to be devalued.

Many economists claimed that an adequate rate of growth in the American economy required a gradual price inflation, but the Eisenhower Administration, which had a premonition that a trade balance problem would develop, had rejected this upward drift of prices. Instead it had sought to secure a "sound dollar"—that is, a completely stable price level—partly because it feared that the persistent (if moderate) inflation of American prices would reduce the foreign demand for American products and accentuate the trade balance problem. The Eisenhower Administration did manage to stop the historic upward drift of prices while maintaining a rate of economic growth that many economists had considered impossible. Yet competitive foreign production grew even faster.

When the balance of trade turned against the United States in 1958, Eisenhower brought pressure on Bonn to assume more of the costs of American troops stationed in Germany. He took further steps late in 1960 to stem an increasing drain of dollars by ordering American dependents home from Europe. The political reaction was costly. Europeans concluded that the United States was going to solve its trade balance problems at the expense of its commitments to defend Europe.

Kennedy's approach to the balance of trade problem was quite different, and he signaled this change in policy by canceling Eisenhower's order to bring back the American dependents. Instead, Kennedy's solution was to link the defense of the American dollar directly to the need for an expanded economy. This new linkage was reflected in the major programs for domestic and foreign policy laid down by Kennedy in a series of messages to Congress during his first four months in the White House. His State of the Union message outlined needed improvements in military, economic, and diplomatic "tools." Barely a week later, he announced a series of executive actions to reduce the unfavorable outflow of dollars and asked the Senate to approve United States membership in the Organization for Economic Cooperation and Development (OECD), a group of NATO countries concerned with economic development and finance. He continued Eisenhower's efforts to induce West Germany—now the third largest national economy in the world—to carry more of the defense burden by subsidizing American forces in Europe and to assume greater responsibility for economic aid to developing nations.

At the end of March, Kennedy elaborated on the economic tools referred to in his State of the Union message. After the spectacular successes of the Marshall Plan, American economic assistance had resulted in a mixture of success, failure, and frustration. Kennedy did not doubt that aid could be useful. By the beginning of his Administration, friendly critics of foreign aid consisted of those who wanted stricter economic criteria used and those who saw economic assistance as a political tool with which to reward friends and friendly acts. A second position was pessimistic: it assumed that, all claims to the contrary, the objective of American aid was not to work an economic miracle, but merely to prod other governments into limited changes. Kennedy adopted the first position in principle (although his Administration still used aid as a political tool). His foreign aid program was based on the same optimism that he displayed about the domestic economy. "There exists, in the 1960s," he told Congress

a historic opportunity for a major economic assistance effort by the free industrialized nations to move more than half the people of the less developed nations into self-sustained economic growth, while the rest move substantially closer to the day when they, too, will no longer have to depend on outside assistance.[5]

In contrast to the Eisenhower Administration's propensity to reward client states with economic assistance, the Kennedy Administration held that economic aid should go to states that met certain objective standards of performance specified by the United States. This system, the Administration hoped, would serve as a major incentive for national economic development without entangling the United States in the internal politics of foreign aid recipients.

The core of the Kennedy aid program was the proposal for five-year low-interest loans, so that recipient countries could make long-term plans with confidence.

Five-year loans, however, would not permit the United States to use its annual grant renewals to prod the recipient country into carrying its economic development forward. As it turned out, Congress would not approve the five-year provision, and nothing more was done about this idea until 1966.

MC NAMARA'S DEFENSE PROGRAM AND THE ATLANTIC ALLIANCE

When President Kennedy took office he immediately began to reconstitute the Atlantic Alliance. He made strong diplomatic appointments, devoted attention to NATO affairs, and exchanged official visits with the British, German, and French heads of state. Surprisingly, the Bay of Pigs disaster in April 1961 (see Chapter 7) only temporarily marred the favorable image of the new President in foreign capitals.

What proved to be the most important development of the Kennedy Administration's relationship to America's European allies, however, was not Kennedy's strengthened diplomatic team but the shift in policy initiatives from the State Department to the Defense Department under the strong, often brilliant, and sometimes in-

---

[5] *Documents on American Foreign Relations, 1961* (New York: Harper & Row, 1961), p. 38.

sensitive leadership of its new Secretary, Robert McNamara. The initiatives of the Pentagon, together with De Gaulle's growing resistance to military and economic integration in Europe, became the main features of American relations with Western Europe in the early sixties.

Under Eisenhower, the Defense Department staff had focused on developing the New Look in an effort to achieve economies that would make the United States defense burden bearable over the long haul. But the Kennedy Administration had a different conception of what would help the American economy and different methods for generating new defense policies. It concentrated instead on stabilizing the nuclear "balance of terror."

Propelled by the urgency of the Berlin crisis in early 1961 (see Chapter 7), McNamara had already taken two moves to provide immediate improvements in our defense. He directed the expansion of both the strategic missile program and the military airlift capacity. At the end of February President Kennedy laid before Congress the result of McNamara's far-ranging reappraisal of the defense establishment.

Kennedy recommended additional steps to strengthen American deterrent and conventional forces, to limit the danger of accidents, and to increase the flexibility of American forces. He recommended a quicker phasing-in of the less vulnerable solid-fueled intercontinental missile forces—the submarine-launched Polaris and the land-based Minuteman—and the more rapid phasing-out of the vulnerable liquid-fueled Titan missiles and B-47 bombers. Speeding up the production of Polaris and Minuteman would give us an expanded force by the mid-sixties. For immediate strengthening of the strategic nuclear force, Kennedy proposed steps to reduce the vulnerability to surprise attack—more aircraft on airborne alert, more planes kept on ground alert, and improvement of our detection and warning systems for incoming intercontinental missiles.

To improve American conventional forces and thus widen our range of possible military responses, Kennedy recommended spending more funds on new non-nuclear weapons. To reduce the danger of accidental war and the vulnerability of American forces, nuclear forces would be brought under tighter control through more secure channels of command and communication.

The net increase in defense spending for the following fiscal year was modest. Thereafter, McNamara's defense budgets increased sharply beyond the Eisenhower ceilings. The change reflected the fiscal optimism in the White House. Kennedy had instructed McNamara to "develop the force structure necessary to our military requirements without regard to arbitrary or predetermined budget ceilings."[6] Increased spending also reflected Kennedy's more immediate desire to offer the Russians concrete evidence of the Administration's resolution in meeting the Berlin crisis of early 1961.

The McNamara program sharply distinguished, however, between resolve and provocation. A strategic nuclear force that could survive attack would be under *less* pressure to act in haste than one that would be wiped out by a first strike from the enemy. A force that could survive to deliver a retaliatory strike would give the government more time to consider its actions in a crisis. Underlining the new approach to stabilizing the "balance of terror," Kennedy declared in a speech on March 26, 1961: "Our arms will never be used to strike the first blow in any attack."

The "missile gap" quickly dropped from sight. The issue had rested on projected future disparities in missile strength predicted by Congress in 1959, and the Kennedy Administration had found these projections quite outdated by early 1961. Soviet strength had been considerably overestimated. In addition, McNamara was impressed by Eisenhower's reasons for not responding to the warnings of the air power enthusiasts. Kennedy, like Eisenhower, wanted to make discriminating choices in his defense policies, and luckily, unlike Eisenhower, he had a Secretary of Defense who could offer him such choices.

The new defense policies were part of a complicated negotiating posture Kennedy was constructing. This posture was intended to be tough, with increased military capabilities, but also flexible and conciliatory, with more choices available in military, economic, and diplomatic moves. The conciliation efforts took two forms. First, Kennedy elevated the status of disarmament planning by assembling the staff responsible for it in a new Arms Control and Disarmament Agency. He linked it to the State Department and instructed it to get the test ban negotiations out of the doldrums.

---

[6] U.S., Congress, House, Armed Services Committee, *Hearings on Military Posture,* 87th Cong., 2nd sess., 1962, p. 3162.

Second, he would seek a better working relationship with the Soviet government. Kennedy's pursuit of agreement with the Soviet Union on arms control measures required the active support of the Defense Department, which McNamara's strong leadership assured.

Kennedy's new defense posture immediately aroused suspicions in Europe. McNamara's object was to increase the stability of the strategic balance with the Soviet Union by reducing the vulnerability of our strategic forces—and hence, the need for an American first strike or a hair-trigger response—and by developing a wider range of conventional choices in order to avoid using nuclear weapons if possible. Washington saw this flexibility as making it more feasible for the United States to use its military capabilities on behalf of its allies. But Europeans saw American flexibility as giving the United States the option *not* to defend her NATO allies.

Nowhere was the difference in perspective between the United States and Europe more striking than with respect to nuclear "locks." When Kennedy became President he found on his desk a proposal for installing electromechanical devices on nuclear weapons located in Western Europe that would prevent their being fired without authorization. This idea was consonant with McNamara's efforts, and Kennedy promptly ordered all United States nuclear weapons in Europe "locked up." He wanted to be sure that in a military crisis no American-made nuclear weapons would be set off by the United States or its allies until authorized by the President.

The practical effect of these new controls, however, was to eliminate the prospect anticipated in Europe that NATO's Supreme Allied Commander could use American nuclear forces in Europe to meet a Soviet attack even without clear authorization from the President. With one stroke, the Supreme Command's role had been radically reduced.

In May 1962, in a secret speech to NATO ministers assembled in Athens, Greece, McNamara stated the American strategic axiom underlying the 1961 decision to lock up nuclear warheads: all nuclear forces on "our" side must be controlled from one source in the interest of controlling and terminating nuclear war, should it occur. He repeated this message in a commencement speech at Ann Arbor, Michigan, on June 16, a month later, driving home the import of his axiom for the British and French: "Limited nuclear capabilities, operating independently, are dangerous, expensive, prone to obsolescence, and lacking in credibility as a deterrent."

In McNamara's attempt to formulate the strategic doctrines of American military policy, perhaps the most difficult considerations to analyze or predict were the political functions of NATO and the American role in NATO, partly because the success of these functions depended on their remaining somewhat ambiguous. McNamara's revamping of United States force postures and strategy destroyed these protective ambiguities and raised new uncertainties among Europeans about the American nuclear commitment to them.

The Kennedy Administration's enthusiasm for a build-up of conventional forces in Europe was particularly troublesome. This build-up began in preparation for the Berlin crisis in early 1961, but it took new impetus from the Cuban missile crisis of October 1962. With nerves still strained from the Cuban crisis, Rusk and McNamara argued at the NATO Council meeting in December 1962 for increased contributions of conventional forces by the NATO allies.

McNamara had just undercut Britain's claim to an independent nuclear force by canceling the development of the American bomber-launched missile Skybolt, designed to extend the life of bombers into an era when Russia would have strong air defenses around its major urban centers. For Washington, future status as a nuclear power rested on intercontinental missiles. Britain, however, could not afford these missiles and had staked its future status as a nuclear power on the U.S. Air Force's plans to develop Skybolt. Cancellation of these plans threatened deep political trouble for Macmillan's Conservative government.

Kennedy wanted to repair the damage the Skybolt cancellation caused Macmillan. But the Cuban missile crisis occupied his attention until he was enroute to a meeting with Macmillan at Nassau in December 1962. Improvising, Kennedy agreed to supply the British with Polaris missiles without warheads. The British would arm them and fire them from British submarines yet to be built. The two statesmen also agreed, however, that these missiles would be assigned to a "NATO nuclear force" if one were to be established, and Britain could use them independently only where "supreme national interests" were at stake.

These nuclear arrangements satisfied none of the foreign policy factions in Washington. The Nassau agreement displeased Anglophiles because it reduced the value of the Anglo-American "special relationship" in nuclear matters. The agreement disappointed European integrationists because it did not enhance European solidarity, and it only partly satisfied those who objected to independent nuclear forces, such as McNamara. The reaction in Washington showed the strains of an alliance policy that had to cope with the diverse political goals of its allies while it was coming to terms with the logic of nuclear strategy.

FRANCE AND EUROPEAN INTEGRATION

French President De Gaulle had reacted to McNamara's Athens attack on independent national nuclear forces with such a strongly nationalistic pronouncement that five of his ministers resigned. Offered the same arrangements for Polaris missiles that the British accepted, De Gaulle rejected them. France remained committed to the development of her own delivery systems—first nuclear weapon-carrying bombers and later nuclear-tipped missiles.

At Nassau Kennedy revived the hope for a so-called multilateral nuclear force (MLF), which Secretary of State Herter had proposed at the end of 1960. The MLF would be a European nuclear force under a multilateral military command. It was supposed to renew the credibility of the American nuclear commitment to Western Europe by offering American participation in an integrated force based in Europe. Yet Washington would supply the nuclear weapons and would continue to control an American "safety catch" against the nuclear trigger.

Both the Germans and the British favored the MLF as an acceptable second choice to having a special nuclear military relationship with Washington. France never did support the MLF: De Gaulle was not ready to settle for second choices. He had proceeded with nuclear tests despite the voluntary test moratorium after 1958. He continued to demand that the United States treat France on the same nuclear footing as Britain,[7] and he refused to

---

[7] See for example the press conference remarks of President Kennedy reportedly in response to a French offer "to purchase from the United States several hundred million dollars worth of military equipment, mostly of an atomic nature." *New York Times*, April 18, 1962.

allow the placement on French soil of any nuclear weapons he could not fully control.

Kennedy attempted to cut through the preoccupation of Europe with these secondary questions in order to follow Marshall's example of 1948: to present the challenge to Europeans without telling them how to conduct their own business. He chose July 4, 1962, in a speech emphasizing the themes of independence and federation, to tell the Europeans that the question of their nuclear independence lay in their own hands. If they could establish the political superstructure to act as a unitary nuclear power, the discord with the United States about military command, weapons' custody, and safety catches would all fall by the way.

Later, with his international reputation soaring after the missile crisis, Kennedy visited Western Europe in June 1963 and used the trip to press for this larger view of Europe's relations with the United States. But the approach was stopped by De Gaulle's skillful and intransigent opposition to European political and economic integration. De Gaulle wanted the chance to establish France's national claim to nuclear power status and rejected the terms that Washington now offered Europe—equality only as a region, not for each country. De Gaulle had met Kennedy's challenge, but not on Kennedy's terms.

CONCLUSION

The Kennedy Administration shared with its predecessor a concern that Europe would become too inward looking. The Common Market had been set up in 1956, consisting of France, Italy, West Germany, and the Benelux countries. This union provided a climate for economic expansion in these countries during the late fifties, adding to the great success of the Marshall Plan in the late forties. In the decade from 1948 to 1958 Western Europe had recovered from the war and gone on to unprecedented prosperity. But as customs barriers went up for outsiders and down within the Common Market, the British economy suffered and the United States began to import more than it exported, increasing our balance of trade problem. We thus had a direct interest in resisting Europe's inclination to turn inward and enjoy the fruits of its success. We not only wished to relieve our balance of payments problem but we wanted Europe to pay more of the costs of supporting economic development in the developing countries. Kennedy had spoken pointedly of both goals in his early presidential speeches, and both issues persisted through the eight years that followed. Kennedy invoked the vision of an Atlantic community in order to conduct negotiations with Europe that would lower trade barriers throughout the world, with Europe bargaining from a position of strength for reduced barriers to the United States and other markets. This liberalizing phase in trade negotiations came to be called the "Kennedy Round." Like the Berlin crisis, the "Kennedy Round" was a specific name for what was in fact an extended period of negotiations that would stretch through 1967.

The attention the Kennedy Administration gave to adjusting and reconstructing our relationship with Western Europe seemed at first a serious opportunity for the Atlantic Alliance, yet this encouraging view soon began to sour. The Kennedy Administration was intentionally flexible about its relations with Western Europe in order to encourage European initiatives, but it was also intent upon reasserting American leadership in the Alliance. The direction this leadership took, moreover, was set by the logic of nuclear strategy as viewed from Washington, and this logic required an exclusive nuclear strategic role for the United States, with only nominal British and French nuclear forces. This much assertion of American leadership in the Alliance had not been attempted since the Suez crisis.

Kennedy and Western Europe never agreed on goals for the Atlantic Alliance. Western European states pursued their own divergent goals in their relationships with the United States. All of them—though none as much as De Gaulle's France—wanted greater independence from Washington in military policy. At the same time all of them, including France, were troubled by the more flexible strategy that the Kennedy Administration adopted because it put more of their defense burden on their own conventional forces. The internal difficulties of the Alliance, then, could be attributed to the persistent question about apportioning burdens of military defense.

chapter 7

The Problems of Great Power Status: Moscow, Congress, and the Developing Nations

THE TURBULENT SOVIET–AMERICAN RELATIONSHIP

Kennedy came to office intent on changing the Soviet-American relationship, though scarcely out of a sense of American weakness. Democratic leaders had developed a general line of criticism about Eisenhower's foreign policy. As Stevenson had voiced it, the Atlantic Alliance had not been adapted to reflect the fact that the military threat in Western Europe had diminished; the American position in the developing nations of the world was far too dependent upon military instruments; and a shift from military to economic and political weapons in foreign policy would encourage a détente with the Soviet Union. The ideological conflict with Russia was an impediment to practical understanding and the source of unnecessary rigidities in American policy in the developing countries. At the same time, Democrats—Stevenson among them—had also decried the apparent complacency of the Eisenhower Administration with respect to its defense programs in the face of growing Soviet missile prowess. Another group—Dean Acheson, Paul Nitze, George Ball, and George Kennan, for example—saw Europe as the main strategic prize but split over the hope for a change in the Cold War. Acheson remained a leading spokesman for the view that "situations of strength" were the main assets in coping with the Russians. Stevenson, Ball, and Kennan, along with Averell Harriman and Chester Bowles, emphasized the prospects for negotiations. These differences were largely matters of emphasis, although on specific issues Democratic leaders sometimes argued sharply among themselves. The most persistent difference in emphasis lay in the expectations held for negotiating with the Soviet Union.

Kennedy had stood apart from the foreign policy factions of his party in his carefully executed bid for the Presidency. Once elected, he drew from all elements of his party, recruiting them into his Administration and combining their viewpoints. Indicative of his ability to recruit talent was the fact that Harriman, a former Governor of New York, a serious presidential aspirant in 1956, a major figure in the Truman Administration, and ambassador to Russia under Roosevelt, at sixty-nine graciously accepted the post of Assistant Secretary in the State Department.

Kennedy's optimism about America's economic strength and about the capacity of government to solve domestic and foreign problems sustained an ambitious set of foreign policy objectives. The United States would build up its military strength, but we would stress flexibility, not massive retaliation, and we would expand our economic assistance programs as well. The NATO alliance should be strengthened, but the United States would not permit its European allies to keep it from negotiating directly with the Russians at the summit. Khrushchev had successfully played on European fears about Soviet-American negotiations and on the Eisenhower Administration's fears about summit meetings. Kennedy's combination of hard-line and conciliatory policies toward Russia deflated summitry as a Soviet diplomatic weapon.

THE BAY OF PIGS DEBACLE

At the beginning of 1959, toward the end of Eisenhower's Administration, a long-time military dictatorship in Cuba under Fulgencio Batista fell to Fidel Castro, a leftist who was also backed by Cuba's middle class. A flamboyant intellectual, Castro used the ideology and rhetoric of Marxism generously, but his revolutionary career had been pragmatic.

Castro was originally welcomed by Washington, but during 1959–60 his regime's radical objectives rapidly antagonized American economic interests and Washington. Turning increasingly to the Soviet Union for help, Castro announced his ideological identification with Communism. He appropriated American property in Cuba, imprisoned and expelled American citizens, and proceeded with a far-reaching social and economic revolution that bore no resemblance to the typical palace revolutions of Latin America. By early 1960 it appeared that Eisenhower had permitted the establishment of a Communist dictatorship on our doorstep. Secretly, President Eisenhower decided in March of that year to train Cuban exiles for guerrilla operations in Cuba.

In the last weeks of the Eisenhower Administration at the end of 1960 the United States broke diplomatic relations with Cuba. By this time Washington's secret sponsorship of guerrilla infiltration in Cuba had expanded into a planned invasion of Cuba by Cuban exiles in order to overturn Castro's regime and establish a government more acceptable to Washington. Kennedy was briefed on this more ambitious plan, and in the next few weeks, the project centered wholly on invasion rather than guerrilla operations, but it remained clandestine. Kennedy refused to allow direct American involvement, though unmarked U.S. Navy carrier jets did offer some covert air cover for rebel bomber strikes.

Flying in from Guatemala, B-26s supplied by the CIA and piloted by Cuban exiles tried to knock out Cuban air power on April 15. Some of the pilots landed in Florida and claimed they were Cuban defectors using Castro's own aircraft, but American reporters had found out about the pending operations and quickly stripped away this disguise. A second air strike occurred two days later as an invasion force of 1400 Cuban rebels approached the Bay of Pigs. The strike failed to destroy Castro's air power, however, and his planes helped the Cuban Army to pin the invaders down. Isolated, with ammunition exhausted, they surrendered.

It was a humiliating defeat, and American prestige inevitably suffered when Washington was unable to conceal its involvement in the invasion. United Nations Ambassador Adlai Stevenson, told of the secret plans at the last minute, had dissented strongly, to no avail. Yet Kennedy's prestige as an international and domestic leader suffered only temporarily. In his inaugural address he had spoken of grave threats and setbacks, and as he pressed on for the summit meeting with Khrushchev, the failure at the Bay of Pigs left little permanent impression. Public opinion polls indicate that domestic opinion rapidly rallied to him, and the reaction of many governments abroad was one of respect and relief for the self-restraint shown by the American government.[1]

The euphoria of Kennedy's first weeks disappeared at the Bay of Pigs, for the disaster shattered confidence within the government. A bitter row developed over the errors of the Central Intelligence Agency, which had conceived and executed the invasion plan. The plan depended on either a successful military conquest or a successful uprising triggered by the invasion. Neither was credible. The government's best experts on military invasions had not been consulted on the practical difficulties of the operation itself, and the best estimates of the intelligence division of the CIA about the prospects of a general Cuban uprising were negative.

Kennedy's judgment in permitting the Bay of Pigs invasion was defective. He failed to anticipate that he would have formidable problems as President in keeping informed and maintaining control over such an operation. For one thing, the Cuban exiles' interests diverged from those of the United States. Cuban exile leaders, intent on their goal, did not care if they involved the United States more than we wanted to be involved. Since these exiles were trained and advised by American officials who developed a similar attitude, there were ample reasons why the participants did not want the President to know what he ought to have known. One of Kennedy's advisers, Theodore Sorensen, has summarized the result:

> With hindsight it is clear that what in fact Kennedy had approved was . . . militarily doomed from the outset. What he thought he was approving appeared at the time to have diplomatic acceptability and little chance of outright failure. That so great a gap between concept and actuality should exist at so high a level on so dangerous a matter reflected a shocking number of errors in the whole decision-making process—errors which permitted bureaucratic momentum to govern instead of policy leadership.[2]

[1] Arthur M. Schlesinger, Jr., *A Thousand Days* (Boston: Houghton Mifflin, 1965), p. 512.

[2] Theodore C. Sorensen, *Kennedy* (New York: Harper & Row, 1965), pp. 301–02.

Out of the Bay of Pigs debacle came an administration skeptical of expert judgments and determined to probe for new options—attitudes that served Kennedy well in the Cuban missile crisis sixteen months later. But a more fundamental failure of judgment was also involved. Kennedy had been worried about right-wing criticism if he should cut off the Cuban operation, particularly since he had criticized the Castro regime during his campaign in appealing to conservative elements in the Democratic party. He evidently viewed Cuba only in terms of its impact on domestic American politics. His failure to probe the CIA plans indicated that he lacked insight into the depths of popular discontent in Cuba over economic and social conditions and was unaware of the entrenchment of the Castro regime. More ominously, it indicated that he overestimated the capacity of the United States to intervene successfully in another country in order to support one set of political interests against another. The Bay of Pigs did not shake Kennedy's optimism about guerrilla warfare, which he shared with many of his leading officials. His high expectations about the use of American military power to achieve political change in other countries, so conspicuous in the Bay of Pigs operation, would help to draw the United States into Vietnam.

Even in hindsight, Sorensen did not get to the more fundamental question about clandestine operations: who should authorize them? The Congress avoided raising a constitutional issue over the Bay of Pigs operation. Yet only from Capitol Hill could such an issue be effectively raised. Behind the formalities of the constitutional problem lay practical issues: what means of counseling and accountability will assure that Congress is not faced with an accomplished fact—a government overthrown, a provocative military operation under way?

Since World War II presidential latitude had been favored in recognition of the Pearl Harbor problem, made more serious by the prospect of surprise attack in nuclear war. The Korean war had begun with an assertion of presidential power that Congress tidied up after the fact. Before Korea was over the main constitutional issue had shifted to the President's scope of authority over his principal military field commander (General Douglas MacArthur). With Congress failing to assert a constitutional role in the case of overt operations, it was scarcely likely that a serious attack would be launched against Kennedy over the Bay of Pigs operation, although the question of whether the President's war powers gave him such latitude was raised—perhaps with some prescience: unacknowledged CIA operations in Laos would soon become a regular part of the American intervention in Indochina.

THE CONFERENCE AT VIENNA

At the height of the Cuban Bay of Pigs crisis in April 1961 Khrushchev threatened Soviet involvement if the United States did not end its "aggression." Kennedy riposted firmly, and neither statesman carried the matter further. On the contrary, they proceeded with arrangements for private talks at their embassies in Vienna in early June.

The accounts we have of the Vienna conference indicate that Kennedy wanted to establish ground rules for Soviet-American coexistence in order to cope with political change in the uncommitted areas of the world. He assumed that any attempt by one great power to change the status quo in these areas would be countered by the other. Perhaps thinking of Laos and the Congo, Kennedy argued that both great powers should avoid becoming involved in political changes in areas in which neither the Soviet Union nor the United States was already involved and where the balance of power would not be affected. Both countries would expect to become involved, however, in political changes that affected the balance of power or involved the other party.

Kennedy's thesis was in effect a diplomatic supplement to McNamara's efforts to stabilize the "balance of terror" through changes in military strategy. McNamara's "flexible options" doctrine held that it was extremely dangerous and unnecessary for the United States to be faced with a stark choice between capitulating to Russia and escalating to massive nuclear attacks. Similarly, Kennedy talked at Vienna about the dangers of getting "cornered." Evidently he hoped that an agreement to maintain the status quo would avoid putting either side into a situation in which it would be forced to act out of desperation.

Khrushchev would not accept Kennedy's thesis. For him the "status quo" included support of political trends that (according to Communist dogma) would ultimately favor Russia. To interrupt these trends—even by failing to cultivate them—was to upset the status quo as perceived in Moscow. Disagreement about defining the status quo, then, was symptomatic of much more profound disagreements between the United States and Russia.

Kennedy's efforts to reach agreement on these matters reflected his association with the Stevenson Democrats rather than the cold warriors led by Acheson. Kennedy came away chastened by the effort and more receptive to Acheson's position, though still temperamentally closer to Bowles and the other Stevensonians.[3]

BERLIN POKER: KENNEDY'S ROUND

On no issue had Kennedy's attempt at Vienna to establish a general understanding with Khrushchev about the status quo been more futile than on the status of Berlin. The American position in Europe rested in part on its backing of the West German regime, which depended in turn on affirming German reunification as a national objective. At that time, no West German government could repudiate or undermine this goal of reunification and hope to survive. Berlin played an important role in keeping the issue of reunification open, for its vulnerable location inside East Germany offered an impetus for future change.

The Soviet Union, on the other side, was committed to a shabby regime in East Germany that suffered from a seemingly fatal manpower hemorrhage into West Germany. The Soviet Union could not maintain a status quo composed of a dying client with her lifeblood of young workers pouring out through West Berlin.

The quarrels over Berlin centered around Soviet demands to change what the United States considered the status quo: the independence of West Berlin from the East German government, with assured access routes to the West. For Russia, on the other hand, preserving the status quo required ensuring the continued existence of a viable East Germany. Kennedy might well have expected to be frustrated in discussing with Khrushchev a status quo that the two statesmen perceived so differently.

---

[3] The above has drawn heavily from Arthur M. Schlesinger, Jr. Though he has been properly classed as a Stevensonian, Schlesinger has written with admirable detachment about these factions in *A Thousand Days*. See especially pp. 299–301.

This difference between Soviet and American perspectives had already produced a series of crises over the Berlin enclave in the late fifties. In 1960 Khrushchev had threatened that unless the West agreed to a settlement to unify Germany in East Germany's favor, Russia would grant East Germany the right to control the access routes into Berlin, thus effectively allowing East Germany to seal off Berlin from the West. But after Eisenhower's summit meeting with Khrushchev that year, the Russian leader failed to carry out this threat.

During Kennedy's first month in office the central crisis he faced was that of Berlin's status. He had come to office assuming that a summit meeting with Khrushchev was unavoidable; but he was able to delay the meeting, and he also quickly took steps to change the impression that had developed in the late fifties that a summit meeting was a concession to the Russians. Finally, to signal his resolve to defend Berlin, Kennedy made a second State of the Union message on May 25, just before the Vienna conference, to request an additional $225 million for the American Army and Marine Corps.

After Vienna, Khrushchev set the end of 1961 as the deadline by which Russia would turn over to the East Germans control of the access routes to Berlin. This step would effectively ensure a blockade of Berlin by the East Germans and isolate the city from the West. Khrushchev underlined his resolve by announcing an increase in Soviet military expenditures equivalent to $3.5 billion. In response Kennedy asked Congress for an additional $3.2 billion in defense expenditures and for the authority to increase conventional military strength immediately.

Washington, expecting the next stage of the crisis in October, busied itself with highly visible preparations. In mid-August, while these preparations were under way, Soviet authorities sealed East Berlin off from West Berlin, cutting its manpower losses to a trickle. The Soviets began cautiously, giving Washington time to react if it chose. First simple traffic barriers were thrown up, then these were replaced with barbed wire. Finally, the barrier was completed with deliberate thoroughness by using brick and mortar. The Berlin Wall was now a fact.

Washington's failure to respond to the Soviet efforts to seal off West Berlin has been attributed to indecision, inattention, inability to coordinate quickly enough, overly centralized and slow military command and control arrangements, and finally, caution. Rarely do governments decide important issues for a single reason. It is possible that Kennedy decided not to respond to the erection of the Berlin barriers because he felt they would stabilize the East German situation and thus reduce the pressure on Moscow to change the status of West Berlin. And in fact building the Wall actually accomplished just that.

The immediate repercussions of the Berlin Wall were adverse. West Berlin was stunned by it and by American acceptance of it. Having permitted the Wall, President Kennedy sent Vice President Lyndon Johnson to Berlin to encourage the West Berliners, and he sent a battle group of 1500 United States troops driving up the Autobahn from West Germany to Berlin to reassert the West's right of access and reinforce the American garrison in Berlin.

It is important to note, however, that despite the demonstrations to the contrary on both sides, the Berlin Wall provided the basis for a tacit agreement between the United States and the Soviet Union. The settlement over Berlin remained unspoken because neither Moscow nor Washington wished to articulate the reasons for it. The Soviet Union could not admit that stopping the man-power drain on East Germany made it unnecessary for Russia to ignite the Berlin powder-keg, for such an admission would undermine the legitimacy of the East German government. Similarly, the Kennedy Administration did not wish its failure to stop the sealing off of East Berlin to be viewed as an intentional concession to the Russians, for we could not make such a concession explicit without substantially damaging our relationship with the West German government or provoking strong domestic criticism in the United States.

Since neither side knew at first or could admit that the Wall had provided an accommodation, the Berlin crisis did not abate immediately. It intensified in September when the Soviet Union resumed nuclear testing with a detonation of unprecedented size. Early in November Kennedy announced that the United States would resume testing in order to preserve our nuclear superiority. The tardiness of the American resumption of testing—more than seven months after the Soviet resumption—indicated that the United States had not been prepared for the Soviet initiative.

Moreover, the American negotiating position on Berlin was by no means in order. The Western allies would not have time to agree on a common position if serious negotiations were to get under way on the status of Germany and Berlin before the end of the year. Also, the Kennedy Administration lacked congressional support for anything but a weak response to Poland's and Yugoslavia's appeals for economic assistance to give them greater independence from Moscow—assistance that would have provided an opportunity for us to drive a wedge into the Soviet bloc. On the other hand, the Administration made it distinctly clear that we had definite strategic nuclear superiority over the Soviet Union and intended to maintain it.[4]

THE CUBAN MISSILE CRISIS

The Cuban missile crisis was the starkest confrontation of Soviet and American nuclear might since the first detected Russian nuclear bomb was detonated in 1949.

After the Bay of Pigs fiasco Cuba moved increasingly closer to the Soviet Union. Castro had immediately declared Cuba a Socialist state, and Moscow began shipping its new client military equipment. Castro then turned his talents to the business of exporting revolution partly through trained guerrillas sent abroad.

The United States government, responding more than it cared to admit to the threat of social revolution raised by Castro and other elements in Latin America, expanded its economic assistance to this region. In October 1962, at a conference of American foreign ministers in Washington, United States officials also began to build a diplomatic wall around Castro. Campaigning for Democratic congressional candidates that month, Kennedy declared that his Administration was "taking a lot of steps to try to isolate Castro." The Cuban missile crisis erupted while the Inter-American Economic and Social Council met in Mexico City in October.

In September 1962 the Soviet government had once again postponed the negotiation of a separate peace treaty with East Germany. The purpose of the postponement became evident in Washington only a few weeks before our congressional elections. American

[4] See for example Roswell Gilpatric's speech in the *New York Times*, October 22, 1961.

aerial reconnaissance detected that the Russians were secretly attempting to deploy nuclear-tipped ballistic missiles to Cuba by rapidly constructing offensive missile and bomber bases. Khrushchev evidently intended to reveal their presence at the United Nations General Assembly meeting in New York scheduled for after the election.[5]

If the Russians succeeded in establishing bases in Cuba, vital targets in the United States and Latin America would lie within missile range. More important, missiles launched from Cuba could not be detected by the elaborate electronic warning screens the United States had aimed northward against Soviet missiles in Europe and Asia. Cuban bases would make it possible for Moscow to strike the United States virtually without warning, while holding its main intercontinental nuclear missile force in reserve for a possible second-strike American response. The Cuban missile bases posed a critical test of American resolve. Kennedy had repeatedly made clear during his year and a half in office that he intended to stabilize the Washington-Moscow relationship by maintaining the status quo. The installation of Soviet nuclear missile bases in the Western Hemisphere would be a radical intrusion into a traditional sphere of American influence and security. To permit this intrusion would reduce the credibility of American commitments in Europe, the Middle East, and Asia as well.

As Kennedy's chosen course of action indicates, he did not think the Russians would become more accommodative if he accepted their Cuban nuclear deployment as a reasonable adjustment of the status quo. But several government advisers offered other assessments of the situation. In his first reaction, Secretary of Defense McNamara viewed the Soviet missiles as a tolerable alteration of the status quo, and a common assessment compared Soviet missiles in Cuba with the American missiles that had been positioned in Turkey and Italy since the fifties. Ambassador Stevenson proposed trading American withdrawal of these missiles and the closing of the American naval base at Guantánamo in Cuba for the withdrawal of the Soviet missiles from Cuba. Dean Acheson, on the other hand, proposed destroying the Soviet missile bases through American air strikes.

[5] Sorensen, p. 667.

For the next week the Kennedy Administration secretly worked at a furious pace to arrange and implement American responses to the Soviet missile emplacements. Troops were moved to Florida, air and naval forces were deployed toward the Caribbean, and strategic nuclear forces were put on the alert. It now became necessary to make the crisis public.

Several factors made it impossible to handle the missile crisis privately. One was the Russian efforts to mislead Kennedy through private messages—including an outright lie.[6] It would also have been politically difficult at home and abroad for Kennedy to have responded satisfactorily to such a blatant Russian effort to change a long-established status quo without including some *public* demonstration of his intentions. Nor could a private response have been accompanied by the type of concrete actions the Administration prepared for without these actions quickly becoming known to the public. Finally, a public disclosure was a demonstration of Kennedy's unwillingness to play out the crisis on Moscow's terms.

Rejecting an invasion for the time being, Kennedy chose a "quarantine" (a modified naval blockade) to stop the Russian build-up. First, he briefed congressional leaders; he dispatched presidential envoys to explain the American action to foreign governments; and speeches and proposals for the United Nations and the Organization of American States (OAS) were drafted, all with remarkable secrecy.

On October 22, a week after seeing the photographs of Russian missile installations, Kennedy told the nation in a television broadcast about the Soviet actions, calling them "a deliberately provocative and unjustified change in the status quo which cannot be accepted by this country, if our courage and our commitments are ever to be trusted again by either friend or foe." He announced what he termed "initial" steps in response, particularly our quarantine on all offensive military equipment under shipment to Cuba, and declared that the United States would hold Moscow responsible for any missile attack launched on the United States from Cuba and would respond in full retaliation against the Soviet Union.

Kennedy's appeal brought no significant public dissent from American leaders. In the short run, at least, most Americans were

6 *Ibid.,* 668.

behind the President. The Organization of American States prompt-ly (and somewhat surprisingly) approved the naval quarantine, and even Mexico and Brazil, which had opposed previous United States efforts to isolate Cuba diplomatically, supported the Ameri-can actions. At the United Nations, Stevenson dramatized his gov-ernment's position with blown-up reconnaissance photographs of the missile sites. Some European leaders, however, reacted skep-tically to Kennedy's initial claims. British parliamentary critics, for example, suspected adventurism in Washington. On October 27, five days after Kennedy's first broadcast the *Economist,* a British periodical that was usually pro-American, deplored "forcing a showdown over the shipment of Russian arms to Cuba."

Privately, however, Kennedy's envoy, Acheson, had convinced Britain's Prime Minister Macmillan. De Gaulle, perhaps gratified that Washington was demonstrating the vital role of independent national behavior in a real nuclear crisis, stood behind Washington like a rock—after pointing out to Acheson that Kennedy had handled his allies the way De Gaulle would have—by informing but not consulting them. The cohesion within the United States and among its allies that was demonstrated in the face of the Soviet threat became a major asset for Washington.

After a tense week, the Soviet Union turned its ships back from the quarantine area. Khrushchev first acknowledged that Russians controlled the missiles and then agreed to stop work on the missile sites and withdraw the missiles. The United States agreed not to invade Cuba and worked out face-saving procedures for American inspection of the Russian missile withdrawal.

There was a flutter of doubt in Washington, but it was not sustained. Some, such as the eminent military strategist Bernard Brodie, advised that Kennedy could successfully have pushed even further. The Soviets, he argued, are willing to take calculated risks and to back off if they misfire.[7] Others worried about the practical difficulties of enforcing the pullback of Soviet missiles. Since Castro had refused to allow the United States or the United Nations access to the Soviet sites in Cuba, Republican critics of the Administra-tion voiced the fear that the missiles would be hidden in caves for

[7] Letter to the editor in the *New York Times,* November 13, 1962.

the time being and that sites would eventually be constructed with more ingenious camouflage. But the White House maintained its position, evidently confident that American aerial reconnaissance flights could effectively monitor the removal of all missiles. Republicans, despite their criticism of the Cuban settlement, were unwilling to blame what they considered a potential threat to American security on disloyalty within the government. Thus the Administration remained relatively invulnerable to partisan criticism.

Some aspects of the missile crisis still lack satisfactory explanations. One unanswered question is why the Russians thought they would succeed with their venture. Their record of caution elsewhere does not support the theory that they are indiscriminate risk-takers. It is more likely that the Russians thought they could get the missiles into place before the United States detected them.

If the Russians had succeeded in emplacing the missiles, there would still have been the grueling game of mutual deterrence to be played out. The United States had missiles and manned aircraft targeted on the Soviet Union. The immediate effect of the Soviet disclosure would probably have been a breathtaking drop in American prestige in Europe and the developing areas, and perhaps a failure of nerve in Europe and Washington as well. This speculation suggests that Moscow had its eye mainly on Berlin, hoping for a Western backdown. But this new situation would also invite new dangers for the Russians—particularly the danger that the United States would launch a preemptive nuclear strike when it discovered its new vulnerability.

Why would the Russians be willing to run such risks? One explanation is that internal pressures within the Soviet state provided the impetus for the Cuban venture. Contrary to common American beliefs at that time, Soviet foreign policy had not been going well. Moscow's success in winning support and influence in the developing areas had fallen short of expectations, and the Communist-bloc claims of rapidly catching up with the West were proving to be exaggerations. Khrushchev had identified himself publicly with the goal of closing the nuclear gap with the United States. But, as was then becoming apparent in the West, Moscow had chosen not to pay the high resource costs for closing this gap. Instead the Soviet Union had decided in the late fifties, much as the United States had, to forego large-scale ICBM deployment and await the development of the next generation of missiles, which would be cheaper and less prone to obsolescence.

Finally, the Chinese Communists were now in open political conflict with Moscow, and this rift with Peking increasingly forced Moscow to compete for leadership in the bloc. Peking had experimented with post-Stalin ideological liberalization in 1956 but had repressed the movement in 1957. Thereafter, the divergent domestic practices in Russia and China fueled reciprocal suspicion and reproaches. The two governments quarreled secretly over China's ambition to acquire nuclear weapons, and Moscow withdrew its technicians from China and discontinued all technical and economic help in 1960. Publicly, the quarrel was restricted at first to oblique criticisms on both sides, but the rift became quite visible when the Chinese delegation walked out of the Moscow Party Conference in October 1961.

Once the breach began to widen, Peking could attack Moscow's de-Stalinization campaign on two grounds. First, it was a departure from the orthodoxies Moscow had earlier laid down. Second, the de-Stalinization program was a distinct product of the leadership struggle within the Soviet Union in the mid-fifties, as were the more flexible and conciliatory aspects of Russian foreign policy from that time on (including the failure to exploit fully the Soviet missile technology in order to achieve nuclear strategic superiority over the United States). Khrushchev had won a leadership struggle with the soft-line Moscow faction by posing as a hardliner; but he shifted ground and adopted a doctrine of "peaceful coexistence" once he had gathered up the reins of domestic power. As De Gaulle challenged American leadership of the Atlantic bloc, Peking challenged Moscow on the grounds that Moscow's new domestic and foreign policies ran against the interests of other Communist nations. The Chinese claimed that a more belligerent leadership would be far better for the common cause of revolutionary Communism. Success with the missiles in Cuba could have helped the Soviet Union solidify its bloc leadership. It would also have confirmed the merits of Khrushchev's policy of domestic development and limited defense expenditures. Instead, the missile crisis led to a large increase in Soviet strategic nuclear missile efforts by the mid-sixties.

Russian adventurism in Cuba may also have been encouraged by Kennedy's handling of the Bay of Pigs a year earlier. Khrushchev had chided Kennedy at Vienna for lacking resolution in dealing with the first Cuban invasion, and the Russian leader may have interpreted Kennedy's weakness as an invitation for the Soviet Union to venture into the Western Hemisphere.

After the missile crisis, Khrushchev, attempting to save face, claimed that the missiles were placed in Cuba merely to defend the island against United States attack. The explanation is interesting because it appears to reflect Kennedy's claims about the need for Soviet-American agreements to maintain the status quo.

The missile crisis was probably the high point of Kennedy's foreign policy—certainly of his summit diplomacy. Its short run outcome was to boost American prestige throughout the non-Communist world, especially among America's allies. Its longer run effect, however, was to accelerate the Soviet nuclear arms effort. Any thorough assessment of the Cuban missile crisis must take this sad fact into account.

KENNEDY'S FUMBLING WITH CONGRESS

More than any modern President in peacetime, Kennedy built his domestic popularity on his foreign policy. The firm manner in which he took charge of the Presidency brought his popularity to a peak of 83 percent by late April 1961, measured by the opinion surveys—probably a rally-'round-the-flag reaction after the Bay of Pigs. His popularity declined unsteadily over the next eighteen months as Republican leaders attacked him for his "tragic irresolution" over the invasion of Cuba. The bottom was 61 percent, reached just before the Cuban missile crisis. His survey opinion popularity then jumped to 74 percent immediately afterward and remained there into 1963, when it began drifting downward again to a low of 57 percent shortly before his death.[8]

From the beginning Kennedy found it difficult to translate his popularity into legislative support. As had been the case since the

[8] Hazel Goudet Erskine, "The Polls: Kennedy as President," *Public Opinion Quarterly* XXVIII (Summer 1964), pp. 334–42.

late forties, Congress readily increased defense and security-related expenditures, but defense economies, foreign assistance programs, trade liberalization, increased contacts with the Soviet bloc, and a more flexible policy toward Moscow all encountered opposition. The ineffectual management of White House relations with the legislative branch seemed to be one difficulty. Another was the wide gap in Democratic congressional leadership created by Lyndon Johnson's leaving the Senate to become Vice President and by the death of venerable House Speaker Sam Rayburn.

Domestic issues unquestionably limited Kennedy's legislative success more than did foreign policy—rarely is it otherwise. His successful appeals for public support over Berlin in his early months in the White House and his dramatic nuclear missile diplomacy in 1962 were acts of Cold War leadership with potentially high popularity. But Kennedy could not capitalize further on Cold War militancy because many of his other objectives in foreign relations required a restrained posture abroad.

Facing the same problems, though with a vastly stronger popular base, the Eisenhower Administration had popularized foreign aid by making it a weapon for fighting the Cold War. Dulles and Radford had made military posture more appealing by giving it a more militant and economical face. The Kennedy Administration, however, wanted a flexible defense posture; a "secularized" foreign aid program (that is, one that did not stress anti-Communism or Cold War utilities); and a program of active and conciliatory diplomacy with the Soviet Union. The political costs of these policies could be considerable.

Kennedy campaigned in the 1962 congressional elections strenuously and almost exclusively on domestic issues until the missile crisis took him out of the campaign for the crucial last two weeks. A Democratic gain of one or two Senate seats and five or more House seats would make it possible to enact bills dealing with medical care, public works, and urban affairs.

Instead, the Democrats lost four seats in each house of Congress. This was actually a better record than average for an off-year congressional election, since the President's party usually loses seats in nonpresidential elections. Nonetheless, the results fell short of Kennedy's hopes. The Cuban missile crisis appears to have helped the Democrats in the 1962 elections, partly because the complications of removing the Soviet missiles did not become apparent until after the elections were over.

THE NUCLEAR TEST BAN TREATY

The new Congress dealt slowly and not very enthusiastically with Kennedy's program in 1963. Most of his legislative program and even the annual appropriations bills left from the previous spring remained unapproved at the time of his death in November. The Test Ban Treaty was the exception.

The idea of a nuclear test ban had arisen inside the government during the early fifties. Stevenson had made it an issue in the presidential campaign of 1956 against firm Republican opposition. Not until the early sixties, however, did the prerequisites for a treaty fall into place.

Kennedy inherited from the Eisenhower years a voluntary moratorium on atmospheric tests that the United States and the Soviet Union had observed since November 1958. But his legacy also included test ban treaty negotiations that had been bogged down on technical inspection problems and complicated by mutual suspicion between Russia and the United States. Kennedy came to office intent on proceeding with the test ban dialog, but the Soviet generals, it now seems, were then demanding tests for the new weapons developed during the moratorium. Russia broke the moratorium in September 1961, setting disarmament negotiations back temporarily. This action brought increased pressure from the nonnuclear powers on both Moscow and Washington for a clear agreement to stop atmospheric tests.

At the same time prospects had diminished for working out the problems of independent enforcement and inspection required in a test ban treaty. The role the United Nations Secretary General played in the Congo crisis of 1960–61, thwarting Soviet aspirations to establish its influence in the Congo, reinforced strong Soviet suspicions about the true "neutrality" of international agencies that would carry out inspection provisions in a disarmament treaty. The Cuban missile crisis made it even more difficult for Moscow to make further concessions to the United States without compromising its position within its own bloc. Peking had reacted with lurid contempt to Khrushchev's backdown in Cuba. Yet, as the Moscow-Peking differences grew, Russia found it more attractive to reduce its differences with the United States.

Kennedy joined Macmillan in a special appeal to Khrushchev in April 1963 to break the deadlocked treaty negotiations. When this joint venture failed, Washington acted on its own, proposing to limit the three-power negotiations to nuclear tests that contaminated the atmosphere. Within ten days the delegates had actually initialed a draft treaty. The three states would agree to refrain from testing in outer space, in the atmosphere, or under water, and from abetting such tests by others.

The Senate ratified the Test Ban Treaty by an 80 to 19 vote in September. More than a hundred other nations also acceded to the treaty. At last Washington and Moscow had reached an agreement that could slow the arms race. In the euphoric aftermath, the Kennedy Administration negotiated the sale of wheat to Russia, and at the end of 1963 the Soviet government announced cuts in its military budget. President Johnson followed by announcing cutbacks in American military expenditures and production of nuclear materials in January 1964.

We should note, however, that the Test Ban Treaty had not been popular with Congress, despite the huge vote for ratification. Relations with the Soviet Union since the Cuban missile crisis had followed an uneven course, with the Russians at once tough and friendly. Moscow had intermittently heated up and cooled down the Berlin crisis, used the disarmament negotiations to propagandize, and intimidated the United Nations Secretary General. Yet it had worked out the test ban with rare dispatch and by mid-1963 American fears about Soviet cheating in removing its missiles from Cuba had abated. Some observers saw Soviet behavior as clever toughness, others as a result of the rift with Peking. Just prior to the three-power test ban meetings in Moscow in July 1962, a Chinese Communist delegation had also met with the Russians in last-ditch talks to heal Sino-Soviet wounds. They failed, and the Soviet government published a full statement of its grievances against Peking.

Regardless of Russia's underlying motives, however, it was difficult for the Kennedy Administration to make headway with Congress in approving conciliatory and flexible policies toward a nation that displayed such contradictory behavior toward us.

DEALING WITH THE DEVELOPING NATIONS

Although Kennedy had come to the Presidency appealing to the public as a mover and shaker, much of his foreign policy lacked popular appeal. The two previous Administrations had chosen to win public support for foreign policy undertakings by relying on Cold War rhetoric, thus narrowing policy choices to those that fit Cold War molds and thus increasing the formidable difficulties of exploring possible settlements with the Soviet Union. Even an aroused public leaves an Administration with considerable latitude in external relations, but the public's concern with the Cold War set limits that Kennedy found particularly confining in developing policies for the developing areas of the world. Kennedy continued to see Russia as a great power rival, but he perceived the Soviet challenge as more flexible and the issues in developing areas as more complex than the Eisenhower Administration had been willing to depict them. Yet he did not move far from the Eisenhower Administration's position on new and developing states. Kennedy acknowledged that the new states faced issues of development and survival more vital to them than the Cold War—that the effort of Dulles to force the new states to run to one camp or the other was a mistake; yet the Kennedy Administration held that American rivalry with the Soviets made it important to deny Moscow hegemony in the developing areas. The effect of setting this objective was to deal with the new states in terms of the American-Soviet rivalry, although it was in fact largely irrelevant to the concerns of the new states, which needed to be addressed on their own terms. In fact, as the Bay of Pigs debacle illustrates, the Kennedy Administration held a very optimistic view about the powers of the American government to intervene in distant governments to achieve United States objectives, such as in Vietnam.

THE MIDDLE EAST

The fate of the Middle East is a sensitive issue in American politics because of United States investments in oil there and the often competing interest of American Jews in the well-being of Israel. After the Suez crisis the Eisenhower Administration had emphasized the Communist threat in the Middle East as a way to reconstruct the American position there. But the dimensions of the struggle for political power in the Middle East were in fact much broader than just conflict between East and West. By the time Eisenhower retired, American policy in this area had begun to reflect these complexities and Egypt's Nasser had proved to be a relatively competent independent nationalist leader who was not inclined to become a tool of either Soviet or American policies.

In the face of these changes the Kennedy Administration limited its role in the Middle East and attempted to diversify its political friendships there. It quickly recognized the new leftist government faction in Yemen, evidently under the mistaken impression that the traditionalists could not sustain an effective opposition. But when the conflict continued, Washington drew the United Nations into negotiating a withdrawal of foreign support from both sides of the conflict in Yemen. Nasser's forces, however, lingered on in violation of the agreement until the Arab-Israeli war in 1967.

Egypt's failure to comply with the United Nations withdrawal arrangements, coupled with its unremitting hostility toward Israel, induced a direct congressional response. An amendment to the Foreign Assistance Act of 1963, passed over the protest of President Kennedy, denied aid to Egypt if she engaged in or prepared for "aggressive military efforts" against other recipients of American aid.

This amendment, one of several congressional stipulations to limit the President's discretion in administering the foreign aid program, illustrates well the domestic political price Kennedy paid for resisting the temptation to label all forces for change in the Middle East as Communist or dangerous to American interests. By focusing on the specter of direct and indirect Communist aggression in the Middle East the Eisenhower Administration had loosened domestic constraints on presidential discretion. The Kennedy Administration refrained from invoking the Communist "menace" and emphasized instead the realities of nationalist rivalries in Middle East politics. Unfortunately, the effect was to arouse congressional sensitivities about the Arab-Israeli conflict and to reduce congressional support for the President's policies. Seeking broader options in the Middle East, Kennedy's choices were in fact reduced by Congress, and the new constraints ultimately proved embarrassing to the Administration in its Middle East relations.

AFRICA

Most of Africa's new states had gained their independence from colonial rule only in the late 1950s. As Britain had done in India in 1947, Britain and France relinquished their colonial power quite abruptly in their African colonies. In India, however, a competent professional government bureaucracy and army remained, while Black Africa in the late fifties had much less of this human "infrastructure" of government. It lacked trained native government functionaries of every kind, from clerks to diplomats.

Moreover, the new African states suffered from a strong propensity to balkanize themselves: to divide into ethnic groupings within each nation. Without the capacity to police their nations effectively, the central governments had as much difficulty coping with secessionist groups as they did in maintaining law and order.

The change of presidential administration in 1961 increased American diplomatic adaptation to the needs of Africa. Kennedy appointed former Michigan Governor G. Mennan Williams as Assistant Secretary of State for Africa; the new Administration gave more attention than its predecessor to appointments for the new American embassies in Africa and increased economic assistance to Africa. Williams, after an awkward beginning, settled down to dealing with the new national leaders of Black Africa as he found them: generally tough politicians who were addicted to strong, broadly eclectic ideological programs that were part of their efforts to improvise new methods and ideas for coping with the turbulent politics of their new states.

The fate of the Belgian Congo in 1960–61 amply illustrates the problems faced by new African nations and the Kennedy response to the crises posed. In July 1960 Belgium abruptly abandoned its vast African colony to independence, and the Congo quickly split into three centers of power. The nominal central government of the Congo, unable to control or administer the country, called in a United Nations military force to establish law and order—and then demanded that the United Nations forces become the instrument of a rigid, centralist government. The United States supported the United Nations intervention and provided the main logistical support for its operations. The United Nations peacekeeping force did demand the evacuation of Belgian troops that were supporting the secession of the rich mining province of Katanga, but the United Nations refused to suppress Katangan independence directly. When the centrist Premier, Patrice Lumumba, turned to Soviet and Czech support against his internal rivals, he split the central government.

By January 1961 three governments coexisted in the Congo: the central government in Leopoldville; its rival at Stanleyville, headed first by Lumumba and then by Antoine Gizenga and supported from North Africa and Moscow by an anticolonialist bloc; and the rebel government in Katanga, headed by Moise Tshombe and backed by Belgian mining interests. In February Moscow seized upon published reports of the political assassination of Lumumba to demand the withdrawal of the United Nations force in the Congo and the dismissal of Secretary General Hammarskjold as an "accomplice" of the murder. On February 15 Kennedy defended the United Nations role against "any attempt by any government to intervene unilaterally in the Congo."

Debate in the Security Council indicated that most non-Communist governments were anxious to maintain the United Nations force in the Congo. The United States continued to back the United Nations peacekeepers on the grounds that the Congo needed to be held together and, more broadly, that it was important to avoid the balkanization of Africa. But the Katanga secession dragged on. In effect, the United Nations had become a fourth party working at cross purposes with the three Congolese governments. The complex play of internal politics became a lesson to outside powers about the difficulties of pursuing their interests in the new African states.

CONFLICT AND DEVELOPMENT IN ASIA

Pakistani-Indian Rivalry

Before 1958 Washington had been inclined to treat Pakistan as an appendage of the Middle East, though its East wing bordered on Calcutta and Burma. But as American interest in India grew, Washington came to view Pakistan as part of South Asia, locked into this region partly because of its bitter territorial dispute with India over control of Kashmir. The Pakistani government had been taken over in 1958 by its British trained Army Chief, Mohammed

Ayub Khan, who promptly instituted economic and political reforms. By 1961 Pakistan's new regime boasted impressive economic growth rates, had demonstrated considerable administrative competence, and was moving methodically toward broader political participation with indirect parliamentary elections.

Since its independence India had been ruled by the Congress party, headed by its preindependence leader, Jawaharlal Nehru. The party consisted of a broad variety of state parties, and the locus of its power reflected the considerable strength of the state governments. From its beginning, India achieved a remarkable degree of democratic participation, thus attracting the special sympathy of the Stevensonian Democrats in the late fifties and the support of Kennedy as a Senator.

The Stevenson Democrats could win support from the Truman Democrats with the argument that India was large, competently governed, and relatively stable—hence, a potentially important ally for the United States. On the other hand, India's decentralized political system made economic development difficult, because the powerful state governments and party organizations controlled the public production and distribution of food.

Pakistan, on the other hand, with a moderate constitutional autocracy, could implement economic development plans more expeditiously. As part of his effort to consolidate the new regime, Ayub Khan decided to emphasize the development of the private sector. Pakistan achieved a considerably higher rate of economic growth than India did, and for a cost that was compatible with the structure of the Pakistani regime: a growing disparity in income distribution, which in turn helped to consolidate the military-business-civil service oligarchy.

Kennedy's inclinations were to favor India over Pakistan, as he demonstrated by appointing the Harvard economist and brain-truster of his campaign, John Kenneth Galbraith, as ambassador to New Delhi. Nonetheless, economic assistance to Pakistan increased proportionately more than our aid to India under Kennedy.[9]

---

[9] The annual average of Pakistan's total economic assistance for the three fiscal years of the Kennedy Administration, 1962–64, was 47 percent higher than the annual average for the four years preceding, 1958–61. The equivalent figure for India was 42 percent. Computed from Agency for International Development, *U.S. Overseas Loans and Grants and Assistance from International Organizations, 1945–66* (1967), pp. 11 and 28.

Ayub Khan, worried about Kennedy's known sympathy for India, arranged to pay a state visit to Washington in 1961, just when the Administration found itself in trouble getting its first foreign aid bill through Congress. The White House arranged to have Ayub address a joint session of Congress. His performance helped pass the bill and deterred the Administration's efforts to shift its support to India.

The balance of American support did ultimately shift toward India, however, as a result of Chinese attacks against the Indian border outposts in Ladach and Assam in 1962. India was able to contain the Ladach attack, but Chinese forces in Assam carried their incursion down the slopes of the Himalayas, inflicting a humiliating defeat against the Indian forces there and greatly alarming the Indian government with the prospect of a major Chinese invasion. Washington and London promptly responded with military aid. To Pakistan, however, the generous United States military aid to India not only appeared to indicate United States sympathies but it tipped the Indian-Pakistani military balance against Pakistan. Ayub promptly set about negotiating with the Chinese over disputed borders and improving trade relations with the Soviet Union. Pakistan, the American client of the fifties, would over the next decade enjoy favored treatment from Peking as well as Washington.

The Kennedy Administration's policies toward Pakistan and India did not produce immediate difficulties for it with Congress or with the public; helping India to stave off a Chinese attack was a popular step. But United States military assistance to India ultimately opened the door to future trouble: when India and Pakistan renewed their old quarrel over Kashmir in 1965, American weaponry was used by both sides to fight one another! The Johnson Administration would pay for Kennedy's policies in this area in lost popularity with Congress and the public.

The Island Nations

In Indonesia the Kennedy Administration was able to maintain a policy of friendly aloofness, partly because the Sukarno regime faced no direct challenge from within. Washington refused to meet the demands of Sukarno's government for increased United

States aid; it bore with patience the wild fluctuations of policy from Sukarno's increasingly ineffective regime as the Indonesian economy drifted into stagnation; and it declined to become visibly involved with any effort to find an alternative to Sukarno.

In Japan, as in Indonesia, the Kennedy Administration's main impact was exerted through diplomacy. The Japanese economy had boomed in the fifties and continued to do so with only minor faltering in the early sixties. The boom brought Americanization and modernization to Japanese culture and business methods, new confidence in domestic politics and external relations, and the rise of strong left-wing political sentiment. This was coupled with the pacifism that was a legacy of the Japanese defeat, the atom bomb attacks, and the American occupation. Japan had been pacified and Americanized only to find that the United States was not pacific; it had been neutralized by the American occupation under Mac-Arthur only to be used by the United States as a military base and then encouraged by Washington to carry some of the military burdens of defending the Far East.

Anti-American attitudes throughout Japan had erupted in civil disorders that forced the cancellation of Eisenhower's state visit in 1960. In 1961 Kennedy appointed Edwin O. Reischauer as ambassador to stem this tide. A distinguished scholar of Japan, with a Japanese wife and a thorough fluency in Japanese, Reischauer set about restoring the "broken dialog" with the United States, bringing Japan into a closer orientation to American culture, politics, and foreign policy.

Indochina: Limited Commitment in a Peripheral Area

American involvement in Southeast Asia was to remain a minor aspect of United States foreign policy until the Johnson Administration, but the roots of this involvement can be traced back to the end of World War II. At that time the United States helped the European colonial powers—Britain, France, and the Netherlands—to reclaim their colonial territories in Southeast Asia from the defeated Japanese, who had seized these areas during the war. The United States supported its European allies at first by default. During the war Roosevelt had postponed the development of an alternative American policy for these areas, and no other postwar provision had been made for governing the liberated territories. Later, however, even when the full extent of nationalist opposition to colonial rule became evident, the United States continued to side with the colonial powers in Asia. (We readily accepted the revolution in Indonesia against Dutch rule.) "Primarily because of our disinterest in Asia and our concern over the sensitivities and political problems of the colonial powers in Europe," Reischauer has written, "we chose to ignore Asian nationalism, except in our own domain of the Philippines."[10]

When the Kennedy Administration came into office, it cautiously attempted to reduce American commitments in Indochina in the face of growing difficulties with our position there. Kennedy did not want to exacerbate the situation in Indochina or call attention to it. At the time, the Test Ban Treaty with Russia took precedence. He feared that growing trouble in Asia would jeopardize future Senate ratification of the treaty.

Kennedy's attention to Indochina began in Laos, which posed the most urgent problem in Southeast Asia at the outset of his Administration. Laos, Cambodia, and Vietnam were the three states created at the Geneva Convention of 1954 when the French gave up colonial Indochina. According to the Geneva settlement, Laos was to be a neutral state, but since 1954 the Eisenhower Administration had attempted to support an anti-Communist regime there. By 1961 Eisenhower's efforts to "deneutralize" Laos had so antagonized the strong neutralist-nationalist faction in that country that it was driven first into diplomatic alliance with Moscow, and then into active military cooperation with the Pathet Lao, a Communist faction organized and supported first from North Vietnam and then from Moscow itself. A few days before Kennedy's inauguration the United States had openly violated the Geneva accord by sending its Laotian client Nosavan Phoumi (a right-wing military figure) fighter bombers and military advisory teams; by doing so we lent further legitimacy to Soviet military support of the Pathet Lao. By the time of the inauguration the United States was isolated in its sponsorship of the Phoumi faction, joined only by Thailand and

[10] Edwin O. Reischauer, *Beyond Vietnam: The United States and Asia* (New York: Vintage, 1967), p. 21. The historical summary given above depends in part on Reischauer's account, pp. 20–27.

South Vietnam, from which clandestine American material support came by airlift.

After rejecting direct military intervention the Kennedy Administration strengthened the Phoumi faction, moved U.S. Marines to Thailand, alerted troops on Okinawa, and deployed the Seventh Fleet into the South China Sea. These actions were intended to demonstrate that we wanted nothing less than the neutralization of Laos. Meanwhile, Kennedy assured the Russians publicly and privately that we wanted both nothing less and nothing *more* than neutralization. Khrushchev agreed to reconstitute the Geneva Commission and indicated that he had no desire to "take risks over Laos" when "it will fall into our laps like a ripe apple."[11] With this, the crisis subsided.

At the Vienna conference in June Kennedy obtained Khrushchev's commitment to reneutralize Laos, and a coalition government was gradually put together after lengthy negotiations at Geneva. The government was established in June 1962 and heralded by simultaneous announcements from Khrushchev and Kennedy. Thirteen states, including the United States, the U.S.S.R., Communist China, the Vietnams, and India, signed the Declaration of Geneva in July.

But the Laotian coalition government soon lost the support of the Communist Pathet Lao. As a result, the neutralist faction in the coalition moved away from the Pathet Lao and toward Phoumi in order to defend Laotian independence against a Communist faction supported from Hanoi. The neutralist faction gradually gained ascendency over right-wing Phoumi's faction in the coalition government, winning indigenous support for its independence, while the Pathet Lao continued to operate in the mountains. Laos was now a divided but more stabilized state.

Kennedy had used negotiations to limit the American commitment to Laos, but he had failed to consider the more fundamental question of American interests in Indochina. After all, if a satisfactory status in Indochina could be worked out at reasonable costs, then why not strive for it? Interests that we recognized as limited justified limited involvement (but not more). This was a step in the right direction in moving away from the rigid fictions about Cold

---

[11] Schlesinger, p. 334.

War frontiers in Asia. But limited interests justified even limited American intervention *only if it would work*. During the early sixties, the important contingency of failure received only cursory attention. It was not a serious element in the American calculations about involvement in Indochina. Perhaps it was a victim of the self-confidence of the Kennedy Administration.

A related issue was the Soviet role and interest in Laos. Soviet material help was clearly involved, but to what purpose? Would Moscow continue to help if it simply meant that Hanoi rather than Russia gained control of Laos? Khrushchev's remark to Kennedy was misleading in a way that would harm the interests of both Moscow and Washington: Laos was not going to fall into Russia's lap; it would fall, if anywhere, to Hanoi.

Khrushchev's rhetoric had a special purpose—to identify Moscow with Communist aspirations in developing areas in order to offset Peking's challenge of Soviet leadership. Kennedy Administration officials, however, saw this rhetoric as reinforcing their Cold War assessment: that Laos hung in the balance between the Communist bloc and the free world.

The problems Kennedy faced in determining the appropriate degree of American involvement in Vietnam were similar to those presented by Laos. In both areas the Administration suffered the frustrations of dealing with an area it was willing to treat only as peripheral to our interests, yet defined by quite stark Cold War doctrine. In both areas Kennedy's goal was to hold down American involvement and expenditures in order to concentrate on other areas deemed more important to our interests, such as India, Africa, and Latin America. In Laos, Kennedy's policies succeeded, but in Vietnam they laid the foundation for substantially increased American involvement.

When the French returned to Vietnam after World War II they found Ho Chi Minh's Communist movement established in the North and receiving de facto recognition from Chiang Kai-shek's Nationalist government in China. At first Ho's regime took an uneasy role within the French Indochinese Federation, but the two were at war by 1946.

The prevailing United States sentiment in mid-1945 opposed the restoration of prewar colonial regimes in Asia. As Japanese rule collapsed in Indochina, the United States refused transport for

French troops returning to Vietnam. (By contrast, American transports moved Nationalist Chinese troops into Manchuria and elsewhere in the wake of the Japanese collapse.) Yet American officials could do very little to remain neutral with respect to the French colonial empire because the United States was more concerned about enhancing the stability of Western Europe and about its relations with metropolitan France than it was about Southeast Asia. A Pentagon Papers author has concluded that "no French government is likely to have survived a genuinely liberal policy toward Ho [the nationalist-Communist leader in North Vietnam] in 1945 or 1946."[12]

At the outset of the conflict with Ho, then, the French reluctance to let Indochina go was the root of the problem. It was aggravated by the precarious status of France itself as a defeated and occupied power during World War II. For the French government and for American officials, even the Communist background of Ho was not at that time used to claim that he was part of a worldwide conspiracy directed by Moscow. A State Department intelligence estimate about Southeast Asia in the fall of 1948 found "evidence of Kremlin-directed conspiracy . . . in virtually all countries except Vietnam." The estimate speculated that Moscow had probably exempted Vietnam from the rigid directives that appeared to guide other Communist movements in the region. It also noted that the French colonial press was far more anti-American than was the Vietnam press.[13]

Given Washington's concern about Europe, however, it had no choice: it had to support France. A more liberal colonial policy, including more autonomy and independence for Vietnam, was a secondary objective about which Washington fruitlessly prodded a succession of French governments from 1946 to 1954. Some revisionists have seen our failure to apply pressure to France as evidence of our own sympathy with colonial interests. Clearly, we gave priority to our relations with Paris over the interests of nationalist aspirations in Indochina. Secretary of State Marshall first approved direct economic aid for Vietnam in 1946—a $160 million credit for Vietnamese industry.

[12] *Senator Gravel Edition: The Pentagon Papers,* 4 vols. (Boston: Beacon Press, 1971), vol. 1, p. 52.

[13] *Ibid.,* p. 34.

For Washington, the picture changed significantly as Chiang lost ground in China. A National Security Council assessment of the situation, approved after Cabinet-level discussion with President Truman in December 1949, held:

> The United States should continue to use its influence in Asia toward resolving the colonial-nationalist conflict in such a way as to satisfy the fundamental demands of the nationalist movement while at the same time minimizing the strain on the colonial powers who are our Western allies. Particular attention should be given to the problem of French Indo-China and action should be taken to bring home to the French the urgency of removing the barriers to the obtaining by Bao Dai [the French-picked nationalist leader] or other non-Communist nationalist leaders of the support of a substantial proportion of the Vietnamese.[14]

As this statement indicates, the United States had gone along with France's handling of the French-Indochinese war, including its characterization of the political issues of the war, then in its third year.

In May 1950 the Truman Administration began sending direct material aid to the pro-French Saigon regime in its efforts against Ho's Vietminh government, ending a long period in which we had supplied heavy economic aid to France that had in turn enabled France to carry on its colonial war. Our new direct aid to the Saigon regime reflected the growing belief in Washington that Communist expansion in Asia was a single, coordinated effort, along with a recognition that it was futile to attempt to change the behavior of our essential allies.

Since World War II a viewpoint had persisted in Washington that the American goal in Asia should be to aid the former colonial areas to achieve independence and statehood. Washington had applied effective pressure on the Dutch in that direction with respect to their East Indies colony, and could take some minor credit for Indonesia's becoming an independent state during 1951. Similar hopes for Indochina were submerged in the late forties because French cooperation in NATO was more essential than Dutch (and because the constant changing of political leadership in France pre-

14 *Ibid.,* p. 39.

cluded a target for sustained American pressure). Starting direct American aid to Saigon in 1950 marked the further submergence of future independence for Vietnam.

As noted in Chapter 5, the war in Indochina reached a climax in 1954 when the French enclave at Dien Bien Phu in the North fell under siege to the Vietminh. At the Geneva Conference that spring France and the Vietminh agreed to divide Vietnam along the 17th parallel and set up an international control commission. A separate agreement provided for elections in 1956 to reunify Vietnam. The Geneva agreements represented a face-saving package for the French.

Britain, Communist China, and the Soviet Union—but not the United States—assented to the proposed 1956 elections in Vietnam. Whether this assent meant that they expected South Vietnam to fall to Hanoi and Ho Chi Minh in two years is unclear. It *is* clear, however, that the Eisenhower Administration had no such expectation; in fact Dulles organized SEATO in part to give South Vietnam the protection of a regional security pact. The United States also installed a new ruler in Saigon, anti-French mandarin Ngo Dinh Diem, and strengthened his regime through subsidy. Clandestine American operations by the CIA also evidently helped Diem to weaken his rival political groups.

Under the moral umbrella of the Cold War, political expediency was intermingled with the aura of a vague moral objective. Since the Eisenhower Administration (and most Americans) perceived the Communist world as morally inferior and monolithic, it viewed a Vietminh victory as a clear gain for the Soviet-led Communist enemy—a prospect that strengthened the moral criteria for American support of the South Vietnamese regime. All forms of American intervention in Vietnam—economic assistance, military training and equipment, and sub rosa operations by the CIA—were being used elsewhere by the United States as well, usually with a similar justification.

Moreover, the Administration's level of intervention in South Vietnam was actually lower than what we had contemplated to save the French at Dien Bien Phu a few months earlier. But moral issues were to become more important later on. As the inhumane side effects of the war on both sides grew and became more visible, our moral position came to seem questionable. As the French had discovered earlier about their own defensive colonialism, however, American participation in the war's inhumanities might have received less notice had we been winning.

Underlying Washington's political considerations was a facile, unexamined premise: that American intervention was justified despite its costs because South Vietnam would otherwise become a part of the world Communist empire. This assumption was based on poor estimates of costs and benefits to the United States and to the Vietnamese. Washington generally underestimated the costs and overestimated the benefits of avoiding Communist rule. It also overestimated the likelihood and the attractions of a non-Communist and independent government as a viable alternative to a Communist government in South Vietnam. In any case, it was difficult at that time to establish consensus about reasonable expectations for government in Vietnam—North, South, or united—according to American political and social standards.

Moral issues nonetheless became increasingly prominent in American debate over Vietnam. To begin with, measured by the standards of advanced democracies, the new Diem regime was not particularly attractive. Washington expected it to be more honest, efficient, and democratic than the French colonial regime. The expectation was unfulfilled. Yet Diem's regime was not conspicuously less appealing than the other alternatives in Vietnam or than other American clients—in Taipei, Seoul, Baghdad, Lisbon, and Havana, for instance. Given our earlier support for the French effort to hold Indochina, Diem seemed to represent a distinct improvement in our moral position.

The American sponsored government in Saigon was only partially successful in consolidating its power over South Vietnam. Many hard-core Vietminh had stayed in the South after 1954. Dubbed by Diem as the "Vietcong," these Southern forces became the heart of the resistance, spreading their control over the rural population with a shrewd combination of service and terror that was often superior to the government's combination of coercion and authority. The Vietcong organized themselves as the National Liberation Front (NLF), a rival government to Diem's.

By the time Kennedy was elected President, Hanoi was supporting the insurgency in the South. In 1961 Ho's government began to infiltrate into South Vietnam some of the estimated 90,000 Vietminh troops that had fled north from the south in 1954.[15]

Kennedy became President at a time of growing demands from Diem for more American supplies and personnel in Vietnam to match the open support of the Vietcong from Hanoi. Kennedy's advisers had been aware of the deepening crisis in Vietnam. Diagnosing the problem as overemphasis on traditional political and military methods, they undertook the development of American guerrilla warfare capabilities. Upon taking office they found that career officials in both the State and Defense departments had anticipated them by starting to prepare a counter-insurgency plan for Vietnam including extensive social and military reforms. In May Vice President Johnson returned from a trip to Southeast Asia to advise Kennedy against American combat involvement in Vietnam. However he recommended changes in our military effort there coupled with more political and economic reforms. Johnson also spoke of a major economic development program for the lower Mekong River basin—in effect, massive American economic intervention.

Diem, however, successfully resisted American pressures for change. With the situation still deteriorating, Kennedy sent a White House team to Saigon in October 1961, headed by General Maxwell D. Taylor. The Taylor team recommended sending 10,000 more United States troops to Vietnam—a virtual doubling of our forces there. The White House found Taylor's recommendations attractive in part because they offset the conciliatory position it had been taking in Laos and its failure at the Bay of Pigs. Kennedy considered the United States overinvolved in Laos and was taking steps to reduce our commitments there. At the same time the Bay of Pigs debacle had left him vulnerable to charges that he was unwilling to stand up to the Communists. After some hesitation he ordered the proposed build-up in Vietnam and for the first time put the American advisers there into uniforms. The uniforms were more than symbolic. Advisers now became "trainer-combat" forces.

Since the Americans in Vietnam had limited access to both government officials and populace, Washington depended largely

---

[15] *Ibid.,* p. 328.

on Diem's government for progress reports. Kennedy's State of the Union message on January 14, 1963, reflected the optimism that prevailed more than a year after he had raised the American commitment there: "The spearpoint of aggression has been blunted in South Vietnam," he said. Earlier, McNamara, on his first visit to Vietnam, had matched this optimistic statement: "Every quantitative measurement we have shows we are winning the war."[16]

In fact, however, the war had not been going well. Our hopes for victory in 1962 had rested on the so-called strategic hamlet program, which was being badly executed by Diem's brother, Ngo Dinh Nhu. American reporters covering Vietnam, resenting the official optimism and the prodding of the United States Embassy in Saigon to "get on the team," began to release news stories that belied the official accounts. By 1963 the discerning American newspaper reader perceived a "credibility gap" between official accounts and other news sources.

The gap continued to grow. The chief American military adviser in Saigon proclaimed a victory for South Vietnamese forces in January at Ap Bac, near Saigon, while American correspondents on the scene filed stories making clear that a victory had not been achieved. Rumblings of failure in the handling of the strategic hamlet program also grew. The program was designed to use military means to increase the security of a spreading geographic area. Village life would be reorganized in the interests of security, and in the process social, economic, and political changes would be carried out. Instead the plan failed to provide security and merely disrupted village life, adding to the antagonisms generated earlier when Diem had abolished local selection of local officials.

The incongruity between press and official accounts of the progress in Vietnam had produced some restlessness among Washington officials by the spring of 1963. Senate Majority Leader Mike Mansfield, for instance, called for a reassessment of American policy in Vietnam. Yet official optimism persisted. In May Kennedy expressed the hope that the United States could begin to withdraw some of its forces by the end of the year. This hope rested on the assumptions that the scale of the North Vietnamese effort would not be significantly increased and that the counter-insurgency efforts

---

[16] Quoted in Schlesinger, p. 549.

of the Diem government would improve. Both assumptions proved incorrect.

The most visible aspect of South Vietnam's problems—a factor that added greatly to the Administration's growing doubts about supporting Diem—was the Diem regime's repressive activities to crush the Buddhist uprising begun in May. The uprising, though urban based, reflected discontent from the countryside as well. In August Diem loosed his special security forces against the Buddhist pagodas, seizing monks, nuns, and school children.

Diem's actions may in fact have been no different from the repression of other ethnic, religious, or political factions elsewhere in Asia, the Middle East, or Latin America. But in this case the growing American involvement made domestic Vietnamese politics newsworthy in the United States, giving Vietnam the very prominence the Kennedy Administration had wanted to avoid.

In August 1963 Kennedy recalled the American ambassador in Saigon since 1961, Frederick E. Nolting, a man closely identified with Diem. Nolting has reported that when he sought an explanation for our official turn against Diem, Secretary of State Rusk told him: "We cannot stand any more burnings."[17] And indeed the Kennedy Administration could not, if it wished to prevent Vietnam from mobilizing the attention of the American public.

Kennedy himself had criticized Eisenhower for identifying the United States with undemocratic regimes in the late fifties. Evidently he believed that not only were these regimes ineffective but that the American public was antagonized by its government's support of regimes that offended democratic standards. The Kennedy Administration could not afford the public antagonism it anticipated if it continued to support the Diem regime.

Kennedy officials in Washington now began to think about letting Diem fall. In a television interview on September 2 Kennedy called the handling of the Buddhists "very unwise" and charged Diem's regime with having "gotten out of touch with the people." He even hinted that Diem's brother, who was in charge of the security forces, might have to be removed from office. Washing-

17 "The Origin and Development of United States Commitment in Vietnam," speech by Frederick E. Nolting, April 2, 1968, *Congressional Record* (May 14, 1968), pp. E 4186–90.

ton followed with selective and unpublicized suspension of assistance in October. These acts effectively allowed for a military junta that toppled the regime and murdered Diem and his brother three weeks before Kennedy's own death.

As American involvement, American costs, and American attention grew, the legitimacy of the Diem regime and its successors were soon to be widely questioned in the United States because of their corruption, repression, and unpopularity. The American association with repressive means to keep the government in power would also be challenged, as would the morality and expediency of opposing the strongly based insurgent forces in South Vietnam. The Kennedy Administration's doctrines had concentrated instead on engineering better methods of countering insurgents. It was too quickly assumed that removing insurgents would reduce political repression and might thus make it possible to get a morally acceptable non-Communist regime.

The Kennedy Administration's decision to let Diem fall reflected its impatience with him, its optimism about the impact of nation building and counter-insurgency, and its anxiety about the political opposition and repressive measures in Vietnam. Diem lost support in Washington because he was not sufficiently concerned about the political and social roots of the insurgent problem—a subject the Kennedy Administration took very seriously. In short, Diem did not appear to be a modern "nation builder."

In general, letting Diem fall made matters worse in Vietnam. The coup that destroyed him swept aside the fragile political structure he had built and left politics in the hands of young military officers. During the next fifteen months three more military coups succeeded in Saigon and still more were attempted. Over the next three years there would be nine different governments. The succession of Army backed civilian regimes and army rulers that followed were less traditionalist than Diem and more tractable to the Americans, but they were hardly more progressive. In fact, the post-Diem regimes were no more capable of winning public support, no less corrupt, no more efficient, and no more responsive to the peasant or worker than Diem had been. Usually dominated by North Vietnamese émigrés who were insensitive to Southern ethnic, religious, and political groupings, these regimes brought no gains in popular rule.

Once the military became the arbiters of the South Vietnamese political order, they repeated the same pattern of behavior that had sapped Washington's confidence in Diem: they remained preoccupied with carrying on a power struggle among themselves and with maintaining the American commitment to South Vietnam—at the expense of political and economic conditions that underlay the country's instability. The Kennedy Administration had let Diem fall in order to give greater weight to improving political and economic conditions. Yet after Diem, the Saigon government's neglect of these problems actually grew. The optimism of the Kennedy Administration about the ability of the United States to carry out direct political intervention and achieve positive results proved utterly wrong when Diem fell.

Two alternative courses of action in the summer and fall of 1963 might have changed political conditions in South Vietnam. First, the Kennedy Administration might have negotiated a political settlement with Hanoi. But this alternative received no serious attention in Washington. In fact the precipitating cause of our letting Diem fall had evidently been the indications that his regime, through the efforts of his powerful brother, was turning toward a neutralist solution for South Vietnam.

Second, the Kennedy Administration might have tried to move into the vacuum left by Diem's removal by supporting a reformist regime with specific programs for improving political and economic conditions. Such a positive political effort would seem to be a necessary step in political intervention. But no such regime had been identified or invented. Washington had made no preparations for filling the Vietnamese political vacuum. The Nuclear Test Ban Treaty had been signed in Moscow on August 5, and when Kennedy withdrew support from Diem in early September the treaty was before the Senate Foreign Relations Committee. The Senate ratified the treaty on September 24, more than six weeks before Diem's overthrow. Kennedy evidently decided at that time, however, that further involvement in Vietnam to secure a new and better regime would jeopardize the Test Ban Treaty. After assessing his priorities, Kennedy chose the treaty over Vietnam. This choice of priorities may also be explained by the penchant among Kennedy officials to underestimate what was required to make political orders like the Saigon regime viable as well as their tendency not to appreciate how viable and resilient hostile political orders such as Castro's in Havana and Ho's in Hanoi could be.

LATIN AMERICA: THE ALLIANCE FOR PROGRESS

Before a glittering audience of Latin American diplomats assembled in the White House in March 1961, Kennedy announced "a vast new ten-year plan for the Americas, a plan to transform the 1960s into a historic decade of democratic progress," repeatedly intoning the plan's Spanish name, *Alianza para el Progreso,* in his Boston accent.

Latin America was changing rapidly. Its birth rate was the highest for any continent, its rate of urban growth phenomenal. Yet economic stagnation persisted. The Alliance, like the Kennedy Administration's other economic aid programs, gave primary attention to economic objectives, though from the beginning the political obstacles to economic development in Latin America proved particularly difficult to overcome.

Most of the Latin American nations had gained their independence in the early nineteenth century, but they were still underdeveloped by mid-twentieth-century standards. United States government officials and American businessmen had had considerable experience with these nations, and they understood in detail the close relationship between their political and economic problems.

Through private investment the United States could provide only a small proportion of the additional capital needed for economic development, and through government grants and loans we could provide even less. The Eisenhower Administration had stressed these limitations when pressed for more economic assistance to Latin America. The Latin American governments needed to take steps to induce saving for capital investment, to stop the flight of their own private capital into foreign investment markets, and to make the investment climate for foreign capital more attractive. The necessary environment for inducing these savings and investments, according to this line of reasoning, could be established through the fiscal and economic policies and business legislation of the Latin American governments involved.

The Kennedy Administration did not deny the importance of private investment. But sole reliance on it, said Kennedy's economic advisers, would only continue the basic conditions of stagnation. The hostile business climate was itself part of the problem. National economic development plans, meeting recognized economic criteria established and enforced by a regional organization (in the manner of the Marshall Plan) rather than by the United States, the advisers suggested, should produce the conditions needed to attract more private investment. The Kennedy Administration was prepared to use American public grants and loans to create those conditions where necessary, channeling funds through public enterprises in the recipient country.

At the same time, prior experience had made it plain that American aid channeled through the recipient government might well reinforce the status quo—by subsidizing it where it was weak and by rewarding its privileged classes—rather than change it. On the other hand, sound economic development plans were more likely to encourage a climate for reforms. Past experience with development plans, however, suggested that merely enforcing economic performance criteria could not assure that the necessary social and economic reforms would occur.

The Alliance needed to be sold in every participating country, including the United States. In the Latin American countries it could succeed only if it could rally the supporters of change against the defenders of the status quo. Public figures in Latin America—to say nothing of the United States Congress—who were potential supporters of the Alliance needed the encouragement and reassurance provided by publicity and political promotion, so that if they ventured to change things they could do so as part of a large and popular undertaking. For these reasons, both the United States and the potential Latin American beneficiaries surrounded the Alliance with strong rhetorical flourishes—with a mystique.

Economic aid for the first year would be covered by the $500 million left over from the Eisenhower Administration's Inter-American Fund for Social Progress. In his March 1962 foreign aid message, Kennedy proposed $3 billion in development funds for the Alliance in the next four years, including $600 million for the fiscal year 1962–63. This proposed expansion of American appropriations brought the first annual stock-taking of the Alliance. Complaints came from all directions. Latin American countries criticized Washington for bureaucratic delays while their own economic and social reforms lagged. Critics in Congress charged that the Latin Americans had shown no clear intention to do their share. In the bill authorizing the appropriations, Congress cut Kennedy's fund proposals modestly and added the Hickenlooper Amendment forbidding aid to countries that expropriated American-owned property without prompt and adequate compensation. Kennedy, to offset a mood of disappointment in Latin America, visited Venezuela and Colombia at the end of the year.

The exchange of recriminations was not the only indication of disagreement between Washington and its Alliance partners. An important divergence of views appeared over what seemed to be a central agreement reached in 1963: the need for stronger multilateral control over the Alliance. The idea had originated in a report by former Presidents Kubitschek of Brazil and Lleras of Colombia, approved at the annual meeting of the Alliance at São Paulo in November. For the Latin Americans, stronger multilateral control through an inter-American committee could help to reduce United States control over the disbursal of assistance funds yet maintain some of the United States pressure on them that they needed. For the United States, the committee could set and enforce performance standards. This would relieve Washington of the uncomfortable roles of auditor and overseer that would otherwise be unavoidable for us as the principal financial contributor. A multilateral Alliance could also protect the United States from the charge that we were using economic aid as an instrument of political manipulation.

Since the United States and Latin America never fully agreed on Alliance objectives, however, bilateral aid remained a vital part of United States policy. And it was a persistent way to manipulate domestic politics in Latin America, as the experience with Brazil indicates. Brazil, the largest and most populous country in Latin America, had a federal form of government and relatively broad participation in its domestic politics. The defense of the status quo was maintained by a wide variety of political groups who benefited from the long-prevailing high rates of inflation. During 1961 the United States discreetly supported the Brazilian National Assembly's successful effort to clip the powers of new President Goulart when he seemed to be drifting to the left. Two years later, when Brazilian criticism of Goulart had declined and his constitutional powers had been restored, Washington provided $400 million in financial aid to help rescue the faltering financial structure of the Brazilian economy. Goulart, however, failed to cope with the mounting inflation, and the United States canceled its assistance. The cancellation conformed to the Kennedy approach in economic assistance: setting and enforcing performance standards. But our action also amounted to using economic aid for political manipulation—the very thing the Kennedy economic assistance program was supposed to avoid.

Had Washington been willing to risk Brazil's failure, it could have restricted its role to the enforcement of performance criteria. But "playing it cool" was difficult for the Kennedy Administration where the United States was actually involved. Concerned about political developments in Brazil, the Kennedy Administration had used economic aid first to discourage, then to encourage, and finally to penalize the Goulart government. With the fate of Brazil at stake, American officials were not content merely to await performance and enforce standards.

The first years of the Alliance saw a noticeable drift toward the right in Latin American politics. The military intervened in the politics of Argentina, Ecuador, and Peru in 1962, and in Guatemala, the Dominican Republic, and Honduras in 1963. Military intervention does not necessarily lead to the establishment of dictatorships—in Latin America, as elsewhere, the military have often played a stabilizing role in national politics. But military intervention did hamper the Alliance objective of democratic development in these nations.

CONCLUSION

Kennedy, like Eisenhower, came to the Presidency apparently determined to make major revisions in foreign and domestic policies. Unlike Eisenhower, he was prepared to use to the fullest the power and status of the Presidency to accomplish his goals. He increased United States military flexibility and military expenditures in an effort to get away from the stark choice between massive retaliation and surrender that he identified with the strategy of the

Eisenhower Administration. He modified the clichés of the Cold War by relying less heavily on the Communist threat to justify foreign programs and actions than either Eisenhower or Truman had, and he dealt with the developing nations more in terms of their own needs and less in terms of their place in the bipolar conflict. Finally, Kennedy talked with rare candor about the limits of American nuclear power. Because American strategic power could not be invincible, reasoned Kennedy, it would be to our advantage to stabilize the balance of terror. He worked to reach accommodations with the Soviet Union about strategic forces and about geographically remote areas, such as Africa, where the interests of both great powers were peripheral. In both efforts Kennedy was reacting against the rigidities that he and other critics had attributed to the Eisenhower Administration. And in all Kennedy's attempts at change he demonstrated an unusual capacity to articulate and publicize public issues.

Kennedy's style in foreign policy was to dramatize to the public the seriousness of the predicaments he was attempting to address. He treated the Berlin crisis this way throughout most of 1961, and during the following two years he made similar appeals, notably during the Cuban missile crisis. In effect, he appealed to the public to "rally 'round" the President without worrying about details—an appeal that was equivalent to Eisenhower's and Dulles' use of Cold War rhetoric to win general public support for foreign policy. But by diminishing the use of Cold War rhetoric Kennedy diminished the onus attached to negotiating with the Soviet Union. In fact the test ban negotiations demonstrated that negotiating with the Russians could actually be converted into a political asset at home.

In appraising the Kennedy Administration's conduct of foreign policy, the main difficulty lies in the disparity between the extraordinary articulation of policy that preceded every attempted change and the Administration's actual performance. After all the fanfare that preceded the Alliance for Progress, for example, this program came to look like a rather ordinary (and not very successful) effort to deal with the very persistent problems of political and economic development in Latin America.

The disparity between policy explanations and actual performance would come to assume tragic dimensions in Vietnam. The Kennedy Administration, after energetic efforts to gain Soviet agreement on neutralizing Laos, inched into deeper commitments in Vietnam. Kennedy then left to President Johnson the stark choice between propping up the shaky junta that succeeded Diem or letting the political situation in South Vietnam deteriorate into irredeemable chaos. However one resolves the puzzle between American extrication in Laos and implication in Vietnam, the latter casts a shadow across the foreign policy achievements of the Kennedy Administration.

More generally, the optimism of the Kennedy Administration about its capacity to govern and about the potential of the United States for international leadership predisposed the Kennedy men toward activism in foreign relations. The question "Where do our priorities lie in foreign relations?" had rarely been dealt with seriously in American public life, and never in a sustained and systematic way. The Kennedy Administration came to power after several years of criticizing the Eisenhower Administration for its emphasis on military alliances, its reluctance to indulge in summit diplomacy, its neglect of areas of secondary importance to the United States such as Latin America and Africa, and its apparent general complacence. These deficiencies appeared amenable to ready correction. Kennedy improved diplomatic representation for the new African states, started "a decade of development" for Latin America, met Khrushchev in Vienna, and increased defense expenditures— but to what purpose? The Cold War rationale had begun to unravel, but the Kennedy Administration offered nothing in its place.

Probably the major constraint on both ideological and policy changes was the problem of generating domestic political support for American foreign relations, which had not changed appreciably since the Truman era. As noted in Chapters 2 and 3, the rigid framework of anti-Communism and bipolarity was used heavily by the Truman Administration in order to justify to Congress and the public its foreign, military, and economic aid policies. The Kennedy Administration, by its own assessment, was driven by the same forces that had so preoccupied the Truman officials.

For several reasons Kennedy worried about the gap between what he believed the United States should do in foreign affairs and what the American public would support. He had come to office on a narrow electoral margin, he had a large appetite for foreign achievement, he was politically vulnerable to right-wing critics, and the general conditions of American politics had not changed since the late forties. Accordingly, Kennedy's style of public arousal through dramatic crises in foreign policy was reminiscent of Truman. The politics of public opinion mobilization helped to generate support for Kennedy's policies.

In the early sixties, as the late forties, much of the attention of the highest officials of the United States government seems to have been directed toward the attainment of domestic political support and consent for foreign policies, with too little attention given to priorities and to what the special role should be of the United States, given the Administration's perception of America's power and leadership status. Kennedy preserved these domestic chains of the Cold War left from the forties. Thus, the worst features of the Kennedy Administration—the Bay of Pigs and the beginnings of the Vietnam involvement—occurred out of concern with public reactions to foreign policy outcomes. Kennedy, in explaining his efforts to shore up the South Vietnamese, stated: "Strongly in our mind is what happened in the case of China at the end of World War II when China was lost. . . . We don't want that."[18]

The optimism of Kennedy officials produced several other serious shortcomings. In the first months of the Kennedy Administration, Khrushchev had declared that "wars of national liberation" were a legitimate form of political change that his government supported. Khrushchev's statement originated in Peking's challenge in the developing states to Moscow's worldwide leadership of the Communist movement. The term "wars of national liberation" was read in Washington to mean Soviet-sponsored insurrection. To deal with this challenge, the Kennedy Administration encouraged the development of innovative doctrines, tactics, equipment, and forces (such as the Army's Special Forces). The resulting innovations were mediocre. The main outcome was an increased inclination to intervene in complex and unknown local political situations, principally in Indochina. Oddly, the same Administration that set a precedent by sending as ambassador to Japan a leading American scholar of Japanese culture, Harvard historian Edwin O. Reischauer, sent special forces and military advisers to Vietnam and Thailand who were

---

[18] Department of State *Bulletin* (June 8, 1964), p. 890.

only superficially prepared to cope with local culture and conditions.

In a similar vein, the Kennedy Administration cultivated relations with leftist Social Democratic parties in Europe and Latin America to demonstrate American acceptance of variations in democratic institutions; yet we developed a defense posture that was insensitive and even hostile to the national aspirations and domestic political interests of other NATO members as reflected in their military policies and priorities. The main clash here, as noted, was with De Gaulle's France, for De Gaulle used military strategy and defense policies as an important element in his successful efforts to reestablish the viability of the French regime. Dulles' insensitivity to French national aspirations were succeeded by the policies of an equally insensitive Kennedy Administration, intent upon promoting NATO Alliance policies made unilaterally in Washington.

Dulles had been intolerant of "neutralist" states. Democratic critics had scored the Eisenhower Administration heavily on this point; yet they adopted an equivalent rigidity in their highly developed, highly coherent, and highly American military alliance policies.

In sum, the Kennedy Administration was unable to transcend the internal political constraints that kept America trapped in Cold War rhetoric and behavior; it failed to develop a diplomacy that recognized the legitimate political-military interests of other states; it failed to establish enforceable criteria for caution and selectivity in choosing areas for local intervention; and it failed to recognize the complex political dimensions of the Communist world. For all the apparent change and for all the innovations in the way Kennedy governed foreign affairs, the output from Kennedy's Administration remained remarkably unaltered from the Truman and Eisenhower eras.

chapter 8

Johnson's Foreign Policies: Europe, Latin America, and the Shadow of China

Lyndon B. Johnson was fifty-five when he took the oath as President of the United States in his native Texas on November 23, 1963, following President Kennedy's assassination in Dallas. Johnson had been a Congressman for twelve years, a Senator for fourteen years, and Vice President for nearly three. He had risen to prominence as a remarkably able Senate majority leader for six years and had gone to the 1960 Democratic convention as a major presidential contender. Johnson's search for delegate strength had been confined to the party regulars, while Kennedy had proceeded to demonstrate in several state presidential primaries that he had strong popular appeal. After Kennedy won the Democratic nomination on the first ballot he picked Johnson as his running mate. Johnson balanced the ticket, helped unite the party, and carried crucial Southern states in the election. When Kennedy's death made Johnson President, he had established an impressive record as legislative and sectional leader, but he had not yet become an important *national* figure.

Franklin D. Roosevelt's Presidency fascinated Johnson as well as Kennedy. It was Roosevelt's innovative spirit and his management of presidential power that appealed to Kennedy. It was

Roosevelt's success in aggregating broad political support and winning consensus that attracted Johnson. While President himself, Johnson became nearly obsessed with consensus and with Vietnam.

Johnson's early success in politics had come from identifying with Roosevelt's New Deal. Switching from a congressional constituency to the statewide Senate constituency in Texas, Johnson had moved to the right politically, winning support from the money and power of Texas business. When his status in the Senate and in national politics rose, he moved back toward the social values he had supported in the thirties. In identifying with Kennedy's program, Johnson was not only carrying out the Vice President's role but was also reasserting the goals of his early political years and adapting to a national constituency, much as Roosevelt had adapted his personal background to the constituencies of New York State and then national politics. Johnson in these later years was a "swash-buckling master of the political midstream."[1]

It fit Johnson's own goals to identify with the Kennedy record in establishing the continuity of the Presidency after Kennedy's assassination. In his first speech to Congress on November 27, 1963, in the leaden atmosphere of grief over Kennedy's death, Johnson drew upon Kennedy's political legacy: "No memorial oration or eulogy," he said, after reminding Congress of his own record in supporting civil rights measures in 1957 and 1960, "could more eloquently honor President Kennedy's memory than the earliest possible passage of the civil rights bill for which he fought." A few weeks later, in his State of the Union message in January 1964, Johnson announced his determination to wage a "war on poverty." In May of that year, during the presidential campaign, he was to state his major aspirations for domestic welfare efforts to achieve what he called "the Great Society."

Johnson at first kept Kennedy's major Cabinet appointees and even Kennedy's White House staff. He also made Kennedy's ambitious legislative program his own. Kennedy had laid the groundwork for the legislation's passage, but the program was stalled in Congress when he died. With a month left in the first session of the 88th Congress, Johnson pushed through the appropriations bills

---

[1] Philip Geyelin, *Lyndon B. Johnson and the World* (New York: Praeger, 1966), p. 15.

and a badly tattered foreign aid bill. He failed to win approval of a civil rights bill, but he demonstrated his interest in that objective.

In 1964, Johnson would go on to establish a brilliant legislative record, and on August 19 he could declare:

> This has been a year without precedent in the history of relations between the Executive and the Legislative branches of our government. This session has enacted more major legislation, met more national needs, disposed of more national issues than any other session of this century or the last.

During the next two years Congress was to approve new medical aid programs, aid to education, voting rights legislation, reformed immigration laws, a higher minimum wage law, an extension of the War on Poverty, and a new program to counter urban blight.

In foreign affairs, as in domestic affairs, Johnson's main goal on taking office was to maintain continuity with the Kennedy policies. The prospects for success in the areas central to American interests, however, appeared less encouraging than at home. The Alliance for Progress was lagging. Laos represented a well-publicized stabilization of Soviet-American affairs, but next door Vietnam was becoming a growing drain on American resources. NATO had become bogged down with the Multilateral Force (MLF) and its implications for nuclear war, and Western Europe was harkening to De Gaulle's nationalism. Kennedy's work for détente with the Soviet Union had produced a test ban treaty, but it had also resulted in compensatory congressional restrictions on trade with and aid to the Iron Curtain countries.

Vietnam would ultimately affect all these issues, dominating Johnson's foreign policy. At the beginning of his Administration in 1963, however, other matters appeared to be more important than Vietnam. The Kennedy legacy in Western Europe and Latin America seemed particularly important.

STANDING BY IN WESTERN EUROPE

The principal business pending with Europe in late 1963 consisted of the MLF and the so-called Kennedy Round of trade negotiations. Trade relations had been in intermittent negotiation since the Trade Expansion Act of 1962. The United States sought better access for its exports to the Common Market in return for lowered trade barriers to American markets. More generally, it sought an "outward looking" European trading system—one that would enlarge the scope of the original Common Market to include Britain in particular. The 1962 Trade Expansion Act had been drafted on the assumption that the United States would negotiate mutual tariff reductions with a single trade area in Europe. However, in January 1963 France had broken off negotiations of the Common Market countries with Britain concerning her entrance into the market. For the next five years the British government continued trying to gain entrance to the Common Market, and France continued to exclude her.

Similarly, France opposed the development of the MLF. Johnson stayed the hands of the MLF enthusiasts when he became President but came out supporting it fully by April 1964. By November Washington and Bonn could announce a new military accord that seemed to clinch the German commitment to the MLF and assure support from other West European governments, if only to prevent the formation of a German-American bilateral nuclear force. French participation would not be essential. De Gaulle, however, threatened to withdraw from the Common Market and to deny French cooperation in attaining European unity if Bonn did not accede to France's agricultural trade demands and abandon the MLF. De Gaulle had touched raw nerves. In West German politics European unity meant German reunification, and taking France out of the Common Market would also hurt the German economy seriously. (Withdrawal would have hurt the French economy too, but it was in better order than Germany's.) Bonn wavered. Johnson pulled back on the MLF in December 1964, leaving the burden of finding a solution to the Europeans.

At the same time McNamara supplied the opening for a solution. Europe could rely on American nuclear protection, he told the NATO Council. Forty percent of the American nuclear stockpile was either in West Germany or allocated to the defense of Europe. Their planned targeting, he claimed, would effectively prevent the United States from defending itself without defending Europe as well. In an earlier effort to reassure the other NATO members, the United States had already invited NATO observers to take up posts at Strategic Air Command (SAC) headquarters in Omaha, which they had done. Now McNamara proposed a select committee to participate in the operational planning for American strategic nuclear forces in NATO. The sharing of American information and staff roles with other NATO members was intended to deflect allied demands away from sharing in the command of nuclear forces toward support for an integrated, common nuclear force instead.

Arrangements for the select committee proceeded while De Gaulle withdrew French land and air forces from all NATO commands (as he had already done with French naval forces). When Bonn questioned the status of the French forces remaining in West Germany under national rather than NATO command De Gaulle coldly stared Bonn down: did Bonn want French forces there or not? The answer was yes. France was still a member of NATO but no longer a participant. In March 1966 France informed her allies that they had one year to remove themselves and their headquarters from French territory. During 1967 NATO headquarters moved to Belgium.

Both the MLF and the new information sharing and planning procedures were marginal to the main course of American foreign policy. Neither one required much change in Washington's co-operation with other countries in deploying and controlling nuclear weapons or in generating strategic plans and doctrines. American alliance policy remained dominated by the inner logic of American strategic doctrine, which stressed the unilateral American control of all nuclear capabilities in NATO.

Johnson's withdrawal of support for the MLF could be taken as a blow to supranationalism in Europe. But the MLF was not a sound building block for European integration in the mid-sixties. With the declining sense of Soviet military threat, military integration in Western Europe hardly carried the value that it had during the Korean war.

Encouraging commercial and political links with *Eastern* Europe, by contrast, would have allowed Johnson to soften the division of Europe between the North Atlantic and Warsaw pacts and thus to outflank De Gaulle in his appeal for a Europe "from the Atlantic to the Urals." Johnson had raised that prospect in his State of the Union message in January 1965, and he made some preparations to pursue the linking of Eastern and Western Europe as an important aspect of American policy. Yet, as his attention increasingly riveted on Southeast Asia, these efforts became a silent casualty of the war.

In 1965 De Gaulle extended his boycott of the Common Market to block the further development of other supranational economic institutions in Europe. (He forestalled, for example, the consolidation under a single executive office of the Coal and Steel Community, EURATOM, and the Common Market.) Challenging the trend toward European integration meant challenging objectives that Washington had supported for twenty years. De Gaulle also challenged the American presence in Europe and American policies elsewhere, particularly in Vietnam. In January 1964 France recognized Communist China, enhancing Peking's prestige at a time of increasing American involvement in Vietnam.

Washington used De Gaulle's behavior in the sixties as the main explanation of the fissile tendencies evident in NATO. In fact, however, other factors contributed to these tendencies as well: the national aspirations of the other European NATO members were making them increasingly independent, as De Gaulle sensed, and after 1963 the United States turned its attention increasingly to Vietnam. De Gaulle was thus a significant symptom of Western Europe's malaise, particularly in relations with the United States.

Some accommodations with De Gaulle were worked out nonetheless. For example, early in 1966 the French boycott of the economic community stopped when the machinery of the community was changed to meet De Gaulle's criticism. The new arrangements permitted economic integration to proceed toward a confederation that would allow for more national independence. It was also possible to gain agreement on other difficult issues once the effort to win De Gaulle's consent was abandoned. For example, in December 1967 the NATO ministers (without the presence of a French delegation) ratified the American strategy of a flexible military response.

Few initiatives were being taken in European affairs in 1966 and 1967, and De Gaulle's behavior was not the only reason for this. The war in Vietnam distracted the United States from changing the political structure of Europe and strained America's relations both with her European allies and with Russia, thus making attempts at political change more difficult for both the East and West.

Any distraction of American interests from Europe was likely to cause difficulties with our European allies, if only because their interests received less attention from us. But Vietnam in fact caused less antagonism from European governments than had the Korean war (despite intensely hostile public demonstrations against Vietnam from certain opinion groups). Official patience in Europe over Vietnam reflected the changed world conditions since the Korean war. Russia seemed less of a threat in the early sixties than in the early fifties; almost no one feared that Russia would escalate the Vietnam war, while in 1950 many Europeans had shared Washington's view that Korea marked a new phase of Soviet belligerence. Europe, moreover, was stronger and less dependent on the United States than it had been in the fifties, and the Soviet bloc more divided than in 1950.

There were advantages to this situation for the United States. For example, our European allies largely avoided public criticism of our Vietnam involvement in the mid-sixties (if one ignored De Gaulle), though its absence was not evidence of European support for the Vietnam war. Their criticisms of American conduct of the Korean war had reflected their nervousness in trying to influence a sponsor whose patronage was indispensable. In the mid-sixties the silence of Europeans indicated their interest in getting along with the United States while not being highly dependent upon us.

THE ALLIANCE FOR PROGRESS AFTER KENNEDY

Kennedy's Alliance for Progress, as we saw, had already lost some luster by the time he died. Many of its difficulties were inherent in the politics of development. The slow pace of appropriations bills in Congress during 1963 had added to Latin American anxieties. Sharp congressional reductions in foreign aid funds had not spared the Alliance in 1962 or 1963. The $850 million Kennedy requested in January 1963 had diminished to $590 million in the final version of the bill Johnson pressed through Congress after the assassination.

Under Johnson a definite shift in tone occurred in the Alliance. Johnson appointed Thomas C. Mann as Assistant Secretary of State for Inter-American Affairs and put in his hands responsibility for economic aid as well as diplomatic tasks. Kennedy had promoted a program of economic assistance by surrounding it with a mystique of social and political development along democratic lines. Mann neglected the mystique, turning instead to an older theme: nonintervention by the United States in Latin American domestic affairs. The change of tone upset both United States and Latin American liberals. They had become disillusioned with the nonintervention doctrine, seeing it as a defense of the status quo.

In March 1964, just as a dispute over these changes began to sharpen, Brazil's President Goulart fell to a military coup. The Brazilian Army abandoned long-observed standards of constitutional restraint to establish a caretaker government under General Castello Branco that initiated a program of social, economic, administrative, and political reform and tried to stop Brazil's galloping inflation.

But to do so the new regime deliberately suppressed democracy and postponed political activity until it could complete the structural changes in Brazil's economy and policy that it considered essential. Local political activity resumed in 1968, but a decade after the coup, Brazil continued to be ruled by its caretaker military elite.

The coup was designed to wipe out chaos as much as Communism, though Washington found it convenient to emphasize that the military takeover had forestalled Brazil's drift toward Communism. The United States became a strong sponsor of the new regime, expecting it to carry out major economic and political reforms that had eluded governments based more on popular support. And to some extent it did. Alas, however, when it fell short of its goals, Washington's stake in its success made it difficult to withhold economic assistance as an inducement for satisfactory economic performance, as the United States had done with Goulart earlier. Not until 1968, after four years of close identification and economic support for the new order in Brazil, did Washington draw back to a more normal distance.

Washington's strong support of the military regime in Brazil made the democratic development issue more muddled than before: Kennedy had held out the prospect of economic *and* democratic development; Mann, under Johnson, insisted that economic development might require the sacrifice of democratic development.

Kennedy's view about the developing countries proved too optimistic for the sixties. No country had yet matched the most impressive model of economic development in this century, created in the Soviet Union and carried out from 1920 to 1950 under highly authoritarian rule. In the 1960s other states with authoritarian regimes made notable strides in economic growth beside Brazil—France under De Gaulle, Pakistan under General Mohammed Ayub Khan, Iran under the Reza Shah, and Korea under Park. In each case, the regime suppressed political factionalism and political activity in favor of a more stable and expanding economy.

Social unrest and insurrection persisted in Latin America, sometimes representing a driving force for reform and sometimes against it. In September 1964 Chile elected Eduardo Frei President by a large majority. A Christian Democrat, Frei pledged "a profound revolution within liberty and law." He quickly emerged as a leading spokesman for democratic change in Latin America, without posing the value conflicts between democratic politics and economic change that Castello Branco represented in Brazil.

Latin American reformers and oligarchs alike continued to be plagued by Castroism. Cuba had become a rallying point and a training center for radical revolutionaries, and a source of colorful revolutionary propaganda—mainly romantic and/or leftist-Marxist (such as Ernesto "Ché" Guevara). Since Marxist concepts and rhetoric have been widely used in Latin American economic and political writings of every complexion, the propaganda from Cuba reached a wide though often skeptical audience.

The United States led the effort to isolate Cuba diplomatically and economically, often with only grudging cooperation or public noncooperation from regimes eager to avoid antagonizing their own leftist political groups. The Caribbean, however, provided Johnson with an even less auspicious occasion to seek Latin American cooperation when the Administration needed to be extricated from its intervention in the internal politics of the Dominican Republic. A left-wing military group seized control there in April 1965, deposing the Cabral regime, which had ruled in Santo Domingo since its military coup in 1963. The new regime proposed to restore to leadership Juan Bosch, the constitutionally elected President who was then in exile. A countercoup led by a general of narrow perspective, Wessin-y-Wessin, moved against the pro-Bosch group, which was now in jeopardy. The latter asked for American assistance but were denied help on the grounds that the United States ought not to intervene in an internal matter.

Within hours, however, the tide had turned. The Wessin-y-Wessin faction now asked in writing for the aid of United States troops. Washington denied the request by specifying that the United States would intervene only if American lives were in danger. The Wessin-y-Wessin faction promptly disclaimed responsibility for American lives and property, the United States ambassador requested United States troops, and Johnson, after agonizing over the issues for a few hours, sent in troops and notified Congress, the Organization of American States, and the American public of his action.

Johnson justified his intervention at first as necessary to rescue and protect United States and other non-Dominican citizens. In fact our intervention helped the Wessin-y-Wessin faction by separating the combatants. It soon became evident that President Johnson had acted out of undue fear of another radical revolution like Castro's in Cuba, based on exaggerated reports from the United States Embassay in Santo Domingo of threats to the lives of United States citizens and reports of a Communist menace. Johnson's anxieties may have been real, but they were misplaced. Critics charged that he had set the clock back thirty years in American relations with Latin America. As more facts about the intervention became available, it became apparent that Johnson had fabricated his explanation for it.

The United States now found itself in a situation comparable to the Lebanese crisis. Its forces stood between two national factions, and it was virtually impossible not to favor one side or the other. Washington wanted our disengagement. It turned first to the OAS, obtaining endorsement for United States forces as peacekeepers and receiving help from the OAS, principally from Brazilian troops. A coalition government was painfully put together and the peacekeeping force phased out. Eight thousand peacekeepers lingered on, but the United States had extricated itself. A Dominican national election in 1966 brought a competent moderate to the Presidency; Bosch accepted electoral defeat and soon retired to Spain. The Johnson Administration made amends by promising to give preference to democratic over nondemocratic governments and promising the Dominican Republic additional economic aid. But Mann's initial doctrine of nonintervention lay in shambles.

By 1966 the mystique of the Alliance and the level of American economic aid had diminished, and Congress was again reluctant about foreign aid. The Administration shifted its emphasis in Latin America back to the private sector—trade and business development. In Washington the new stance looked like a return to the Eisenhower era. For Latin America, however, there was no turning back from expectations aroused by the Alliance. At a Panama meeting of the OAS in the spring of 1966 Latin American representatives demanded formal United States commitments to pay higher prices for their principal export products—in effect, United States subsidies for Latin American products—in recognition of the claim that raw material producers were at a disadvantage in the international markets. Just as the United States resisted European efforts to tie its nuclear arm to NATO, the Johnson Administration withstood Latin American pressures for subsidies and countered with a drive for Latin American economic integration instead. This shift in policy was a distinct departure from Kennedy's Alliance. Comparable changes in American posture occurred in other regions as Washington sought to draw back on its other external commitments in order to cope with Vietnam.

Integration and regional interdependence were goals of American foreign policy dating back to World War II. They were the main objectives of the Marshall Plan and others like it. The shift that occurred in American foreign policy during the mid-sixties challenged these goals. The Johnson Administration began a new disengagement from our allies and new efforts to reduce their dependence on the United States. In the 1970s this disengagement would become the Nixon Doctrine and serve as an impetus for new friendship with Peking and Moscow.

CHINA AND THE PEACE OF ASIA

There was a good deal of the affected quality of the "good neighbor" in the Alliance for Progress as well as some genuine acceptance of Latin American and other countries as simply different from the United States and less developed. Yet during the first half of the sixties Americans had a growing vision of the special power (and sometimes the morality) of their country in the world. The United States economy leapt forward in the early sixties while economic growth rates in Europe declined and the Soviet Union appeared to be more and more plagued with the common problems of sustaining growth and meeting increased demands for domestic consumption. By the late sixties, moreover, Eastern Europe's unity could no longer be taken for granted.

Johnson became President at a time when the disunity of Western Europe was growing and De Gaulle's vision of a united Eastern and Western Europe was gaining ground with the growth of trade through the thinning Iron Curtain. In 1966 Johnson launched a program designed to open contacts with Eastern Europe, following up Kennedy's Test Ban Treaty and his wheat deal with the Soviet Union. But, like other potential initiatives, overtures to the East remained undeveloped because of the Administration's preoccupation with Vietnam.

The United States remained preeminent as a world power; and the Soviet Union and the United States remained the major nuclear and world powers. Other nuclear powers (such as Britain and France) and other economic powers (such as West Germany, Japan, Britain, and France) stood well back from the two superpowers. The Soviet Union and the United States, partly through their special nuclear power relationship, shared certain interests not always harmonious with those of their respective allies. Kennedy and Johnson had both asserted the special relationship between the United States and Russia by reopening Soviet-American negotiations despite West Germany's fear of an East-West settlement without Bonn's participation. In the mid- and late sixties a tacit Soviet-American accommodation seemed to be growing in Asia as well as Europe.

During the Korean war American relations with China had frozen into a persistent effort to isolate Peking diplomatically and to institute trade embargoes in order to undermine the technical and economic basis for China's military power. The diplomatic isolation had partially succeeded. Not only had the United States and some of her allies refused to establish diplomatic relations with Communist China, but Peking had been kept from membership in the United Nations. American attempts at economic isolation, however, did not succeed. By the late sixties, more than 70 percent of China's trade was with the non-Communist world.[2]

The problem of American relations with Communist China has been often a partisan issue, but the positions of the two major political parties have not been far apart. The Eisenhower Administration attached much value to the potential trouble that Taiwan could make for Peking. Yet it was Dulles who got Chiang Kai-shek to renounce his objective of invading the mainland in 1958. The Kennedy Administration, for all its resolve to recast the Cold War, did not begin to change the relationship between the United States and Communist China.

The Eisenhower Administration had developed an alliance structure for Asia that assumed China to be aggressively expansionist. In the mid-fifties China seemed on its way to becoming a major economic power. The plans for a "great leap forward," announced in 1957, seemed to confirm the impression of phenomenal Chinese development. But the image was inaccurate. By 1959 the Chinese economy was in a tailspin. Natural disasters, Soviet withdrawal of aid, bureaucratic problems, and economic mismanagement contributed to a major fiasco that changed the whole outlook for China's future. China's foreign trade did not return to its 1959 level until the late sixties.

Having split with Russia, Peking now claimed to be the true spokesman for Communist revolution. Her verbal belligerence sustained her aggressive image during a period of actual weakening in her aggressive capabilities. China's attack on India in 1962, although provoked by inept Indian behavior, appeared in some capitals—Washington among them—to demonstrate this belligerence. India's reaction was profound. China had been considered a friend; now it became the principal threat to Indian security. The United States sprang to India's aid. But our involvement led us to take a closer look at the Chinese threat, and we began to realize the limitations of Chinese power in South Asia. Gradually, New Delhi came to share the American view that the Chinese posed only a very limited direct military threat to India.

In October 1964, when the Test Ban Treaty was hardly more

---

[2] Edwin O. Reischauer, *Beyond Vietnam: The United States and Asia* (New York: Vintage, 1967), p. 167.

than a year old, China detonated her first nuclear device. In the next two years four more detonations occurred, and in June 1967 China tested a hydrogen bomb. The first detonation boosted China's reputation enormously with non-nuclear powers and made it very difficult for nuclear power aspirants—particularly India—to refrain from turning their own nuclear resources to the development of military weapons.

The Chinese detonations began when the United States was considering a heavy commitment to Vietnam. They added to the fear in Washington and elsewhere that escalating the American commitment—particularly by bombing North Vietnam (begun in February 1965)—would bring China directly into the Vietnam war. Making his own assessment of the risk, Johnson chose a steady increase in the American war involvement, which could have been halted if signs of dangerous reactions from China appeared. They did not, perhaps because of Chinese caution, perhaps because its Cultural Revolution was about to be launched.

The Chinese Cultural Revolution was a drastic program of reform that turned into an upheaval. It was undertaken by the old revolutionary leaders in the central government of Communist China to restore revolutionary enthusiasm and root out what they considered the increasingly harmful influence of technicians in the bureaucracy. The course of the factional infighting was difficult to follow in the West, but the dominant theme of the revolution was clear. It was xenophobic and ideological, evidently resisting trends toward a Communist technocracy that had long been evident in the Soviet Union. In effect, the Cultural Revolution became an internalization of the ideological conflict with the Soviet Union.

All indications were that the revolution would cost the Chinese government a high price in future economic development. It was causing substantial civil chaos and evidently the crushing of personal initiative in the administrative apparatus of China. A whole generation of technicians lost a year of their education. Another target of the Maoist reformist faction was the professional military. Apparently reluctant to increase dependence on its own military wing, Peking is reported to have notified the United States through indirect diplomatic channels that it would not intervene in Vietnam provided the United States did not invade China or North Vietnam or bomb the Red River dikes in North Vietnam. The

United States was reported to have replied that we had no intention of attacking these areas. Following this exchange, war talk in Peking died down.[3]

The Chinese nuclear detonations had given impetus to negotiations for a treaty to prevent the spread of nuclear weapons to states that did not already have them. The nuclear powers pursued the treaty out of mixed motives. The Soviet Union wanted to keep Germany from gaining control of nuclear arms, and she also used the negotiations to divide NATO members through their fears of German military power. Within its own bloc, Moscow could use this fear of Germany to rally Eastern Europe and turn these countries against Communist China's nuclear aspirations. From Washington's viewpoint a nonproliferation treaty would isolate France and Communist China, the newest nuclear powers, and reduce the likelihood that India, Israel, Sweden, and other states would acquire nuclear weapons. In June 1968 the United Nations General Assembly approved a nonproliferation treaty that the Soviet Union and the United States had drafted. France and several nuclear-aspirant powers did not vote for approval, but the heavy majority favoring the treaty assumed that it would bring strong pressure against new national nuclear weapons programs.

China's growing nuclear power also led to an important new phase in the arms race—the decision in Washington to build a "thin" defense system against nuclear-tipped missiles (a so-called antiballistic missile system—ABM). McNamara had long delayed this decision because of the system's limited capability. But with ABM capabilities gradually improving, with the Russians apparently deploying a thin ABM system of their own, and with considerable pressure in Washington not to hold back any longer, he acceded. The thin ABM, he explained, was intended to eliminate the possibility that the Chinese could coerce the United States with nuclear threats. It was not meant to protect American cities from a Soviet attack. But the ABM decision raised the prospect of a new generation of weapons on both sides.

The nations on the periphery of China manifested mixed developments and expectations in the late sixties. South Korea's econ-

[3] Diplomatic exchange reported in *U.S. News and World Report,* January 15, 1966.

omy was booming, while its rulers became more authoritarian. The Philippine economy was chaotic, and its political system was showing signs of disintegration. The Philippines were (except for a rural insurgency that had been contained in the fifties) only now in the first stages of anticolonial agitation against their strong ties to the United States economy.

Indonesia had been rescued from a Communist takeover in 1965 by a military countercoup and was now being ruled by a Western-oriented military regime intent upon reform and national reconstruction. Although many prominent Indonesian military officers had received training in the United States, Washington kept somewhat aloof from Indonesia after the coup. The dramatic shift of Indonesia from a leftward drift to a Western orientation seemed to confirm the utility for Washington of a hands-off policy in Asia.

Similarly, when Pakistan attacked India in 1965 in the hope of seizing the disputed territory of Kashmir, Johnson cut off aid to both sides and delayed the resumption of economic assistance even in the face of famine in India. American officials recognized that the central government in India, chaotic and sometimes paralyzed, operated under many pressures. In 1966 Johnson used the threat of American economic cutbacks to get the Indian government to adopt tougher development policies. When economic aid was resumed that year, the precedent of the American cutoff and the conditions of resumption indicated that the Johnson Administration was willing to force responses from the Indian government—something the Kennedy Administration had not done.

The presence in Southeast Asia of Britain—the last of the European colonial powers—had gradually diminished. Britain scheduled the pullout of her remaining military forces in Hong Kong and Singapore first for 1972 and then for 1970.

Japanese power, on the other hand, had grown immensely. By 1967 Japan was the third industrial power in the world. Her gross national product was larger than that of all Latin America together. Her population growth was under control, her economic growth rate phenomenal, and she had stemmed a drift toward the left in the late fifties, which might have made Japanese politics vulnerable to Chinese Communist manipulation. Even the vexing issues raised by the Chinese nuclear weapon developments were calmly faced by Japan. By 1966 Japan had begun to assume a role as a regional power in Asia. Japan had to overcome the hostility generated by its aggressive policies of the thirties and early forties—and the memory of its brutal occupations throughout Southeast Asia. But Japan could rely on a residue of good will from the same period for eliminating European colonial rule in much of Asia. In the foreseeable future, Japan could be more powerful in international affairs than Communist China; and by assuming a greater role in Asia, Japan might reduce the pressures on Washington to counterbalance China on that continent.

CONCLUSION

The circumstances under which Johnson came to the Presidency heavily predisposed him to emphasize domestic programs at the beginning. Kennedy's legislative program was in the doldrums, and Johnson was confident of his ability to salvage it. Johnson needed continuity with the fallen President and was personally disposed toward domestic reforms anyway. In the first weeks of his Presidency, Johnson asked his Cabinet to avoid foreign crises—incidents that would draw public attention and require government action—so he could promote Kennedy's domestic legislative program. After winning his own electoral mandate in November 1964, his legislative success continued through 1965, only to be slowed down by growing political opposition to Vietnam and by the war's drain on our resources. But even with the slack years after 1965, Johnson's legislative record was impressive.

As a result, however, he was never able to give foreign policy the priority that it deserved. Kennedy had been able to turn his handling of foreign relations into a means for achieving the national standing that he needed. Johnson found a comparable vehicle in his extraction of domestic legislation from Congress. He may have intended to give greater priority to foreign relations later, as his legislative agenda was fulfilled, but when this time came he was in no position to take the initiative in foreign relations. Vietnam had pinned him down.

The secondary priority accorded foreign relations by Johnson meant that his promise as an international negotiator went untested. His Senate record showed that his grasp of political negotiations was extraordinary. Its potential transferability to foreign relations was suggested by Johnson's graceful deflation of the MLF project and other points of confrontation with De Gaulle. In particular, Johnson's promise as an innovative international negotiator might have been fulfilled by his pursuit of a détente with the Soviet Union. Kennedy had started a movement in that direction with the Test Ban Treaty, demonstrating that domestic political gains were possible from settling issues with the Soviet Union. As more of a cold warrior than Kennedy, Johnson was in a better position to retain the public's trust during such negotiations. His Administration had successfully carried through tortuous negotiations of terms for a treaty—with Moscow, our allies, and other United Nations members—to hinder the spread of nuclear weapons.

Johnson had planned to go further in exploring the common interests between the two nuclear superpowers and in promoting a reconciliation between East and West in Europe by "building [economic] bridges." What the outcome would have been had he continued to pursue these goals, however, must remain speculative. It is quite possible that if Johnson's negotiations with the Soviet Union had become prominent in American politics, he would have been hampered by his heavy-handed methods of winning public support. (His handling of Vietnam, covered in the next chapter, suggests this inference.)

Finally, our perspective on Johnson suffers from the aura that sprang up around President Kennedy's achievements after his death —particularly the Alliance for Progress. The change of tone in the Alliance that many observers throughout the hemisphere noted after Johnson took office had really begun before Kennedy died. As we saw in the last chapter, much of the Alliance's appeal lay in the accompanying rhetoric, and Johnson lacked the rhetorical style that had won sympathy and support for Kennedy among European, Asian, and Latin American leaders and intellectuals.

chapter 9

Vietnam
Defeats Johnson

GOLDWATER AND THE
1964 DEMOCRATIC LANDSLIDE

One cannot easily recapture the atmosphere of confidence in Johnson as a partisan political leader in 1964, looking back on his problems of the next four years. No incumbent except perhaps Eisenhower in 1956 enjoyed such a prospect of popular support.

The moderates of the Republican party had not coveted a presidential nomination in 1964 until it was too late. When Senator Barry Goldwater's success in the presidential primaries made him the Republican frontrunner, first New York Governor Nelson Rockefeller and then Pennsylvania Governor William Scranton tried in vain to head him off.

In the primaries Goldwater had made ill-considered extreme proposals that drew attention but limited his popularity. For example, he proposed dismantling some federal social welfare programs. He wanted to make social security assistance "voluntary." And he had suggested that not only the President but also the NATO Commander should have the right to order the firing of strategic nuclear weapons. He also revived some of the right-wing phrases that Eisenhower had buried—"rollback," "brinksmanship," "total victory"—and brought back a strong ideological version of the

Cold War. The rhetoric did not change when Goldwater became the Republican candidate. Goldwater had learned from Kennedy how to use presidential primaries to gain control of state party organizations, and through them, the national party. But Goldwater had failed to learn that it was necessary to unite his party after nomination in order to broaden his electoral appeal. His failure helped to assure Johnson's reelection.

In fact, Goldwater used the campaign to articulate the long-endured agony of right-wing Republicans, torn between militarism and libertarianism. "We must make clear that until [Communism's] goals of conquest are absolutely renounced and its relations with all nations tempered," Goldwater had declared in accepting the nomination, "Communism and the governments it controls are the enemies of every man on earth who is or wants to be free." He advocated militant assertions of American power, including the bombing of North Vietnam. Yet, predisposed against government action, Goldwater asked for an end to the draft and a 5 percent income tax cut in each of the next five years. His coupling of militant anti-Communism with opposition to government was not a credible combination for most voters. Goldwater thus left the political advantage wholly to Johnson.

As though oblivious to his own strong position, Johnson argued with a heavy hand for a moderate approach to foreign and domestic issues: "We don't want our American boys to do the fighting for Asian boys," Johnson declared at Eufala, Oklahoma, in late September, paraphrasing a famous campaign statement of Eisenhower's and echoing Roosevelt's campaign rhetoric from 1940. Two weeks before the election he told a university audience in Ohio: "There is only one road to peace and that is to work patiently, deliberately, wisely, step by step, year by year, never to become weary of the journey and irritated with folks who may not agree with you the first time you talk with them." Johnson took the high road—or seemed to—and won 61.4 percent of the popular vote in 1964. Some prominent Republican candidates refused to endorse Goldwater, partly to survive the surge of voting against him. Johnson carried thirty-eight more Democrats into the House of Representatives with him, giving Democrats more than a 2–1 ratio over Republicans. In the Senate, already Democratic by 2–1, the Republicans lost two more seats.

AFTERMATH OF THE ELECTION

It was a great political triumph, but an ephemeral one. Johnson had carefully manipulated the Vietnam issue to prevent a groundswell of public impatience against him and to amass an electoral landslide. But after the election, Johnson's response to events in Vietnam spread suspicions that he had misrepresented his intentions conspicuously during the campaign and misled the public through his moderate and reassuring statements about the war. Johnson himself nourished these suspicions by later remarking to at least one reporter that he had made up his mind to bomb the North as early as October 1964.[1] After the election, when he adopted a policy of escalating the war in Vietnam, he dissembled about it, and this dissembling became apparent. It eroded his credibility and his political following. To understand more of what happened, we must go back to Johnson's earliest Vietnam decisions.

When Johnson became President in November 1963, South Vietnam urgently needed a government that was stable and effective enough to cope with the insurgent threat. Kennedy had avoided giving prominence to the small but important role American military advisers and civilian officials had come to play in the Vietnam war during his Administration. As Vice President, Johnson had opposed military assistance to Vietnam and had recommended a major economic development program for the Mekong River basin—a conspicuously nonmilitary "solution" to Vietnam. He remained concerned about limiting American involvement in Indochina during his first year as President, yet became immersed in the urgent problem of keeping the Saigon regime afloat after the fall of Diem.

The main White House objective about Vietnam throughout 1964 was "keeping it quiet" for domestic reasons, according to one of Johnson's aides.[2] There was no assurance against events overriding that objective, however, and one event did—at least temporarily.

[1] Charles Roberts, *LBJ's Inner Circle* (New York: Delacorte Press, 1965), p. 20.

[2] Tom Wicker, *JFK and LBJ: The Influence of Personality on Politics* (New York: Morrow, 1968), p. 244.

In early August—three months before the election—small un-identified naval craft attacked an American destroyer on a recon-naissance mission in the Gulf of Tonkin that took it closer than usual to North Vietnam. Johnson's response was to order the Navy to destroy such attackers in the future. Two days later, when American naval forces in the Gulf reported new attacks, he ordered air raids against North Vietnam in retaliation, reinforced air and sea units in the Vietnam theater, and demanded that Congress authorize him to "take all necessary measures to repel any armed attacks against the forces of the United States and to prevent future aggression." Congress did so by passing the Tonkin Gulf Resolution of 1964. As Eisenhower had done in 1957 for his Middle East policy, Johnson used a crisis to induce Congress to endorse his Vietnam military policies, including future actions. The Tonkin Resolution, by winning bipartisan congressional endorsement for the most visible American military action to date in Vietnam, helped assure that Vietnam would not hurt Johnson in the 1964 election.

The controversy over the Tonkin Gulf incident came to occupy a special place in the criticism of Johnson's leadership. It was charged that as an excuse to escalate the war, Johnson fabricated the crisis by provoking a North Vietnamese attack or by misrepresenting the facts about it, or both. Rarely are the available data about a military event examined with as much diligence as Senate investigators did in this case, yet they neither established nor disposed of the charge of fabrication. However, other easily substantiated criticisms can be leveled over the Tonkin Gulf episode. The naval patrols asserted greater American participation in the war with their presence in a hitherto avoided area. They were a provocation to the North Vietnamese, though their presence would probably be considered justified to anyone who shared the Administration's objectives at that time. It should have been obvious that Hanoi might react with a naval attack. Given this potential for a hostile response, Johnson's military measures and his demand for a congressional resolution were all out of proportion to the event itself.

Even more fundamental economic problems were generated first by Johnson's early decisions about military preparedness and then by military escalation itself. In both periods, successful adjustments of the American economy depended on accurately anticipating the fiscal and economic consequences of military undertakings. The margin for error was small. Unlike circumstances at the beginning of both World War II and the Korean war, the Vietnam mobilization occurred when our economy was already operating close to optimum, while constrained by a weak balance of trade position in relationship to our major allies. Johnson in fact exceeded the small margin for error the situation allowed. First, he delayed too long in restricting fiscal policies to offset the increased government expenditures. As a result, inflation got under way. Then, over the next four years he consistently erred in planning the federal budgets by assuming that the war would not continue beyond the next fiscal year—this despite McNamara's Defense Department reforms that emphasized the importance of taking a serious five-year look ahead at the implications of any major defense budget decisions.

THE ESCALATION OF 1965

In his State of the Union message in January 1965 Johnson sketched the broad scope of his intentions now that he was President in his own right. Not even the ponderous imagery of the "Great Society" obscured his ambition to attack the major recognized social and economic problems of the day. He further intended to pursue rapprochement with the Soviet Union, and he apparently envisioned a wholesale transformation of the conflictive relationship underlying the Cold War. In both respects his message was a remarkable vision of the future. But his actions took him in quite a different direction. By summer of 1965 he had become committed to a major conventional military involvement in Vietnam on the mainland of Asia.

Two days before the 1964 election a Vietcong mortar attack had destroyed six B-57 bombers and killed five Americans at a South Vietnamese air base at Bien Hoa. Johnson did nothing. When a similar attack occurred at Pleiku in February 1965 he ordered air strikes against North Vietnam in retaliation and then continued them on a regular basis against a restricted set of targets. At the same time, McNamara announced a major expansion of the South

Vietnamese army and a small increase in the number of American advisers in Vietnam.

The bombing and the increased military assistance were insufficient to stabilize the beleaguered Saigon government. Anticipating American public opposition to another major commitment by us on the Asian mainland, Johnson apparently hoped to ride out criticisms by securing a dominant American military presence before the congressional elections in 1966—or at least before the 1968 presidential election.

The build-up of ground forces, like the air attacks, became incessant. In May 1965 American forces numbered 35,000; by September they totaled 130,000; by the end of the year, more than 180,000; by mid-1966, 270,000; by year's end, 380,000. In 1967 they increased another 100,000, and by mid-1968, another 60,000.

During the first months of the build-up the military effort reached a scale so large that Americans had to assume a major share of the fighting burden. As the build-up continued, the military performance of the South Vietnamese armed forces ceased to be vital. The extensive role that American military forces assumed in the war robbed Saigon's armed forces of the incentive to fight effectively. American economic assistance and civil government aid similarly reduced incentives for the South Vietnamese government to perform well. In fact, the Saigon regime's own special interests—at least in the short term—lay in keeping the Americans heavily involved in the war. Its major costs for the Vietnamese did not fall upon its governmental leaders; they benefited disproportionately from the immense resources that Washington poured into Vietnam.

American officials in Washington and Saigon agonized over this situation, but did not appreciably alter it. Evidently they expected to show Hanoi and the National Liberation Front (NFL), the political arm of the Vietcong southern units, that the United States was prepared to increase the engagement of its own vast military power until the insurgent conflict in Vietnam was stopped.

The escalation was by no means one-sided. An important phase in the escalation from the North began in 1964 when organized units of North Vietnamese regulars became the major manpower traffic southward. (They may have been encouraged by President Johnson's very moderate statements made in the months before the

1964 election.) The rate of infiltration from the North remained a matter of dispute. Despite heavy losses (according to American claims) the total number of North Vietnamese troops in the South continued to increase, sometimes faster than the United States build-up.

The size of the American ground force commitment eliminated the possibility that the Vietcong would win a military victory over the United States. Two other outcomes—both with grave implications for American interests—remained possible. First, even if overwhelming United States military strength could "defeat" the Vietcong, Washington could not provide a stable political order for South Vietnam. Unless the political situation improved considerably, the United States would face the difficult choice between a long and unpleasant occupation or a pullout that would lead to collapse of the South Vietnamese government.

Hanoi clung to the possibility that American losses in Vietnam and political pressures could force the United States to pull out, as the French had. Hanoi made no secret of these expectations. The North Vietnamese saw that Washington's demonstrations of resolve by escalation could easily be offset by signs of serious division at home about the war. The Johnson Administration was acutely aware that the vocal domestic criticisms of expanding United States air and ground operations were undermining the Administration's strategy of coercing Hanoi. Johnson in fact told his critics that they were comforting the enemy. His remarks added to their alienation from his Administration.

THE DOMESTIC IMPASSE OVER VIETNAM

Vietnam spelled trouble to any American politician with a memory of Korea. A continuing limited war inflicting United States casualties, requiring increased draft quotas, and producing daily newspaper reports and radio and television broadcasts penetrates public consciousness as nothing else does, while offering little gratification in return. Depicting the violence of war may encourage public resolve, but it also becomes frustrating and irritating as the coverage becomes monotonous and the goals remain unattained.

On a more personal level, even a limited war demands public attention when it threatens to involve family and friends in dangerous military service. Its electoral consequences for an incumbent government are gloomy. In a crisis, public opinion can be rallied by a vigorous response to a threat, as Kennedy showed with the Berlin crisis in 1961 and during the Cuban missile crisis in 1962. But a protracted threat, requiring a persistent and costly response, can be expected to produce wide dissatisfaction; and electoral dissatisfaction becomes a vote against the incumbent.

Doubtless the men of the Kennedy and Johnson Administrations knew that a protracted war in Vietnam would hurt them politically. Exactly a week after Johnson's election in 1964, McNamara's chief civilian assistant on Vietnam, John T. McNaughton, evaluated a proposal for cautious and limited escalation in Vietnam as "inherently likely to stretch out and to be subject to major pressures both within the United States and internationally. As we saw in Korea, an in-between course of action will always arouse a school of thought that believes things should be tackled quickly and conclusively."[3] McNaughton's deputy questioned whether such a limited military effort could be *"carried out in practice* under the klieg lights of democracy, in view of its requirement that we maintain a credible threat of major action while at the same time seeking to negotiate, even if quietly? . . . The parallel to Korea in 1951–53 is forbidding."[4]

The bombing of North Vietnam that began in February 1965 reduced Johnson's opposition on the right, but it opened a large fissure within his own party. The peace wing of the Democratic party became the chief opposition to Johnson on the war. Its main base was in Congress. Senator Frank Church of Idaho had dissented against American policy in Vietnam as early as the summer of 1963. In March 1964 Senator J. William Fulbright had attacked many popular Cold War tenets as "old myths." The temperate public response to Fulbright's speech invited Johnson to move away from the Cold War, but he did not accept the invitation. With a presidential election eight months away, moderating the frozen hos-

---

[3] *Senator Gravel Edition: The Pentagon Papers,* 4 vols. (Boston: Beacon Press, 1971), vol. 3, p. 617.

[4] *Ibid.,* p. 648. Underlining in original.

tility to China and Russia would raise issues that he was unwilling to face.

When the bombing of North Vietnam began a year later, fifteen Democratic Senators signed an appeal to Johnson to stop it; many more shared the view. A similar protest came from the House of Representatives. Much criticism rested on the argument that if the bombing stopped, Hanoi would negotiate. Johnson stopped bombing for eight days in May but resumed it when he concluded that Hanoi remained unwilling to negotiate. He coupled the resumption with another call for negotiations—"unconditional discussions"— as he put it. Hanoi refused, and a propaganda duel developed with both sides firing broadsides.

In mid-December United States forces made their first air strikes against major industrial targets near Haiphong. But the bombing failed to achieve Johnson's goals—to reduce the flow of supplies and men to the South and coerce Hanoi into a settlement. The flow continued, and Hanoi showed no interest in settling on any terms satisfactory to Johnson.

Johnson's preference for domestic consensus was also unsatisfied. By 1966 Johnson had alienated vital congressional supporters. Many resented his obvious manipulation of them in winning the Gulf of Tonkin Resolution and then escalating the war. Congressional leaders came to believe that Johnson had violated the trust that must underlie relations between the executive and legislative branches. In his efforts to cope with a public opinion that was expected to be hostile to the war, Johnson had lost the support of the men he knew how to handle best—his Senate colleagues.

THE LINK BETWEEN VIETNAM AND DOMESTIC ISSUES

A dissident core of activists had formed in this country during the fifties and early sixties on behalf of civil rights, drawing whites as well as blacks from the staffs and students of northern colleges, the clergy, the arts, and other sources. The civil rights movement recruited members for closely knit political activity and increasingly for political action. Vietnam and civil rights were issues that had been linked on the college campuses before 1965, but the bombing drew the two issues closer together. The humanitarian concerns of domestic affairs were now directed toward the victims of American bombing in North Vietnam.

The civil rights movement had developed methods of peaceful resistance in the mid-fifties as a means of legally challenging state and local laws in the federal courts. Its methods were initially non-violent, though in practice they needed to provoke government actions that could be challenged in the courts. But they did not always remain nonviolent, particularly under the provocation of white supremacists. Moreover, the civil rights movement generated a revolution of rising expectations among blacks that had helped produce explosive conditions in the black urban ghettos of the North by the early sixties. Demonstrations were peaceful there at first, too, but by 1963 they had become angry melees in which lives were lost. In the summer heat of 1965 violent anomic rioting burst out in the Watts section of Los Angeles, followed by riots in Washington, Baltimore, Chicago, and other cities during that and successive summers.

College students from northern campuses, applying what civil rights workers had learned in the South, attempted a more calculated program of nonviolent coercion. At Berkeley in 1964 students and nonstudents first demonstrated that a major university could be easily paralyzed. Direct action, in the tradition of the Abolitionists, became a familiar form of protest over the war and other issues. Draft cards were burned, marches and demonstrations staged, and public assemblies picketed and disrupted. Civil rights and the war in Vietnam had politicized the college student.

Johnson coped with his antiwar critics by agreeing to bombing pauses and by offering to negotiate. His offer, however, quickly became entangled in a nettle of issues. He was criticized for excluding from negotiations the National Liberation Front, which claimed political status in South Vietnam, for claiming he would negotiate "unconditionally" when he would not, and for changing the conditions he originally set for negotiations.

Johnson continued his plans for the Great Society; his executive budget for 1966 was an ambitious guns-and-butter program. But Vietnam cost him support in Congress. Legislators could hardly fail to honor his military requests for authority, men, and war materiel, but they could resist his domestic program—which they did. By 1967 he had considerably lowered his sights for domestic legislation and expenditures, and even then he encountered strong opposition on Capitol Hill. Nineteen sixty-five had been a vintage year for presidential programs in Congress; 1967 was a mediocre one, and 1968 no better.

For the first time in the twentieth century the United States was waging war under strong fiscal limitations. The Korean war rearmament had occurred when the United States was in a very strong balance of payments position, with a slack economy and modest consumer expectations. In that situation it was possible to allocate resources to the war and permit private consumption to grow without interruption (under price and monetary controls) while holding back public welfare programs only a little. By the late 1960s, however, all these conditions had changed. A balance of payments problem had persisted since 1958; any setback in the economy could be expected to aggravate it. Johnson had adopted Kennedy's objective of managing the national economy to induce a high rate of expansion; for all practical purposes, the economy had no slack, or reserve capacity, that could absorb an expanded military program. Finally, the public had been led to expect that federal spending power should and would be used to deal with a large agenda of domestic welfare problems. It might have been possible to meet the public's expectations about domestic programs without Vietnam, but the budget could not accommodate both.

The direct costs of the war rose rapidly in 1965 to more than $25 billion per year. Johnson's guns-and-butter assumptions that year had rested on a serious underestimation of the costs of the war and of the inflationary impact of defense spending. The Administration persistently assumed that the war would be over within six months. Also, the counter-inflationary measures—a squeeze on credit and a tax increase—came too late. As a result, the sustained attack on the American dollar grew to a crisis in the international money markets by the end of 1967. On New Year's Day 1968 President Johnson announced an emergency program to cope with it, including temporary mandatory controls on domestic investments abroad and an unprecedented plan for the control of a major source of dollar exports—American tourist expenditures abroad.

With diminishing congressional support for his Administration, Johnson was unable to gain approval for an income tax increase in 1967. He had already reduced his annual domestic budget requests for the second time. To gain the tax increase in 1968 he had to permit still deeper congressional slashes in domestic programs.

WHAT WENT WRONG?

Large-scale American intervention was to continue in Indochina for another five years—until 1973. The size of American ground forces began to decline during the Nixon Administration in early 1969 and continued steadily until only a small force remained by the time of the 1972 election. Their decline was somewhat offset by increased American naval and air operations and increased assistance in building up South Vietnam's forces. The costs of the war in human lives on both sides, in physical destruction to the countryside, and in the shattering of Vietnamese families and traditional culture would also continue to accumulate. But the main American involvement and escalation occurred during the Johnson Administration. How big a mistake was it? Why did it occur?

MISCALCULATIONS IN VIETNAM

Had American intervention in Vietnam achieved its avowed objectives, it is likely that few Americans would have been seriously dissatisfied. These objectives included ending the Vietcong insurgency in South Vietnam and the support of it from North Vietnam as well as establishing a viable Saigon regime. However, the failures of the United States in attempting to achieve these objectives, at significant human and financial costs, apparently forced many Americans to reconsider the appropriate role of this country abroad. The enthusiasm for supporting the United States as world policeman seems to have been destroyed for many Americans by the Vietnam debacle.

The mechanized American style of fighting wars wrought extensive damage to our Vietnamese "beneficiaries." High altitude carpet bombing, chemical defoliation, search-and-destroy area sweeps with ground force units, and free fire zones were relatively destructive and indiscriminate applications of war technology. The accumulating effects of these tactics on the populace—for example, the growing number of Vietnamese who had become homeless and landless—and the persistence of corruption and ineffectiveness in the Saigon regime suggest that American intervention was much worse for the South Vietnamese population than the extension of Hanoi's rule over South Vietnam would probably have been. Similar claims about the Korean war had drawn little attention. Once reconciled to a negotiated peace in Korea, Americans generally accepted its human costs—about which they had never been keenly aware—as necessary to discourage military aggression and contain the Communist bloc. The validity of this assumption had crumbled by the seventies. Considering the Sino-Soviet dispute and Hanoi's ability to conduct her foreign policies independently of close direction from Moscow or Peking, the expansion of North Vietnam's hegemony over all Vietnam would not be a victory for Communists everywhere. In fact, it might further reduce Communist-bloc unity by encouraging the type of nationalism among smaller Communist states that Tito's Yugoslavia had achieved.

In sum, Johnson's Vietnam policies exaggerated the connection between local political conflicts and the broader structure of international power, drew too stark and simple a picture of the bipolar world, and were overly resistant to political change in Asia and other third-world areas. These shortcomings in perception and interpretation, however, scarcely begin to explain Vietnam, for the officials of the Johnson Administration were generally aware of them. To explain why they did not fully credit them and failed to heed them will require probing deeper into the way government works.

THE CREDIBILITY GAP

The Johnson Administration suffered from several internal problems that made it difficult for it to evaluate what was happening in Vietnam. There was an appalling lack of knowledge within the government as to precisely what was happening there—what American and South Vietnamese operations were accomplishing, what the situation was on the other side, and so forth. This official ignorance and misperception had been exposed as early as 1962 by the journalists in Saigon. Symptoms of official errors were the numerous revisions of American military estimates and the inaccurate predictions that persisted through early 1968 about the course of the war. These symptoms had already created a credibility gap between government statements and information from other sources in Vietnam before the 1965 election. The gap widened as the Administration unconvincingly depicted its decisions to increase American commitments in Vietnam as dramatic responses to dramatic threats.

Inaccurate reporting within the government had plagued Kennedy as well as Johnson. The problem was closely linked to the difficulties of working through a client regime—particularly one dependent upon the United States for its very existence, as Saigon was. For Kennedy these difficulties were identified with Diem. For Johnson the problems shifted with the changes in the Saigon regime, settling eventually upon young military men of narrow perspective and experience. The most prominent of them was a Northerner, Marshal Nguyen Cao Ky, Premier in the military junta in 1966 and Vice President after the national election in 1967. During the American congressional election campaign in 1966 Ky publicly refused to negotiate with the National Liberation Front of the Vietcong and called for an invasion of North Vietnam. He argued that if this step did bring the Chinese into the fight it would be better to deal with them now than later. Ky's statement greatly embarrassed the Administration both at home and abroad. Under American pressure he backed away from that position. But his statement indicated a gulf in purpose between the United States and the client government of South Vietnam that persisted, much as the Formosa Straits crisis in 1958 had highlighted the differences between Nationalist Chinese and American purposes in dealing with Communist China.

Attempts to work with client governments in putting pressure on the enemy are risky ventures. In this case one objective had been to coerce Hanoi, but it was not clear how to coerce that regime or when it was coerced. It was therefore prudent for the military commanders to seek more resources—more troops and more fire power—in order to provide for more contingencies. Brawn thus became a substitute for brains; lacking any other solution, the American forces were expanded in the expectation that the sheer weight of military power would provide one. At the very least they could change the conflict from an insurgency to a conventional war, which they were better prepared to fight.

Johnson's behavior in other foreign policy matters added to the credibility problem already apparent by 1964. In April 1965, during the early stages of the build-up of American military strength in Vietnam, Johnson ordered American marines to intervene in a political crisis in the Dominican Republic. As explained in the last chapter, the intervention rapidly became an embarrassment to Johnson. In justifying the act he aggravated his credibility problems with the press and the public by claiming that the Dominican Republic was in danger of a Communist takeover from within—a statement later proved to be completely unfounded.

The credibility gap also widened because of real disagreements over facts about the war; in addition, instances of Cold War dissembling under previous administrations compounded public and congressional suspicions about the government. The official lie by the Eisenhower Administration in the 1960 U-2 crisis and the American-instigated Bay of Pigs invasion under Kennedy in 1961 had doubtless attracted the widest attention.

To answer the question "Who is to blame?" it is easy to make a case against President Johnson—as indeed it should be in the American constitutional system. He evidently became personally obsessed with the conduct of the war. To be more precise about his role, one can concentrate on his interaction with his staff. He inherited Kennedy's advisers. According to this view, they worked well for Kennedy but not for Johnson. Kennedy kept up an easy interchange with them that enabled him to examine issues thoroughly. He also bypassed them as needed, reaching down into the executive agencies. Johnson respected men like McGeorge Bundy, the Special Assistant for National Security, and Secretary of State Rusk, but he asserted his authority over them more than did Kennedy. With Johnson they were less inclined to disclose their misgivings about Vietnam. Furthermore they were still confident activists about foreign relations in general and Vietnam in particular and thus predisposed toward escalation and involvement.

One can help to explain our Vietnam involvement by watching Johnson with his advisers. One can explain it by other means as well. The director of the Pentagon Papers studies, Leslie Gelb, saw

Johnson "more as a captive than as a Commander."[5] Johnson's staff, civilian and military, according to this viewpoint, made him a captive of their own opinions. A common problem (one that had also been prominent during the stalemate of the Korean war) was the exchange of charges and antagonism between civilian and military leadership. For example, General Maxwell D. Taylor served President Kennedy first as a special military adviser, then as chairman of the Joint Chiefs of Staff, and still later as ambassador to Vietnam. Although assigned both civil and military roles in Washington and in Vietnam, Taylor could later write that the trouble with the war was the civilians. His view expressed the common frustration of military men with policy constraints on operations.

In turn, civilians such as Defense Department officials Townsend Hoopes and Chester Cooper noted that as the American war effort expanded, military operations took on a life of their own. This perception of military dominance also became exaggerated. In fact, civilian officials—Secretary McNamara was probably among them—tended to nourish the perception that in wartime military judgments prevailed because it was easier to gain acceptance for American wartime policies by emphasizing the prominence of the military in making them. A thorough explanation of the forces that generated our Vietnam involvement must include all these elements of the American governmental processes engaged in Vietnam.

Another explanation about Vietnam has emphasized the incremental nature of the decisions taken and the cumulative effect of our involvement. According to the "quagmire" theory, each successive American President who made decisions that increased our involvement in the Vietnam war considered our objectives to be limited. Faced with the continuing prospect that South Vietnam would lose, and resolved not to let that happen during *his* administration, each President took steps that involved the United States more and more in a war to save the Saigon regime. No one wanted to get in; but no President or presidential adviser wanted to be held responsible for South Vietnam's collapse. Short-range incremental decisions were made to assure that the war would not be

[5] Leslie H. Gelb, "The Pentagon Papers and *The Vantage Point*," *Foreign Policy* VI (Spring 1972), pp. 33–36.

lost in the short run; but in the long run the United States sank deeper and deeper into the quagmire. This thesis is useful in pointing out that policy making is usually or necessarily composed of a series of incremental decisions that are likely to be based on short-term considerations. This is all the more likely when policy making is reactive and only of secondary importance to a major power like the United States, as the Vietnam issue was at first. The quagmire metaphor is also useful because it takes note of the domestic political pressures that were an important part of the Vietnam policy making.

The most important mistake about Vietnam—one that bred most of the others—was the failure to concentrate on making the Saigon regime into a viable government, or the failure to recognize that doing so lay beyond the means of Washington. Kennedy's envoys had noted the inadequacies of the Vietnam government in their first serious appraisal in 1961. Two years later the Diem regime was abandoned by Washington only when it appeared hopelessly ineffective and the opposition to it substantial. The next year, during the 1964 presidential election, a summary of national intelligence estimates about the other side pictured the political situation in South Vietnam in the same terms:

> The basic elements of Communist strength in South Vietnam remain indigenous: South Vietnamese grievances, war-weariness, defeatism, and political disarray; VC terror, arms capture, disciplined organization, highly developed intelligence systems, and ability to recruit locally; and the fact that the VC enjoys some status as a nationalist movement. The high VC morale is sustained by successes to date and by the receipt of outside guidance and support.[6]

In short, American officials in Washington and in Saigon were aware that the South Vietnamese government was ineffective and corrupt. The problem arose over what to do. Given their resolve that South Vietnam not fall into the hands of the North Vietnamese government, American officials had few choices. They chose to assume that the Saigon regime would improve if given a chance. They avoided facing the contingency that the regime might fail to improve, and

[6] *Gravel Edition*, vol. 3, p. 653.

if so, that the United States would have to accept a negotiated loss to Hanoi or intervene even more massively to reform the Saigon regime.

Beginning with the Taylor-Rostow report in 1961 the view prevailed that the Saigon regime would be able to improve its effectiveness if American efforts provided it with time—"room to breathe." This view misperceived the incentives and motivations of Saigon officials in a military government quite willing to remain dependent on the United States. American intervention provided American substitutes for the Saigon regime's effectiveness and offered opportunities for Vietnamese officials to pursue other objectives instead— usually private interests. According to one account, during the chaos of the Tet offensive of 1968, the province chief in Hue, which was overrun by Vietcong forces, devoted himself to stealing relief supplies rather than regrouping his forces.[7] That would not have been possible if the security of the area really depended on him. Progress in one area was persistently being offset by failures in another largely because the Americans had created major incentives for the South Vietnamese to remain clients of the United States.

Viewed in this light, the escalation of 1965 was a giant step in the wrong direction. Attacking North Vietnam by air, increasing material aid to the South Vietnamese ground forces, and finally, providing direct ground support with American troops were all part of a growing coercion of Hanoi that in fact relieved the pressures on South Vietnam for effective reform. Military escalation almost assured that the Saigon regime would remain a "kept" government predisposed to corruption.

American policy rested on the faulty premise that Saigon and Washington had common interests because Washington wanted South Vietnam to survive and prosper. In fact, Washington's interests were not congruent with those of Saigon officials. And the interests of Saigon officials failed to reflect those of the South Vietnamese people in significant ways—as demonstrated by the willingness of these officials to accept the death and suffering of Vietnamese people and damage to culture and countryside as costs of American intervention. For Saigon officials, the prudent course was to gain what advantage they could from the American presence in Vietnam

[7] Francis Fitzgerald, *Fire in the Lake* (Boston: Little, Brown, 1972), p. 397.

and to assure that it continued as long as possible, while reducing the risks of associating themselves conspicuously with the Americans. Perpetuating South Vietnam's ineffectiveness furthered these goals by increasing dependence on the United States.

To assure an actual congruence of purpose, Washington needed to pay close attention to the incentives that it generated for the Saigon regime to become more effective. While the Johnson Administration carefully orchestrated the application of coercive instruments against Hanoi, it only haphazardly pressured the Saigon government to perform better. This was particularly unfortunate for the political future of South Vietnam. While Hanoi was establishing its independence from both Peking and Moscow and enhancing its legitimacy as a national government, the American presence overshadowed the Saigon regime, diminishing its legitimacy and maintaining its dependence. The downfall of Diem demonstrated that the Americans would not tolerate a government that went its own way. The event was scarcely helpful in establishing the Saigon regime's political legitimacy. American officials, mindful of the problem of legitimacy (though not prepared to confront it fully), put up with noncooperation and sometimes defiance in Saigon while perpetuating Saigon's dependence on the United States. In this way Washington gained the worst of two worlds. Similarly, the American escalation of 1965 contributed to the legitimacy of Hanoi while limiting the legitimacy of Saigon.

Taking a broader look, one might ask whether there is some validity in the revisionist thesis that the American involvement in Vietnam was at least partly encouraged by the predisposition of the United States to be imperialistic. Did we stumble into Vietnam; were we drawn in; or was such a massive enterprise by the United States more purposeful? If our objectives were obscure to most people, were they perhaps clear to the powerful people who ran the war—to President Johnson (and later President Nixon) and the civil and military directors of the war?

The Pentagon Papers offer a glimpse into the thinking within the government about Vietnam. These documents suggest that official government thinking was muddled, with goals ill-defined and shifting. A prominent revisionist, Gabriel Kolko, while acknowledging the apparent befuddlement, argues that the Vietnam war was "the culminating yet unavoidable miscalculation in a global effort that began well before the Indochina crisis . . ." to save "vast areas of the world for its own forms of political and economic domination." [8] Yet Washington does not appear to have had such a clear vision of goals in Vietnam. American officials, reflecting attitudes of the American public in general, were all too inclined to see Vietnam as a test case closely linked to the balance of the Cold War and thus requiring, as Kolko correctly states, "resistance to Communism." The "domino theory"—what had more commonly been called "no appeasement" in the fifties—was applied to Vietnam: if it fell, so would all Southeast Asia. But to interpret such misconceptions as long-range strategy is to confuse sentiments with plans.

Once begun in earnest, the war developed a powerful momentum. The American armed services at first acted reluctantly. Vietnam was not the kind of war they wanted to fight. Like Korea, it was the "wrong war, at the wrong place, and with the wrong enemy." The Army had successfully resisted involvement in Vietnam in 1954, during the first Vietnam crisis. Involvement had at that time been promoted by the chairman of the Joint Chiefs of Staff, Admiral Radford, whose extreme views about the uses of air power were scarcely representative of the Chiefs in the mid-sixties. Once American participation in the war began, however, Army reluctance gave way to demands for men and material in sufficient quantity to assure success by familiar means—which meant highly mechanized conventional war.

Revisionists share with a larger segment of the war's critics the view that the United States became involved in Vietnam partly because American business interests backed the war as a business opportunity for the "military-industrial complex." The links between the private and government interests are doubtlessly a significant force in the American political system, and the military-industrial complex is a conspicuous part of that force. The military-industrial complex is scarcely a unified set of interests, however, nor are they the only powerful interests within the American economic and political system. The Vietnam war harmed important economic

[8] Gabriel Kolko, "The American Goal in Vietnam," in Noam Chomsky and Howard Zinn, eds., *Senator Gravel Edition: The Pentagon Papers,* 5 vols. (Boston: The Beacon Press, 1972), vol. 5, p. 2.

interests while it aided others. On one hand, Vietnam benefited construction and service contract firms in Southeast Asia and manu-facturing firms producing war equipment; on the other hand, the war generated economic pressures that affected other economic in-terests adversely.

The domestic political constraints that helped make the war a foreign policy debacle induced President Johnson to adopt fiscal and monetary policies that produced economic stagnation and in-flation—conditions that harmed American business interests in gen-eral. Even the industrial sector most dependent upon defense con-tracts, the aerospace industry, went through a severe contraction during the height of the Vietnam war effort. These losses must be considered along with the gains in weighing American economic interests in the Vietnam war.

The United States did not become involved in Vietnam be-cause the government was subservient to powerful economic in-terests intent upon promoting war or American domination in Viet-nam. The energy of collective interests flowed the other way, if at all, from within the government in Washington outward. Successive administrations did act in anticipation of public attitudes and did respond to group pressures—but they acted selectively and on their own terms. The revisionists have properly concerned themselves with the processes of government in explaining how foreign policy evolves. For example, they have been skeptical about the rationale of "national security" that Cold War prophets have virtually equated with our national interest. The revisionists have inherited venerable insights from nineteenth-century writers who were con-cerned with explaining economic imperialism. But the political sys-tems of the dominant socioeconomic elites of nineteenth-century Western European regimes were quite different from the political system of the United States today. In our contemporary system, po-litical participation is broader, social structure more fluid, economic interests more numerous and diversified, and government more independent of special interests than was the case in late nineteenth-century Europe. For better or worse, the American government—more broadly, the American public sector—is itself a set of interests to be reckoned with, and never more seriously than when it is pur-suing its own vision of our national interest such as the American stake in Vietnam.

THE DOVES DEFEAT JOHNSON

A UNIFIED FRONT IN THE
EXECUTIVE BRANCH

Johnson's most effective demonstration of leadership in the growing crisis over Vietnam was his command of the executive branch. In the United States no administration is a monolith. The President must live with men of independent political means who have direct access to the press and Congress. Yet Johnson managed to deny his critics outside the government any rallying points within his Administration.

A likely potential critic around whom to rally was the field commander of Vietnam military operations from 1963 to 1968, General William C. Westmoreland. When a commander is unable to win, he may question the adequacy of the forces assigned to him. His prominence will assure that he gets a hearing. Hence, an administration runs a considerable political risk when it permits military disgruntlement to grow. But Westmoreland was not a general who would ask for military resources the Administration, or at least the Pentagon military chiefs, were unwilling to give him. He continued to back Johnson's policies.

The Johnson Administration was able to keep all its prominent members from joining its critics. Nonetheless, there is ample evidence of a schism between the military leaders and a civilian faction that was increasingly skeptical of military claims and solutions. Secretary of State Dean Rusk continued to align himself with the military hawks, while Robert McNamara, Secretary of Defense until April 1968, evidently became a civilian skeptic, but left the Administration quietly; to Johnson's dismay, McNamara's successor, Clark Clifford, immediately joined the skeptics within the government.

Johnson's congressional opponents were constrained at first by the logic of his coercive strategy. Neither Mike Mansfield, Senate majority leader, nor Senator Fulbright condemned the resumption of the bombing of North Vietnam in January 1966. Yet both called for more vigorous efforts to negotiate, and Fulbright conducted television hearings that made it respectable for Congressmen to follow him into open opposition to the Administration. Robert Kennedy,

Attorney General in the Kennedy Administration and now a Senator from New York, became a major rallying point for disgruntled Democrats, although it was Fulbright who criticized the Administration's foreign policy systematically and persistently. Critics charged that legitimacy for Saigon was hopeless. In Washington a major policy review during the spring of 1967 confronted officials with the same question that President Kennedy's envoys had raised (and then neglected) in 1961: what to do about the political weakness of the Saigon regime? As in 1961, contingencies in case of failure were never worked out, leaving only the question of means and the persistent, ineffective concern about incentives.

Ambassador Robert Komer, in charge of political development efforts in Saigon, challenged a military proposal to increase troop strength in Vietnam from 470,000 in 1967 to 680,000 by 1968 on the grounds that it neglected "the tougher, slower and less certain measures required to make the Vietnamese pull their weight."[9] In assessing proposed measures, the most critical factor, as William P. Bundy put it, "lies in the effect they have on the South Vietnamese."[10] During 1967 Johnson held the scheduled troop increase to 60,000 for 1968 and coupled it with an increase in bombing and quickened efforts to construct an electronic barrier against infiltration from the north.

More significantly, by taking these steps Johnson chose for the first time not to meet most of the demands of his military chiefs. As a result, in August 1967 the Senate Preparedness Subcommittee, after listening to testimony from the Army, Navy, and Air Force chiefs, and from McNamara, condemned the failure of the Administration to follow military advice. Johnson was now having considerable trouble denying outside critics of the war support from within his Administration.

The Tet offensive in February 1968 brought the antiwar criticism into sharper focus. The Vietcong had carefully built up their forces and supplies for months in advance while the American military command in Saigon claimed that the enemy threat was diminishing. The insurgents struck at cities in South Vietnam during the Chinese New Year truce. The strength of their attack

9 *Gravel Edition,* vol. 4, p. 439.

10 *Ibid.,* p. 503.

discredited American claims about the diminishing threat. The insurgent success in preparing for such a massive attack without American discovery indicated the complicity of the local populations in its preparation. The offensive forced South Vietnamese and American forces to abandon rural areas in order to recover control in the cities. It brought urban areas under greater threat than ever before, and the use of American fire power in response caused heavy destruction of urban property to root out the Vietcong.

Tet cost the Vietcong heavy casualties; it cost the Johnson Administration substantial political support at home; and it hurt the Saigon government by demonstrating that the regime could not guarantee the security of its own urban areas. Moreover, Tet was only the beginning of a new phase in the war. The offensive spent itself in a few weeks, but the attacks on the cities soon resumed. Even the later attacks on cities by the Vietcong demonstrated a formidable staying power in the face of the American build-up.

DOMESTIC ELECTORAL POLITICS

The Administration had suffered no more than expected setbacks in the 1966 congressional elections. If anything, the electoral results lent support to its Vietnam policy by putting into office new Representatives who favored stepped-up operations. Yet the slowdown of Johnson's legislative program that year and the next, the increasingly vocal opposition to the war, and the public opinion surveys indicated growing public concern over the war, though no clear opinion on what to do about it.

Draft calls and casualty rates had risen considerably since 1964. Monthly draft quotas averaged 4,000 in the first three months of 1965—16,000 from April through August and 28,000 for the rest of the year. In 1967 they averaged just over 30,000; through May 1968, 38,000. At the end of May 1965 American troop casualties in Vietnam stood at 400 killed and 2,000 wounded. At this time, United States commanders in Vietnam were authorized to commit American ground troops to combat. Three years later casualties had risen to more than 20,000 killed and 130,000 wounded. Press coverage was incessant. By early 1966, as a careful opinion survey by a group of experts gathered at Stanford University indicated, the public had a fairly high level of information about the issues associated with Vietnam.[11]

During 1965–68 Johnson evidently expected that his greatest difficulties in regard to Vietnam would come from the hawks, as in the 1964 election. During the Korean war the opposition had come mainly from that direction. Yet the Korean settlement produced contrary indicators as well. General MacArthur, the leading advocate of escalation, won public acclaim but not support, and the public accepted the modest gains of a negotiated settlement in 1953 with barely a murmur. As domestic and foreign criticism mounted, Johnson claimed that he was doing no less than the public demanded of him. In fact, public support was not demanding a particular course of action but rather had demonstrated its support for any changes in government policy. Presidential popularity had shot up, for instance, when Johnson met with Premier Kosygin of the Soviet Union during Kosygin's visit to the United Nations in September 1967. The Stanford study showed that the President could not justify his war decisions on the grounds that he was forced by public opinion.

JOHNSON'S 1968 CAMPAIGN WITHDRAWAL

Late in 1967 Senator Eugene McCarthy of Minnesota, an unannounced candidate for the Vice Presidency at the Democratic nominating convention in 1964, declared that he would challenge President Johnson in five primary elections in 1968. Vietnam was the main issue that led him into a grass roots confrontation with Johnson. McCarthy made a surprisingly strong showing in the February New Hampshire primary, indicating considerable public dissatisfaction with the Administration over Vietnam as well as McCarthy's political potency. With these results published, Robert Kennedy declared his own candidacy, competing with McCarthy for leadership among strong antiwar Democrats. Johnson now faced open challenges to his control of the Democratic party.

Any President has formidable assets in winning the renomina-

---

[11] S. Verba, R. A. Brody, *et al.*, "Public Opinion and the War in Vietnam," *American Political Science Review* 61 (June 1967), pp. 317–33.

tion of his own party. Truman had demonstrated this fact in 1948, as had William Howard Taft in 1912. No President in the twentieth century has failed to win renomination when he has sought it. Yet Johnson announced at the end of March 1968 that he would not seek or accept renomination.

We will never know whether he would have been renominated and reelected had he chosen to run. He was undoubtedly in deep political trouble. His Gallup poll rating had fallen from more than 80 percent of the public approving of his performance in early 1964 to 36 percent in March 1968. His rating on the handling of the war had fallen even lower that month, to 26 percent. In addition, a White House poll showed Johnson running behind McCarthy by 2 to 1 in Wisconsin, and far behind Kennedy in California. The primary elections promised considerable embarrassment for him, but they hardly forclosed his renomination and reelection.[12]

Before the New Hampshire primary, the Tet offensive had hardened the dove-hawk split within the government. The military chiefs proposed further escalation of the bombing and another 200,000 troops, while Clark Clifford, Johnson's new Secretary of Defense, became an outspoken skeptic. Just a week after the primary Johnson called nine prestigious former presidential advisers in for special consultation. They advised against further escalation of the war and in favor of greater efforts to get peace talks under way.

After the New Hampshire primary, Johnson could scarcely expect that his statements about Vietnam would carry much credibility in Saigon or Hanoi, at least until after the 1968 presidential succession was determined in November. His withdrawal from the campaign could not take Vietnam off the political campaign agenda, but it did strengthen the credibility of the Johnson Administration's resolve to coerce Hanoi into negotiations that would permit the survival of the Saigon regime after a reduction in the American military effort.

Johnson's withdrawal from the 1968 campaign had been coupled with an announcement of limited deescalation of the air war against North Vietnam and a renewed effort to parley with Hanoi. The withdrawal may have been the more important dis-

---

[12] *New York Times,* March 31, May 25, and June 25, 1968; *The* [London] *Observer Review,* April 7, 1968.

closure to Hanoi. At any rate, in May spokesmen for the United States and North Vietnam began negotiations openly for the first time in Paris, while the Vietcong pursued their attacks on the cities in South Vietnam and the American forces kept up their own pressure against the enemy.

Johnson's Vietnam entanglement cut off his presidential tenure at five years instead of a possible nine, and it quenched a brilliant legislative record as President that had lasted nearly two years. By early 1968 the Vietnam war had badly splintered the Democratic party. Hubert Humphrey's nomination on the first ballot at the presidential convention in August left the party divided. The election campaign of 1968 aired the mood of wide public alienation over Vietnam. As usual, domestic issues—mainly law and order—preempted foreign issues. But the impact of Vietnam on the election was nonetheless profound. It eliminated Johnson from the Democratic candidacy and enabled the Republican Nixon to win despite a strong voter preference for Democrats in Congress.

CONCLUSION

The international consequences of Vietnam came to dominate Johnson's foreign policy, and the domestic consequences influenced his domestic political position. In foreign policy, adapting American diplomacy to China's changing role in Asia was the main casualty. A similar paralysis developed toward Europe. Washington's relationships with East and West Europe had been in visible flux over the prospects of a détente in 1964 and planned American initiatives to build "bridges to the East." Increased trade was in prospect, accompanied by improved political relations. These were tasks primarily for Europeans to accomplish, but they required the attention of Washington because of Soviet interest in the East. Our interest diminished with the escalation in Vietnam. Liberal and nationalist forces in the Soviet-bloc countries, however, did not atrophy. Czechoslovakia was liberalizing the most rapidly when Moscow abruptly reoccupied it in August 1968 and began the suppression of a surprisingly resilient national Communist regime. Had Washington been strengthening our bridges to the East instead of abandoning them for two years, the fate of Czechoslovakia might have been different. Such speculations suggest the possible effects on America's worldwide interests of Johnson's concentrating our resources and diplomatic objectives on Vietnam.

The legacy that Johnson inherited from Kennedy in Vietnam strongly disposed him toward greater military involvement there, but it did not predetermine his decisions to increase military commitments or his persistent preference for military over other means. These decisions were prompted more directly by the high domestic political costs of protracted wars—so clear since the Korean war. Johnson, in coping with these inevitable costs, undertook a relatively conventional military solution while not explicitly repudiating the assessment that the main problem in Vietnam was the political viability of the Saigon regime.

In effect, the momentum of the military operations directed and conducted by Americans overrode political objectives that depended heavily on the actions of others whom the Americans could not control. The diplomatic process was a similar casualty of military activities, as it had been to some extent with previous administrations as well. The Truman Administration had, in Churchill's phrase, "armed to parley" with the Communists, but it had never really parleyed or indicated the circumstances under which it would do so. Dulles had turned Churchill's dictum into "arm and beware!" Kennedy had actually followed Churchill's motto by arming *and* parleying. But Johnson, the extraordinary parleyer of American domestic politics, found himself fighting in Vietnam while wanting to parley.

Vietnam, however, did not just happen to Johnson; he helped it to happen. He built up the American forces in Vietnam until they acquired a life of their own. In doing so, Johnson assured that the Saigon regime would remain ineffectual and dependent on the United States. He dealt with the problem of growing political opposition at home by manipulating the press to be more reassuring in its reporting of the war and by manipulating Congress to support him while leaving him a free hand.

Johnson's manipulations of Congress and the press nourished public distrust. Evidently he expected public opposition to grow with the protraction and visibility of the war, and these expectations steeled him against political adversity. Thus the growing opposition to the war did not persuade him to reconsider his strategy.

Johnson was less critical of military enterprises than he should have been, and he was not the master of the broader forums of presidential politics that he was of the Senate. Yet it is not at all clear that another President would have altered the main elements of his Vietnam strategy—to reassure the public while trying to end the war on favorable terms. It is, however, quite certain that future Presidents will avoid committing military forces to a distant area if they foresee being drawn into a protracted conflict.

chapter **10**

Nixon's First Term: Vietnam and the Reelection Timetable

Richard Nixon's presidential era—from 1969 until mid-1974—appeared to be a period of major change in American foreign policy. The American commitment of armed forces in Vietnam and the long isolation of Communist China ended. Relations with Moscow improved, changing the American position in Europe and opening up a more complex and flexible power system in Asia. The United States reduced its foreign commitments in favor of greater "self-reliance" on the part of its clients and allies. The architects of these changes, insofar as they were designed by Washington, were President Nixon himself and Henry Kissinger, first Nixon's Special Assistant for National Security and then Secretary of State.

The Nixon Administration's accomplishments in foreign policy are a complex puzzle. Not the least puzzling is how much it actually accomplished. Some international and foreign policy changes would have occurred anyway. The withdrawal from Vietnam may be one of these. Other changes may prove temporary or inconsequential, such as the warming of American relations with Russia and China. Other changes may prove to have been unwise.

The fact that Nixon resigned from the Presidency rather than

face an impeachment trial complicates these problems of interpretation and evaluation. There is virtually no question by now that
Nixon's aides engaged in illegal activities during his 1972 election
campaign and then obstructed justice and perjured themselves to
cover up the initial violations and to protect the President. It
appears that Nixon joined and led his aides at least in the cover-up
activities of the Watergate and related scandals.

Since Nixon's aides did not benefit financially from their illegal
activities, it seems likely that their motives were, as they declared,
to ensure by any means the reelection of the President. If so, should
we conclude that the same kind of narrow political motives generated most of Nixon's foreign policy decisions? Apparently they
did not.

In this chapter, however, we will concentrate on the area in
which political motives doubtless played a major role—Vietnam.
We will explore how the Nixon Administration extricated the
United States from Vietnam, paying special attention to the domestic political imperatives and restraints that had developed during the war's duration. Two major influences on Nixon's Vietnam
policies were the public reaction to the war and the political timetable imposed by impending 1970 and 1972 elections for Congress
and the Presidency. The next chapter will place the Vietnam war
within the broader context of Nixon's foreign relations, their origins, and their consequences.

THE 1968 ELECTION

Nixon won the 1968 election with a narrow popular vote mar-
gin (43.4 percent for the Republican ticket, 42.7 percent for the
Democratic ticket, and 13.5 percent for the Conservative party's
George Wallace). The Democratic candidate was Hubert Humphrey,
Johnson's Vice President. Humphrey's role in Johnson's incumbent
Administration posed problems similar to those Nixon found in
1960. Humphrey had been an articulate and loyal member of the
Johnson Administration, and he proved less able to disassociate
himself from Johnson's policies than Nixon had from Eisenhower's
in 1960—and much less than Stevenson from Truman's in 1952. As
a result, Humphrey was unable to unite a party that had become

badly divided over Vietnam. Perhaps the clearest example of the impact of Vietnam on domestic politics had been President Johnson's decision not to run for reelection in 1968. His conduct of the war had made him not only unpopular, but unwilling to endure the partisanship and political risks necessary to remain in the White House.

Support for Nixon was in part a reaction against Johnson's handling of Vietnam. The war appears to have contributed substantially to the public dissatisfactions upon which the Nixon campaign was built. Humphrey remained largely on the defensive, coping with the major question of whether his election would bring sufficient change in handling Vietnam. Nixon highlighted the possibilities of change without repudiating the American role in Vietnam. He said it in the phrase "peace with honor."

Like 1952, the outcome in 1968 can be interpreted as choosing a new President to deal with what had become an intractable foreign problem. But this parallel needs strong qualifiers. Both Nixon and Humphrey advocated general changes in the handling of Vietnam without being specific. Domestic politics played its normally large role in the election, and the popular vote outcome showed only a weak preference for Nixon. For the American voter in 1968, choosing a President scarcely meant either repudiating American participation in the war or selecting alternative proposals for the future. However, Nixon's claim to have a "secret plan" to end the war probably made him appear (mistakenly) to assure a more distinct break with the past.

NIXON AND THE INSTITUTIONAL PRESIDENCY

THE PRESIDENT'S ORIGINS AND PERSONALITY

Nixon became President at fifty-six. Born in Whittier, California, he had attended the local schools, and was graduated from Duke University Law School in 1937. Before his wartime services as a Navy supply officer in the Pacific, he worked two years in a government tire rationing office in Washington. Elected from California to the House of Representatives in 1946, and to the Senate in 1950, he drew national attention as a Communist-hunter in the government. After eight years as Vice President, Nixon lost both the presidential race against Kennedy in 1960 and the California gubernatorial race in 1962. His 1968 presidential election victory completed a surprising political comeback.

A balanced treatment of Nixon's political career is yet to be struck. His first campaign, in 1946 against Jerry Voorhis, a respected Congressman, was rough. His Senate campaign in 1950 against a congressional colleague, Helen Gahagan Douglas, was disgraceful. Yet he was not the only dirty campaigner in California politics—just the most successful one. Most of his charges against Mrs. Douglas had been used against her in the California primary by her Democratic rivals. Nixon's campaigning was not original; but it was single-minded in his pursuit of victory. Joining the Eisenhower presidential ticket in 1952 gave Nixon new respectability. A brief foreshadow of the later Watergate scandal occurred during the 1952 campaign when it became known that a special personal expense fund had been set up with gifts from some of his supporters to defray the "extra expenses" of public life that the salary of a Senator did not cover.

Before the 1972 campaign, one close observer of Nixon's record noted that he "substitutes technique for value." He is "a man on the run, watching himself run, criticizing his form as he runs. He *tends* himself."[1] The overwhelming impression of personal observers has been of an "aloof," "self-contained" person who considers other people essentially untrustworthy. This assessment of Nixon was to be reflected in his organization of the White House.

CENTRALIZATION OF THE WHITE HOUSE STAFF

As he organized his own White House, Nixon laid stress on Eisenhower-like arrangements—orderly procedures, structure, and staffing. Presidents often claim that they prefer not to centralize power in the White House but rather to delegate responsibility to

---

[1] James David Barber, *The Presidential Character: Predicting Performance in the White House* (Englewood Cliffs, N.J.: Prentice-Hall, 1972), p. 361.

their appointed officials to run the executive departments. Actual practice is usually somewhere in between. Nixon's was at the other extreme. The White House staff quickly turned into a centralized operation that undercut the authority of Cabinet officers.

Domestic Advisers and Problems of Access

On the domestic side, Nixon appointed Arthur Burns, who had been a White House economist under Eisenhower, counselor to the President with Cabinet rank and apparent authority to coordinate overall domestic policy. This arrangement was reminiscent of Eisenhower's use of the presidential Cabinet as a domestic council; but under Nixon the domestic Cabinet rarely met. Nixon also appointed Daniel Patrick Moynihan as head of an Urban Affairs Council, and during Nixon's first year, Moynihan clearly gained the advantage over Burns in the White House pecking order. Then in late 1969 John Ehrlichman, Nixon's aide, eased Moynihan out and acquired authority over domestic policy in the White House staff.

The shift from Burns to Moynihan to Ehrlichman indicates Nixon's steady movement away from men of independent public status and mind to personal assistants with no such status. Nixon came increasingly to deal with domestic issues through Ehrlichman and with all matters through his Chief of Staff, Robert Haldeman. Both were exclusively Nixon men: their entire public experience was linked to Nixon.

The pressures for access to any American President from Congressmen, executive branch officials, the press, political figures, economic spokesmen, foreign representatives, and others are immense. The President's staff is his shield. Eisenhower was thoroughly experienced in using military staffs in the Army, yet he came under much criticism for permitting his presidential staff to shield him so much. Given Nixon's predilection to work alone or with a few trusted associates, his White House structure outdid even Eisenhower. Nixon's White House staff came to shield the President even from his own Cabinet officers. Two major Cabinet members, George Romney and John Volpe, protested their loss of authority in the first White House reorganization; later Walter Hickel was fired for protesting the inaccessibility of the President to him. In the national security area similar trends occurred. Even Secretary of State William P. Rogers, one of Nixon's closest friends, had difficulty with access. Increasingly foreign affairs were handled through Henry Kissinger, Nixon's Special Assistant for National Security who eventually replaced Rogers as Secretary of State.

The Rise of Kissinger and Flexible Diplomacy

Rogers, an affable lawyer, had been Eisenhower's Attorney General. Nixon's first Secretary of Defense, Melvin R. Laird, was a senior and respected Republican Congressman. The appointment of well-liked Republicans suggests Nixon's intent to reduce the breach with Congress over Vietnam that had developed during the Johnson Administration. From the outset, however, Nixon evidently expected to explore a secretly negotiated settlement with Hanoi through Kissinger, whom Nixon chose to keep closer at hand.

The shift from Rogers to Kissinger in regard to national security was at first parallel to Nixon's shifts among domestic advisers. Kissinger began his service in the White House with considerable professional standing among the foreign policy elites as a Harvard professor and an adviser to Nelson Rockefeller, though he lacked an effective political power base. He was the first foreign-born Special Assistant to the President. A man with distinct published views about foreign relations (unlike his domestic counterparts, Haldeman and Ehrlichman), Kissinger nonetheless established a close working relationship with Nixon. A glimpse at Kissinger's responsiveness to Nixon has been provided by leaked minutes from the Washington Special Action Group, a sub-Cabinet committee set up to deal with diplomatic crises, when this committee was dealing with the Bangladesh war in 1971. Nixon favored Pakistan's effort to repress the revolt in what was then East Pakistan, evidently because Pakistan had been helpful in arranging the first direct contacts with Peking and because he resented India's encouragement of the revolt. Apparently vexed over the committee's failure to be more responsive to Nixon's viewpoint, Kissinger exploded that he was getting "hell every half hour" from the President.[2] This statement reminded committee members that Kissinger and they had no power to move away from the President's own declared views.

Given the particular "importance of proximity" in Nixon's White House, as Moynihan had observed, Kissinger's daily access to the President increasingly outweighed Rogers' preoccupation with State Department duties. Rogers took over the role of speaking for conventional Administration foreign policy positions and for continuity with past policies. He also helped to smooth relations with our allies and acted as a buffer in regional disputes that were not considered urgent enough to warrant Nixon's or Kissinger's direct intervention. For example, Rogers smoothed appearances about West Germany's bilateral treaty making with Moscow in the face of domestic criticism here, and he also handled the Israeli-Egyptian dispute of 1969–70 (as discussed in Chapter 11).

Kissinger, meanwhile, focused his attention mainly on the Vietnam negotiations and on the Peking and Moscow visits. These summit meetings were showcases not only for Nixon but for Kissinger as well. He made the arrangements, and he figured more prominently in the American party than anyone but the President himself. The Vietnam negotiations also gave Kissinger prominence, first within the government and later with the public. At first Kissinger's activities were secret, but during 1972 he became increasingly preeminent as he shuttled back and forth from Paris to Washington, and in the final stages, to and from Hanoi and Saigon.

In most matters involving foreign relations it became increasingly clear to foreigners and to the ubiquitous Washington press corps that Kissinger had Nixon's ear and was the key official to deal with. By 1971 foreign diplomats wanted to see Kissinger rather than Rogers. Such trends can produce personal conflicts, but in this case none ensued. Rogers adapted to his declining role gracefully, while the State Department languished.

Even in matters other than Vietnam and the summit meetings, Nixon's style of conducting foreign policy contributed to Kissinger's growing status. Where possible, Nixon chose to handle matters from within the White House itself. There he could better protect

---

2 Quoted in Henry Brandon, *The Retreat of American Power* (Garden City, N.Y.: Doubleday, 1973), p. 263, from the so-called "Anderson Papers."

his policies from critics in a Democrat-controlled Congress and from the federal bureaucracy, which he distrusted for its alleged hostility to him, his programs, and his party. Most important, Nixon and Kissinger undertook such large-scale changes in foreign relations that they could expect their policies to encounter non-cooperation and resistance if cleared through the State Department and the other units of foreign policy making in government. Nixon was not willing to devote his efforts to winning support in Congress and the executive branch for such changes, as Truman had done. He opted instead to impose change from the White House.

After the Vietnam settlement in early 1973, Kissinger talked briefly of retiring. Nixon delayed taking action in his responses to this talk because of the Watergate scandal, but in September 1973 he appointed Kissinger the first foreign-born Secretary of State in American history.

VIETNAM: HIGHEST FOREIGN POLICY PRIORITY

Vietnam dominated the foreign policy agenda that Nixon faced as a new President. It was by no means the only problem he faced in foreign relations, but it was the most demanding politically. The ongoing costs of the war in American lives and resources and the high level of public attention it had attracted assured that either the Nixon Administration would have to avoid becoming identified with the war or would have to demonstrate that it had taken the initiative in extricating the United States from the war. Otherwise Nixon faced the prospect that public opposition to the war would become a major burden to his Administration. Unless steps were taken to avoid this negative public reaction, the congressional elections of 1970 and the presidential election of 1972 would be likely to undermine the Nixon Administration's interests. This prospect paced the Administration's handling of Vietnam. The handling of Vietnam in turn became the main impetus for accomplishing a fundamental change in American foreign policy by opening relations with Communist China. This step assured that Soviet-American relations would begin to reflect the political diversity within the Communist bloc that the United States had long neglected.

THE JOHNSON LEGACY

When Johnson had started the massive American troop build-up in Vietnam in 1965, Southeast Asia appeared to Washington on the brink of disaster. American officials were still alarmed by the avowed Soviet support for "wars of national liberation," although Khrushchev had been deposed as Soviet Premier in 1964. Indonesia was drifting into the orbit of Peking; South Vietnam seemed near collapse; and China was winning recognition among Communist parties for its own brand of world revolutionary ideology, to the particular embarrassment of Moscow.

By the time Nixon became President, many of these conditions had changed. An internal political upheaval, the Cultural Revolution, had crippled China's government and economy, sharpened her quarrel with the Soviet Union, and interrupted her diplomacy with the developing nations. The Indonesian military, a relatively close-knit faction forged in the years of rebellion against Dutch rule, had taken charge of Indonesia, slaughtering or interning most Indonesian Communists and breaking with Peking. The new regime launched an effective economic development effort and reversed that country's drift toward economic chaos, political disintegration, jingoism, and Peking. South Vietnam was no longer on the edge of collapse. The new Soviet regime had increased its foreign trade and cultural contacts. Soviet doctrines about internal war as well as Chinese pronouncements about worldwide guerrilla war now seemed less threatening, given the Soviet-Chinese quarrel.

Most remarkably, despite these changes in the large political configurations that bore on the Vietnam conflict from 1964 to 1968, Indochina itself had maintained an equilibrium. When Johnson escalated the war he strained that equilibrium. But he also took steps to limit the strain. He repeatedly declined to permit ground attacks on supply routes and staging areas in Laos and Cambodia, the mining of Haiphong harbor (the main port for Hanoi), and the bombing of Haiphong and central Hanoi. These military operations would have broadened the geography of the war effort and brought more foreign personnel and property under fire (particularly ships and other transport, together with their cargoes), raising the risks that Soviet and Chinese military forces would help Hanoi more generously. Earlier, Kennedy had limited our commitments by securing the neutralization of Laos, which was to remain in effect in 1969, and the Cambodian government had actively maintained its own neutrality.

For any American administration intent on ending or significantly reducing the threat to the Saigon regime, however, the equilibrium in Laos and Cambodia had to be jostled. While both sides treated the conflict over South Vietnam as the main contest, North Vietnamese forces used both Laos and Cambodia for supply routes and staging areas. As the conflict in South Vietnam grew, therefore, Hanoi became increasingly dependent upon its sanctuaries in Laos and Cambodia for supply routes and assembly points. The Tet offensive had been launched largely from Cambodian sanctuaries in 1968. The widening of the American war effort through our secret bombing campaign further strained the equilibrium in Indochina.

NIXON'S CAMBODIAN INCURSION OF 1970

A third source of strain was the growing political instability in Cambodia. The Cambodian head of state, Prince Norodom Sihanouk, was deposed by a military coup in March 1970, led by Prime Minister Lon Nol, a "pro-American rightist." Lon Nol promptly set about ridding Cambodian territory of the estimated 40,000 Communist troops within its eastern borders. He failed, and his capital, Phnom Penh, came under Communist attack. He had already appealed to the United States for assistance and had established links with the Saigon regime.

In April 1970, Nixon ordered American ground forces to participate with South Vietnamese (RVN) forces in a military thrust into Cambodia aimed mainly at the North Vietnamese forces building up there. The incursion was justified on the grounds that it would improve the military position of the RVN and enable the continued withdrawal of American forces from Vietnam; but it was also designed to save the Lon Nol regime. Nixon also ordered the resumption of air strikes against North Vietnam to forestall the possibility that North Vietnam would react by striking directly across the demilitarized zone.

The Cambodian incursion was out of phase with the Administration's efforts to reduce public attention to the war in preparation for the congressional elections in 1970. The American public reacted severely enough to the Cambodian offensive to indicate that the Administration could no longer count on a "rally round the flag" response to its Vietnam initiatives. Across the country college campuses erupted with political demonstrations. Many of them closed down immediately, some not to be reopened for the rest of the academic year. Others reopened only under conspicuously modified (usually reduced) academic programs. Four students were massacred at Kent State University in Ohio by undisciplined national guard troops sent to deal with demonstrators. Violent confrontation occurred on other campuses as well. Opposition culminated in a march on Washington in May. Several minor foreign policy advisers resigned from the White House staff in anger or despair.

The American military objectives of the Cambodian incursion remain murky. Reacting to the public outcry, the Administration quickly claimed success (with little evidence to support the claim) and pulled American forces back from Cambodia sooner than it had planned. The pull back of American troops from Cambodia and the continuing withdrawal of American forces from Vietnam soothed the public clamor. That September colleges opened in a calmer mood. Cambodia, however, had become dependent upon the United States for military and economic aid. The equilibrium in Indochina had shifted once again and Washington was now propping up another regime there!

THE LAOTIAN INVASION OF 1971

A year later, South Vietnamese troops invaded Laos on a similar venture, this time supported only by American air power. Again, the campaign objectives were not clear. If it accomplished anything, the invasion lowered the value of Laos as a sanctuary by showing that Laotian territory was not exempt from attack. The attack precipitated heavy fighting. South Vietnamese troops performed unevenly. It was plain that they were becoming more effective, but how effective remained in dispute. The resistance they encountered indicated that the North Vietnamese could still conduct large-scale operations; nevertheless, the North suffered heavy enough casualties to suggest that it might be interested in negotiations.

With the broadened use of air power in Vietnam and the bombing campaigns in Cambodia and Laos, Nixon had resumed and extended the coercive diplomacy of Johnson's earlier Vietnam policy. The use of coercion appears to have been based on our experience in concluding the Korean war—to threaten a removal of American constraints in conducting the war while encouraging negotiations. Johnson had been concerned about the divergent goals of containing the conflict at the same time that he was applying increased coercion. To reconcile these goals he had placed limits on American military operations—mainly on bombing targets and the pace of the war. He had also accompanied changes in military operations with announcements designed mainly to assure Hanoi that each escalative move was measured and limited. Evidently these limitations and announcements reassured North Vietnam that it could endure whatever amount of coercion the United States intended.

Nixon, however, removed some of the constraints that Johnson had imposed; and before achieving an outcome acceptable to him, Nixon would remove additional ones. The consequences of his escalation were more complex than Johnson's, moreover, because the limitations Johnson had maintained during the mid-1960s had allowed him to avoid the labyrinths of Cambodian and Laotian internal politics. Nixon reentangled the United States in the affairs of these two governments.

Nixon's domestic critics converged on a common view: the United States should not allow its plans to withdraw troops from Vietnam to depend on what the Saigon government did. Many critics also rejected a precipitate withdrawal but did want a unilateral one—a course of action that would have eliminated most bargaining assets in dealing with Hanoi. In effect, most domestic opponents to our Vietnam policies had given up the prospects for a negotiated settlement. Their lowered expectations reflected exasperation with Saigon's political weakness and military ineptitude, and the difficulties of making effective use of American armed forces in this setting. By mid-1970 Nixon's own position had approximated unilateral withdrawal, yet in certain important respects it differed from his critics' views. Most important was his commitment to coercive diplomacy. Moderate critics who supported unilateral withdrawal—former Secretary of Defense Clark Clifford, for example—considered it futile to attempt to coerce Hanoi and the NLF, particularly through aerial bombing. Nixon's willingness to continue the use of American forces and to resume air strikes against the North eliminated the option of reducing domestic criticism. Predictably, broadening the use of air power drew heavy criticism from American opponents of the Vietnam war.

During the last two years of his Administration President Johnson had been unable to travel anywhere without encountering embarrassingly hostile demonstrations. The Cambodian and Laotian incursions reestablished siege conditions for the White House.

Nixon had taken care to eliminate a major cause of public attention to the war—the perceived risk to American manpower there. American ground troop strength had peaked in early 1969; during that year and the next Nixon committed himself to withdrawing 225,000 troops from Vietnam by April 1973. By early 1972 Nixon claimed that over 400,000 troops had been withdrawn, and he announced that the remainder would be halved again by May 1 to 69,000 and to 27,000 by December 1. The troop withdrawal deadlines served two purposes—to reassure the American public about the direction of the American effort in Vietnam and to confront the South Vietnamese with the prospect of performing their own security functions. The intense public attention to Vietnam during 1967 and 1968 had declined by 1970 and was never resumed.

American casualties had averaged three hundred per week in 1968. They fell to twenty-six per week in 1971 and four per week during the last five months of 1972,[3] fulfilling an important requirement for Nixon's election strategy. But active hostile minori-

[3] *U.S. Foreign Policy for the 1970's*, A Report to the Congress by Richard Nixon, President of the United States, vol. 4, pp. 44–45.

ties assured that Nixon's staff had to choose and engineer every public appearance carefully. This siegelike state contributed to the view in the White House—all too readily accepted there—that it was surrounded by its enemies.

PEACE NEGOTIATIONS: PUBLIC AND PRIVATE

Meanwhile, the Paris negotiations were getting nowhere. In 1969 the Nixon Administration had begun negotiating with Hanoi in Paris. The United States position at that time was that both sides must withdraw from Vietnam simultaneously and that a coalition government consisting of the Saigon regime and the NLF was unacceptable. As the congressional election of 1970 approached, Nixon assigned David K. E. Bruce, a prestigious American diplomat, to the Paris Vietnam negotiations to restore their dwindling status. In early October Bruce introduced a proposal for a cease-fire in place and the immediate exchange of prisoners (an issue that was rapidly assuming importance to the American public). The proposal won back some of the domestic support that had been lost by the Cambodian incursion. Senator Mansfield, the majority leader of the Democratic-controlled Senate, praised it, and the American press gave it near-unanimous editorial backing.

In late 1969 Kissinger had begun secret meetings in Paris with the Hanoi delegation. Kissinger's secret negotiations in Paris were intended to assure a more reliable communication link to Hanoi. The public Paris conferences often served both sides as a propaganda forum, handicapping their use for serious negotiations. In May 1971 Kissinger had presented a major new American position —in effect a proposal for settling military issues only, with other questions to be left for direct negotiations between the Saigon regime and the NLF. Washington was trying to drive a wedge between Hanoi and the NLF. Hanoi responded by stalling the secret negotiations while joining the NLF in a propaganda barrage in the public meetings.

By mid-1971 Washington's political timetable had put the Americans in a position of wanting progress in the Paris negotiations much more than did the Communist side. In August the

United States added a sweetener to its terms: an American-financed reconstruction plan available to both sides. Hanoi nonetheless broke off negotiations in November. In January 1972 Nixon tried again to move them along. With the concurrence of the Saigon regime, he made an additional offer: a presidential election in South Vietnam "organized and conducted by an independent body representing all political forces in South Vietnam, including the National Liberation Front." By early 1972, however, the Nixon Administration had moved into a much stronger stand than Saigon against collaborating with the Communist side and decided to draw away from Hanoi. Nixon did so by declaring: "Will we collude with our enemies to overturn our friends? Will we impose a future on the Vietnamese people that the other side has been unable to gain militarily or politically? This we will never do."[4]

This was the state of negotiations between the Communist side and the American side (including the Saigon regime) when negotiations resumed in July 1972, after the Peking and Moscow summit meetings.

NEW RELATIONSHIPS WITH PEKING AND MOSCOW

By 1969 Hanoi had demonstrated not only its extraordinary resilience and resourcefulness as a military opponent but also its relative independence from Moscow and Peking. In fact, it played the two rival Communist powers against one another to assure itself the material aid that it needed for its war effort. Given Hanoi's performance by 1969, two things were apparent: (1) Negotiating a Vietnam peace would not mean a direct gain for Peking or Moscow; (2) Washington might be able to use Peking and Moscow as potential pressure points on Hanoi because of Hanoi's dependence upon them jointly for her war effort. Both circumstances were favorable to negotiation.

The possibilities of applying pressure on Hanoi through Peking and Moscow to help settle Vietnam were encouraging. There was reason to believe that both the Soviet Union and the People's Re-

[4] *Ibid.*, p. 49.

public of China were interested in reducing the conflict. The material costs to each had mounted, but most important were their deteriorating relations with one another. In March 1969 Moscow had announced that Chinese Army units staged an "armed provocation" on their common Ussuri River border, giving public notice to a growing confrontation that had already drawn the attention of other powers. The border actions were indicators of a deeper conflict, a political and military rivalry that had generated reciprocal fears of strategic military coercion and attack. Russian fears had been accelerated by the Chinese acquisition of nuclear weapons. (China had detonated its first atom bomb in 1964.) The Russians, for their part, could bomb Chinese targets with nuclear missiles or amass conventional forces on the Chinese borders. But the Soviets could still ponder the nightmare of a future hostile China with a first-strike capability and worried about what the Soviets might do.

The nightmare for Peking was more immediate. The Soviets already had the nuclear forces to inflict major damage on China, possibly to eliminate Chinese hopes for attaining major nuclear military prowess. The Chinese braced for a major Russian attack in 1971. When it did not occur, China shifted to longer-term preparations against Soviet threats.

By 1969 Peking's priorities had shifted toward improving its competitive position in the conflict with the Soviet Union. Not only were signs to this effect obvious in Washington in the first year of the Nixon Administration, but Peking signaled in several ways her interest in improving relations with the United States.

Moscow's problems were different. She had gained little from Hanoi's dependence on Soviet assistance except to preclude the expansion of Chinese influence. In view of these limited gains, she wished to acquire more mobility elsewhere in Asia to pursue her anti-Chinese policy. For example, ending her assistance to Hanoi would improve her prospects with India, which feared the aggressive interests of Hanoi and particularly Peking.

The Sino-Soviet rift paved the way for a classical three-power relationship with the United States, which could deal with each of two conflicting Communist powers to further her own interests. It was not a new prospect, but an improved one. The Sino-Soviet border clashes increased Washington's confidence in the conflict's potential, and Vietnam forced the issue. America's China policy had been frozen into a rigid stance since the beginning of the Korean war. Since then, only minor changes had occurred in our position —reductions in the lists of items forbidden for sale to mainland Chinese customers; reduced opposition to trading with the Chinese by other countries; and a greater willingness to deal directly with representatives of Communist China in Warsaw (where both governments had accredited ambassadors).

THE ROADS TO PEKING AND MOSCOW

By late 1970, Canada and then Italy had established diplomatic relations with Peking, responding to a new outward-looking phase in Chinese official behavior. At the United Nations General Assembly meeting that November the United States shifted its tactics on the issue of admitting Communist China (partly to postpone the time when admission would be approved). We softened our opposition to the annual resolution to seat Communist China and expel Nationalist China; we merely emphasized the injustice of expelling Nationalist China from the United Nations. (Once again, the resolution failed to achieve the necessary two-thirds vote for its approval.) Without actually saying so, the United States had adopted a "two-China" policy. Close observers attributed no more to this change than the "growing pressure in the world body for the Peking government to be seated," as the *London Times* stated on November 30, 1970.

During its first three years, the Nixon Administration appeared to be losing the battle of diplomatic isolation for China both in the United Nations and in terms of diplomatic recognition. In 1970–71 Nixon bypassed the two issues by arranging to make a state visit to Peking.

Secret preparations began during 1970 for a high-level direct meeting with Peking. Vice President Agnew set the stage in June 1971 with a five-week, ten-nation tour around the southern rim of Asia and into Europe. His conspicuous, highly publicized trip produced a good deal of right-wing political schmaltz in the American press. Traveling in five jet transports with a party of 141, including eleven reporters and two armored limousines, Agnew denounced the American press in press-censored Singapore, and praised the one-man rulers of the Congo, Kenya, and Ethiopia for their moderation—in contrast to what he termed the "querulous complaints and constant recriminations" of American black spokesmen.[5] In Spain he joined the regime's anniversary celebration for Franco's military victory in the Spanish Civil War of the 1930s. While this road show proceeded, Henry Kissinger flew secretly to Peking and returned. On July 15, Nixon announced the result from Washington: he had made arrangements to visit Peking sometime before May 1972. The theatrics had been well staged. Foreign and domestic reactions were heavily favorable, exaggerating the import of the announced summit. On July 23 Senate leaders Mike Mansfield and Hugh Scott introduced a bipartisan resolution commending the President "for his outstanding initiative."

Nixon's announcement that he had made arrangements to go to Peking greatly reduced the opposition to what was to become a major shift in American foreign policy—the abandonment of a twenty-year effort to keep Communist China in diplomatic isolation. The planning and conduct of a Peking summit exemplified the advantages the Nixon Administration gained from centralizing its foreign policy making. The Administration facilitated the changing of long-established policies by quietly preparing diplomatic initiatives in the White House rather than by moving conspicuously through the State Department and other government agencies. This approach was effective in commanding short-run support from the public and Congress, though it made generating longer-term support more difficult.

Plans had also been in the making for a Soviet-American summit. Relations with Moscow had scarcely been easy from the beginning of the Nixon Administration. Moscow's foreign policy leadership had resorted to its most authoritarian methods in late 1968 to crush the nationalist uprising in Czechoslovakia, spreading gloom in Western Europe that deepened with the Soviet justification for the brutal suppression of the "Prague Spring." Soviet Premier Brezhnev claimed for the Soviet Union the right to intervene in the internal affairs of any Communist country to protect the

[5] *London Times,* July 29, 1971.

Communist government. Superficially cast much like the Truman Doctrine of 1947, the Brezhnev statement differed vitally: whereas Truman had announced in 1947 that the United States would help any democratic government that was endangered by Communism, he never suggested intervening against the preferences of an established government. The Brezhnev Doctrine claimed the right of the Soviet Union to do just that.

Expanded Soviet military programs indicated that Moscow intended to improve her competitive position in relation to the United States. Russian nuclear forces had grown substantially in relation to American nuclear strength since the Cuban missile crisis in 1962, and Soviet naval forces were also expanding; their new strength in the Eastern Mediterranean was already complicating matters for the American Sixth Fleet there. In addition, the Soviet Union had played an active role in undermining a cease-fire along the Suez Canal in 1970 (discussed below).

Nonetheless, by the early 1970s Russia needed to reduce competition with the United States. The Sino-Soviet conflict raised less urgent threats for Moscow than for Peking, but Russian anxieties about China had plainly mounted. (From Washington's more detached viewpoint they seemed to be exaggerated.) Moscow had also relaxed tensions in Europe, partly reflecting Russian worries about its Chinese borders, and partly demonstrating an improved capacity for flexible diplomacy. Russia signed a peace treaty with Bonn that ratified the status of Berlin and recognized West Germany's legitimacy—to the consternation of the East German government. Moscow also treated a new liberal-national trend in Poland with a light hand—a striking if quiet contrast to Russia's swift military thrust into Prague in 1968.

Furthermore, the Russian economy had been stagnating. The high economic growth rate of the fifties—averaging 12 percent of the gross national product until 1958—had declined in the sixties to an average of 6 percent for that decade, and then drifted still lower. By the late sixties the Russians had begun to hope for a higher growth rate by importing technology from Western Europe and the United States as a byproduct of increased trade. However, closer Russian economic ties to the West would make it more difficult for Moscow to manage East European bloc relations through repressive measures. In fact, similar economic conditions suggested that the East European states would also need to build economic bridges to the West. Hence, Moscow faced difficult problems in balancing its interests in Eastern Europe with those in Asia and in reconciling its internal resource needs with the demands of external interests and national security. These balances could be helped by rendering the relationship with Washington more predictable.

Finally, there was the prospect of a Sino-American rapprochement. Moscow could scarcely view such a development with anything but alarm. If it chose, the United States could use its satellite warning systems to supply Peking with vital early warning of a Soviet strategic attack on China—information that would weigh heavily in affecting the Soviet-American military balance. Over the longer term, the United States could supply China with the technology that her economy—like the Soviet economy—needed for expansion. Moscow had denounced the prospect of a Sino-American rapprochement following the announcement in July of the planned Washington-Peking summit—after a long delay that indicated serious conflict within the Soviet government about the significance of the planned summit.

It was against this background that Kissinger negotiated the final arrangements with the Soviet government for a Moscow summit. In October 1971, Washington and Moscow announced plans for President Nixon to visit Moscow in May 1972.

THE PEKING SUMMIT

Nixon's Peking trip took place in February 1972. As the presidential campaign season approached, intensive negotiations with Hanoi and the NLF lay ahead, with the prospect that the declining American presence in Vietnam would reduce the war as an issue in the election. Since further American force withdrawals had already been announced, some critics charged that Nixon had already yielded his main bargaining assets with Hanoi. However, troop withdrawals had bought him time—and more time meant more room to maneuver in negotiations. For Hanoi and the NLF, an important question would be whether to settle with the Nixon Administration before the November election or await its outcome and deal with the winner. When it appeared that the Democratic candidate would be Senator George McGovern, who was likely to be less demanding in a peace settlement than Nixon, the Communist side faced a peculiar set of speculative choices. It could wait, and in the unlikely event that McGovern won, it could anticipate the best outcome: a quick settlement on generous terms. If it settled before the election, Nixon would be likely to make some concessions in the interest of keeping the negotiations moving ahead. Hanoi faced the least promising outcome if it waited and Nixon won the election. For with the assurance of four more years in office, he would be likely to demand more than he had before the election. Hanoi chose not to wait.

Nixon visited Peking during the last week of February 1972. His trip drew extensive press and television coverage in the United States, China, and around the world. Its main accomplishments were "atmospheric." The trip began a process of normalizing relations between the two countries but did little to settle outstanding issues. It finessed the most conspicuous bone of contention, the status of Chiang Kai-shek's regime in Taipei: both governments agreed on the *principle* that there is "but one China." They did not reestablish the conventional norms of diplomatic relations between Peking and Washington: both sides agreed to establish a "liaison office" in the other's capital and to shift the formal site of diplomatic communication from Warsaw to Paris. The Peking summit served mainly to reduce the extraordinary isolation of the Chinese leadership from direct contacts outside China and to signify that Sino-American relations were (or could be) an important factor in international affairs.

International politics can be significantly affected by anticipation. The mere announcement of the planned meeting in Peking had wide impact in Asia, for example, and rocked Japan's domestic politics, where deference to American foreign policy leadership was taken for granted. Japan would soon suffer a second shock resulting from Washington's decisive efforts to deal with an increasingly serious balance of payments problem.

No doubt the Peking and Moscow summits presented troublesome prospects for Hanoi as well. On March 3, two months before the 1972 Moscow summit, the official North Vietnamese Army daily newspaper, *Nhan Dan,* noted, with special attention to the Soviets, that Communists "never set national interests against the interests of the world revolution nor place private national interests above the common interests of the world revolution, much less serve their own national selfishness."

Midway between the Peking and Moscow summits, on March 30, North Vietnam launched a frontal assault on South Vietnam across the demilitarized zone, scoring large territorial gains, including the capture of Quang Tri city, a provincial capital (later recaptured by South Vietnamese forces). Damage was heavy. The offensive produced more than a million refugees in the South. Some South Vietnamese forces broke under the invasion, but more performed creditably, aided by American air power.

In response, American negotiators arranged a secret meeting with the North Vietnamese in Paris on May 2, seeking deescalation and settlement. It failed. According to Nixon's later account: "On May 8, faced with aggression in Vietnam and intransigence in Paris, I announced that we were mining all major North Vietnamese ports and were resuming air and naval attacks in North Vietnam to interdict the flow of troops and supplies into the South."[6]

The mining of Haiphong harbor had long been advocated by American military spokesmen but opposed by moderates and skeptics. The blockade begun in May was effective, and casualties as well as damage to supplies and facilities were heavy. Hanoi had evidently undertaken the "Easter invasion" as a last major military initiative prior to the United States election of 1972. It would scarcely have done so if it had correctly anticipated the American response. Under duress of the bombing, Hanoi officials would return to Paris negotiations in July, after the Moscow summit.

THE MOSCOW SUMMIT

Nixon's escalation of the Vietnam war just two weeks before the scheduled Moscow summit in May enhanced its dramatic weight with foreign as well as American audiences. No doubt the Soviet Union had supplied provisions for Hanoi's Easter invasion of South Vietnam. Even Washington, however, distinguished between general provisioning and directing the attack, for by then

6 *U.S. Foreign Policy for the 1970's,* vol. 4, p. 47.

Hanoi had gained a reputation for independence. When Nixon decided upon a severe military response, Moscow faced a difficult choice between Hanoi and Washington.

Nixon's innovative diplomacy was undeniably linked to internal American political pressures. Similarly, when faced with the Easter invasion, Nixon gambled with strategic and domestic political stakes. Moscow needed only to call off the summit and stall negotiations to complicate Nixon's electoral strategy. Evidently the factions within the Soviet government that supported détente with Washington judged that course of action too costly.

Washington and Moscow had been moving cautiously toward limited cooperation in their nuclear strategic forces, pursuing a mutual interest in stabilizing their nuclear military competition. They had signed a treaty designed to slow the spread of nuclear weapons in November 1969, just after the opening of the Strategic Arms Limitation Talks (SALT) in Helsinki. Moderation of the arms competition with the United States could free Soviet resources to cope with domestic economic stagnation and with the Chinese military threat.

Nixon's first Moscow summit had to achieve more tangible goals than the Peking event, though both served a common symbolic purpose in signifying his Administration's capacity for diplomatic mobility. Given the history of numerous working contacts between American and Russian officials, general "good will" discussions in Moscow like the talks in Peking would have been poor political theater for the Nixon Administration. Something more substantial would have to result from a Soviet-American summit. Thus Nixon undertook steps to ensure adequate preparations beforehand and reasonable grounds to expect concrete beneficial outcomes. Concrete results, moreover, would confirm for the United States (though scarcely for the Soviet Union) the value of the Peking summit. For Nixon's domestic supporters, both the adequacy of preparations and the significance of the Moscow summit's results would be tested. To assure optimal results, the two governments arranged to have the Moscow summit conclude and ratify several negotiations previously undertaken between them.

The major result of the Moscow summit was the first SALT agreement. It limited the deployment of Soviet and American ballistics missile defenses by treaty. A five-year interim agreement set maximum numbers for the main nuclear forces on each side. A second outcome of the summit was the removal of obstacles to improved economic relations between the United States and the Soviet Union.

THE 1972 ELECTION

The Democratic candidate for the Presidency in 1972 was North Dakota Senator George McGovern. Like Goldwater in 1964, McGovern gained the advantage within his party through an early dedication to the presidential primaries. He even defied political custom by declaring his candidacy a full year early, in January 1971. While Goldwater had run unchallenged in the early primaries, McGovern faced several rivals clustered in the middle of the political road. By taking a distinctly radical position, he won by splitting support among the moderate candidates.

It was later revealed that McGovern unknowingly received support from a somewhat unexpected group of skilled campaigners —aides from the Nixon reelection committee. They preferred McGovern as the weakest possible Democratic candidate, and they used illegal tactics to discredit and defeat his leading rivals in the primaries that doubtless had some effect.

Like Goldwater, having swept the primaries, McGovern won his party's nomination without having to accommodate himself to the major elements that composed the Democratic party. Also, like Goldwater, McGovern failed to alter his campaign style to unite his badly divided party. His campaign faltered from the outset, beginning with his inept choice of a vice presidential candidate with a politically troublesome personal history, and followed by the graceless way McGovern handled the awkward problem of replacing him.

The style that had worked to advantage in the primary contests now became a liability on the national stage: proposals were launched without careful scrutiny and retracted or revised in seeming confusion. The handling of domestic and international issues was often contentious and divisive. McGovern's own record on Vietnam (he was an early advocate of withdrawal) might have made him a formidable candidate, someone who could fight Nixon on that and other issues. But McGovern never became more than a factional leader, an outsider in the traditional party.

Nixon had succeeded in removing the Vietnam issue from serious partisan exploitation by his opponent. In a late preelection Gallup poll, seven out of ten Nixon voters and nine out of ten McGovern voters said that getting out of Vietnam was the prime factor in their choice of candidates.[7] From the opening of McGovern's campaign opinion surveys had given Nixon a 60 percent majority.[8] Backed by the massive efforts of a lavishly financed campaign organization, and further assisted by the use of unethical and illegal "dirty tricks," Nixon easily held the upper hand. Before the end of September, it had become widely accepted that a McGovern victory was unlikely.

Some have asked why Nixon's aides resorted to tactics that reflected so badly on the Republican party and that were unnecessary in light of his strong campaign lead. Part of the answer is that Nixon's campaign was run by men whose primary loyalty was to his personal political career, rather than to the Republican party. Their determination to take no chances after the very close 1960 and 1968 presidential elections partly accounts for the "overkill" of their efforts against such a weak opponent.

During October 1972, as the election approached, Hanoi pressed intensively to complete an agreement, dropping the demand that the United States agree to change the Saigon regime into a coalition government that included Communists. Kissinger, on a rising tide of optimism, pronounced that "peace is at hand." A week before the election, in a last-minute move to force Washington to sign, Hanoi broke the secrecy of the negotiations and disclosed their terms. They were generally reasonable. The Nixon Administration held out for the clarification of (1) linguistic differences, which it claimed affected the interpretation of the agreement; (2) the strength of the international control machinery; and (3) the status of the demilitarized zone. In the remaining days before the election it became apparent that the negotiations were paralyzed.

[7] *New York Times,* October 8, 1972.

[8] American Institute of Public Opinion, August 19 and August 29, 1972.

McGovern charged that the negotiations had been an election stunt. Nixon, with a touch of bravado, announced that he would not be forced into an agreement by an election deadline.

Nixon won the election with 61 percent of the popular vote, carrying every state except Massachusetts. He did not help his party much, however. Republicans lost seats in both the Senate and the House, leaving the Congress with increased Democratic majorities in both houses. The last-minute disappointments over peace negotiations proved of little importance in the election.

THE FINAL ROUND OF VIETNAM NEGOTIATIONS

Paris negotiations on Vietnam resumed in late November, after Nixon's reelection, but stalled again. Nixon broke them off and authorized a new bombing campaign against an expanded target list in the Haiphong and Hanoi areas. At the same time, he increased pressure on Saigon to acquiesce to a cease-fire in place. After three weeks of costly bombing—costly both to North Vietnam and to the American air force—the attacks stopped and negotiations resumed. They were finally completed in late January.

In the last stages of the negotiations, from October to January, Hanoi periodically probed Washington's link to Saigon. The "linguistic differences" that Washington wanted clarified included a translation problem designed to divide Saigon from Washington: Hanoi's Vietnamese language version differed from Hanoi's English language version in a way that made it unacceptable to Saigon. The final terms were scarcely reassuring to Saigon. At best they did not explicitly doom the Saigon regime. Saigon had not lost, but neither had it won the war. The terms of the agreement made it clear that for the Saigon regime the war was not yet over.

Nixon's critics claimed that the delay beyond October gained nothing. Technically, they were wrong. The terms of the final agreement were considerably more specific than the October draft. For instance, the status of the Saigon regime was clarified by removing ambiguous phraseology that could have implied approval of the much disputed coalition government. In fact, the People's Republican Government (the political successor to the National Liberation

Front) was not treated as a government coequal to the Saigon regime, despite the insistence of the PRG.

In general, however, the agreement mainly limited both Hanoi's and Washington's military roles in South Vietnam, but did not underwrite the Saigon regime against its rival Communist forces there. The principal gain for the United States in the last weeks of negotiation and fighting was to restore some of the credibility it had lost in the late sixties by demonstrating its resolve to use force to achieve its ends in international politics. It may be unfair to suggest that Moscow's repression of Czechoslovakia in 1968 parallels the Nixon Administration's handling of the last stages of negotiation and coercion over Vietnam, but it is nonetheless instructive. Having made its point in 1968, Moscow was able to pursue a more flexible policy toward Eastern Europe than seemed possible after the "Prague spring" ended. Similarly, the manner in which the United States withdrew its armed forces from Vietnam may have helped the Nixon Administration to restore the prerequisites for handling some types of international political matters more flexibly.

CONCLUSION

The conditions that produced United States involvement in Vietnam were numerous and complex. The main ones were (1) bureaucratic momentum—the perpetuation and gradual extension of past policies and operations rather than a reappraisal that would lead to an unpopular and difficult decision; (2) the propensity of presidential administrations to overprotect themselves on national security threats—what might be called "the fall of China syndrome"; and (3) doctrinaire Cold War anti-Communism that reduced the issues concerning Vietnam to stark and simplistic alternatives. These factors reinforced one another.

In Nixon's case, his political future lay in the reverse direction —extricating us from Vietnam on acceptable terms. He might have avoided becoming identified with the war by merely continuing withdrawal on Johnson's timetable, but Nixon chose to take on the burdens of the war and make them fit his own timetable. Thus the American withdrawal during the Nixon Administration was paced by the domestic political and electoral clock—in effect, a "Vietnam syndrome." The election politics of 1970 and 1972 generated the energy for change in our Vietnam stance. And if Vietnam accomplished nothing else for the United States, it established the Vietnam syndrome as an alternate political risk to those risks associated with the "fall of China syndrome"—that is, the unpopularity of an administration that allows itself to be drawn into a local foreign war versus the unpopularity of not intervening to stop a local Communist advance. The Vietnam experience may thus help to discourage the escalation of future American military commitments and actions.

On balance, however, it should be noted that despite the political incentives for getting us out of Vietnam and the rigid timetable for doing so, the Nixon Administration's actions in Vietnam reflected broader considerations as well. For example, as noted earlier, Nixon refused to make concessions to Hanoi in the last weeks of the 1972 campaign in order to ensure a Vietnam cease-fire by election eve, although he could not rule out the remote possibility that a last-minute cancellation or postponement in the negotiations, with Hanoi's skillful propaganda, could reverse the outcome of the 1972 presidential election. In sum, his Administration did not handle Vietnam merely as an artifact of American electoral politics.

What induced the North Vietnamese to settle? The available evidence is not conclusive about Nixon's coercive diplomacy making the difference. Hanoi may have wanted to settle anyway. But it appears that the combination of concessions and threats by Nixon influenced the outcome.

Nixon's personal style and behavioral propensities, together with Kissinger's negotiating style, were also doubtless factors in the settlement. Kissinger and Nixon were very good with competitive and hostile negotiations that were appropriately secretive and manipulative. In addition, Nixon had made the war *his* war, which increased the credibility of his threats. His aggressive responses to events in Indochina—the Cambodian and Laotian incursions and the attacks on Haiphong and Hanoi—demonstrated this trend.

Finally, it should be said that Vietnam was a gross misdirection of American efforts. We spent approximately $100 billion and concentrated much of our attention in foreign affairs for nearly eight years on Vietnam. Yet the stakes involved for Americans did not begin to justify this allocation of our material and political resources. Nor did the objectives of the Saigon regime justify their people's costs in lives, maiming, family and cultural disruption, and property damage. Because of the disparity between actual costs and aims, the moral issues of our involvement came to the fore through the war's critics. The powerful can be damned for failing to intervene as well as for the consequences of intervening. For example, progressive Latin Americans have criticized Washington for failing to intervene in helping them to further their domestic aspirations, but they have demanded that the principle of American nonintervention be upheld under other circumstances. These positions are not wholly inconsistent. These critics recognize that the United States cannot absent itself from Latin America. It can only be more or less active in wielding its influence. The "power realists" recognize these dilemmas and reject the claim that unqualified nonintervention per se is more moral.

The assessment of the full moral costs of Vietnam is still incomplete, and the war issue will continue to pit power realists against idealists in foreign relations. Largely neglected so far in the assessment of Vietnam have been America's lost opportunities to deal with other moral issues because of her preoccupation with Vietnam—issues such as international food and population problems, for example. For the power realists, other important opportunities were foregone. The next chapter will consider these other issues as we look at the rest of the Nixon Administration's foreign policy in the context of larger international developments from 1969 to 1974.

11

Nixon and the New "Era of Negotiations"

The last chapter traced Nixon's Vietnam policies through their climax in January 1973. This chapter will deal with the other major developments in his Administration's foreign policy.

The Nixon Administration showed an early interest in changing relations with allies and clients in Europe and the Third World areas. Until 1973, however, Vietnam dominated American foreign policy, relegating these other areas to secondary priority. The Nixon Doctrine, for instance, put the best face on Washington's new determination to reduce America's commitments abroad; yet at the end of 1972 it remained little more than a series of pronouncements. Far more important for Washington's Third World allies was what they could deduce for themselves in the Vietnam stalemate and in the domestic reaction to it in the United States: Washington was no longer likely to take up regional political disputes merely because one side could depict the issue in Cold War (anti-Communist) terms.

Another example involved trade and monetary policy. A monetary crisis in 1971 (to which the costs of Vietnam contributed) enabled Nixon to break some traditional restraints in monetary relations with America's major trading partners. But in this case, also, the follow-up from Washington achieved little beyond handling the immediate crisis. Similarly, little changed in the Middle East until the Yom Kippur war opened up new opportunities and posed new risks for American policy at a time when Kissinger could turn his attention away from Vietnam.

Even the Vietnam cease-fire agreement, signed in January 1973, however, did not free Nixon and his Administration to devote their attention to foreign relations in other areas. By the beginning of 1973 the Watergate scandals had begun to take over Nixon's attention, sap his political strength, and impede his foreign policy initiatives. Eighteen months later American foreign policy came to a virtual standstill while the transition to President Ford was effected.

These political conditions marked the boundaries within which the non-Vietnam aspects of American foreign policy were conducted during the Nixon era. In the following sections we will consider these policies in greater detail.

THE ATLANTIC ALLIANCE OF THE 1970s

The Vietnam involvement had become a major impediment to adaptive change in American foreign policy after 1964, as Washington's trans-Atlantic relations indicate. By 1969, when Nixon became President, Europe presented a special problem for Washington. By then, our failure in Vietnam had forced leaders of both this country's political parties to note that Europe deserved a special priority that it was not getting among American interests. Furthermore, it was becoming more difficult to assert the American role in Europe. Western Europeans no longer looked to the United States for economic and political leadership. More than a decade of prosperity had generated self-confidence, preoccupation with their own interests and problems, and less concern with the shadow of Soviet and American power across Europe.

The Soviet suppression of Czechoslovakia in 1968 changed this situation only briefly. The Western European reaction, after an initial flare of alarm, was surprisingly mild—scarcely what the suppression of Hungary in 1956 or the Czech coup in 1948 had generated. European reactions to an American war in Asia in the sixties, compared with European reactions to the Korean war seventeen years earlier, suggested the same trend: that European security concerns had become less sensitive to United States policy at the very time that a consensus was growing in Washington that Europe deserved more attention.

More broadly, the decade of prosperity also brought increased international interdependence among developed states, and in the early 1970s some economies had grown faster than others. West Germany and Japan, after steady rapid growth, were the third and fourth largest economies in the world, after the United States and the Soviet Union. These changes had major implications for changing United States relations with both allies and adversaries—Eastern as well as Western Europe. Yet initiatives to deal with them, like Johnson's "bridges to the East" to expand relations with Russian satellite nations in Europe, had been abandoned in the general preoccupation with Vietnam.

THE NIXON DOCTRINE AND THE EUROPEAN ALLIANCE

The American entanglement in Vietnam did provide impetus for a major policy innovation that directly affected our European allies and our Asian "client" states (to be discussed later). The difficulties of the United States in Vietnam led President Nixon to articulate a policy that emphasized new reliance on local and regional forces and resources in an effort to reduce dependence on the United States.

The Nixon Doctrine, as this policy was called, was part of the new flexibility in foreign relations assumed by Nixon and Kissinger both toward our traditional adversaries and toward our European allies. Nixon and Kissinger were more successful than Eisenhower had been during the 1950s in introducing flexible diplomacy, mainly because they were now able to demonstrate that the United States was no longer confined to a static bipolar conflict with the Soviet Union.

The Nixon doctrine followed the rationale of détente. It recognized that the United States and the Soviet Union had some common interests that could serve as the basis for closer cooperation.

In place of Dulles' vision of military specialization within the American-centered alliance system, Nixon stated that the United States would not use nuclear power "against any aggression," but solely to counter nuclear threats. In his annual foreign policy report in February 1971, summarizing the development of this rationale to date, he offered other states a protective nuclear umbrella to discourage the spread of nuclear weapons. In this way he set the United States apart from her allies, sharing an interest with Moscow: "the spread of nuclear capabilities would be inherently destabilizing. . . . Accordingly, while we maintain our nuclear forces, we have encouraged others to forego their own. . . . The Soviet Union has done so as well."[1]

Previously, the United States and Europe had shared interests that served as the basis for cooperative economic and security policies. But shared interests had long frustrated American efforts to get Europeans to assume more of the non-nuclear military burden for a common defense. Europeans lacked the incentives to carry a larger portion of the burden because, by the same logic of shared interest, the United States could be induced to carry more if they would not. Washington occasionally threatened, but threats lacked credibility as long as the European allies knew that Washington assessed the Soviet bloc threat to Europe as seriously as they did and considered the defense of Europe against Soviet dominance a vital American interest.

BILATERAL NEGOTIATIONS BY EUROPEAN ALLIES

American policy began to change when Kennedy nudged American political sympathies in Europe leftward toward leaders, such as the West German Premier Willy Brandt, who were interested in improved relations with Eastern Europe and the Soviet Union. This change in American policy gained more weight when the Nixon Administration went along with Brandt's *Ostpolitik*, his campaign for reconciliation with the Soviet bloc. Brandt re-

[1] *U.S. Foreign Policy for the 1970's,* A Report to the Congress by Richard Nixon, President of the United States, vol. 2, 1971, p. 14.

turned from a state visit to Moscow and Warsaw in August 1970 wth signed treaties that recognized as inviolable the postwar boundaries of Russia, Poland, and the Germanies. The West German parliament held up ratification of these treaties pending the positive outcome of four-power talks on the status of Berlin started earlier that year. That outcome, the Berlin agreement, which was completed in 1971, was a major concession by Moscow to reconciliation with West Germany. Russia accepted responsibility for access to Berlin from Western Europe and guaranteed it. This was a blow to East Germany, for her sovereignty had long been identified with her control of access to Berlin. The old Stalinist who headed the regime, Walter Ulbricht, immediately retired. Bonn, in return for guaranteed access, dropped its objection to East German representation in international bodies.

The 1971 four-power Berlin accord, taken with the Moscow treaty, had major implications for potential change in European and American relations with Moscow that both Moscow and Washington were slow to appreciate in full. The linked agreements demonstrated a serious Soviet interest in improved relations with Western Europe, and Russian motivations were readily apparent. The Russians wanted Western technology as a boost to their economy, and they wanted a more secure western border because of tension with China. It was less immediately apparent that the Soviets also made it easier for other members of the Atlantic Alliance, including the United States, to deal with Moscow bilaterally.

The problem of negotiating with Moscow had long been a source of embarrassment in Atlantic community relations. It would have been unthinkable in 1956, or even much later, for Bonn to deal directly with Moscow in the way that it did in 1970. To have done so would have alarmed Bonn's allies, who would have feared that an agreement had been reached at their expense. Kennedy had challenged Europeans to unite if they wanted to deal as an equal of the United States with Moscow; by implication, they would not have American support if they tried it without uniting first. Johnson had taken a somewhat less doctrinaire position, encouraging the development of ties, particularly economic ties, with Eastern Europe. But he had scarcely endorsed the idea of bilateral political agreements. In fact, during the early and mid-sixties, diplomatic initiatives eastward had been associated with efforts to reduce the cohesion of the Atlantic Alliance and challenge Washington's leadership of it. Before Brandt launched his *Ostpolitick*, France was the main West European power seeking direct links to Moscow. Taken with De Gaulle's other foreign policies—his hostility toward NATO, his pretense of independent nuclear military prowess, his exclusion of Great Britain from the Common Market—Washington expected that any Paris-Moscow treaty would advance French interests at the expense of American and Atlantic Alliance interests. West Germany had less competitive national objectives, and *Ostpolitik* therefore did not pose similar difficulties, as its outcome proved. *Ostpolitik* redefined Western bloc solidarity by demonstrating that NATO alliance members could work out new arrangements with Moscow bilaterally without jeopardizing the alliance— indeed, that they could benefit common interests of alliance members by pursuing their own national objectives within an alliance framework, for Bonn's initiatives improved the legal status of Berlin.

In sum, during the first half of the Nixon Administration, while it was still heavily preoccupied with Vietnam, it had mainly responded to initiatives in European diplomacy undertaken by West Germany. By 1973, after the Vietnam ceasefire and before Kissinger became Secretary of State, Washington tried, with little initial success, to take the initiative in Atlantic Alliance relations. United States efforts were hampered in part by the strained relations with our allies that had resulted from major changes we made in our trade and monetary policies abroad during 1971 in order to meet increasing financial crises.

NEW RELATIONS THROUGH MONETARY AND TRADE DIPLOMACY

Kissinger's position was not preeminent until the Vietnam settlement was completed. While Kissinger was becoming increasingly preoccupied with Vietnam and the Moscow-Peking diplomacy, Nixon turned to his Secretary of the Treasury, John Connally, to handle a major foreign trade and monetary crisis that developed during 1971. The crisis was an important event in American foreign economic relations because it marked a change in the way the

United States used its economic power. It was also an important indicator of Nixon's interest in breaking out of the constraints that Washington's traditional ways of dealing with its allies and trading partners had imposed on American foreign relations. The Nixon Administration's new posture of diplomatic mobility over Vietnam was in fact compatible with Nixon inclinations about international negotiations. The way he handled the monetary crisis of 1971 indicates that he was quite willing to reshape long-established relationships with other states in order to accomplish his objectives.

Given its importance to foreign policy, one may wonder why John Connally was Nixon's agent in this crisis. In fact, however, Kissinger was conspicuously less interested in foreign economic than in political issues, and the Secretary of the Treasury usually plays a major role in foreign economic policy. Nixon may also have wanted to test Connally for a larger role as Secretary of State or candidate for the Vice Presidency in Nixon's second term.

THE GROWING AMERICAN DOLLAR DEFICIT

United States foreign trade and monetary policy had been constructed after World War II, when American exports and dollars dominated international trade. At that time the government was heavily committed in principle to free trade, but principle had to come to terms with a gross imbalance in favor of American exports that justified trade barriers in Europe and Japan as well as developing states. The General Agreement of Tariffs and Trade, a multilateral instrument intended to structure and institutionalize trade relations, served to drive conventional trade barriers down, but left standing important indirect obstacles with America's chief trading partners in Europe and with Japan. Another American objective, the political and economic unity of Europe, further compromised the American goal of lowering trade barriers. A build-up of heavy dollar debts abroad during the postwar reconstruction period that turned the dollar into the dominant world reserve currency became an additional complication.

These circumstances prevailed over the next twenty-odd years. The fact that the dollar was the main reserve currency in the world monetary system deprived the United States of options other governments enjoyed in managing their currencies, for monetary controls undertaken to cope with internal American economic and fiscal problems would immediately affect the world monetary system. As a result, beginning in the late fifties, Washington took the lead in pressing for a comprehensive reform of the international monetary system, at first clumsily and with little support from other governments. The expansion of dollar credits as an international currency ended in 1958, when Washington first began to run annual trade deficits. By the mid-sixties, dollar balances in Europe were backing loans in Europe, providing the further expansion of international monetary units. This was one way America's trading partners were able to deal with the problem of monetary inflexibility created for them as well as the United States government when the postwar dollar became the major reserve currency.

The Nixon Doctrine was the first articulated attempt to change the frame of reference in dealings with developing nations that were allies of the United States by declaring that, past commitments aside, they would have to undertake to meet their own security needs first. Nixon seemed to be saying (the threat was not explicit) that states that did not make the effort might not be rescued by the United States.

For the developed countries—Japan and Western Europe, primarily—the Nixon Doctrine and its rationale meant several other things as well. The trade deficit with Europe could be attributed to several factors. Yet negotiations with European governments over sharing the foreign exchange burdens focused mainly on the costs incurred in maintaining United States troops there. West Germany, where most American forces were stationed, agreed to "offset payments" to help reduce the trade deficit. Offset payments were guarantees by Germany to import an agreed minimum amount of American goods and services. But the agreement was merely a palliative. Germany would have imported many of these goods even without this arrangement. A more fundamental corrective would have been to revalue the German mark. For its own reasons, the Federal Republic kept its currency undervalued in the world market—in effect, penalizing the German consumer in order to sustain a high foreign (including American) demand for German products. Washington's willingness to settle for offset payments in the late sixties indicated that it was more concerned about the effect the trade imbalance would have on Congress' willingness to maintain American troops in Europe than about the economic problems that lay behind it.

The Japanese case, despite certain differences, was remarkably similar. After World War II rearmament was at first prohibited in both countries by the occupying powers. After 1954, however, West Germany was encouraged to rearm, and it quickly assumed a major share of Western Europe's defense burden. Japan did not rearm, and through the fifties and sixties the United States in effect carried the Japanese defense burden with a "mutual defense" treaty that assigned American military forces to Japan's defense. While the United States maintained a defense burden ranging from 6 to 10 percent of our GNP, Japan spent trivial sums on her Self-Defense Forces. In a similar spirit, conventional trade barriers were lowered on both sides, yet Japan maintained substantial indirect barriers (and certain direct ones as well) against the inflow of foreign goods and capital. The Japanese also kept the yen highly under-valued in international trade—even more than West Germany undervalued the deutschmark.

As long as American trade was in surplus, these asymmetries in trading relations were justified or went unexamined. By the time the balance of trade shifted in favor of Japan and Western Europe in the early sixties they had become venerable conditions in the international system of trade. Furthermore, through the sixties the United States trade deficits were not considered alarming. Heavy defense spending abroad, foreign aid, and large private outflows of investment capital accounted largely for them. This period of uneasy complacency ended, however, when the adoption of a cheap money policy in the United States in 1970 to counteract domestic recession precipitated an international monetary crisis. During 1971 a massive outflow of dollars from the United States occurred. In particular, the volume of dollar outflow soared as investors sought higher interest rates abroad and speculative gains from the dollar's declining value.

DRASTIC AMERICAN MONETARY ACTIONS

At first the United States government neglected the problem while its major trading partners fell to bickering about what to do. West Germany and Holland floated their currencies while France and others maintained parities by using exchange controls to prevent the excessive inflow of dollars. Then, on August 15, 1971, virtually without warning, Nixon took decisive action to reverse the rapidly deteriorating American monetary situation. He suspended gold payments for dollars, and he imposed a 10 percent surcharge on imports, import discriminations against capital goods, and subsidies for American exports. These actions declared his intention to compel Europe and Japan in particular to revalue their currencies against the dollar—a shock tactic that was largely successful.

Nixon also demanded that America's trading partners undertake other measures to help the situation. Secretary of the Treasury Connally followed up on Nixon's mid-August initiatives with an aggressive negotiating effort. His opening position was to insist that the dollar problem be shared with America's trading partners. He argued that the dollar, when it serves as a reserve currency, is a common institution among trading partners, and these partners have an obligation to share in finding a solution for the dollar crisis. Connally's "starting" position also supported maintaining the value of the dollar against gold. Devaluing the dollar came as a latter-stage American concession.

Connally's behavior was reminiscent in certain respects of French diplomacy in the early and mid-sixties. De Gaulle's willingness to run risks and incur the enmity of allies gave him a distinct advantage over the United Kingdom, often over the Federal Republic of Germany, and usually over the governments of Italy and the smaller states in European foreign relations. In effect, Connally forced Washington's nine major trading partners to acknowledge their own interest in a strong dollar and in relatively stable exchange rates and hence greater responsibility than before in the status of the American balance of payments.

The monetary negotiations of 1971 are a distinct reference point in American relations with the non-Communist developed world because they abandoned the established customs of American negotiations with allies and friends. They were an extreme but by no means isolated development. The Nixon Administration's interest in establishing a more assertive American diplomacy in a policy area closely linked to monetary policy—trade negotiations—began modestly in 1969. Over the next three years the Administration became bolder until it came to question the status quo in world trading arrangements. Speaking before the governors of the International Monetary Fund and the International Bank for Reconstruction and Development on September 25, 1972, Nixon said: "Like every leader of the nations represented here, I want to see new jobs created all over the world, but I cannot condone the export of jobs out of the United States caused by an unfairness built into the world's trading system."[2]

THE LINKAGE OF NATIONAL SECURITY AND TRADE POLICIES

Nixon made clear what he meant by "unfairness" when he proposed in April 1973 a Trade Agreement Act that would set aside the long-established statutory constraints on the bargaining power of the United States government in trade negotiations. He sought unlimited authority in negotiating trade agreements with other countries to raise, lower, or eliminate tariffs, and to convert one kind of trade barrier into another. No more would tariffs be the sole target of trade negotiations. In addition, he linked trade and security matters—issues that had theretofore been kept separate. After long delay and some amendments, Congress passed this proposal in late 1974.

Speaking to a national press convention in April 1973, Kissinger declared that the Administration intended to negotiate a new "Atlantic Charter" with European states. He referred to common purposes and drew an analogy to the highly regarded Marshall Plan of the late forties. Yet in fact his linking of the two main concerns shared by Europe and the United States—national security and trade—put aside another long-established custom.

Kissinger's principle of linkage had kept a sense of proportion in Sino-American and Soviet-American negotiations. According to his principle, if major issues are divided up, each segment must be settled on the basis of some principle of balance equity; it then becomes very difficult to agree on segments, much less reach a general accommodation. The linkage principle had apparently fa-

---

[2] *National Journal,* January 13, 1973, p. 45.

cilitated agreement in Moscow in May 1972 partly because it discouraged haggling over details. Linkage, however, meant something quite different to Western Europeans who had survived the onslaught of Connally's monetary diplomacy.

The stable, institutionalized relationships that had grown up in the fifties among the Atlantic partners differentiated the way trade, economic aid, monetary, political, and military matters were handled by common institutions. Kissinger, by emphasizing linkage, opened the whole Atlantic relationship for review. As a working alliance, NATO had adjusted incrementally. Linkage could be used by a state intent upon changing the status quo to assert more influence, and Europeans recognized this fact. The British Foreign Secretary, Sir Alec Douglas-Home, questioned the feasibility of linking monetary, trade, and defense issues in a single set of negotiations, noting that "established institutions are already working on most of the issues" and "the time scales of their discussions differ."[3] British and French spokesmen rejected Kissinger's effort to link defense and economic issues. By denying linkage, they supported alliance procedures that protected the status quo against the change-oriented Americans.

AMBIVALENT RELATIONS
WITH OUR ALLIES

Just how much the Nixon Administration could change the nature of the Atlantic Alliance depended upon how thorough it was in changing its own diplomacy as well as on its diplomatic prowess and what interests were at stake. Nixon did not abandon the main features of established Atlantic relationships. In 1970, under pressure from Congress to reduce American troops in Europe, he used NATO machinery to create the appearance of an expanded European military effort. The European Defense Improvement Plan was supposed to increase the defense expenditures of West European powers by 3 to 4 percent. In fact these increases were made mainly on paper. In this case, NATO institutions and processes served Washington in its claims—made in appealing for domestic political

[3] As quoted in "Reflections on the Quarter," *ORBIS,* Vol. XVIII, No. 1 (Spring 1973), p. 9.

support—that European members had met the conditions required for undiminished American support. Similarly, while the Nixon Doctrine pointed strongly to greater self-reliance among our allies, Washington resisted European efforts to use the French and British nuclear forces as the core of an independent European nuclear force intended to reduce Europe's strategic dependence on the United States. Self-reliance evidently did not extend to nuclear matters. Kissinger's "Atlantic Charter" speech made the same point. Indeed, among the guidelines for Atlantic partnership relations was one that sounded much like Kennedy in challenging Western Europe to unify itself politically. Kissinger's distinction between a regionally oriented Western Europe and the United States with "global" interests said much the same thing.

If there was anything about 1973 that made it the "year of Europe," the Yom Kippur war and the ensuing OPEC (Organization of Petroleum Exporting Countries) oil embargo ended these conditions. Western Europe proved to be acutely aware that it was heavily dependent upon Middle East oil for its economic well-being. To Washington's dismay and anger, most of our European NATO allies denied landing rights to cargo aircraft taking military supplies to Israel. British, French, and German officials were in turn dismayed and alarmed when Washington called for a strategic alert without consulting them when Soviet forces were found preparing to intervene directly in the Middle East. Further, when the oil embargo began, the Atlantic powers failed to cooperate among themselves in establishing common policies and sharing oil inventories in an effort to cope with oil shortages. Atlantic solidarity simply collapsed. Britain and France entered into negotiations with Arab oil suppliers for long-term contracts without consultation with the United States. That December, speaking to the Pilgrim Society in London, Kissinger complained that "some Europeans have come to believe that their identities should be measured by Europe's distance from the United States."

Washington's relations with Europe improved after the Yom Kippur war. Kissinger offered cooperation in coping with the new energy situation; but the Administration floundered for more than a year over its own energy policy, and was therefore unable to provide credible leadership to Europe or Japan in coping with the prospect of future oil embargoes. An oil consumers' conference held in early 1974 reestablished a limited basis for cooperation among the Atlantic partners in dealing with OPEC. France held out for an independent approach, but found itself isolated. Meanwhile, President Ford had negotiated the Vladivostok agreement with Soviet leader Brezhnev in a new effort to contain the strategic arms race.

NATO was weakened by the withdrawal of Greece in mid-1974. Italy and the United Kingdom continued to suffer severe economic effects from the oil crisis. The Portuguese regime, after a progressive military coup, had fallen into the hands of a leftist group. Washington was in no position to negotiate with Moscow from a "situation of strength" in Europe, but the United States saw some promise of success in view of evidence that the Soviet regime had its own internal reasons to negotiate.

THE PENTAGON PAPERS AND THE WATERGATE SCANDALS

THE LEAKING OF CLASSIFIED INFORMATION

In the spring of 1971 Daniel Ellsberg, an MIT researcher and former analyst for the Defense Department who had served in Vietnam, released to the press the so-called Pentagon Papers. These consisted of the major portions of a historical study of American policy in Vietnam from 1954 through 1968 that was classified "Top Secret."

The newspaper publication of the Pentagon Papers and related government files in mid-1971 panicked the White House even though they dealt only with the period before 1969. The main apparent purpose of these releases was to discredit the American involvement in Vietnam or particular people connected with it by revealing embarrassing details of how it came about. The opponents of the Vietnam war already knew most of the detailed information the Pentagon Papers provided; some of them had authored its documents and studies. The ring of authenticity lent by the Papers may have provided war critics with new weaponry, but there was little to use against the Nixon Administration specifically.

American laws concerning official secrets were on shaky grounds when applied to the release of the Pentagon Papers. These criminal statutes outlawed actions by traitors and spies, and they applied to information that, if disclosed, would harm national security. But the Pentagon Papers mentioned no current negotiations or military operations, and by no stretch of the imagination was Ellsberg a spy (though some officials considered him a traitor). His trial during 1972–73 thus also became a test of these statutes as they applied to an American citizen who was not in league with a foreign power. If the statutes were struck down, the government's document security procedures would have to be reconstructed. Neither Ellsberg's guilt nor the validity of the statutes was resolved, however, for the case was thrown out of court in May 1973 when much of the government's evidence was declared inadmissible because it had been acquired through illegal wiretaps and other "misconduct."

The major significance of the Pentagon Papers release was not in supplying Administration opponents with ammunition but rather in increasing the President's already obsessive concern with maintaining executive branch secrecy. Within a week after the Papers began to appear in the *New York Times,* President Nixon authorized a White House secret special investigations unit, nicknamed "the Plumbers," designed to "stop security leaks and to investigate other sensitive security matters."[4]

THE WATERGATE MORASS

In preparation for the 1972 election, and in an atmosphere of siege, Nixon established a Committee to Reelect the President (CRP), headed by his friend John Mitchell, former United States Attorney General.

Under the direction of Mitchell and Nixon, the committee turned normal political fund raising into a large-scale and often illicit enterprise. The committee accepted illegal contributions from business firms; it actively sabotaged the campaigns of leading Democratic presidential aspirants in the state primaries; it used FBI wiretaps to provide campaign information; and in the matter-of-fact

[4] As quoted in "Chronology of Related Events," *The White House Transcripts* (New York: Bantam Books, 1974), p. 814.

spirit of industrial espionage or police undercover work, the CRP "bugged" the Democratic national headquarters and other lesser Democratic campaign offices.

In June 1972, Washington police caught red-handed a wiretapping team that included an employee of the CRP during a burglary at the Democratic headquarters, located in the Watergate complex. Through White House intervention, the links between the burglars and the CRP were covered up until after the November 1972 presidential election. Then, however, the CRP involvement began to come to light.

As it did, the President and key members of his immediate staff undertook additional cover-up efforts that in turn became the targets of press investigation and criminal prosecution. By April 1973, several White House officials, including John Ehrlichman and H. R. Haldeman, came under enough suspicion to force their resignations from the White House staff.

During the summer, the Senate established a special Watergate investigating committee that held televised hearings. As the Watergate episode unraveled, other questionable operations were uncovered—greatly broadening the suspected scope of the Administration scandals. In addition to the illegal activities of the CRP itself, other efforts by Administration officials were revealed: the establishment and conduct of the Plumbers' unit, which among other things had burglarized a Los Angeles psychiatrist's office in search of information to discredit Daniel Ellsberg; use of the Internal Revenue Service to persecute those who opposed the President's policies; the selling of ambassadorships and other government favors; and questionable practices by President Nixon himself that had resulted in significant underpayment of income taxes for several years. In response to an investigation by Congress, Nixon promptly complied with the ruling of a House tax subcommittee that he owed $467,000 in back taxes.

By mid-1974 the President's personal lawyer, two members of his White House staff, a former Attorney General, and three former members of the CRP had confessed to federal crimes. Three former members of the President's Cabinet and his two closest former White House advisers (Ehrlichman and Haldeman) were under indictment or had been tried.

Nixon himself was being investigated by the House Judiciary

Committee to determine the critical issue of whether the President should be impeached for "high crimes and misdemeanors." With few exceptions, all charges against Nixon and his associates alleged illegal activities for partisan political goals, and the evidence that accumulated against them indicated an intense preoccupation with manipulating political power.

In July 1974, the House committee investigating possible impeachable offenses by Nixon drafted and passed by majority vote three articles of impeachment. Shortly afterward, new evidence proved Nixon's involvement in the cover-up even more clearly, and he resigned as President in August 1974 in order to avoid a vote of impeachment against him by the full House.

WATERGATE AND FOREIGN POLICY

Nixon's Watergate-related behavior remains puzzling. It seems likely that he badly overestimated his ability to "contain" the situation and badly underestimated the public's reaction to the blatant immorality of the political fund raising, "dirty tricks," and cover-up activities that came to light. As cover-up expediencies failed, Nixon seems to have turned to his record in foreign affairs as a means of personal escape and vindication as well as to rally his special assistants. For example, in a late evening telephone conversation with Ehrlichman on April 14, 1973, the President mused:

> You know, what the hell, it is a little melodramatic, but it is totally true that what happens in this office in these next four years will probably determine whether there is a chance—and it's never been done—that you could have some sort of an uneasy peace for the next 25 years. . . .
>
> And that's my—whatever legacy we have. Hell, it isn't going to be in getting a cesspool for Winnetka; its going to be there.[5]

Nixon's musings notwithstanding, the Watergate scandals undermined the credibility of his Administration domestically and paralyzed its foreign policy initiatives while attention was directed toward the increasing domestic crisis. During Nixon's last six

[5] *Ibid.,* p. 422.

months in office his foreign policy activities were increasingly interpreted as efforts by the President to divert attention from Watergate or to bolster the claim that he was indispensable.

One effect of the President's weakened status was to enhance Kissinger's foreign policy status. Kissinger's own actions to preserve secrecy within his National Security Council staff raised congressional suspicions. But he was able to fend off critics mainly through his prestige.

When he had first joined the Nixon Administration, Kissinger's lack of political standing must have been one of his attractive features for Nixon. But by 1973 Kissinger's prominence in international negotiations and his colorful public personality had generated a popular following at home and abroad that did not diminish even as Nixon fell. When Gerald Ford became President in August 1974, he gave primary emphasis to keeping Kissinger on as Secretary of State in his actions to maintain continuity with the Nixon Administration.

TURBULENCE AND
ACCOMMODATION WITH MOSCOW

Each presidential administration in the postwar era has relied upon public hostility toward the Soviet Union to sustain general support for its military posture and foreign policies. This trend has made it difficult to pursue détente with Moscow without reducing public support for foreign policies designed—or at least justified—for their intended value in conducting such negotiations. Presidents have thus found it difficult to compete with the Soviet Union while also attempting to parley with it. Truman had postponed negotiations to build "situations of strength." Of the postwar Presidents, Eisenhower had been the most conspicuously worried about creating public expectations that could not be fulfilled through summit diplomacy; but each had encountered the strain between vigilance and reconciliation. Kennedy had been sobered by his Vienna summit meeting with Khrushchev and had not attempted to resume general negotiations with the Soviets until 1963, after the Cuban missile crisis had strengthened his reputation for vigilance. Johnson had started toward a conciliatory position, but gave it up because it was incompatible with the public mood he considered necessary to support the Vietnam war.

NEW FLEXIBLE DIPLOMACY

Nixon's attitude was not radically different from his predecessors in his views about vigilance, and yet he achieved a different outcome. Doubtless Kissinger played a significant role in making the difference. He persuaded Nixon to abandon his support for nuclear superiority in favor of parity (which Nixon had denounced during his 1968 campaign) in order to establish a flexible negotiating position. At the same time, Nixon assumed a strong "arm to parley" posture, demanding congressional approval of the Safeguard missile defense system and the appropriations to modify nuclear-tipped missiles to enable them to carry multiple warheads before any explicit agreements were achieved with the Soviets. These steps would help assure that a détente with the Soviets would not soften congressional support for the planned missile systems. This was scarcely a Kissinger-inspired position. It was pure Nixon—a tough starting position comparable to his monetary policy actions of August 1971.

During the Nixon era both Moscow and Washington established a record of toughness and flexibility that might encourage the other to believe summit diplomacy could be productive. In their foreign relations each demonstrated that it had the capability and will to use military power to achieve its ends. Both also showed a flexibility that indicated they had the license to make concessions and the authority to honor agreements.

Moscow had been expanding its strategic forces rapidly since the mid-sixties, and it had suppressed the Czech revolt in early 1968. Yet it coped adaptively with a political outburst in Poland the following December. Soviet Foreign Minister Gromyko had attacked the United States for resuming its diplomatic contacts with the Chinese in Warsaw in 1969. Moscow attempted to place offensive nuclear-missile–carrying submarines in Cuba in 1970, and it helped undermine cease-fire arrangements between Israel and the Egyptians that year. Also, Russian support encouraged India to intervene in the Bangladesh war of independence against Pakistan, while Washington took the other side. Yet Brezhnev scheduled a summit meeting with Nixon in Moscow for May 1972, while the Vietnam war was still in progress, and did not cancel it despite Nixon's order to blockade Haiphong harbor. In October 1973, Moscow undertook preparations for major direct intervention in the Middle East. A year later Russia's strategic forces continued to grow in strength.

Washington followed a somewhat similar course. Nixon had been reluctant to start the SALT negotiations in 1969. He had provoked Moscow by visiting Rumania the same year. His overtures to China were conspicuous evidence of a new diplomatic flexibility in Washington and particularly pointed evidence to Moscow because of its quarrel with Peking. The American response to the discovery of Soviet submarine activity in Cuba in 1970 was tough but restrained. We were careful to preserve Soviet prestige when the Russians gave private assurances that they would not locate offensive missiles in Cuba. Washington accepted this concession discreetly. On the tough side, Kissinger indicated that Russia's role in supporting India and Bangladesh against Pakistan could jeopardize the impending Nixon visit to Moscow. Nixon's decision to blockade Haiphong harbor and resume the bombing of North Vietnam just weeks before the Moscow summit of 1972 was tough, even audacious, considering Nixon's domestic stakes in that summit. Furthermore, at the height of the 1973 Yom Kippur war, Nixon quietly ordered a strategic alert in response to observed Soviet preparations to send Russian troops into the war. The American troop alert apparently induced the Soviets to stop. (As in the 1970 Cuban incident, the Nixon Administration did not publicize either the alert or the Soviet backdown.)

THE COMPLICATIONS OF DÉTENTE

Both the Nixon Administration and the Soviet regime thus mixed toughness with discreet diplomatic initiatives on behalf of negotiated settlements. Several complications resulted from this style of quiet diplomacy. The Nixon era began with a mood of strong public distrust of the President and of government in general. Unpublicized successes represented lost opportunities to improve public confidence in the Administration. More than that, they risked increasing public suspicions when they were detected but still unexplained. Both the Cuban submarine crisis and the Middle East strategic alert were insufficiently explained to the public to forestall suspicions that they were unnecessary or worse. Congress and the press still remembered Johnson's exploitation of the Tonkin Gulf attack to win support for escalating the Vietnam war. Without full disclosure later military alerts inspired similar suspicions about Nixon. The 1973 Middle East alert occurred as the Administration became increasingly enmeshed in the Watergate scandal. It alarmed our European allies and generated suspicions at home. To the irritation and resentment of the White House, the press speculated that it was staged to offset Watergate setbacks. By the time of Nixon's second summit meeting in Moscow in June 1974, House impeachment proceedings had become serious business, further contributing to suspicions that Nixon would make unwise concessions to the Soviet Union in his effort to achieve new breakthroughs in détente.

Nixon claimed that his personal relationship with Brezhnev was an important ingredient in his ability to negotiate. The claim attracted heated criticism of Nixon for using foreign policy accomplishments as justification for overlooking the mounting evidence of abuses in the White House. As the 1974 summit approached, Nixon's home base was further weakened by an increasingly visible faction centered in the Defense Department that challenged the optimistic expectations about SALT II. In a Washington press conference on June 17, 1974, Secretary of Defense James Schlesinger reassured newsmen, however, that the President would not sacrifice national interests to help him out of his own predicament with Watergate because he was a "visceral patriot."

Other critics of Soviet-American détente looked inside Russia to evaluate the effects of détente and found ample cause for concern. For example, in early 1974 a group of British and American authorities on Soviet and international affairs published an evaluation of détente that criticized it for enabling Moscow to reverse liberalizing trends within Russia. They declared:

> While *détente* does not mean the abandonment of the Soviet posture
> of ideological struggle, it tends to foster in the West the idea that it
> has to accept tacitly Soviet political practices as a necessary condition

for avoiding a nuclear war. This false alternative provided in the past the underlying premise for those advocating unilateral Western disarmament. Today it is Western government spokesmen who often use this simplified dichotomy to justify an attitude of silent indifference toward victims of Soviet persecution.[6]

This and similar criticism gained the endorsement of Senator Henry M. Jackson, a prominent Democratic presidential aspirant and a major critic of Nixon's foreign policies. Jackson had criticized the SALT I agreement, alleging its overreliance on American technological superiority, which could only be temporary, he asserted. He challenged the terms of American trading arrangements with Russia, including the "wheat deal" in 1972; and he had made a point of criticizing the Soviet government's harassment of intellectual dissenters and opposition to emigration by Russian Jews. Jackson had long been identified with the conservative wing of his party, but détente exposed an issue that appealed to the center and left in both parties: political conditions inside Russia.

Senator Fulbright, the retiring chairman of the Senate Foreign Relations Committee, stated a quite different view in a Senate speech in June 1974. Warning that the Soviet Union is a great and proud nation "that is not likely to yield indefinitely to foreign pressures" for the reform of its internal practices, he declared that "there were larger issues at stake, issues more directly related to the national interests of the United States." The main one was "the cultivation of an international atmosphere of security and cordiality in which the danger of nuclear war could steadily abate."[7]

Unquestionably, a Soviet-American détente affects the internal politics of both great powers, and intrabloc politics as well. Doubtlessly, the Soviet regime did use détente as critics charged—to make the handling of internal dissent easier—just as Nixon used it for that purpose in the United States. Détente also served both powers in dealing with their own allies and with what Kissinger once called the "gray areas," such as the Middle East and Southeast Asia. Euro-

[6] "Détente: An Evaluation," *International Review,* No. 1, Spring 1974, as reprinted in U.S., Congress, Senate, Armed Services Committee, "Détente: An Evaluation," Committee Print, 93rd Cong., 2nd sess., 1974, p. 3.

[7] "Normalizing Relations with the Soviet Union—Avenues and Obstacles," Statement to U.S. Senate Committee on Foreign Relations, June 27, 1974, p. 4.

pean officials complained that Washington failed to consult them on negotiating positions before dealing with Moscow. Peking also attacked Soviet-American summitry. Such reactions were to be expected. Indeed, from the perspective of the late fifties, it was surprising that a Soviet-American détente had not led to the complete disintegration of NATO or to Russia's renewed suppression of Eastern Europe. Even in the mid-seventies it was surprising how flexible Moscow's relations with Eastern Europe remained, and how mild West European protests were about direct American negotiations with Russia.

Nixon's centralized conduct of foreign relations, with initiatives and innovations instigated from the top, facilitated his Administration's accomplishment of great power détente and increased flexibility in other diplomacy. It remains to be seen, however, how compatible these procedures are with the internal political requirements for American foreign relations. For the Nixon Administration constructed its foreign policy on the same principles of presidential initiative and secretiveness that had exacerbated public disillusionment over Vietnam.

EAST-WEST BLOC NEGOTIATIONS

The character of multilateral negotiations between the Western and Soviet blocs changed to reflect the new Soviet-American diplomatic flexibility. During autumn 1973, two multilateral East-West conferences got under way—an arms reduction conference in Vienna (Mutual Balanced Force Reductions) and the European Security Conference in Geneva. The bilateral Soviet-American SALT II negotiations also began in Geneva. The two multilateral conferences indicated that Soviet-American diplomatic initiatives were subjecting the East and West blocs to internal stresses, to the initial advantage of the Western bloc. On the other hand, some Americans who had been alarmed by the outcome of SALT I and were disappointed by the limited results of SALT II assessed bilateral developments as favoring Moscow.

The Russians had for several years wanted to hold a conference on European security that would exclude non-Europeans (that is, Canada and the United States). Washington had also wanted to start a multilateral conference that would offset the narrow Soviet-American SALT negotiations and deal with broader arms control issues as well. Moscow initially saw European security negotiations as a way to divide the Atlantic Alliance and bring pressure on its European members. In the course of gaining agreement to the conference, however, the Russians had to accept Canada and the United States as members. Moscow's East European partners were eager to participate. Tedious negotiations about the ground rules settled the charged question of which states would be participants. Moscow was apparently more embarrassed at the prospect of exposing the Warsaw Pact's internal stresses in an open, multilateral meeting than were the NATO members.

Mutual Balanced Force Reductions (MBFR) was an old proposal. It dated from the last year of the Johnson era. The Nixon Administration adopted it in 1971 to head off domestic critics who wanted to reduce United States forces unilaterally and to meet the demands from NATO powers for more of a role in arms talks. Moscow at first resisted MBFR. France came to oppose it because it feared West Germany's domination of Europe if the United States left. Washington, in turn, wanted to negotiate the reduction of American forces along with others, anticipating that American forces would have to be reduced in any case. These shifts in support indicated that pragmatic political considerations controlled participation on both sides, including assessments about the comparative effects of force reductions on the NATO and Warsaw Pact alliances.

STRATEGIC ARMS LIMITATIONS TALKS

The SALT II negotiations were supposed to produce a major new agreement about strategic arms limitations between the Soviet Union and the United States by mid-1974, in time for Nixon's next scheduled visit to Moscow. They did not. At Moscow in June, Nixon and Brezhnev approved minor agreements. SALT I had given the Soviets a numerical advantage in nuclear missile throw weights and numbers, relying on the qualitative advantage of American missiles in their performance and in multiple warheads (MIRVs). These were temporary agreements that would be satisfactory until more carefully prepared long-term agreements could be worked out.

This meant that time was on the Russian side, and the lack of progress in the SALT II negotiations induced considerable disappointment in Washington. Paul Nitze, the senior member of the American delegation, resigned shortly after the President's return from Moscow, complaining of inadequate communication between the White House and the delegation and raising questions about the true predicament for the United States. The SALT I agreement had been greeted by a Washington euphoria generated by the Peking and Moscow summits in 1972. The mood in Washington over negotiating with the Russians had changed by mid-1974. Only Senator Jackson had demanded qualifiers to the SALT I treaty provisions during the Senate ratification process of 1972. When Nixon returned to Moscow two years later, however, Jackson's skepticism enjoyed more support. The continued turbulence in the Soviet-American relationship had moderated the American enthusiasm for negotiating with the Russians.

THE YOM KIPPUR WAR AND OIL: RADICAL CHANGES IN THE MIDDLE EAST

TENSION IN THE MIDDLE EAST: 1967–73

The Johnson Administration had subordinated its foreign policy in the Middle East to the objective of maintaining public support for his Vietnam policy. That meant adopting a strongly pro-Israeli position—the most easily defended policy in the face of vocal Jewish pressure groups in this country as well as more general sympathy for Israel as a besieged democracy.

The 1967 Six Day war had enabled Israel to achieve territorial gains that reduced the exposure of its population to guerrilla attack and to Syrian artillery fire from the Golan Heights, and provided the Israeli armed forces warning time and territory in which to maneuver against an Egyptian attack. Israel acquired control over the Golan Heights and all the Sinai. Now Egypt would have to cross the Suez Canal to attack Israeli forces.

Israeli military plans had not anticipated political consequences. The Six Day war produced a fresh crop of Palestinian refugees and fueled Palestinian nationalism throughout the Middle East. The new territories needed governing. Israeli authorities were impressive but scarcely benevolent rulers over Arabs, who were themselves pressured from outside to leave their homes, or at least not to cooperate with their new rulers.

Israel, though an advanced democracy, was governed by a "wall to wall" coalition of political parties in the tense atmosphere of a state under siege from her neighbors. Increasingly, Israel began to lay permanent claim to the occupied territories—Jerusalem for political reasons and the Golan Heights for military reasons. Segments of the West Bank and even the Sinai were being colonized by Israel in an effort to establish permanent claim to territories taken in 1967 to achieve only short-term military objectives.

In early 1969, during the first months of the Nixon Administration, Secretary of State William Rogers took the lead in dealing with the Arab-Israeli conflict, enunciating a new policy of "even-handedness" for the region. Kissinger's inactivity with respect to the Middle East hot spots seems to have been a calculated division of labor between the National Security Council staff and the State Department. Leaving Middle East problems to the State Department had certain advantages. The Department could provide continuity with past policies for American negotiating positions while making tactical adjustments in them. It could also offer the White House some insulation from political pressures by American pro-Israeli interests. Where such politically explosive issues have been involved, however, Presidents have usually taken a more direct hand. Johnson, for instance, had kept relations with Israel under his close scrutiny. Nixon at first left Middle East policy with the State Department, but Kissinger's role came to dominate there as part of the general centralization in the White House.

Since the Six Day war, while Israel was laying political claim to captured territories, Egypt and Syria were turning to the Soviet Union for arms to replace what Israel had captured. By late 1969 a war of attrition erupted across the Suez Canal, again forcing the extension of American support to Israel. The Israeli air force retaliated against Egyptian shelling across the canal with air bombardment, only to find that new aircraft from the Soviet Union (flown by Russian pilots) and Soviet-supplied surface-to-air missiles (SAMs) threatened its mastery of the skies. The SAMs, unglamorous weapons compared to modern jet fighters, were to become a major factor in Egyptian military planning.

Secretary of State Rogers pressed for an Arab-Israeli settlement from the new American position of "evenhandedness." Meanwhile, Israeli and Egyptian military action over the Suez Canal expanded during 1970. Rogers, after assessing the possibilities of Soviet cooperation, proposed a ninety-day cease-fire in place, linked to negotiations supervised by the United Nations Secretary General. This proposal represented the high point of Rogers' involvement. Egypt and Israel agreed to the cease-fire in August 1970. But Egypt violated the agreement, evidently with Soviet cooperation. (The Russians pointed out that they were not party to the agreement and hence not bound by it.)

The Rogers Plan clearly required further personal diplomacy, but that fell increasingly to the Assistant Secretary for the Middle East, Joseph Sisco, who developed a close working relationship with Kissinger. American diplomatic efforts bogged down, however, until Kissinger himself was to step into the conflict in 1973.

The difficulties appear to have been caused largely by new Egyptian leadership. With Nasser's death in 1970, his successor, Anwar el Sadat, assumed an even more belligerent posture toward Israel, apparently to help establish his claim to Nasser's role. In fact, he evidently had much more in mind, as events three years later were to demonstrate.

The Middle East diplomacy was further complicated by the indirect interests of both the United States and Russia. The Arab states were unwilling to acknowledge Israel as a legitimate state, while Israel was unwilling to make territorial concessions from her 1967 conquests. For many reasons, the Arab-Israeli dispute was too important for the major powers to ignore without a mutual agreement not to intervene. Both the United States and Russia had committed themselves to opposing sides of the dispute, and both nations pursued objectives in the Middle East that depended on the balance of power there.

For example, the Russians used Egypt's new dependence on Soviet equipment to gain access to Egyptian port facilities, rapidly increasing their naval presence in the Eastern Mediterranean—to the consternation of Washington. The American Sixth Fleet had dominated the Mediterranean since World War II. By 1971 Soviet naval forces would grow large enough to complicate any application of American sea power in the Eastern Mediterranean. Land-based Soviet aircraft and pilots stationed on Egyptian territory also threatened American naval power in the region.

So long as their concern over the balance of power in the Middle East made Moscow and Washington willing to fuel an arms race there, it was unlikely that the Arab states and Israel would be willing to reach a workable accommodation.

THE YOM KIPPUR WAR

In October 1973, during the solemn Jewish observation of Yom Kippur, Egypt and Syria attacked Israel, catching her by surprise. Syria captured the Golan Heights while Egypt, using ground-launched missiles for air cover, crossed the Suez Canal and overran the front Israeli positions in the Sinai. Israeli forces recovered the Golan Heights in a counterattack on her northern boundaries that quickly carried past the 1967 cease-fire line, but slackened and stopped as Israeli forces were shifted to the Sinai. There they punched and pincered Egyptian forces and struck across the Suez Canal, destroying and disbursing the missiles in order to restore Israeli air cover.

Despite Israel's swift comeback from the initial Arab on-slaughts, however, the overall course of the war left a radically different impression on both sides from that of the 1967 Six Day war. In 1973 Egyptian and Syrian forces performed well, recovering their lost pride in arms and discrediting the myth of Israel's invincibility. Israel's air force and armor had proven highly vulnerable to Arab-launched Soviet missiles. Both sides spent ammunition many times faster than anticipated; equipment losses, particularly aircraft, ran high; and the material and human costs of the war were staggering for Israel. She had come to expect that in war her armed forces would perform brilliantly, and her enemies badly. Only slight changes in the performances on both sides produced a nearly disastrous outcome for Israel. Wholly dependent upon the United States for immediate resupply, Israel had little choice but to accept American conditions as well.

Washington first sought to stop the war. Nixon briefly withheld arms from the Israelis, and Kissinger warned the Soviets that détente could not survive "irresponsibility" from Moscow. When Egypt began to lose, Brezhnev invited Kissinger to Moscow for talks.

It was mainly American prodding, coupled with Soviet concurrence and pressure from the United Nations, that induced both sides to accept a cease-fire in place on October 22. After that, limited adjustments of lines were made, including a separation of forces that removed Israeli troops from the west bank of the Suez Canal. Marathon diplomacy by the tireless Kissinger freed the encircled Egyptian third army in November, after the grim signal of an American strategic alert ordered by Nixon warned off the Russians from rescuing the Egyptians by direct military intervention. Kissinger's diplomacy also arranged for an Israeli-Egyptian prisoner exchange at the beginning of negotiations in Geneva in December, and an Egyptian-Israeli disengagement followed in January 1974. Kissinger's "shuttle diplomacy" was even more predominant in the Israeli-Syrian disengagement in the spring of 1974. During five weeks he visited Tel Aviv eighteen times, Damascus fourteen times, Cairo and Alexandria two times, and Amman, Nicosia, and Riyadh once each. The technique stressed modest, incremental goals: settle now those issues that matter now. Kissinger helped achieve a Syrian-Israeli disengagement, though unstable governments in both states had complicated the negotiations. Militants in Syria resisted following Egypt's lead into agreement with Israel. An election defeat prompted Golda Meir's retirement and the formation of a somewhat younger Israeli cabinet. Meanwhile, Palestinian terrorists threatened Arab peace-makers and mounted more raids into Israel.

Another important element to emerge from the war was Egyptian diplomacy. Sadat had gained the support of wealthy and conservative Saudi Arabia and wealthy and radical Libya before starting the war. During the first week of the war's major fighting, while Israel frantically called for more American arms, Libya's President flew to Moscow to buy Soviet arms for cash. Nearly two years before the Arab attack, Sadat had expelled most of the Soviet technicians and instructors from Egypt. While his armed forces used Russian tactics and training in the war along with Russian equipment (and some Russian military advisers), they were used on Egyptian terms. In 1973 the war experience and its aftermath actually widened the Soviet-Egyptian breach rather than increasing

Egyptian dependence on the Soviets. The 1967 war had begun a period of significant Soviet presence in Egypt and Syria: the 1973 Yom Kippur war severely reduced it.

The reduced role played by the Soviet Union was reflected in its relative lack of influence during the negotiations. As Kissinger moved about encouraging and facilitating negotiations, Soviet Foreign Minister Gromyko was reduced to following him to Cairo and Damascus to dissuade his hosts from cooperating with the American diplomat. Perhaps this was a perverse form of face-saving. At any rate, the Soviets for the moment had little to offer. Sadat's working understanding with Saudi Arabia and the new developments in oil markets reduced Egypt's dependence on Soviet military supplies. Egypt was not an oil exporter. Her main asset was her status as political leader among the Arab states. Sadat had reasserted this role, using war with Israel as the centerpiece in a brilliant combination of moves that gained the solid support of Saudi Arabia and drew Cairo away from a growing alliance with Libya. Egypt could continue to use outside assistance for arms and economic aid; but neither needed to be accepted on undesirable terms from the United States, Western Europe, or the Soviet Union.

THE NEW IMPORTANCE OF OIL POLITICS

The war also thrust oil politics to the fore in Arab diplomacy by precipitating first an oil embargo and then a quadrupling of oil prices for consumer nations. The world demand for oil had been multiplying; by the early seventies it was rising fast enough to seriously worry Western European governments, the United States, and Japan—the major users—because of foreign exchange implications. In 1972 it had been estimated that by 1980 the Middle East oil-producing states would be earning $30 billion more from oil revenues than they would be spending. In fact, the actual figure for 1974 was approximated at twice that sum. During 1971 the oil-producing states, mainly in the Middle East, plus Venezuela, had been able to make effective an oil cartel they had formed a decade earlier called the Organization of Petroleum Exporting Countries (OPEC). In November 1973, the Arab members of OPEC announced an embargo against the United States, Portugal, and the Nether-

lands, and a monthly 5 percent reduction of oil shipments to Western Europe and Japan. Japan, the most vulnerable, was hard hit.
Imported oil, mostly from the Middle East, supplied almost all her
energy needs. Europe was hit next hardest; and the United States
the least. Americans depended mainly on domestic and Western
Hemisphere production. Most of Europe shifted foreign policies to
favor the Arab states. (France, already pro-Arab, had anticipated
this problem.) Japan held to its pro-Israeli policy at first, but shifted
in late November.

The oil boycott split the United States from Western Europe
and divided the Europeans. Europeans criticized Washington for its
support of Israel and for achieving a temporary Middle East settlement at the cost of a massive increase in oil prices that hurt European economies more than the United States. In December 1973
Kissinger called for a common front of oil-consuming powers.
Western European states, fearing Arab reprisals, failed to respond.
Britain and France negotiated separately with Arab states for long-
term agreements to exchange manufactured goods and arms for oil.
Italy pursued similar objectives. This rivalry among our allies precipitated critical remarks in Washington about Atlantic solidarity.
Faced with the Arab oil cartel, the Europeans were unable to co-
operate effectively.

When the oil boycott ended in the early months of 1974, it left
the major oil-consuming states to ponder the new dimensions of
international trade and economic power. Western Europe and
Japan suffered sharp economic setbacks from the oil price increases,
aggravating a worldwide inflation. By mid-1974, Britain and Italy
were drifting toward political and economic chaos.

THE NIXON DOCTRINE IN ASIA

President Nixon first declared his objective of a new American
relationship with smaller powers during a trip through Asia in 1969
when he talked about the values of regional and local self-reliance—
what he later dubbed the Nixon Doctrine. Critics have claimed a
parallel between the Nixon Doctrine and Eisenhower's embarrassing
phrase "let Asians fight Asians." As long as the world was viewed as
Dulles saw it—as a worldwide struggle between Communism and

freedom in which neutrality was irresponsible and immoral—one could scarcely justify an American policy of letting Asians fight Asians. That would have put the United States into the very neutralist position that Dulles criticized.

But the situation was entirely different if the Cold War bipolar premise was discarded or softened, as the Nixon Administration did. Nixon accepted Kissinger's interpretation that the bipolar conflict reflected the structure of the international political system and could include not only conflict between the major adversaries but competition and cooperation as well. Despite appearances, it was not a stark ideological dispute. Toughness toward and cooperation with Moscow were equal political requirements for the United States. Similarly, the Nixon Doctrine objective of local self-reliance took into account the strains and risks of bipolarity and the propensities of relations between great and small powers to deteriorate into dependency linkages that corrupt both powers (as had happened for the United States in the Vietnam war particularly). Nixon's new policies drained the phrase "let Asians fight Asians" of its most objectionable connotation: using Asians to fight wars to protect the interests of the United States. Because Nixon (perforce or by preference) viewed America's position in the world in a different light, the Nixon Doctrine acquired a meaning that its antecedents in the Eisenhower era lacked.

In Asia, the Nixon Doctrine's emphasis on local self-reliance was addressed in particular to those regimes that had become dependent on their special relationship with the United States for survival or for other types of assistance. Washington's new flexible diplomacy raised the practical question of how these governments would actually adapt to the American demand for self-reliance and what changes would occur in Washington's policies toward them. The Bangladesh war of independence provided some answers to both questions.

BANGLADESH: THE DISMEMBERMENT OF PAKISTAN

The balance of power in Southern Asia had long been a concern of the United States—at least since the early fifties, when

Eisenhower started a close military alliance with Pakistan to offset India's potential strength. Since the mid-fifties American diplomacy in South Asia had been quite inflexible. During 1971–72, in anticipation of the Peking summit, our policies became extraordinarily rigid.

Pakistan was a geographic monstrosity. East Bengal, its smaller, more populated wing, bordered on the Bay of Bengal and India's northwest boundary. Pakistan's west wing, the old northwest frontier of India, was a thousand miles across India. Though united by a common Moslem faith, East and West Pakistan were divided not only by India but by ethnic differences and by growing economic and political differences. After the 1958 military coup Pakistan was governed by an authoritarian civil-military autocracy dominated by West Pakistanis. The American-subsidized economic development of the 1960s benefited mainly West Pakistan. Increasingly East Pakistan served West Pakistan as an internal colony—a source of raw materials and a market for manufactured products.

In 1970, however, Bengali leaders won a parliamentary majority in the national election. The national regime in Islamabad would not accept the result. A bloody repression of East Bengal by the Pakistani army followed in March 1971 in an attempt to maintain domination over the east wing. Millions of East Pakistanis fled across their border to neighboring India, burdening India's economy and inviting India's involvement in the conflict. New Delhi prepared to dismember Pakistan. First, India armed and trained the Mukti Bahini, an East Pakistani resistance force that took a heavy toll against West Pakistani troops in the next eight months. Then the Indian army itself invaded East Bengal and crushed West Pakistan's rule there in a well-organized two-week war that was a sensational success with the Indian public. Bangladesh was born— a satellite of India, famine-ridden, and impoverished; and Indira Gandhi's government stood at the peak of its popularity in New Delhi.

These events unfolded while Nixon and Kissinger were arranging their Peking visit, using the good offices of the Pakistani government, which had well-established relations with Peking and regular airline service to China's capital city. The Bangladesh war divided the White House and the Pentagon from the State Department, for Nixon correctly perceived the State Department to be pro-India, while the White House and the armed services favored Pakistan. Nixon was concerned about two incompatible objectives: his access to Peking and the regional power balance on the Indian subcontinent. The breakup of Pakistan served India's purposes as a growing regional power interested in weakening her immediate neighbors.

The Bangladesh crisis illustrates the dual pressures faced by the Nixon Administration in attaining its goals: on one hand, to ensure that any foreign policy issue was handled in a way that was compatible with the President's outlook; on the other hand, to subordinate lesser crises to the goals of Nixon's great power summit diplomacy.

JAPAN: RECOVERY FROM THE "TWIN SHOCKS"

Nixon's announcement in July 1971 of his plans to visit Peking caught the Liberal-Democratic government in Japan by surprise, with important and far-reaching results for Japanese-American relations. Since the end of the American postwar occupation of Japan, the Liberal-Democrats, a relatively conservative coalition of government and business interests, had maintained control of Japan's increasingly competitive parliamentary system. Their main challengers were the Socialists, and one of the Liberal-Democrats' main vulnerabilities was their close identification with the United States. Premier Sato, like his predecessors, looked to the United States to assist Japan's postwar prosperity and to offer military protection against her traditional rivals in East Asia—China and the Soviet Union. Sato himself had gestured toward independence from Washington, but mainly to moderate Japanese domestic pressures of emotional anti-Americanism. Washington responded to his predicament by agreeing to turn Okinawa over to Japan, and the visible identity with Washington continued.

An American rapprochement with Peking would alter Japan's military and economic situation significantly, for China was feared as a threat to Japan's security but eyed as a major trading partner. It was apparent when Nixon announced his plans to visit Peking that the Sato government had been neither consulted nor forewarned. This shock was followed barely a month later by Nixon's announcement of import surcharges and other measures to bolster the sagging dollar during the monetary crisis of 1971. These twin shocks demonstrated that Japan's special relationship to Washington counted for little even when matters vital to Japan were at stake.

Adjustments immediately began within the Liberal-Democratic party that resulted in a change of leadership. In early July 1972 the election of Kakuei Tanaka as party leader and Premier broadened the base of power in the party, for Tanaka had campaigned against the traditional government-business elites. He had also promised major changes in foreign policy, and he promptly set out to honor this commitment. That September he visited Peking, established formal diplomatic relations with the People's Republic of China (PRC) and severed relations with the Nationalist regime in Taiwan, going beyond the American initiatives. Trade relations promptly expanded as the PRC energetically pursued its new policy of using trade to acquire technological advances that would in turn encourage modernization in her own economy.

Considering the initial reaction in Tokyo to the double shocks from Washington, Japan's political system adapted with surprising facility. First, a long-standing inhibition about relations with Communist countries was set aside. Japanese-American relations became more distant, and remained so. Nixon and Kissinger both continued to be regarded in Tokyo as insensitive—even hostile—to Japanese interests. Japanese dependence on the United States diminished more because of the faltering American economy than because of the abrupt change in Washington's Cold War alignments.

OTHER ASIAN DEVELOPMENTS

A similar salutary effect seemed at first to be under way in the Koreas. Shortly after the announcement of the Peking summit, the North and South Korean governments announced an agreement about definite measures to reduce tensions between them, with the purpose of moving toward reunification. But by Nixon's second Moscow summit in June 1974, the Park Chung Hee regime in South Korea had become severely repressive, and relations with North Korea had returned to a more familiar hostility. The opportunity for political reconciliation in the Koreas, if there had been one, had passed. Park had been unable to take advantage of reduced Sino-American tensions to effect reconciliation with North Korea. Washington, fearing that North Korea would misunderstand any official American signs of disapproval of Park's regime and start a new Korean war, found itself trapped once again in reluctant support of a small power with unattractive features in the interest of keeping local order.

The Philippine Republic had been drifting along with a ramshackle but durable political and economic structure when President Ferdinand Marcos declared martial law and suspended parliamentary government to launch an authoritarian regime emphasizing economic development. Indonesia, ruled by a military oligarchy since 1965, was becoming increasingly authoritarian. Thailand, under the stress of adjusting to changes in neighboring Indochina, had overturned its government, but essentially maintained a centralized authoritarian regime.

These internal changes were scarcely the result of changed relations with Washington, or of the softened Sino-American rivalry in Asia, or of the growing Sino-Soviet conflict. Yet there was some discernible relationship among internal politics, the structure of regional power, and the great power alignments. South Korea and the Philippine Republic had drawn some of their authority from their alignments with the United States. As these alignments softened, they had to adapt. South Korea and the Philippines moved toward the right in adjusting to Washington's new relationship with Peking. Developments in India were in this respect instructive. Following the stunning defeat of Pakistan's army of repression in Bangladesh, Indira Gandhi's supporters in the Congress party won an important victory in state elections, strengthening her hold on the government. Gandhi detonated an Indian nuclear device in 1974 to strengthen the government's domestic prestige as it faced a national railway strike—and increased its reliance on prestigious symbols rather than on internal political or economic accomplishments. With India's intractable internal economic problems, this trend was likely to continue. The external consequences of this policy were apparent in India's alignment with Moscow against China and in the United States' resistance to India's expanding regional power at the expense of smaller powers such as Pakistan.

CONCLUSION

By mid-1974, the Nixon-Kissinger diplomacy had gained considerable flexibility for the United States in dealing with allies and third world countries as well as with our principal rivals, the Soviet Union and Communist China. The new American assessment of China as representing less of a threat to its neighbors also reduced the incentives we offered Japan and the smaller powers to isolate China and maintain a conspicuous anti-Communist foreign policy. Each client state and ally was thus compelled to adjust its own foreign policy to the local configuration of political forces.

At its best, the new situation meant more independence for regional powers and less need for the United States to be their general guarantor. Being relieved of the latter task had come to be a valued goal for Washington after the disappointments of underwriting the Saigon regime for so long. At its worst, the new situation meant that the United States would tolerate political suppression in South Korea, for example, while continuing to provide military assistance to Seoul. The alternative would be to withdraw support from South Korea and severely reduce the American presence in Asia. The new Nixon policies excluded intervention to establish democracy in Korea—a lesson from Vietnam. Similar dilemmas arose in Europe and the Middle East. In short, policy had changed, but major issues persisted. As long as the United States had the power to intervene for "good" reasons, the question would remain as to whether it should exercise that power.

Nixon's diplomatic initiatives had achieved notable but precarious settlements of the Vietnam and Middle East conflicts and in strategic arms limitations. A breakdown in any of these agreements could seriously discredit this new diplomacy, but would not by itself be likely to return the United States to the rigid foreign policy of 1967–68, when the American public was highly aroused over the Vietnam war and demanded action. The Nixon-Kissinger diplomacy had partially returned foreign policy to the status it had previously enjoyed in American politics, with public support based mainly on public deference to government authority. The experience of Vietnam, however, left public confidence in government less stable than before. Moreover, Nixon's style of foreign policy making, to say nothing of his shocking political conduct, made foreign policy more vulnerable to partisan political challenge. The return of public deference to authority in American foreign policy in the mid-1970s was illustrated by the relatively smooth transition from the Nixon resignation to Ford's Administration, with Kissinger's widely approved continuance as Secretary of State.

Nixon's style of conducting foreign policy contributed substantially to the reduced visibility of specific foreign policy issues and thus to public deference (as was seen in the Eisenhower era). Nixon undertook major foreign policy initiatives without first arranging bipartisan support in Congress. Instead he relied on the direct popular appeal of his initiatives to win the support needed. Maintaining public support for foreign policy has been a fundamental problem in the postwar era, and Nixon did not ignore it. Until Vietnam, maintaining congressional support for an administration's foreign policy had been tantamount to maintaining public support.

The breakdown of both congressional and public consensus over Vietnam made it essential that any President seeking to restore consensus deal with public opinion directly as well as with congressional opinion. Nixon in fact went further. He chose to win short-run public support through the inventiveness and audacity of his policies, rather than to work toward developing a stable long-term base of public opinion by first building consensus in the executive branch and then in Congress, as his predecessors had generally done. It had been their practice to follow extensive clearance procedures within government for foreign policy initiatives. This practice helped to achieve consensus and minimize criticism by foreign policy opinion leaders. It also tended to reduce the risk of mistakes caused by inadequate prior examination of policy choices that existed within the range of established consensus, although it discouraged fundamental questioning of policies by foreign policy opinion leaders.

An example of a Nixon Administration mistake that might have been avoided if moderated by prior consultation within the government was the Russian wheat deal of 1972. The Administration arranged to permit the Russian government to buy one-quarter of the American wheat crop on concessional financing terms when market conditions were already pushing the price of wheat upward.

As it turned out, Russian traders were able to buy wheat at low prices subsidized by the United States Treasury. This transaction then drove the price of wheat up, eliminating price subsidies and presenting the American consumer with substantially increased costs for wheat products. Wheat price increases marked the beginning (though not the cause) of a major inflationary rise in the American economy that lasted into 1975. The Administration neither wanted nor anticipated these effects.

In sum, Nixon's popular success with flexible diplomacy initiatives freed American foreign policy from traditional restraints in the short term, but his unwillingness to seek bipartisanship in negotiating and implementing foreign policies opened the way for major partisan conflict over the merits of these policies. This potential for partisan conflict was inherited by his successor, Gerald Ford.

chapter 12

Where Have We Been?
What Lies Ahead?

PRESIDENTIAL POWER AND
THE POSTWAR CONSENSUS

Perhaps the most consistent pattern among the postwar Presidents is the fact that, regardless of their relative success, all of them devoted much of their attention to foreign affairs, even when they entered the White House (as Johnson did) intending to minimize the intrusions of foreign policy on domestic matters.

Several factors have contributed to this emphasis on foreign policy. First, domestic issues can be highly frustrating to the President as principal actor on the national political scene. Too many diverse interests are affected by any specific policy issue to allow the President the satisfaction and prestige of choosing the "right decision" and thus of making a distinct political gain by carrying out his policy successfully. This sharing of power lowers presidential risks in making domestic policy and helps to spread the burden of defeat if necessary. On the other hand, the President who does make a clear gain usually finds that his victory horse is crowded with fellow riders.

Foreign policy, on the other hand, is a far less crowded political domain. In addition, the President enjoys certain advantages over political rivals that are not available to him in domestic affairs. His main advantage in foreign policy issues is the greater deference accorded him by the public and the media on the assumption that he has greater knowledge of the issues than his critics. Despite the "credibility gaps" and media attacks of the past decade, the President remains—perhaps by default—acknowledged as more expert in handling the intricacies of specific foreign policy issues. Presidents generally want to be regarded as statesmen; and with all its risks, foreign affairs is the domain that offers the greatest promise of attaining that goal. Regardless of whether they have attained this larger goal, however, the postwar Presidents have generally been able to glean more immediate advantages from their foreign policies. All of them have drawn political strength and prestige from their special status as chief of foreign relations in dealing with Congress and with political rivals and critics.

Conversely, they have suffered political setbacks from domestic dissatisfaction over their handling of foreign relations. In addition, the increasing use of discretionary presidential power in regard to Vietnam during the 1960s and early 1970s has revived perennial questions about the level of appropriate constitutional power for Presidents in foreign affairs. Public recognition of this issue was generated in particular by Johnson's and Nixon's flamboyant use of presidential power in regard to Vietnam—including Nixon's use of a vague "national security" rationale to justify illegal acts in the Watergate affair. Public and congressional questions about the limits of presidential foreign policy making powers suggest that the issue of presidential power will remain entangled with the merits of specific foreign policies until a new consensus about the President's role is achieved.

THE RIGIDITIES OF
THE COLD WAR STANCE

Truman, Eisenhower, and Johnson all left office suffering from public alienation over their conduct of foreign relations. Truman suffered at first from public anxieties that his Administration was not tough enough in fighting Communism abroad. After 1948 criticism focused on Truman's Asian policies, and the suspicion of Communist subversion in Washington aggravated public distrust.

The Korean war drew a positive public response at first, but as the war drifted into stalemate, public awareness and impatience grew. Political discussions turned on particulars. Should MacArthur have been fired? Should the United States bomb Communist China? Who were the Communists in the government who let China fall? The war's important political effect, however, was a general decline in public confidence that damaged the Truman Administration's legislative program after 1950 and diminished its authority in foreign relations.

Behind the foreground of Dulles' scurrying about, the Eisenhower Administration stood self-possessed for more than five years. It operated with a restraint in foreign relations that was closely related to its view about limited national government in domestic affairs. In part as a result of this restraint, public confidence in Eisenhower's conduct of foreign and domestic affairs remained high through his first term. The election of 1956 indicated a broad public confidence in Eisenhower, a feeling of security in knowing that he was President when the Suez war occurred. Yet Eisenhower's critics were able to capitalize on public anxiety over his apparent complacency about foreign developments that Sputnik triggered in 1957.

A reassessment of foreign relations followed the launching of Sputnik. The Eisenhower Administration now acted in response to its critics and to its own new perceptions of external conditions. Among these conditions were problems of political unrest in Japan and Latin America, the American interests perceived as being at stake involved in Southeast Asia, the diverging interests of the newly prosperous NATO member nations, the new strengths and weaknesses of the Soviet Union, and changing perceptions throughout the world about the nature of the Cold War.

The 1960 election reflected the corrosive effects of these anxieties on public confidence: the nomination of two young candidates, Nixon and Kennedy, and the theme of renewal and reinvigoration expressed by both.

Kennedy came to the Presidency without the political stature that Eisenhower had possessed in 1953. But though Kennedy lacked political status, he was favored by purpose and circumstance, which permitted him to use foreign policy as an opportunity. The widespread public anxiety about Eisenhower's seemingly underactive stewardship in foreign relations, coupled with Kennedy's own activism, allowed him to capitalize on the demands of foreign policy—

quickly expanding his popularity. By the time of his death in 1963, however, some dissatisfaction, particularly on foreign aid, had set in from his politics of arousal in the first two years. He had, moreover, demonstrated an odd sense of proportions. He had drifted into the Bay of Pigs debacle with his attention on the wrong issues. He had helped to embroil the United States in Vietnam while worrying about the Test Ban Treaty. He had devoted such generous attention to the public relations component of an aid program for Latin America that unrealistic expectations developed on both sides about what the Alliance for Progress would and would not do.

We will never know what Johnson—or Kennedy, had he lived—might have been able to accomplish in foreign relations without the burden of Vietnam. Its massive political effects dwarfed the consequences of all other foreign policy issues. Johnson's decision to strive for a military solution to the Vietnam problem made all other foreign policy considerations secondary from 1966 to 1973. Yet even without Vietnam Johnson might well have suffered the public alienation encountered by Truman and Eisenhower.

Johnson confronted—and contributed to—a revolution of rising domestic expectations that put heavy pressure on the government to limit our external commitments in order to give domestic reforms higher national priority. In addition, Johnson's style of national politics often alienated the very opinion leaders he was attempting to persuade, as his handling of our Dominican intervention (to say nothing of Vietnam) showed. Finally, the legacy of Kennedy's politics of arousal and his priorities in foreign relations included some formidable problems, which Johnson inherited: high expectations and growing discontent about the Alliance for Progress; a settlement in Laos that helped Hanoi support the insurgents in South Vietnam along the Ho Chi Minh Trail; an unstable and inept regime in Saigon with no arrangements for reform in it; a European alliance that had put aside political logic to pursue a narrower, more efficient, and more disruptive military logic; a new military link to India (after the Chinese attack) that had already been handed over to the economic and military technicians; and a minor détente with Khrushchev, who would soon be succeeded by less amenable Soviet leaders.

The Johnson Administration's performance, particularly in regard to the Vietnam war, represented the culmination of American foreign policies that had been largely unchallenged and unexamined since the end of World War II. The extent of our failures in Vietnam and the resulting public dissatisfaction with Johnson's Administration were to force a sharp reassessment of axioms our nation had clung to for nearly twenty years without taking into account changes in our own status or in world conditions.

At the end of World War II, American internationalists had affirmed that the United States ought to be concerned with foreign affairs. They gained support for this general principle in the early postwar years, but no specific priorities or principles of selectivity were established to determine where or when the United States should become involved in foreign affairs. Two conditions prevented more careful thought on these issues: the need to mobilize American consent for a continuing international role in the postwar period and the consensus among American opinion leaders, more convenient than realistic, that the Communist world was monolithic.

Both these conditions had encouraged American leaders to present foreign policy objectives as designed to counter Communist political threats around the world. During the early postwar years, foreign intervention could be justified in the face of the urgent need to help European states under threat of economic collapse and political domination from Moscow. By the time the threat in Europe no longer commanded unchallenged priority, the United States had entered a period of economic prosperity and nuclear military superiority that sustained an illusion of omnipotence. This illusion obscured the limits of American power, even during the Korean war, and made the establishment of principles for selective foreign involvements seem unnecessary.

The tendency to avoid making discriminating judgments about appropriate intervention abroad was accentuated among American policy leaders by the adverse public reaction to the Truman Administration for appearing to "let China fall" to the Communists. Washington officials themselves recognized that different local situations involved American interests to different degrees, and they were capable of deciding to ignore local conflicts they considered to be of little interest to the United States. But the prospect of facing a serious domestic political reaction if an administration failed to act became a potent force for nonselective intervention abroad. It be-

came more prudent and required less public explanation for suc-
ceeding administrations to adopt a "cover all bets" strategy—that is,
to support any regime identified with us throughout the world
that appeared or claimed to be under Communist threat from outside or through internal subversion.

VIETNAM: A SHATTERED CONSENSUS AND NEW FLEXIBILITY

By 1967, however, the increasing public visibility of our government's problems in Vietnam forced government officials and public
opinion leaders to reevaluate the facile tenets underlying our
foreign policies for the past twenty years. First, unlike World War
II or the Korean war, the Vietnam war brought the United States
up against the political and economic limits of its international
power. The huge financial and human costs of the war and our
lack of success demonstrated that American power was finite—both
materially and politically. Vietnam was only a modest aspect of the
worldwide interests and commitments of the United States, even in
the 1960s. Yet the war concentrated vast American resources and
attention on remote military operations and limited objectives, at
the expense of other commitments. The government's distortion of
priorities is illustrated by the fact that at the high point of our
involvement, a half million American men were in Vietnam, and
our government incurred costs of approximately $100 billion over
most of a decade.

The new recognition of the limits to American influence abroad
virtually shattered the delicate postwar consensus about foreign
relations, polarizing foreign policy leadership opinion. The bipartisanship of the early postwar era, on uncertain ground since the
Korean war, was destroyed by the rising public concern over Vietnam. Bipartisanship at best had been an imperfect collusion among
Republicans and Democrats designed to avoid a level of controversy that would arouse the public over foreign policy issues. Vietnam brought about such a high level of public visibility and
controversy that both sides lost incentives for bipartisanship. And,
in fact, dissident Democrats were even more willing than many Republican leaders to arouse public attention and recommend changes
in our policies.

Critics of the war used the Vietnam issue to raise much deeper questions about morality, national interest, and the appropriate exercise of power in foreign affairs. Specifically, critics were raising the possibility of a major reduction in our foreign policy commitments by demanding that the United States turn first to the achievement of its own domestic objectives and by recommending that this country apply consistent moral standards at home and abroad. Moreover, for the first time since the fall of China, a prominent group of American opinion leaders offered a countervailing viewpoint to the assumption that all Communist threats everywhere must be met by the United States: they suggested instead that foreign intervention could very well lead to disaster and was even likely to be immoral. The effect was to call for a reassessment of what American interests really consisted of and to highlight the need for more selective criteria for foreign intervention.

President Nixon took full advantage of the new climate. In response to the broad questions evoked by the Vietnam debacle, Nixon reduced the ideological component of American foreign relations and introduced a more flexible diplomacy into relations with major rivals and allies.

In order to accomplish this, Nixon bypassed our relatively stable alliance system and the complex network of bilateral military and economic ties our country had established with other nations over the past twenty years. This network had assisted us and our allies in achieving military preparedness, and it reflected American preferences for stable, institutionalized foreign policy arrangements. But these arrangements had also made our foreign relations quite rigid, impeding flexible American responses to regional and local power situations abroad and to shifts in East-West relations.

The Nixon Administration was able to evade these impediments as well as those created by domestic pressures by launching its initiatives in foreign policy from the top of the government without first securing a new consensus with Congress, with the public, or even within the executive branch. Nixon was able to effect major changes in foreign policy stances, but he avoided the consensus-building processes of American policy making upon which stable public support for foreign policy traditionally depended.

It is perhaps easier to assess the benefits of foreign policy for

Nixon than vice versa. As President, Nixon was able to turn his foreign policy accomplishments into a powerful domestic political asset. Even as the Watergate scandal closed in on him, he took refuge in a summitry redoubt, claiming that he had a unique personal capacity to deal with the Soviet leadership.

It will be some time, however, before we can accurately assess the long-term benefits or problems generated by Nixon's innovations in foreign policy. His Administration's tough bargaining with our allies in Europe and Asia, as well as the détente with Russia and the rapprochement with China, have strained our alliances. These new strains may offset the general benefits of greater American diplomatic flexibility and the special benefits of improved relations with Moscow and Peking.

President Ford began his Administration by taking steps to demonstrate continuity with Nixon's foreign policies—most notably by ensuring that Henry Kissinger would remain with the new Administration as Secretary of State. Kissinger continued to be pre-eminent in the early Ford Administration, and decision making continued to be highly centralized around the President and Kissinger. Ford, however, was more solicitous of congressional views than Nixon had been. Ford also displayed a more conciliatory style of foreign relations with our allies than Nixon had shown. The Ford Administration appeared to be less prone to seek diplomatic confrontations with allies or to employ coercive instruments unilaterally against friends or rivals. If "blood and iron" power politics was Nixon's way, it was evidently not Ford's.

FUTURE TRENDS AND FUTURE UNCERTAINTIES

SOVIET-AMERICAN RELATIONS

What have the events of the mid-1970s suggested about the future course of American foreign policy and our impact on international affairs? A continuing aspect will be our relationship with Russia: will détente become institutionalized, or are future confrontations with Russia (or China) likely?

Any assessment about the future must take into account assumptions about Moscow's long-term objectives and tendencies. At

one extreme is a power politics interpretation: Moscow's accommodations to the Nixon Administration appeared to be in response to
the violent actions that Nixon directed against the Communists
while extracting the United States from Vietnam. As its 1968 suppression of Czechoslovakia indicated, the Soviet Union appreciates
the significance of a show of strength. Moscow may have had particular respect and concern for an Administration in Washington
that was able to withstand its own domestic turmoil to strike at
Cambodia and Laos, hold out through the 1972 elections, and then
resume the bombing of North Vietnam. A variant of this interpretation, however, would suggest that if the Soviet-American
détente leads to a weakening of American preparedness and resolve,
Moscow might be tempted into further ventures—even into replay-
ing the Cold War.

Another interpretation emphasizes changes in the conditions
underlying Soviet-American rivalry. As noted, American political
leaders must now consider a new domestic political constituency
that discourages foreign interventions. In addition, American armed
forces have been under severe budget pressures in recent years as a
result of the high inflation rate in military hardware, the rapidly
increasing manpower costs created by conversion to all-volunteer
armed forces under the Nixon Administration, and public hostility
to high military budgets, intensified by Vietnam. The combination
of worsening inflation and recession during the mid-1970s would
indicate a poor economic base on which to establish a militant
foreign policy in Washington.

Changes leading to similar constraints have been occurring in
the Soviet Union as well. In response to Russia's lagging economic
growth, the Soviet government has taken steps to acquire foreign
technology through increased trade with the United States and Europe. These economic objectives have evidently become a serious
consideration in Soviet foreign relations that coincides with Moscow's strategy for handling her rivalry with China. If this line of
reasoning is accurate, a détente between Washington and Moscow
should reinforce the moderate inclinations of Soviet foreign policy.

The period of intransigent hostility between Moscow and
Washington—the classic definition of the Cold War—is perhaps over,
now that the Vietnam experience and the improved relationship
with the Soviet Union have created a more flexible American

foreign policy. But regardless of détente, the prospect of confrontations between Moscow and Washington is not over, and the potential for a "Cold War" in some form continues.

Despite its economic problems during the 1970s, the Soviet Union has been increasing military outlays as measured in several ways—in absolute terms, in terms of the percentage of its gross national product, and in comparison with American military expenditures. Viewed from every aspect, Russian armaments have been growing. Since the United States is unwilling to disarm unilaterally, and since important differences remain between the two superpowers, military confrontation can scarcely be ruled out. For instance, at the end of 1974, the Middle East was more of a tinderbox than ever during the postwar era. The stakes of outside powers in the Middle East were raised by the worldwide energy crisis, and Washington and Moscow were pursuing rival political and military interests there.

The United States must be able to meet the prospect of regional or local crises during the mid- and late-1970s through diplomatic, economic, and military means that will depend on popular support and compliance. Thus the domestic political problem for American foreign policy leaders during the 1970s is remarkably similar to what it was in the late 1940s: how to maintain popular support for foreign relations.

STABILIZING FORCES IN INTERNATIONAL AFFAIRS

During the Cold War period, institutions such as NATO and the Warsaw Pact served a double purpose: they helped to sustain the hostility of the Cold War, but they also acted as stabilizers of the international system. For instance, both NATO and the Warsaw Pact had fairly constant goals, levels of effort, and standard operating procedures.

If, however, a new Soviet-American friendship should induce either or both sides to dismantle their alliance systems, we may expect new uncertainties in the bipolar rivalry. The most likely gain of the Soviet-American détente will probably be to reduce the risk of Soviet-American conflict triggered by lesser allies. In particular, client states on both sides, such as North and South Korea, Nationalist China, or North and South Vietnam, will find it much more difficult to draw their great power sponsors into helping them achieve local or regional power aspirations.

At the same time, the increased power that Congress has recently asserted in foreign relations may create a new source of stability in American foreign policy. During the early 1970s, Congress legislated new limits on the power of the President to take initiatives in foreign affairs without its concurrence. These restrictions were imposed to achieve several goals: to force Nixon to end the American military involvement in Vietnam; to reflect lessons learned in Congress about the conduct of the war; to respond to the Watergate scandal; and more generally, to reassert a larger role for Congress in foreign policy making. The main target of this legislation was the President's power to order emergency military action that could lead to growing foreign involvements.

The import of these congressional restrictions could be exaggerated. It is not in the interest of Congress to assume significant political responsibility for foreign policy. Increased responsibility for Congress means increased vulnerability to political constituency pressures. In the calculus of politics the benefits are unlikely to balance the costs for a Congressman because the President can usually upstage Congress and take credit for foreign policy successes. American politics offers Congress only weak incentives to play a major role in foreign relations.

THE NEW IMPACT OF INTERNATIONAL ECONOMIC FORCES

New forces may well be displacing the Cold War Soviet-American rivalry as major determinants of the structure of the international power system. Now that summit diplomacy has changed the basis for the old Cold War rivalry from relatively intractable ideological differences to negotiable political differences, economic factors are more influential. Changing economic conditions throughout the world are producing a new set of political power issues for the United States and her allies.

As discussed in Chapter 11, nations that produce and export

oil have begun to exert coercive power over both the East and West through an international cartel called the Organization of Petroleum Exporting Countries (OPEC). By quadrupling oil prices at the end of 1973, for example, the oil-producing nations were effectively able to divide members of the Atlantic bloc and weaken the economies of all the industrialized states of the world.

It would be impossible to overestimate the effects of this impressive demonstration of strength by the oil-producing nations and its future implications for the world balance of economic and political power. In the fourth quarter of 1973 the industrial nations ran a trade deficit totaling $10 billion, due mainly to the new price of crude oil. The deficit rose to $41 billion in the first quarter of 1974 and to $51 billion in the second quarter. Looking ahead in late 1974, the managing director of the International Monetary Fund predicted that the current account deficit of oil-importing countries would total about $64 billion in 1975.[1] The massive movement of capital represented by these figures does not tell the whole story, however, for the total deficits of the industrial nations are diminished by the flow of foreign credits back to the oil-consumer nations and to other states as investments.

During 1974 OPEC members earned $133 billion from oil exports. Saudi Arabia and Iran accounted for nearly half that staggering sum. In 1972 their total foreign credits had been only $15 billion. This enormous increase had immediate adverse effects on the highly industrialized states of Europe and on the United States and Japan, to say nothing of developing countries such as India that needed less oil but had an even poorer capacity to pay for it with foreign exchange. Industrial countries at first pinned their hopes on oil price reductions. As late as September 1974, Secretary of State Kissinger advocated that course of action, but he then lowered his expectations and merely tried to prevent further price increases. Hopes had rested on the prospect that oil payments would return to consumer nations in the form of producer-country investments. But this hope must be balanced against the possibility that oil producers will invest their "petrodollars" in the more stable economies—the United States and West Germany, for example—to the further dis-

---

[1] *Los Angeles Times,* November 27, 1974.

advantage of the more embattled national economies, such as Italy.

The impact of multiplied crude oil prices was less severe for the United States than for most other industrialized countries. During the mid-1970s, the United States imported approximately one-third of its petroleum needs from outside the Western hemisphere. Japan, at the other extreme, imported 90 percent of its oil from abroad and depended more heavily on oil as an energy resource than did the United States. But the Japanese economy had been highly competitive; the prospects were that after a year of stalemate Japan would resume growing, though at a slower rate than had prevailed for many years.

In Europe, Britain and Italy were the worst hit by the oil price increases. They were not only heavily dependent on oil and natural gas imports but their economies were weak. As an example of their precarious situation, in early December 1974, the Saudi Arabian government refused to accept British currency in royalty payments from the Saudi Arabian international oil consortium ARAMCO. The immediate effect of this refusal was a drop in the value of the British pound in the international monetary markets. The Saudi action was evidently not part of a general plan. It may have been a reaction to a pro-Israeli gesture by British Prime Minister Harold Wilson, or the Saudi government may have considered the British pound unstable or weak at that time. However, the immense monetary power accumulating primarily in Saudi and Iranian hands was yet to be employed systematically for political purposes, as the oil embargo had been in 1973.

It may be that 1973 marked a historic shift in the international terms of trade (the ratios of raw material prices to the prices of manufactured goods). This shift benefits developing states that mainly export raw materials and hurts the industrialized countries (primarily Western Europe, Japan, and the United States) that import raw materials and mainly export manufactured goods. No world consensus about distributive justice governs these relationships. In terms of per capita income, the richer nations have been getting richer while the poor have become poorer until this shift. The rich industrialized states view population pressures as a major cause of impoverishment. Spokesmen for the developing states instead blame adverse trends in the terms of trade—the fact that over the postwar decades the prices of raw materials have generally declined in relation to the prices of manufactured goods. Oil and gas have now become a dramatic exception to this trend.

The most pressing problem from the standpoint of the United States is oil-related. Those developing states with relatively large oil reserves and large current export capacities (mainly Algeria, Libya, the Middle East Arab states, Iran, Indonesia, Venezuela, and Mexico) will become prosperous or even fabulously rich, while poorer states become further impoverished and the modern industrial powers suffer economic setbacks. The prospects are ominous for the United States, but more ominous still for our industrialized allies that are heavily dependent on imported oil. No other raw materials cartel is likely to wield the power OPEC has acquired, yet OPEC's success has inspired other producer states to try—with coffee and copper, for example.

A world food shortage has developed and will grow over the next decade and beyond. International food and other commodity trading is likely to become charged with economic and political conflicts now that the sellers have gained an advantage the buyers usually held in the past. These conflicts, coupled with the increasing competition to acquire food on reasonable terms and to control raw materials sources, may well generate new tools of economic coercion in the late seventies. Unless international cooperation can forestall this trend, economic weapons will become much more prominent instruments of foreign policy in the future than they were in the first three postwar decades.

Even if this prognosis is accurate only with respect to oil markets, such a trend would be a major event in international politics. Critics of the industrial powers have long claimed that in the past these powers have persistently wielded economic weapons at the expense of the developing states. The Shah of Iran and other major oil producers have made it clear that they intend to raise oil prices again whenever necessary to offset the effects of inflation in the industrial states on the terms of trade. The oil producers clearly intend to maintain their newly advantageous position in world trade—one that will improve further as oil exports grow, oil revenues accumulate, and these revenues are used in turn for foreign investments. It is unlikely that these new economic powers will be any more inclined to give away their advantages than were the industrialized states when they were dominant. Iran, Saudi Arabia, and possibly other large oil producers are likely to become major world powers unless military and political pressures offset their growing strength.

In a peculiar way, these developments may solve the problem of maintaining the necessary public support for United States foreign policy in a period when emphasizing the Soviet Communist threat is no longer an appropriate solution. The domestic effects of the new international economic situation are likely to be keenly felt by Americans. Consumer product shortages such as the 1973 gas crisis have a potentially powerful impact on public opinion because they draw attention to foreign policy issues through personal experience—which the Cold War usually failed to do. Other raw material shortages affecting American consumers directly will probably also attract attention—just as a military manpower draft has a wide public impact under conditions like those experienced during the Vietnam war. Political leaders will have a less urgent need to invent ways to draw and sustain public support and a more urgent need to shape domestic consensus toward constructive ends if the future brings an increasing use of economic instruments of international bargaining and coercion.

One senses in the mid-seventies the convergence of major forces bringing about important changes for the United States as a world power. The Soviet-American hostility appears to have been brought under better joint management by the two superpowers. They still carry on their military competition—now within generous guidelines marked by the SALT agreement. The dangers of their military rivalry have probably been reduced, although by how much is hard to say. For the Soviets, the China problem looms forebodingly over the long term. Moscow presently copes with a quietly stagnant economy and restless satellites. The United States also faces a sick economy and restless allies; in addition, we face the prospect that international affairs will be increasingly dominated by economic power politics, as dramatized by the energy crisis. The rigid Cold War stance of American foreign policy has been replaced by a more flexible diplomacy. It is too soon, however, to assess how well this new flexibility will survive major shocks in American foreign policy.

Bibliographical Essay

AMERICAN FOREIGN POLICY: AN OVERVIEW

Public opinion surveys are compiled by issue in each number of the *Public Opinion Quarterly*. In addition, several extensive works treat American public opinion behavior as it pertains to foreign relations on the basis of numerous opinion and voting surveys:

* Alfred O. Hero, *Americans in World Affairs* (Boston: World Peace Foundation, 1959), is an excellent summary of how voting studies structure the electorate. * Gabriel A. Almond, *The American People and Foreign Policy*, rev. ed. (New York: Praeger, 1960), provides an important description of the social structure of public opinion formation, and his new introductory essay comments on public opinion behavior during the 1950s. * Bernard C. Cohen, *The Public's Impact on Foreign Policy* (Boston: Little, Brown, 1973), handles the complexities of public influence clearly. H. Bradford Westerfield, "Congress and Closed Politics in National Security Affairs," *Orbis* (Fall 1966), pp. 737–53, describes foreign policy making as an example of "secret politics." * Leon V. Sigal, *Reporters and Officials: The Organization and Politics of Newsmaking* (Lexington, Mass.: D. C. Heath, 1973), analyzes the mutual and manipulative dependence of press and government that complicates these "secret politics." Victor Marchetti and John D. Marks, *The CIA and the Cult of Intelligence* (New York: Knopf, 1974), is highly revealing about which secrets the clandestine services prefer to keep.

The intrepid reader can go further. V. O. Key, Jr., *Public Opin-*

* Asterisk indicates a paperback edition.

ion and American Democracy (New York: Knopf, 1961), maps the dimensions of public opinion and adduces its rationality. Samuel Stauffer, *Communism, Conformity and Civil Liberties* (New York: Doubleday, 1955), relates public perceptions of external threats to political beliefs and behavior during the Korean war "Red scare"; * Lloyd A. Free and Hadley Cantril, *The Political Beliefs of Americans: A Study of Public Opinion* (New Brunswick, N.J.: Rutgers University Press, 1968), analyzes the bases of American public opinion reactions on specific issues; Hadley Cantril, *Patterns of Human Concerns* (New Brunswick, N.J.: Rutgers University Press, 1966), uses cross-national surveys with basic issue categories to provide extensive evidence of broad public perception about public issues. Archibald T. Steel, *The American People and China* (New York: McGraw-Hill, 1966), uses survey techniques to examine public awareness, perception, and information levels about China as a foreign relations issue. * Bernard R. Berelson, Paul F. Lazarsfeld, and William N. McPhee, *Voting: A Study of Opinion Formation in a Presidential Campaign* (Chicago: University of Chicago Press, 1954), is a panel study of the 1948 election. * Kenneth N. Waltz, *Foreign Policy and Democratic Politics: The American and British Experience* (Boston: Little, Brown, 1967), develops criteria for foreign policy performance and thoughtfully compares the postwar performance of the two countries. Manfred Landecker, *The President and Public Opinion: Leadership in Foreign Affairs* (Washington, D.C.: Public Affairs Press, 1968), describes how Presidents Roosevelt and Truman aroused public opinion to support their foreign policies. * John E. Mueller, *War, Presidents and Public Opinion* (New York: Wiley, 1973), analyzes and compares public support for the Korean and Vietnam wars.

A full and sober revisionist statement about the Cold War—arguing that it was an avoidable tragedy—is Denna F. Fleming, *The Cold War and Its Origins, 1917–60,* 2 vols. (New York: Doubleday, 1961). A more recent compilation on the subject is * David Horowitz, ed., *Containment and Revolution* (Boston: Beacon Press, 1967). See also * David Horowitz, *The Free World Colossus* (New York: Hill & Wang, 1965); * William A. Williams, *The Tragedy of American Diplomacy,* rev. ed. (New York: Dell, 1962); Joyce and Gabriel Kolko, *The Limits of Power: The World and United States Foreign Policy 1945–1954* (New York: Harper & Row, 1972); and

* Walter LaFeber, *America, Russia and the Cold War 1945–1966* (New York: Wiley, 1968). A more plausible revisionist position, though less thorough than Fleming, is * Ronald Steel, *Pax America* (New York: Viking, 1967). Robert James Maddox, *The New Left and the Origins of the Cold War* (Princeton, N.J.: Princeton University Press, 1973), and the more measured Joseph M. Siracusa, *New Left Diplomatic Histories and Historians: The American Revisionists* (Port Washington, N.Y.: Kennikat Press, 1973), demonstrate poor historical practices by revisionists.

THE TRUMAN ADMINISTRATION

For the origins of the Cold War a good general source is still * William H. McNeill, *America, Britain and Russia: Their Cooperation and Conflict, 1941–1946* (New York: Johnson Reprint, 1953). Reflecting more recent concerns about the subject and also excellent are Louis J. Halle, *The Cold War as History* (New York: Harper & Row, 1967); * William L. Neumann, *After Victory: Churchill, Roosevelt, Stalin and the Making of the Peace* (New York: Harper & Row, 1967); and particularly * John Lewis Gaddis, *The United States and the Cold War* (New York: Columbia University Press, 1972). An interesting thesis about Truman's foreign policy and public opinion is presented in Richard M. Freeland, *The Truman Doctrine and the Origins of McCarthyism* (New York: Knopf, 1972). Charles L. Mee, Jr., *Meeting At Potsdam* (New York: M. Evans & Co., 1975), argues that the major powers—the United States, Russia, and Great Britain—all had reasons for avoiding definitive settlements or negotiating lasting agreements at Potsdam.

Indispensable on the Truman Administration are * Harry S Truman, *Memoirs,* Vol. 1: *Years of Decisions;* Vol. 2: *Years of Trial and Hope* (New York: Doubleday, 1958); and Dean Acheson, *Present at the Creation* (New York: Norton, 1969). An excellent account is * Cabell B. Phillips, *The Truman Presidency: The History of a Triumphant Succession* (New York: Macmillan, 1966). Richard F. Haynes, *The Awesome Power: Harry S. Truman as Commander in Chief* (Baton Rouge: Louisiana State University Press, 1973), reviews Truman's military decisions.

Seyom Brown, *The Faces of Power: Constancy and Change in*

U.S. Foreign Policy from Truman to Johnson (New York: Columbia University Press, 1968), Part II, concentrates on the perceptions of policy makers in the Truman Administration. Edward S. Flash, Jr., *Economic Advice and Presidential Leadership: The Council of Economic Advisors* (New York: Columbia University Press, 1965), traces the development of the CEA, an important agency that first came into its own during our Korean war rearmament. Warner R. Schilling, Paul Y. Hammond, and Glenn H. Snyder, *Strategy, Politics and Defense Budgets* (New York: Columbia University Press, 1962), pp. 1–378, is valuable on congressional and presidential policy making.

Arthur H. Vandenberg, ed., *The Private Papers of Senator Vandenberg* (Boston: Houghton Mifflin, 1952), provides a rich view of bipartisanship in action by a Senate Republican statesman. H. Bradford Westerfield, *Foreign Policy and Party Politics* (New Haven: Yale University Press, 1955), examines bipartisan cooperation on foreign policy from Pearl Harbor to Korea.

Thomas G. Paterson, *Soviet-American Confrontation: Postwar Reconstruction and the Origins of the Cold War* (Baltimore: Johns Hopkins University Press, 1973), deals with the economic roots of American foreign policy. Harry B. Price, *The Marshall Plan and Its Meaning* (Ithaca, N.Y.: Cornell University Press, 1955), assesses the European Recovery Program in retrospect; Coral Bell, *Negotiations from Strength* (New York: Knopf, 1963), advances interesting interpretations of the Cold War stance of the Truman Administration; and * Joseph M. Jones, *The Fifteen Weeks* (New York: Harcourt Brace Jovanovich, 1955), and George F. Kennan, *Memoirs, 1925–1950* (Boston: Little, Brown, 1967), Chapters 11–20, both provide accounts by State Department participants of how the Marshall Plan was mapped out in Washington. * John Morton Blum, ed., *The Price of Vision: The Diary of Henry A. Wallace, 1942–1946* (Boston: Houghton Mifflin, 1973), provides a participant's alternative view of the growing Soviet-American rivalry.

* Tang Tsou, *America's Failure in China, 1941–1950*, 2 vols. (Chicago: University of Chicago Press, 1963), treats its subject definitively. Trumbull Higgins, *Korea and the Fall of MacArthur* (New York: Oxford University Press, 1960), is clever and quite sound; Walter Millis, *et al., Arms and the State* (New York: Twentieth Century Fund, 1958), surveys the military side of the U.S. re-

sponse to the Cold War, including an interesting treatment of Mac-
Arthur (Chapter 7).

THE EISENHOWER ADMINISTRATION

Herbert S. Parmet, *Eisenhower and the American Crusades*
(New York: Macmillan, 1972), is the best study so far.

Robert J. Donovan, *Eisenhower: The Inside Story* (New York:
Harper & Row, 1956), is an account of Eisenhower's first term by
an independent journalist with special access to the White House.
* Dwight D. Eisenhower, *The White House Years*, Vol. 1: *Mandate
for Change, 1953–1956* (New York: Doubleday, 1965), reveals little
but is a valuable and authoritative survey. Vol 2: *Waging Peace,
1956–1961*, recounts events of Eisenhower's second Administration
from the President's vantage point. Sherman Adams, *First-hand Report* (New York: Harper & Row, 1961), is sometimes quite revealing
about Eisenhower's Presidency, though less comprehensive and orderly. * Arthur Larson, *Eisenhower, the President Nobody Knew*
(New York: Scribners, 1968), is candid and often illuminating.
* Richard E. Neustadt, *Presidential Power: The Politics of Leadership* (New York: Mentor, 1960), diagnoses Eisenhower's leadership
problems through comparisons with Truman.

Louis L. Gerson, *John Foster Dulles* (New York: Cooper Square
Publishers, 1967), is highly informed but cryptic. Richard Goold-
Adams, *The Time of Power: A Reappraisal of John Foster Dulles*
(London: McClelland, 1962), is a superb appraisal and keen ex-
planation. Emmet J. Hughes, *The Ordeal of Power* (New York:
Atheneum, 1963), is a revealing critical memoir. Michael A. Guhin,
John Foster Dulles: A Statesman and His Times (New York: Co-
lumbia University Press, 1972), is appreciative and persuasive.

Glenn H. Snyder, "The 'New Look' of 1953," in Schilling,
Hammond, and Snyder, *op. cit.,* pp. 379–524, is illuminating and
definitive on the changes in our strategy and defense postures during this period. * Samuel P. Huntington, *The Common Defense*
(New York: Columbia University Press, 1961), is a scholarly work on
defense policy and politics throughout the Eisenhower Administration. Maxwell D. Taylor, *The Uncertain Trumpet* (New York:
Harper & Row, 1960); and Matthew B. Ridgway and H. H. Martin,

Soldier: Memoirs of Matthew B. Ridgway (New York: Harper & Row, 1956), discuss defense policy making from the viewpoint of two generals.

* Adam B. Ulam, *Expansion and Coexistence: The History of Soviet Foreign Policy, 1917–1967* (New York: Praeger, 1968), is comprehensive and scholarly. * Philip E. Mosely, *The Kremlin and World Politics* (New York: Random House, 1960), is a collection of essays by a scholar-diplomat. Arnold L. Horelick and Myron Rush, *Strategic Power and Soviet Foreign Policy* (Chicago: University of Chicago Press, 1966), discusses Soviet policy since 1954 and includes a provocative account of how the Russians exploited Sputnik. See also Lincoln P. Bloomfield, Walter C. Clemens, Jr., and Franklyn Griffiths, *Khrushchev and the Arms Race: Soviet Interests in Arms Control and Disarmament, 1954–1964* (Cambridge, Mass.: Massachusetts Institute of Technology Press, 1966). Bernard G. Bechoefer, *Postwar Negotiations for Arms Control* (Washington, D.C.: Brookings Institution, 1961), is a major work on disarmament negotiations by a participant. Leonard Beaton and John Maddox, *The Spread of Nuclear Weapons* (New York: Praeger, 1962), is an early, somewhat alarmist survey of nuclear proliferation.

Many books offer valuable insights into the Eisenhower Administration's policies in specific areas of the world. On the Eisenhower policies in the Middle East, John C. Campbell, *Defense of the Middle East: Problems of American Policy,* rev. ed. (New York: Praeger, 1960), is a solid account of the Eisenhower period. * Anthony Eden, *Full Circle* (Boston: Houghton Mifflin, 1960), is the British Prime Minister's memoir on the Suez crisis. Herman Finer, *Dulles Over Suez: The Theory and Practice of His Diplomacy* (Chicago: Quadrangle, 1964), is angry and unfair but nonetheless illuminating. Terence Robertson, *Crisis: The Inside Story of the Suez Conspiracy* (New York: Atheneum, 1965), is cool and independent inside journalism. Anthony Nutting, *No End of a Lesson* (London: Potter, 1967), is a revealing memoir.

* Melvin Gurtov, *The First Vietnam Crisis* (New York: Columbia University Press, 1967), is sound and definitive on the 1953–54 period. Morton H. Halperin and Tang Tsou, "United States Policy Toward the Offshore Islands," in John D. Montgomery and Albert O. Hirschman, eds., *Public Policy, 1967* (Cambridge, Mass.: Harvard University Press, 1967), pp. 119–38, recounts the Formosa Straits

crisis. American relations with Europe are analyzed by an American, Robert E. Osgood, *NATO: The Entangling Alliance* (Chicago: University of Chicago Press, 1962); and by a European, Jacques Freymond, *Western Europe Since the War* (New York: Praeger, 1964). * Theodore Draper, *Castroism: Theory and Practice* (New York: Praeger, 1965), is a thoughtful account of the establishment by revolution in 1959 of the Castro regime in Cuba.

THE KENNEDY ADMINISTRATION

On the 1960 election, see * Theodore H. White, *The Making of the President, 1960* (New York: New American Library, 1967), which emphasizes Kennedy's campaign, and Richard M. Nixon, "The Campaign of 1960," in his *Six Crises* (New York: Doubleday, 1962), pp. 293–426.

Indispensable on Kennedy are three memoirs: * Arthur M. Schlesinger, Jr., *A Thousand Days* (Boston: Houghton Mifflin, 1965); * Theodore C. Sorensen, *Kennedy* (New York: Harper & Row, 1966); and * Roger Hilsman, *To Move a Nation* (New York: Dell, 1967).

Heavy-handed correctives to Kennedy euphoria are Louise Fitzsimons, *The Kennedy Doctrine* (New York: Random House, 1972); and Richard J. Walton, *Cold War and Counterrevolution: The Foreign Policy of John F. Kennedy* (New York: Viking, 1972). An additional viewpoint now available in English is Anatolii Andreievich Gromyko, *Through Russian Eyes: President Kennedy's 1036 Days* (Washington, D.C.: International Library, 1973), by the son of the Soviet Foreign Minister. Seyom Brown, *op. cit.,* is a valuable analysis. * John F. Kennedy, *The Strategy of Peace,* edited by Allan Nevins (New York: Harper & Row, 1960), presents Kennedy's early foreign policy views. In Seymour E. Harris, *Economics of the Kennedy Years, and a Look Ahead* (New York: Harper & Row, 1964), a modern if venerable economist surveys economic policy.

On our defense policies under the Kennedy Administration, William W. Kaufmann, *The McNamara Strategy* (New York: Harper & Row, 1964), is authentic McNamara. Maxwell D. Taylor, *Responsibility and Response* (New York: Harper & Row, 1967), is a memoir from Kennedy's closest military adviser. * William B. Bader, *The United States and the Spread of Nuclear Weapons* (New York:

Pegasus, 1968), is especially valuable on the diplomacy of the test ban and nuclear proliferation during the Kennedy and Johnson Administrations. See also Bloomfield, Clemens, and Griffiths, *op. cit.,* and Horelick and Rush, *op. cit.* on the Soviet Union's foreign relations and views on arms control.

On the Kennedy Administration's policies in specific areas of the world, several works are valuable. Jean Edward Smith, *The Defense of Berlin* (Baltimore: Johns Hopkins, 1963), thoroughly examines the Berlin crisis. On the Cuban missile crisis see two excellent analyses: Arnold L. Horelick, "The Cuban Missile Crisis: An Analysis of Soviet Calculations and Behavior," *World Politics* (April 1964), pp. 363–89; and Albert and Roberta Wohlstetter, "Controlling the Risks in Cuba," *Adelphi Papers* (London: 1965). Elie Abel, *The Missile Crisis* (Philadelphia: Lippincott, 1966), gives excellent detail.

John C. Dreier, ed., *Alliance for Progress* (Baltimore: Johns Hopkins, 1962), records the origins of the Alliance and the early expectations for it; but William D. Rogers, *Alliance for Progress* (New York: Random House, 1967), is a more thorough survey and appraisal.

On the background of American intervention in Vietnam and developments in Asia, see first and foremost * *Senator Gravel Edition: The Pentagon Papers: The Defense Department History of United States Decisionmaking on Vietnam,* 4 vols. (Boston: Beacon Press, 1971), and * *The Pentagon Papers,* as published by the *New York Times* (New York: Bantam Books, 1971). See also Gurtov, *op. cit.;* * Edwin O. Reischauer, *Beyond Vietnam: The United States and Asia* (New York: Random House, 1967); * Arthur M. Schlesinger, Jr., *The Bitter Heritage: Vietnam and American Democracy, 1941–1966* (Boston: Houghton Mifflin, 1966); and * George M. Kahin and John W. Lewis, *The United States in Vietnam* (New York: Dell, 1967). Of particular value is * Robert Shaplen, *Lost Revolution: The U.S. in Vietnam* (New York: Harper & Row, 1965). David Halberstam, *The Making of a Quagmire* (New York: Random House, 1965), is a journalist's account of the Buddhist uprising and American operations during the Kennedy Administration. * Donald S. Zagoria, *Vietnam Triangle: Moscow/Peking/Hanoi* (New York: Pegasus, 1967), examines the problems faced by the principal foreign supporters of the insurgency.

THE JOHNSON ADMINISTRATION

Lyndon Baines Johnson, *Vantage Point: Perspectives of the Presidency, 1963–1969* (New York: Holt, Rinehart and Winston, 1971), is a strong self-justification.

Eric F. Goldman, *The Tragedy of Lyndon Johnson* (New York: Knopf, 1969), the first memoir on the Johnson Administration to appear, probes personalities and examines Johnson's fall from popularity.

In addition, three valuable works by journalists are * Rowland Evans and Robert Novak, *Lyndon B. Johnson: The Exercise of Power* (New York: New American Library, 1966), especially strong on Johnson's Senate experience; Philip L. Geyelin, *Lyndon B. Johnson and the World* (New York: Praeger, 1966), a reflective contemporary interpretation; and * Tom Wicker, *JFK and LBJ: The Influence of Personality upon Politics* (New York: Morrow, 1968), valuable on Johnson's handling of Vietnam. Hugh Sidey, *A Very Personal Presidency* (New York: Atheneum, 1968), is excellent on Johnson's personality. On the 1964 election see * Theodore H. White, *The Making of the President, 1964* (New York: Atheneum, 1965).

On the Vietnam war a number of works are illuminating. Bill D. Moyers, "One Thing We Learned," *Foreign Affairs* (July 1968), pp. 657–64, offers the reflections of a former close adviser to Johnson on the relationship of public opinion to the Vietnam war. Townsend Hoopes, *The Limits of Intervention* (New York: David McKay, 1970), describes the opposition to the war within the Johnson Administration by a participant. Chester L. Cooper, *Lost Crusade: America in Vietnam* (New York: Dodd, Mead, 1970), is also a participant's viewpoint. Sidney Verba, Richard A. Brody, Edwin B. Parker, Norman H. Nie, Nelson W. Polsby, Paul Ekman, and Gordon S. Black, "Public Opinion and the War in Vietnam," *The American Political Science Review* (June 1967), pp. 317–33, demonstrates that the public is concerned but deferential. Seymour M. Lipset, "Doves, Hawks, and Polls," *Encounter* (October 1966), pp. 38–45, surveys the polls to make a similar point. Press coverage of Vietnam is described in John Hohenberg, *Between Two Worlds: Policy, Press and Public Opinion in Asian-American Relations* (New York: Praeger, 1967), Chapter 6.

* J. William Fulbright, *The Arrogance of Power* (New York: Random House, 1967), is an angry and eloquent attack on the Administration's Vietnam policies by a leading Senate critic. David Halberstam, *The Best and the Brightest* (New York: Random House, 1972), is pretentious, provocative, and engaging. Thomas Powers, *The War at Home: Vietnam and the American People, 1964–1968* (New York: Grossman, 1973), traces the opposition to the war from the early 1960s. * Staughton Lynd and Thomas Haydon, *The Other Side* (New York: New American Library, 1967), is the account of revisionist visitors to Hanoi.

Several works are valuable on other aspects of Johnson Administration policies. On the Dominican crisis, see Theodore Draper, "The Dominican Crisis: A Case Study in American Policy," *Commentary* (December 1965), pp. 33–68; and * Tad Szulc, *Dominican Diary* (New York: Dell, 1966). Alastair Buchan, ed., *China and the Peace of Asia* (New York: Praeger, 1965), is a competent survey. See Bader, *op. cit.*, on negotiations with the Russians on arms control under the Johnson Administration.

THE NIXON ADMINISTRATION

The best general book on Nixon so far is Garry Wills, *Nixon Agonistes: The Crisis of the Self-Made Man* (Boston: Houghton Mifflin, 1970). The enigma of Nixon is explored through a psychoanalytic approach by Bruce Mazlish, *In Search of Nixon: A Psychohistorical Inquiry* (New York: Basic Books, 1972), and examined more systematically and soundly through adaptive psychology by James David Barber, *The Presidential Character: Predicting Performance in the White House* (Englewood Cliffs, N.J.: Prentice-Hall, 1972), Chapters 10–12. John Osborne, *The Nixon Watch* (New York: Liveright, 1970), shows grudging appreciation. Theodore H. White, *The Making of the President, 1972* (New York: Atheneum, 1973), is broadly relevant and White's best of four books on presidential elections. Carl Bernstein and Bob Woodward, *All the President's Men* (New York: Simon & Schuster, 1974), recounts the Watergate exposé.

Henry A. Kissinger, *American Foreign Policy* (New York: Norton, 1969), is the last major publication of Nixon's principal diplomat before he joined the Nixon Administration. Marvin Kalb and

Bernard Kalb, *Kissinger* (Boston: Little, Brown, 1974), is sympathetic, illuminating, and independent. Stephen R. Graubard, *Kissinger: Portrait of a Mind* (New York: Norton, 1973), is rigorous, admiring, and clarifying. David Landau, *Kissinger, The Uses of Power* (Boston: Houghton Mifflin, 1972), is critical of personal characteristics that allegedly prolonged the Vietnam war.

On contemporary issues, Mason Willrich and John B. Rhinelander, eds., *SALT: The Moscow Agreements and Beyond* (New York: Free Press, 1974), explains and assesses the SALT I accords. F. C. Langdon, *Japan's Foreign Policy* (Vancouver: University of British Columbia Press, 1973), predicts a looser alliance with the United States. In A. Doak Barnett, *Uncertain Passage: China's Transition to the Post-Mao Era* (Washington, D.C.: Brookings Institution, 1974), a major authority predicts growing military influence in Chinese politics and activism with moderation in foreign policy. Luigi R. Einaudi, ed., *Beyond Cuba: Latin America Takes Charge of Its Future* (New York: Crane, Russak, 1974), explores Latin American prospects. Louis J. Mensonides and James A. Kuhlman, eds., *The Future of Inter-Bloc Relations in Europe* (New York: Praeger, 1974), surveys the prospects for further changes in East-West relations in Europe. S. David Freeman, *Energy: The New Era* (New York: Walker, 1974), surveys the energy problem and offers proposals for government policy.

Appendix:
Maps

MULTILATERAL MILITARY SECURITY ORGANIZATIONS

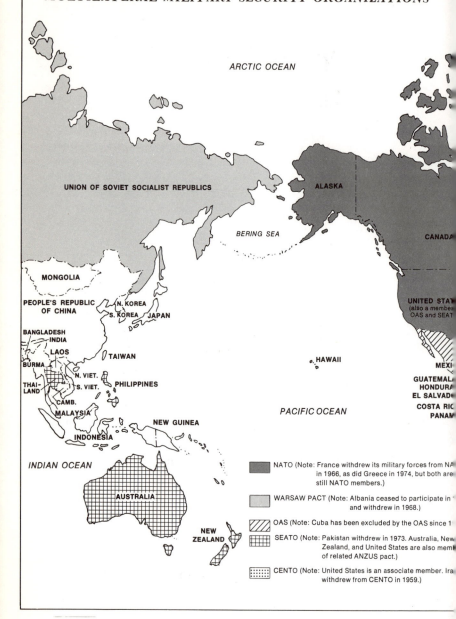

ARCTIC OCEAN

UNION OF SOVIET SOCIALIST REPUBLICS

ALASKA

BERING SEA

CANADA

MONGOLIA

N. KOREA

S. KOREA JAPAN

UNITED STAT
(also a member
OAS and SEAT

PEOPLE'S REPUBLIC
OF CHINA

BANGLADESH
INDIA
LAOS
BURMA
TAIWAN

HAWAII

MEXI

GUATEMAL
HONDURA
EL SALVAD

N. VIET.
THAI-
LAND
S. VIET.
PHILIPPINES

COSTA RIC
PANAM

CAMB.
MALAYSIA

PACIFIC OCEAN

NEW GUINEA

INDONESIA

INDIAN OCEAN

AUSTRALIA

NATO (Note: France withdrew its military forces from NA
in 1966, as did Greece in 1974, but both are
still NATO members.)

WARSAW PACT (Note: Albania ceased to participate in
and withdrew in 1968.)

OAS (Note: Cuba has been excluded by the OAS since 1

SEATO (Note: Pakistan withdrew in 1973. Australia, New
Zealand, and United States are also mem
of related ANZUS pact.)

NEW
ZEALAND

CENTO (Note: United States is an associate member. Ira
withdrew from CENTO in 1959.)

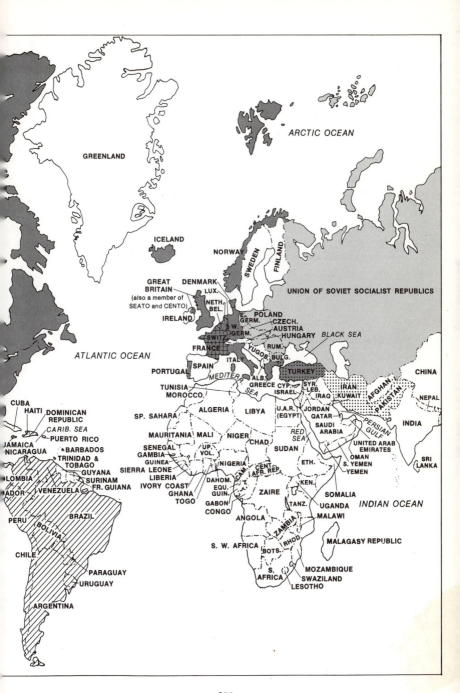

ARCTIC OCEAN

GREENLAND

ICELAND

NORWAY

SWEDEN

FINLAND

UNION OF SOVIET SOCIALIST REPUBLICS

GREAT BRITAIN
(also a member of SEATO and CENTO)

DENMARK

LUX.

NETH.

BEL.

IRELAND

E. GERM.

POLAND

CZECH.

W. GERM.

AUSTRIA

HUNGARY

BLACK SEA

SWITZ.

FRANCE

ITALY

YUGO.

RUM.

BULG.

ATLANTIC OCEAN

PORTUGAL

SPAIN

ALB.

GREECE

CYP.

TURKEY

SYR.

LEB.

IRAN

AFGHAN.

CHINA

MEDITER. SEA

ISRAEL

IRAQ

KUWAIT

PAKISTAN

NEPAL

TUNISIA

MOROCCO

CUBA

HAITI

DOMINICAN REPUBLIC

CARIB. SEA

PUERTO RICO

JAMAICA

NICARAGUA

BARBADOS

TRINIDAD & TOBAGO

GUYANA

SURINAM

FR. GUIANA

LOMBIA

ADOR

VENEZUELA

SP. SAHARA

ALGERIA

LIBYA

U.A.R. (EGYPT)

JORDAN

QATAR

SAUDI ARABIA

PERSIAN GULF

UNITED ARAB EMIRATES

INDIA

SRI LANKA

MAURITANIA

MALI

NIGER

CHAD

RED SEA

OMAN

SENEGAL

GAMBIA

GUINEA

UP. VOL.

NIGERIA

SUDAN

S. YEMEN

YEMEN

SIERRA LEONE

LIBERIA

IVORY COAST

DAHOM.

CENT. AFR. REP.

CAM.

ETH.

GHANA

TOGO

EQU. GUIN.

ZAIRE

KEN.

SOMALIA

GABON

CONGO

TANZ.

UGANDA

INDIAN OCEAN

PERU

BOLIVIA

BRAZIL

ANGOLA

MALAWI

CHILE

S. W. AFRICA

ZAMBIA

RHOD.

MALAGASY REPUBLIC

PARAGUAY

BOTS.

MOZAMBIQUE

URUGUAY

S. AFRICA

SWAZILAND

LESOTHO

ARGENTINA

351

MAJOR MULTILATERAL ECONOMIC ORGANIZATIONS

ARCTIC OCEAN

UNION OF SOVIET SOCIALIST REPUBLICS

ALASKA

CANADA

BERING SEA

MONGOLIA

PEOPLE'S REPUBLIC OF CHINA

N. KOREA
S. KOREA JAPAN

UNITED STATE

BANGLADESH
INDIA
LAOS
BURMA
TAIWAN
N. VIET.
THAI-
LAND S. VIET. PHILIPPINES
CAMB.
MALAYSIA
INDONESIA

NEW GUINEA

HAWAII

MEXICO

GUATEMALA
HONDURAS
EL SALVADOR
COSTA RICA
PANAMA

PACIFIC OCEAN

INDIAN OCEAN

AUSTRALIA

NEW
ZEALAND

COMMON MARKET

COMECON (Note: Albania ceased to participate in 1961 and withdrew in 1962.)

OPEC (Note: Gabon is an associate member.)

352

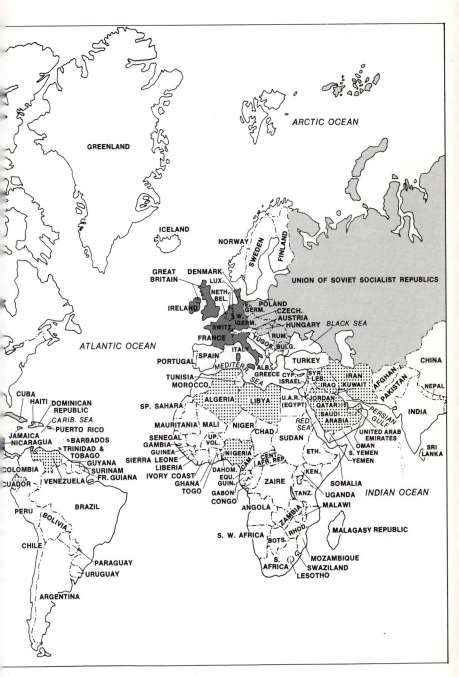

ARCTIC OCEAN

GREENLAND

ICELAND

NORWAY

GREAT
BRITAIN

DENMARK

UNION OF SOVIET SOCIALIST REPUBLICS

LUX.
NETH.
BEL.

E. POLAND
W. GERM. CZECH.
GERM. AUSTRIA
HUNGARY

IRELAND

SWITZ.
FRANCE

BLACK SEA

YUGOS. RUM.
BULG.

ATLANTIC OCEAN

ITALY

TURKEY

PORTUGAL

SPAIN

MEDITER.
SEA

ALB.
GREECE CYP.
ISRAEL

SYR.
LEB.
IRAQ

IRAN

AFGHAN.

TUNISIA

MOROCCO

PAKISTAN

CUBA
HAITI

DOMINICAN
REPUBLIC

CARIB. SEA
PUERTO RICO

SP. SAHARA

ALGERIA

LIBYA

U.A.R.
(EGYPT)

JORDAN
KUWAIT

QATAR
SAUDI
ARABIA

PERSIAN
GULF

CHINA

NEPAL

INDIA

JAMAICA
NICARAGUA

BARBADOS
TRINIDAD &
TOBAGO

MAURITANIA

MALI

NIGER

CHAD

RED
SEA

UNITED ARAB
EMIRATES

SRI
LANKA

COLOMBIA

GUYANA
SURINAM
FR. GUIANA

SENEGAL
GAMBIA
GUINEA

UP.
VOL.

SUDAN

OMAN
S. YEMEN
YEMEN

CUADOR

VENEZUELA

SIERRA LEONE

NIGERIA

CAM.

CENT.
AFR. REP.

ETH.

PERU

BRAZIL

BOLIVIA

IVORY COAST
GHANA
TOGO

DAHOM.
EQU.
GUIN.

GABON
CONGO

ZAIRE

KEN.

SOMALIA

UGANDA

INDIAN OCEAN

TANZ.

ANGOLA

ZAMBIA

MALAWI

CHILE

S. W. AFRICA

BOTS.

RHOD.

MALAGASY REPUBLIC

PARAGUAY
URUGUAY

S.
AFRICA

MOZAMBIQUE
SWAZILAND
LESOTHO

ARGENTINA

353

THE WAR IN INDOCHINA

Note: The boundaries of North and South Vietnam, Laos, and Cambodia were established by the international Geneva Convention in 1954 when the French Indochinese empire collapsed. The boundaries have remained the same to the present.

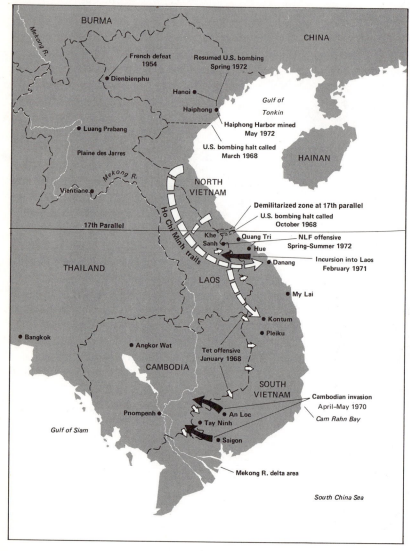

1973 PARIS PEACE ACCORD: SOUTH VIETNAM

Note: Truce teams were composed of members from two groups: the Joint Military Commission consisted of the United States, South Vietnam, North Vietnam, and the Vietcong. The International Commission for Control and Supervision consisted of Hungary, Indonesia, Poland, and Canada (Canada withdrew and was replaced by Iran).

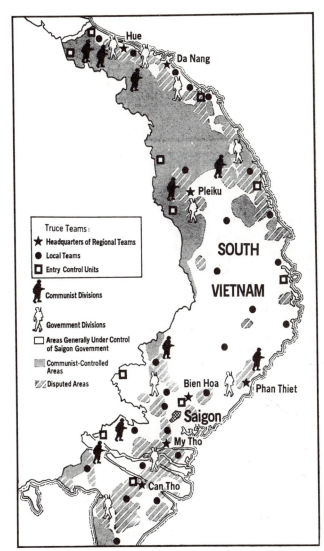

Truce Teams:
★ Headquarters of Regional Teams
● Local Teams
□ Entry Control Units

Communist Divisions

Government Divisions

□ Areas Generally Under Control of Saigon Government

Communist-Controlled Areas

Disputed Areas

SOUTH

VIETNAM

Hue
Da Nang
Pleiku
Bien Hoa
Phan Thiet
Saigon
My Tho
Can Tho

From *New York Times,* January 28, 1973

THE COURSE OF THE KOREAN WAR

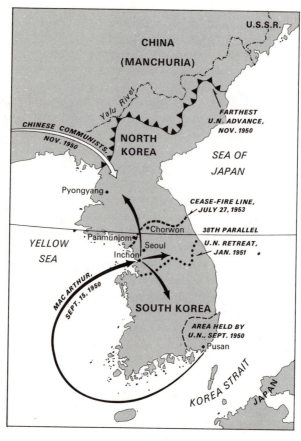

POSTWAR EVENTS IN THE MIDDLE EAST

From *New York Times,* November 18, 1973

357

1974 GENEVA PACTS: ISRAEL, SYRIA, AND EGYPT

1974 Syrian-Israeli Pact (below)

Note: Area from Jordan River to line A: occupied by Israeli forces. Area
between lines A and B: United Nations buffer zone (no Syrian or
Israeli forces allowed). Area from line B to Damascus: Syrian forces.
Dotted line indicates farthest Israeli advance in 1967 war.

1974 Egyptian-Israeli Pact (facing page)

Note: Area from Suez Canal to line A: limited Egyptian forces only. Area
between lines A and B: United Nations buffer zone (no Egyptian or
Israeli forces allowed). Area between lines B and C: limited Israeli
forces only. Area beyond line C in Sinai Peninsula: occupied by
Israeli forces.

From *New York
Times,* June 2,
1974

358

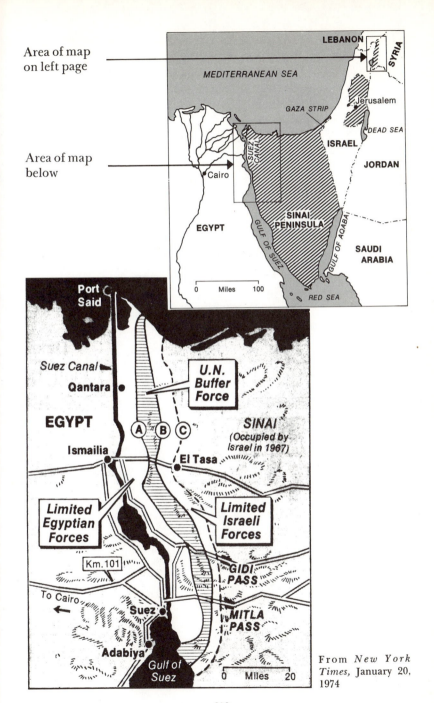

Area of map on left page

Area of map below

LEBANON

SYRIA

MEDITERRANEAN SEA

GAZA STRIP

Jerusalem

DEAD SEA

ISRAEL

SUEZ CANAL

JORDAN

Cairo

EGYPT

SINAI PENINSULA

GULF OF SUEZ

GULF OF AQABA

SAUDI ARABIA

0   Miles   100

RED SEA

Port Said

Suez Canal

Qantara

U.N. Buffer Force

EGYPT

(A)(B)(C)

SINAI (Occupied by Israel in 1967)

Ismailia

El Tasa

Limited Egyptian Forces

Limited Israeli Forces

Km.101

GIDI PASS

To Cairo

Suez

MITLA PASS

Adabiya

Gulf of Suez

0   Miles   20

From *New York Times,* January 20, 1974

Index

C 7
D 8
E 9
F 0
G 1
H 2
I 3
J 4